# EXPLORATIONS IN ECONOMIC SOCIOLOGY

# EXPLORATIONS IN ECONOMIC SOCIOLOGY

*Richard Swedberg*

EDITOR

RUSSELL SAGE FOUNDATION
NEW YORK

# THE RUSSELL SAGE FOUNDATION

The Russell Sage Foundation, one of the oldest of America's general purpose foundations, was established in 1907 by Mrs. Margaret Olivia Sage for "the improvement of social and living conditions in the United States." The Foundation seeks to fulfill this mandate by fostering the development and dissemination of knowledge about the country's political, social, and economic problems. While the Foundation endeavors to assure the accuracy and objectivity of each book it publishes, the conclusions and interpretations in Russell Sage Foundation publications are those of the authors and not of the Foundation, its Trustees, or its staff. Publication by Russell Sage, therefore, does not imply Foundation endorsement.

**Library of Congress Cataloging-in-Publication Data**

Explorations in economic sociology / Richard Swedberg (ed.).
    p.   cm.
    Includes bibliographical references and index.
    ISBN 0-87154-840-2
    1. Economics—Sociological aspects.
HM35.E96   1993
306.3—dc20                                                      92-41592
                                                                    CIP

RUSSELL SAGE FOUNDATION
112 East 64th Street, New York, New York 10021

10 9 8 7 6 5 4 3 2 1

# Contents

# PART III
# THE SOCIAL CONSTRUCTION
# OF ECONOMIC INSTITUTIONS:
## Money, Markets, and Industries

# PART IV
# THE PERFORMANCE OF FIRMS
# AND THEIR ENVIRONMENTS

# PART V
# SMALL FIRMS IN NETWORKS

# Acknowledgments

Without the kind help of friends, family, and colleagues it would have been very difficult to edit this book. First of all, there are of course the contributing authors, who all in goodhearted manner let me bully them about deadlines, missing references, and the like. I am in particular grateful to Frank Romo, who at one stage of this book's materialization saved it from going under. Mark Granovetter was crucial to this book, not the least in his capacity as main organizer of the seminar. My wife Cecilia gave me many good ideas for how to organize the material. And, finally, I have to thank all the great people at the Russell Sage Foundation who helped me with this book and who in general made my stay at the Foundation during 1990 to 1991 into a delightful experience: Sara Beckman, Eileen Ferrer, Jamie Gray, Bianca Intalan, Pauline Jones, Vivian Kaufman, Lisa Nachtigall, Christina Paterniti, Pauline Rothstein, Madge Spitaleri, Eric Wanner, and Camille Yezzi.

Richard Swedberg
*New York, August 1991*

# Notes on Contributors

**Ronald S. Burt** is professor of sociology and business at Columbia University, and director of the Strategy Laboratory at Columbia's Center for the Social Sciences. His current research concerns envy and entrepreneurial opportunity in the social structure of competitive environments. Recent works include *Structural Holes* (1992) and *Social Contagion* (1992).

**Mark Granovetter** is professor and chair of sociology at the State University of New York at Stony Brook, and is currently at work on a book entitled *Society and Economy: The Social Construction of Economic Institutions* to be published by Harvard University Press, from which the chapter in this book is drawn. He is the author of numerous papers on economic sociology, and of *Getting A Job: A Study of Contacts and Careers* (1974).

**Paul M. Hirsch** is James Allen Distinguished Professor of Strategy and Organizations at Northwestern University's Kellogg Graduate School of Management. He has published numerous articles on economic sociology and mass communication.

**Mark Lazerson** is assistant professor of sociology at the State University of New York at Stony Brook. He has worked and lived in Italy for many years. He is presently engaged in a project on understanding how social relations determine prices within the Italian women's stocking industry.

**Patrick McGuire** is an assistant professor of sociology at the University of Toledo, Ohio. An author of several articles on U.S. state and industry formation before 1930, he is co-authoring a book with Mark Granovetter and Michael Schwartz titled *The Social Construction of Industry*. He is a contributor and co-editor (with Don McQuarie) of a book on Marxist Sociology, *From the Left Bank to the Mainstream* (1992).

**Marshall W. Meyer** is professor of management and Anheuser-Busch Term Professor in the Wharton School and professor of sociology at the University of

Pennsylvania. His books include *Environments and Organizations* (with several co-authors), *Change in Public Bureaucracies, Limits to Bureaucratic Growth, Bureaucracy in Modern Society* (with Peter M. Blau), and *Permanently Failing Organizations* (with Lynne G. Zucker). Professor Meyer is currently associate editor of *Administrative Science Quarterly.*

**Mark S. Mizruchi** is professor of sociology at the University of Michigan. His research includes an examination of corporate political behavior and (with Linda Stearns) a longitudinal study of organizational responses to capital dependence. His books include *The American Corporate Network, 1904–1974* (1982), *Intercorporate Relations* (1987, co-edited with Michael Schwartz), and *The Structure of Corporate Political Action* (1992).

**Charles Perrow** is professor of sociology at Yale University and the author of several books, including *Complex Organizations: A Critical Essay* (3rd edition) and *Normal Accidents: Living with High Risk Technologies.* He is endlessly (he notes) working on a book to be titled *A Society of Organizations* that will examine the development of U.S. society from 1820 from an organizational point of view. His contribution here is a part of that book.

**Frank Romo** is assistant professor of sociology at the State University of New York at Stony Brook. He is the author of numerous articles on the substance and methodology of network analysis and is currently finishing a book on the dynamics of social networks.

**Charles F. Sabel** is Ford International Professor of Social Science at MIT. He is co-author with Michael Piore of *The Second Industrial Divide: Possibilities for Prosperity* (1984) and has written a number of articles on industrial policy.

**Michael Schwartz** is professor of sociology at the State University of New York at Stony Brook. He is the co-author (with Beth Mintz) of *The Power Structure of American Business,* co-editor (with Mark Mizruchi) of *Intercorporate Relations,* and editor of the Rutgers Press Series *Social Foundations of the Policy Process.*

**Charles W. Smith** is professor of sociology at Queens College, CUNY, a member of the Sociology Graduate Faculty of CUNY, and the Acting Dean of the Social Science Division of Queens College, CUNY. He is the author of *Auctions: The Social Construction of Values* (1989; paperback, 1990); *The Mind of the Market* (1981; paperback 1983), and *Critique of Sociological Reasoning* (1979), as well as numerous articles.

**Linda Brewster Stearns** is an associate professor of sociology at the University of California, Riverside. At present, she is working on a comparative analysis of the ideologies and the institutional structures that promote or impede the involvement of business and government in long-term economic and social planning. In addition, she has been working with Mark Mizruchi on an extended study of the organizational responses to capital dependence. Her publications include *Politics of Privacy* and recent articles in such journals as *Administrative Science Quarterly, Theory and Society,* and *Social Forces.*

**Richard Swedberg** is associate professor at the University of Stockholm, Sweden. He is the author of *Economics and Sociology* (1990), *Schumpeter—A Biography* (1991) and other books in economic sociology. Professor Swedberg is currently working on a book on the European Community.

**Michael Useem** is professor of sociology and management at the University of Pennsylvania. He is completing a book on corporate restructuring and the organization of senior management. With the support of Columbia University's Institutional Investor Project, he is also directing a study of the corporate response to institutional investors.

**Harrison C. White** is professor of sociology and director of the Center for Social Sciences at Columbia University. He is the author of a series of books and articles on economic sociology, including *Chains of Opportunity: System Models of Mobility in Organizations* (1970) and "Where Do Markets Come From?" (1981).

**Viviana A. Zelizer** is professor of sociology at Princeton University. She is the author of *Morals and Markets: The Development of Life Insurance in the United States* (1983) and *Pricing the Priceless Child: The Changing Social Value of Children* (1987).

# Preface

There is a famous story from around the turn of the century about a meeting between Vilfredo Pareto, as always a vigorous advocate of analytical economics, and Gustav von Schmoller, the leader of the socially oriented Historical School of Economics. Pareto was well aware that Schmoller was critical of his idea that one could establish physics-like laws in economics, and once when Pareto was lecturing in Geneva Schmoller noisily interrupted him by shouting, "There are no laws in economics!" Pareto got annoyed and decided to teach Schmoller a lesson. He got his chance the next day when he saw Schmoller in the streets of Geneva. Pareto approached Schmoller and hid his face, pretending to be a beggar (which was not too difficult since Pareto was a shabby dresser). "Please, Sir," Pareto said, "Can you tell me where I can find a restaurant where you can eat for nothing?" Schmoller replied, "My dear man, there are no such restaurants, but there is a place around the corner where you can have a good meal very cheaply." "Ah," said Pareto triumphantly, "so there *are* laws in economics!"

This story is usually told to illustrate the naivete of the proponents for a social and historical approach in economics: they simply do not understand the hard economic realities, as codified in the economists' laws.[1] But today, nearly a century after the meeting between Pareto and Schmoller, it is not so clear that all the laughter would be on Pareto's side. There are several reasons for this. One is that the days are over when it was realistic to believe that economics could develop physics-like laws, valid for all times and countries. Another is that today's economists, following Pareto et al., have gone much too far in eliminating social and historical elements from their analyses. It is no doubt true that neoclas-

[1] For the Pareto-Schmoller anecdote, see, for example, Pareto (1935:xviii). A latter-day version reads "there is no such thing as a free lunch."

sical economics has many splendid accomplishments to its name. But it is equally clear that the current type of analytical economics has failed to integrate a social perspective into its analyses, and that this prevents it from ultimately becoming a truly successful social science.

It is in this situation that economic sociology comes into the picture.[2] *Economic sociology* may be defined as the attempt to analyze economic phenomena as social phenomena or as resulting from human interaction, within the context of broader social structures. As a distinct type of analysis, economic sociology was invented in the 1890s, primarily by Max Weber who was deeply disturbed by the polarization of economics into an historical branch and an analytical branch in the so-called Battle of the Methods *(Methodenstreit)*. But Weber was not alone in his interest in economic sociology; Durkheim and Simmel (and later Schumpeter) were also fascinated by this new approach to economics. All the time, in the background, there was of course also the magnificent work of Karl Marx, formerly in political economy but sociological to its core.[3]

Despite the fact that all the founders of sociology (including Comte!) felt that it was extremely important to develop a sociological analysis of the economy, the topic somehow got lost during the twentieth century when sociology was professionalized and grudgingly accepted into the universities. Sociologists shied away from what they saw as purely "economic" topics (which were left to the economists) and only approached the more social-looking economic problems, often under the protective cover of some relatively innocuous-sounding name such as "consumer sociology," "industrial sociology," and the like. Talcott Parsons, Neil Smelser, and Wilbert E. Moore made a vigorous effort in the late 1950s and early 1960s to revive economic sociology, but failed. Exactly why the topic did not catch on during all these years is not clear. It was actually not till the 1980s that economic sociology got some fresh wind in its sails. Public discourse now shifted to economic topics, especially to the market, and what was soon to be called "New Economic Sociology" started to develop, first slowly and then with increasing speed.[4] This new

---

[2] Throughout this introduction we shall use the term *economic sociology,* since this is the term used—and defined—by Max Weber *(Wirtschaftssoziologie),* Emile Durkheim *(sociologie économique),* and Joseph A. Schumpeter *(Wirtschaftssoziologie* and *economic sociology).* A particularly fine outline of the tasks of economic sociology can be found in Chapter 2 of *Economy and Society* (Weber 1978:63–211).

[3] For the history of economic sociology, see Swedberg (1987; 1991).

[4] See, for example, the work of Mitchell Abolafia (1984), Wayne Baker (1984), Nicole Biggart (1989), Fred Block (1990), Ronald Burt (1983), Paul DiMaggio (1990), Robert Eccles and Dwight Crane (1988), Amitai Etzioni (1988), George Farkas and Paula England (1988), Roger Friedland and A. F. Robertson (1990), Mark Granovetter (1974,

type of economic sociology, it should be noted, is considerably more aggressive than its predecessors. It does not respect the economists' turf, but takes on such "economic" topics as markets, insurance, price formation, and the like. The present volume is the most recent product of this new and more ambitious economic sociology.

## The Origin of the Russell Sage Seminar in Economic Sociology (1990– )

From the viewpoint of economic sociology in general, the decision by the Russell Sage Foundation to start a seminar series in economic sociology, beginning in 1990, was very important. The reason for this is that, even though there are a number of sociologists today who are interested in economic topics, the field of economic sociology itself has been very little institutionalized. Because of its history during most of the twentieth century, little effort has been made to provide economic sociology with the kind of infrastructure that is natural for a major field in sociology. There does not exist, for example, a section devoted to economic sociology in the American Sociological Association; there does not exist a journal (or yearbook) in economic sociology; and there does not exist an association or newsletter for scholars who are interested in economic sociology. Sociologists who do work on economic topics have now and then been able to gather together at the ASA around an isolated session on "the sociology of markets," "the sociology of banking," (or, more recently, simply "economic sociology"). There are also the yearly meetings of the Socio-Economic Society, which are interdisciplinary in nature and where sociological approaches are welcome. But, on the whole, there exists far too little sustained interaction between economic sociologists, and this makes the decision of the Russell Sage Foundation to hold its monthly seminar particularly welcome.

The decision by the Foundation to organize a seminar on economic sociology goes back to its efforts, already expressed in 1987, to "open up economic issues to more socially and behaviorally informed approaches."[5] Originally, this interest in alternative approaches to economics was exclusively centered on behavioral economics; the Foundation thus decided in the late 1980s to co-sponsor a program in this field with the Sloan Foundation. A need to complement behavioral economics with

1985), Gary Hamilton and Nicole Biggart (1988), Beth Mintz and Michael Schwartz (1985), Walter Powell (1987), Susan Shapiro (1984), Arthur Stinchcombe (1983), Harrison White (1970, 1981), Viviana Zelizer (1983, 1985), and Sharon Zukin and Paul DiMaggio (1986).

[5] Eric Wanner in a letter to Mark Granovetter, December 1, 1987.

a more socially oriented type of analysis was, however, soon felt. In the spring of 1988, for example, the idea of putting together a group of economic sociologists at the Foundation was explored. For advice the Foundation turned to Mark Granovetter, who by the mid-80s had emerged as one of the key proponents of New Economic Sociology. In 1989 the Foundation decided to support Granovetter's project for a major theoretical treatise in economic sociology, and it was also agreed that he should help organize a seminar at the Foundation. The seminar, it was understood, should coincide with an effort from the Foundation to invite a few visiting scholars who were particularly interested in economic sociology. By the fall of 1990, the whole set-up was clear: a few visiting scholars had been assembled (Charles Perrow, Frank Romo, and Richard Swedberg), and a date had been set for the seminar.

The first meeting of the seminar took place on October 15, 1990, and nine sociologists attended, mostly from the New York region. The group quickly expanded over the year, and by the time of the last meeting, in June 1991, there were sixteen regularly attending members.[6] Most of these people have contributed chapters to this book. Occasionally, specially invited guests such as Alessandro Pizzorno, Lynne Zucker, and Siegwart Lindenberg attended the seminars. The meetings took place in the library of the Foundation and were chaired by Mark Granovetter. At a typical meeting, two people would present papers, which were then discussed and criticized. Most people presented a few samples of their works-in-progress, which usually meant that four to five papers were read for each session. The seminar series was not centered on a single theme, such as money, markets, or networks in the economy. As a result, there was great diversity of methods and topics in the papers that were presented.

## The Major Themes of this Book

The 1990–1991 seminar at the Foundation was mainly exploratory in nature, and this is reflected in the chapters that have been included in this book as well as in its title. Still, it is clear that certain questions were more discussed than others, and an attempt has been made to group together the chapters so as to reflect this. One of these questions had to do with *the way economic relationships are analyzed in the social sciences* (Part

[6]The sixteen members were: Ronald Burt, Paul DiMaggio, Mark Granovetter, Paul Hirsch, Mark Lazerson, Mark Mizruchi, Marshall Meyer, Charles Perrow, Frank Romo, Charles Sabel, Michael Schwartz, Charles Smith, Richard Swedberg, Michael Useem, Harrison White, and Viviana Zelizer.

I). This topic is obviously central to economic sociology, and a series of different positions are possible: only economics should deal with economic topics; only social (as opposed to neoclassical) approaches should be used when analyzing economic phenomena; and a mixture of economic and social approaches can be used. Two of the chapters in this volume directly address this issue: Mark Granovetter's "The Nature of Economic Relationships" (Chapter 1) and Richard Swedberg's "On the Relationship between Economic Theory and Economic Sociology in the Work of Joseph Schumpeter" (Chapter 2). Both authors argue that one should use a *mixture* of social and economic approaches. Granovetter, for example, finds support for this thesis in his reading of economic anthropology. "The evidence makes clear," he says, "that both supply and demand *and* social structure effect prices and quantities in tribal and peasant markets".[7] Swedberg analyzes Schumpeter's thesis that a complete economic analysis must simultaneously draw on four approaches: economic theory, economic history, economic sociology, and statistics (e.g., Schumpeter 1954:12–21). As Swedberg points out, Schumpeter claimed that a good economist must be trained in all four of these fields—but the specific way that one puts together the concrete analysis is necessarily different from case to case.

Neither Granovetter nor Swedberg spell out in any detail how one is to travel the golden middle road between excesses in economic theory and economic sociology. One can, however, point to two implicit conclusions of their arguments. One is that any kind of economic analysis that does not contain, at some level, a genuinely *social* approach will ultimately fail to get a handle on most economic reality. The other is that the need for a genuinely social approach does not rule out that some of the basic ideas of mainstream economics are very useful. All in all, the two articles by Granovetter and Swedberg thus contain an advocacy for cooperation between economists and sociologists around economic problems.

Another theme that emerged in the seminar has to do with the role of *trust, cooperation, and competition in economic life (Part II)*. According to neoclassical theory, certain social institutions are necessary if the economy is to function properly. Or, as economists sometimes formulate it: Economic mechanisms can only operate within a distinct framework of institutions.[8] Several chapters in this volume, however, go directly counter to this view of things. This is the case with Ronald Burt, "The Social

---

[7] Mark Granovetter, "The Nature of Economic Relationships," page 36, this volume.

[8] See, for example, the introduction to Schumpeter's *History of Economic Analysis*.

Structure of Competition" (Chapter 3), Charles Sabel, "Studied Trust: Building New Forms of Cooperation in a Volatile Economy" (Chapter 4), and Paul Hirsch, "Undoing the Managerial Revolution? Needed Research on the Decline of Middle Management and Internal Labor Markets" (Chapter 5). According to these authors, the economic arena itself (as opposed to the institutional framework that supposedly surrounds it) is not something nonsocial, where everything is decided by demand and supply. Instead, the economic arena consists of a number of mechanisms that are truly social in nature, such as trust, cooperation, and competition. Economists have paid relatively little attention to these three forms of interaction; and when they have discussed them at all, they have usually done so in purely economic terms. But as Burt, Sabel, and Hirsch show, these forms are much more complex than that; and they need to be theoretically reconstructed from a *social* perspective if they are to become truly useful as theoretical tools.

Burt's essay, it should be noted, represents the first sustained attempt by a sociologist to develop a general theory of competition; he does this through a networks approach. The basic idea is that competition consists of a subtle form of social interaction—an attempt to close "social holes," in Burt's terminology—where it is more *the possibility* of a relationship than an actual relationship that is important. How far one can go with Burt's type of analysis is not clear. It is, however, obvious that his whole approach is radically different from that of mainstream economics, where the emphasis is on isolated actors in various combinations (monopoly-oligopoly-perfect competition and so on).

Trust and cooperation, on the other hand, are topics that sociologists have paid quite a bit of attention to over the years, both in the United States and elsewhere.[9] The main point has usually been to show that neither society in general nor some particular institution can exist without trust and cooperation. The two chapters by Sabel and Hirsch attempt, however, to make a different point. Sabel's main contribution consists in laying bare the difficulty in *constructing* trust in employer-worker relationships. Hirsch similarly notes that once trust is destroyed, it can have disturbing ripple effects elsewhere in the economy. His empirical focus, however, is on a different group than Sabel, namely middle managers.

---

[9] The literature on cooperation goes back to Marx and Durkheim. Though Simmel (1978) discussed the notion of trust (he was the first sociologist to do so), it was not until the 1970s and 1980s that this concept was integrated into mainstream sociological theory. The most sophisticated theoretical approach to trust is probably that of Luhmann (1979); for an overview of the literature, see, for example, Shapiro (1987).

Another theme that emerged during the seminar had to do with *the social construction of economic institutions,* such as money, markets, and industries (Part III). It is clear that much of the work that pioneered New Economic Sociology in the 1980s was centered on economic institutions, and it seems that this topic continues to fascinate economic sociologists. It would be premature to say that there already exists a new and exciting sociological theory of economic institutions. It seems, however, that such a theory is well under way; and the reader can get a sense of what it will probably look like in its final version by reading the following four essays: Harrison C. White, "Markets in Production Networks" (Chapter 6); Charles W. Smith, "Auctions: From Walras to the Real World" (Chapter 7); Viviana Zelizer, "Making Multiple Monies" (Chapter 8); and Patrick McGuire, Mark Granovetter, and Michael Schwartz, "Thomas Edison and the Social Construction of the Early Electricity Industry in America" (Chapter 9). All these chapters emphasize that economic institutions are basically to be understood as a kind of *social construction.* This term is primarily associated with Berger and Luckmann's famous book *The Social Construction of Reality* (1966) and comes from the work of Alfred Schutz (see Granovetter 1990:108–109). Most of the people who use it, however, are not particularly inspired by Schutz (who had picked up the key ideas from Weber). Instead they use the term *social construction* in a rather loose sense, mainly to indicate that an institution is not something given, but rather the result of a complicated construction through social interaction.

One consequence of this social construction perspective is that the neoclassical vision of how institutions come into being (New Institutional Economics) is seen as hopelessly flawed.[10] This comes out with particular clarity in the essay by McGuire, Granovetter, and Schwartz on the electric utility industry. Another consequence is a strong emphasis on the need for a historical perspective: a "construction" begins by definition at a certain moment in time and evolves from there. It also seems that today's economic sociologists reject the economists' idea that there exist only a few basic economic institutions and that these are unitary in nature. According to economic theory, there is, for example, only *one* type of money, *one* type of market, and *one* type of auction. But the authors of Chapters 6 through 9 argue that there exists a real multiplicity

[10]The main sociological argument against New Institutional Economics is that the emergence and functioning of social institutions cannot be explained in terms of cost efficiency. While people such as Coase and Williamson argue that a corporation is used rather than the market because it is cheaper to proceed in this manner, sociologists claim that this type of analysis falls into the old trap of functionalism: everything is said to exist because it fulfills some function that is constructed ex post (see Granovetter 1985).

of different types of monies, markets, and auctions. Another sign of multiplicity that incidentally characterizes these four chapters is that they all use different approaches and material to get at their topics. Harrison White uses model building; Smith, ethnographic material; Zelizer, social and cultural history; and McGuire, Granovetter, and Schwartz, business history. This multiplicity of material and approaches also hints of the pluralism that currently characterizes economic sociology.

A further theme in this book has to do with *the performance of firms and their environments* (Part IV). Sociologists have for a long time been interested in large corporations and used a number of different perspectives in analyzing these, especially those of Marx, Weber, and organization theory. Some of this interest has today been channeled into an interest in economic sociology. Four essays in this section exemplify this tendency: Marshall Meyer (in collaboration with Kenneth O'Shaughnessy), "Organizational Design and the Performance Paradox" (Chapter 10); Linda Brewster Stearns and Mark Mizruchi, "Corporate Financing: Social and Economic Determinants" (Chapter 11); Michael Useem, "Shareholder Power and the Struggle for Corporate Control" (Chapter 12); and Frank Romo and Michael Schwartz, "The Coming of Post-Industrial Society Revisited: Manufacturing and the Prospects for a Service-Based Economy" (Chapter 13). These chapters also focus on a much-discussed problem in recent organization theory: the interaction of firms with their environments. A particular theme that unites them further is that of performance. Marshall Meyer, for example, analyzes why there is so little correlation between various performance measures. Linda Brewster Stearns and Mark Mizruchi approach the topic of firms, performance, and their environments from a different angle: when does a corporation need to borrow money and what role does its relationship to financial institutions play in this process? Michael Useem analyzes the way an old interest group—the owners—have recently made a comeback in the modern corporation and what consequences this may have. And, finally, Frank Romo and Michael Schwartz suggest that the vitality of regional economies depends on how tightly linked individual corporations (as well as whole industrial sectors) are to one another.

Finally, two additional chapters on corporations were presented at the seminar that also deal with performance in relation to the corporate environment. Since both of them, however, focus on small firms, it seemed more appropriate to discuss them in a separate section centered on the theme of *small firms in networks* (Part V). One of these chapters is exclusively devoted to a case study—Mark Lazerson's "Future Alternatives of Work Reflected in the Past: Putting-Out Production in Modena" (Chapter 15)—and the other is more general in nature, Charles Perrow's "Small

Firm Networks." Both, however, agree that the significance of small firms in production networks extends well beyond their actual role in the economy. From the vantage point of his research, Lazerson thus states that "the sun is setting on the epoch of centralized production." And Perrow argues that the existence of small firms networks is one of the very few phenomena that go counter to the general trend in modern society for the large corporation to absorb ever more of social life.

## Concluding Remarks

When the seminar at the Russell Sage Foundation was initiated, it was hoped that it would help to further the development of economic sociology. We can now present the contribution made by the seminar in 1990–1991 in a more concise form. There is, first of all, the insight or proposition that economic sociology and economic theory often complement each other and that one has to draw on both for an adequate analysis. This was particularly emphasized in the more general essays (Granovetter, Swedberg). Or to cite two concrete examples: when a price is decided, both social elements and demand-supply forces are involved (Granovetter); and when a corporation decides to borrow money, this decision is influenced not only by its need for new funds but also by its social network (Stearns and Mizruchi). Markets, it was also emphasized, are primarily to be understood as social structures, which means that many of the more un-social premises of neoclassical theory definitely have to be scrapped (White).

A further contribution of this volume is represented by the attempt to lay bare certain intermediate processes that are fundamental to economic life, such as trust, competition, and cooperation. As to trust, two important theoretical points were made: that trust is difficult—but not impossible—to create in economic relationships (Sabel); and that the destruction of trust in one area of the economy may have destructive ripple effects in other areas (Hirsch). An interesting and ambitious attempt to develop a theory of competition was also presented at the seminar (Burt). This was centered on the idea of "structural holes," and is a further example of how important networks analysis has become for today's economic sociology.

Another interesting development in New Economic Sociology, which was also represented at the seminar, has to do with the attempt to develop a sociological theory of economic institutions. This theory is currently associated with the slogan "the social construction of economic institutions," and is being simultaneously worked on by a number of people with very diverse interests. This book contains, for example, chapters along these lines in the sociology of money (Zelizer), on auctions (Smith) and on production markets (White). A fascinating attempt to account for the emergence of a whole industry was also made (McGuire, Granovetter, and Schwartz).

Sociologists have also continued to make advances in the study of business corporations. The decision made at the seminar to focus attention on performance is definitely innovative (Meyer); as is the attempt to analyze why corporations borrow (Stearns and Mizruchi). There are also promising signs that economic sociologists are becoming more sophisticated in their discussions of major public issues concerning the economy, such as deindustrialization (Romo and Schwartz) and the relationship between owners and managers in the huge corporations (Useem, Hirsch). Novel contributions to the old debate about the advantages of small versus large corporations were also made (Perrow, Lazerson).

For a variety of reasons, a number of important issues were *not* raised during the Russell Sage seminar in 1990–1991—but, it is hoped, will be discussed during the years to come. One lacks, for example, a comparative perspective or a gender perspective in many of the chapters that have been included in this book. And no author tried to analyze the momentous events that are currently going on in the economies of Eastern Europe and in what was once the Soviet Union. Some of the classic topics in economic sociology were also passed over in silence, topics such as consumption, the international economy, and the relationship between religion and economic life. It also seems that, although many sociologists today have some knowledge of economic theory, there is little equivalent knowledge of economic history. This is a pity because some of the best works in economic history—such as those by Henri Pirenne, Marc Bloch, and Alexander Gerschenkron—show a natural affinity with economic sociology. So perhaps this is the time to recall once more Schumpeter's dictum that a sound analysis of economic topics (or what he called *Sozialökonomik*) must simultaneously draw on several approaches: economic theory, economic sociology, economic history, and statistics.

# References

ABOLAFIA, MITCHELL. 1984. "Structured Anarchy: Formal Organization in the Commodities Futures Market." In Patricia A. Adler and Peter Adler eds., *The Social Dynamics of Financial Markets*. Greenwich, CT: JAI Press, pp. 129–150.

BAKER, WAYNE. 1984. "The Social Structure of a National Securities Market." *American Journal of Sociology* 89:775–811.

BERGER, PETER, and THOMAS LUCKMANN. 1966. *The Social Construction of Reality: A Treatise in the Sociology of Knowledge*. New York: Doubleday.

BIGGART, NICOLE. 1989. *Charismatic Capitalism: Direct Selling Organizations in America.* Chicago: University of Chicago Press.

BLOCK, FRED. 1990. *Postindustrial Possibilities: A Critique of Economic Discourse.* Berkeley, CA: University of California Press.

BURT, RONALD. 1983. *Corporate Profits and Cooptation: Networks of Market Constraints and Directorate Ties in the American Economy.* New York: Academic Press.

DiMAGGIO, PAUL. 1990. "Cultural Aspects of Economic Action and Organization." In Roger Friedland and A. F. Robertson eds., *Beyond the Market Place: Rethinking Economy and Society,* New York: Aldine, pp. 113–136.

ECCLES, ROBERT G., and DWIGHT B. CRANE. 1988. *Doing Deals: Investment Banks at Work.* Boston: Harvard Business School.

ETZIONI, AMITAI. 1988. *The Moral Dimension: Towards a New Economics.* New York: Free Press.

FARKAS, GEORGE, and PAULA ENGLAND. 1988. *Industries, Firms and Jobs: Sociological and Economic Approaches.* New York: Plenum.

FLIGSTEIN, NEIL. 1990. *The Transformation of Corporate Control.* Cambridge, MA: Harvard University Press.

FRIEDLAND, ROGER, and A. F. ROBERTSON, eds. 1990. *Beyond the Market Place: Rethinking Economy and Society.* New York: Aldine.

GRANOVETTER, MARK. 1974. *Getting A Job.* Cambridge, MA: Harvard University Press.

––––––. 1985. "Economic Action and Social Structure: The Problem of Embeddedness." *American Journal of Sociology* 91:481–510.

––––––. 1990. "Interview." In Richard Swedberg, *Economics and Sociology: Redefining Their Boundaries—Interviews with Economists and Sociologists,* Princeton: Princeton University Press.

HAMILTON, GARY, and NICOLE BIGGART. 1988. "Market, Culture, and Authority: A Comparative Analysis of Management and Organization in the Far East." *American Journal of Sociology* 94:S52–S94.

LUHMANN, NIKLAS. 1979. *Trust and Power.* New York: Wiley.

MINTZ, BETH, and MICHAEL SCHWARTZ. 1985. *The Power Structure of American Business.* Chicago: University of Chicago Press.

PARETO, VILFREDO. 1935. *The Mind and Society: A Treatise on General Sociology.* New York: Dover Publications.

POWELL, WALTER. 1987. "Hybrid Organizational Arrangements: New Form or Transitional Development?" *California Management Review* 30(1):67–87.

SCHUMPETER, JOSEPH A. 1954. *History of Economic Analysis.* London: Allen & Unwin.

SHAPIRO, SUSAN. 1984. *Wayward Capitalists: Targets of the Security and Exchange Commission.* New Haven, CT: Yale University Press.

––––––. 1987. "The Social Control of Impersonal Trust." *American Journal of Sociology* 93:623–658.

SIMMEL, GEORG. 1978. *The Philosophy of Money*. London: Routledge & Kegan Paul.

STINCHCOMBE, ARTHUR. 1983. *Economic Sociology*. New York: Academic Press.

SWEDBERG, RICHARD. 1987. "Economic Sociology: Past and Present." *Current Sociology*, 35(1):1–221.

———. 1991. "Major Traditions of Economic Sociology." *Annual Review of Sociology* 17(1991):251–276.

WEBER, MAX. 1978. *Economy and Society: An Outline of Interpretive Sociology*. Berkeley: University of California Press.

WHITE, HARRISON C. 1970. *Chains of Opportunity*. Cambridge, MA: Harvard University Press.

———. 1981. "Where Do Markets Come From?" *American Journal of Sociology* 87:517–547.

ZELIZER, VIVIANA. 1983. *Morals and Markets: The Development of Life Insurance in the United States*. New Brunswick: Transaction Press.

———.1985. *Pricing the Priceless Child: The Changing Social Values of Children*. New York: Basic Books.

ZUKIN, SHARON, and PAUL DiMAGGIO eds. 1986. "Structures of Capital." (Special Double Issue) *Theory & Society* 15(1–2):1–313.

# I

# ECONOMIC RELATIONSHIPS AND THE SOCIAL SCIENCES

# 1

# The Nature of Economic Relationships

## MARK GRANOVETTER

If economic action is embedded in networks of relations (cf. Granovetter 1985), it is logical to begin our investigation by discussing the nature of those relations. A main issue is how much economic activity is carried out between individuals who have personal knowledge of one another that affects their economic action, and how this compares with the rather impersonal relations implicit or explicit in most neoclassical economic theorizing. Where such personal knowledge is important, we need to identify the dimensions of these relationships along which variation affects economic outcomes.

Much of this chapter discusses economic activity in tribal and peasant societies. This is not because I think the subject is more critical there than in the modern industrial setting, but rather because the vast majority of studies that shed light on the texture of personal economic relations have been carried out in nonindustrial societies. In the more "modern" setting, economists' training disinclines them to study such matters, and, as documented in Granovetter (forthcoming), sociologists are only beginning to do so.

It is among some of those who study nonindustrial societies that we find what one might call the "strong" embeddedness position—the argument that modern economic analysis sheds *no light whatsoever* on these settings, because economic action and institutions are totally embedded in and submerged by other social institutions, having no recognizable separate existence. Thus I begin by laying out the main elements of the debate on this issue in the literature on economic anthropology, focusing especially on the important dispute between "substantivists" and "formalists." Subsequently I assess the value of these various viewpoints for understanding several aspects of economic life and try to indicate how my argument about embeddedness draws back from the strong embeddedness position, in order to better clarify these issues.

# The Substantivist-Formalist Debate in Anthropology

In the 1950s a bitter debate broke out among two groups of economic anthropologists, who came to be known as "substantivists" and "formalists," the former proclaiming the irrelevance of formal economic analysis to the economic institutions of tribal societies, the latter its explanatory power. On the whole, the substantivist view was closer to the main line of anthropological thought, stressing the primacy of the whole community and opposing the reduction of events to the motives and actions of individuals; it has attracted many more eminent anthropologists than the formalist view.

Substantivists would argue, correspondingly, that the texture of economic relations cannot be understood without analyzing the culture and institutional structure of the society as a whole. As William Davis notes, the two views are special instances of a longstanding split in anthropology between adherents of a " 'superorganic' viewpoint and the adherents of methodological individualism, or 'actor-oriented' models. . . . The basic issue . . . is the level of organization that provides the main locus of social processes. Individualists . . . hold that individual persons are the principal concrete elements in social dynamics. . . . [S]uperorganicists argue that individual persons cannot be the loci of process for they are themselves constituted by specifically social processes that do not exist at the individual level. Individuals desire the goals they seek, have the means they command, and make the decisions they express primarily as a result of the imposition on them of processes that are inherent in the external constraints themselves . . ." (1986: 167–168). This depiction of the debate suggests, and I will argue, that the substantivist-formalist split corresponds to that which I have identified between over- and undersocialized views in other work on economic action.

The substantivist school of economic anthropology was founded by a Hungarian refugee economic historian who held no regular academic positions during most of his life: Karl Polanyi (1886–1964).[1] Polanyi's

---

[1] Polanyi's most important work for our purposes was accomplished at Bennington College in the 1940s and at Columbia University after World War II, from which he retired

influence rests on three productions: his 1944 book *The Great Transformation: The Political and Economic Origins of our Time;* an important 1947 article published in the journal *Commentary,* "Our Obsolete Market Mentality"; and a volume edited with Conrad Arensberg and Harry Pearson, *Trade and Market in the Early Empires* (1957). The first is an analysis of the emergence of the self-regulating market in nineteenth-century Europe, especially England. Sounding what was to become a main substantivist theme, Polanyi observed that all types of societies "are limited by economic factors. Nineteenth-century civilization alone was economic in a different and distinctive sense, for it chose to base itself on a motive only rarely acknowledged as valid in the history of human societies, and certainly never before raised to the level of a justification of action and behavior in everyday life, namely, gain" (1944:30). Markets had been important, of course, Polanyi observed, at least from the 16th century on. But "there was still no sign of the coming control of markets over human society. . . . [T]he very idea of a self-regulating market was absent. [There was a] . . . sudden changeover to an utterly new type of economy in the 19th century" (1944:55).

Polanyi argued that the self-regulating market, in order to set prices and function without external intervention, had to make abstract commodities out of labor and land. But this enterprise, in his view, would have destroyed the social fabric if successfully completed. To "separate labor from other activities of life and to subject it to the laws of the market was to annihilate all organic forms of existence and to replace them by a different type of organization, an atomistic and individualistic one. . . . [T]he noncontractual organizations of kinship, neighborhood, profession and creed were to be liquidated since they claimed the allegiance of the individual and thus restrained his freedom." And land "is an element of nature inextricably interwoven with man's institutions. To isolate it and form a market out of it was perhaps the weirdest of all undertakings of our ancestors" (1944:163, 178).

For Polanyi, the reign of the self-regulating market came to an end in the crisis of the 1930s, and one can summarize the process in the formula that nineteenth-century civilization "disintegrated as the result of . . . the measures which society adopted in order not to be, in its turn, annihilated by the action of the self-regulating market. . . . [T]he conflict between the market and the elementary requirements of an organized social life provided the century with its dynamics and produced the typical strains and distresses which ultimately destroyed that society. External wars merely hastened its destruction" (1944:249). In the 1947 article

in 1953 to Canada where his wife "had settled because McCarthyism had prohibited her from living in the United States" (Block and Somers 1984:51).

on the "obsolete" market mentality, Polanyi pushed the comparative ideas farther. In market society, an " 'economic sphere' came into existence that was sharply delimited from other institutions in society. . . . Ranging over human societies, we find hunger and gain not appealed to as incentives to production, and where so appealed to, they are fused with other powerful motives. . . . Man's economy is, as a rule, submerged in his social relations. The change from this to a society which was, on the contrary, submerged in the economic system was an entirely novel development." In primitive societies, "the individual is not in danger of starving unless the community as a whole is in a like predicament." And though markets and merchants are familiar in many kinds of society, "isolated markets do not link up into an economy. The motive of gain was specific to merchants, as was valor to the knight, piety to the priest, and pride to the craftsman. The notion of making the motive of gain universal never entered the heads of our ancestors." Polanyi decried the separation of material and ideal motives that he saw as specific to market society and pleaded "for the restoration of that unity of motives which should inform man in his everyday activity as a producer, for the reabsorption of the economic system in society . . ." (1947:111–116).

Polanyi thus set himself squarely in the tradition of those mid-century modernization theorists who saw a sharp break between earlier and modern societies in the level of societal differentiation and in the underlying principles that governed all human relationships, such as those dichotomies indexed by Talcott Parsons's "pattern variables" and earlier by the distinctions between status and contract made by Henry Sumner Maine or between *Gemeinschaft* and *Gesellschaft* by Ferdinand Toennies. As Polanyi himself summed up the line of intellectual descent: "It is now possible to say that status or *gemeinschaft* dominate where the economy is embedded in noneconomic institutions; *contractus* or *gesellschaft* is characteristic of the existence of a motivationally distinct economy in society" (1957:70).

In *Trade and Market in the Early Empires* (1957) Polanyi, with his collaborators, turned more seriously to the comparative and historical work required to flesh out the earlier claims. This book, more influential among anthropologists than the earlier work, collects a series of empirical papers on trade (especially long distance) in ancient empires, and several important theoretical papers, the key one being Polanyi's "The Economy as Instituted Process." Here Polanyi distinguishes two fundamentally different meanings of the word *economic*. One is the formal meaning, which "derives from the logical character of the means–ends relationship, as apparent in such words as 'economical' or 'economizing.' " The other is the substantive meaning, which "derives from man's dependence for his living upon nature and his fellows. It refers to the interchange with his natural and social environment, in so far as this results in supplying him with the means of material want satisfaction." He goes on to claim that these two meanings "have nothing in common. The [formal] . . . derives from logic, the [substantive] . . . from fact. . . . It is our proposition that only the substantive meaning of 'economic' is capable of yielding the concepts that are required by the social sciences for an investigation of all the empirical economies of the past and present" (1957:243–244). Formal economics refers to choice situations that arise from an insufficiency of means—that is, situations of scarcity, as represented in price-making markets. But outside of such markets, "economic analysis loses most of its relevance as a method of inquiry into the working of the economy. A centrally planned economy, relying on nonmarket prices is a well-known instance" (1957:247).

The economy, then, is an "instituted process"; it is "embedded and enmeshed in institutions, economic and noneconomic. The inclusion of the noneconomic is vital. For religion or government may be as important for the structure and functioning of the economy as monetary institutions or . . . tools and machines . . ." (Polanyi 1957:250). Polanyi distinguishes three ways in which actual economies are integrated: reciprocity, redistribution, and exchange. Reciprocity characterizes an economy dominated by symmetrically organized structures such as kinship groups. Redistribution presupposes a strong central organization that collects and redistributes goods. Exchange integrates the economy under a system of price-making markets. As Pearson suggests, these three principles of integration correspond respectively to the dominance of social, political, and economic principles of order in society (Pearson 1977:xxxv).

Polanyi stresses that dyadic acts of exchange cannot produce overall integration of the system in the absence of the appropriate institutional framework. Thus, the reciprocative behavior of gift exchange and kinship transactions results in important economic institutions only when the environment is "symmetrically organized," redistribution is meaningless in the absence of strong allocative centers, and "only in the presence of a system of price-making markets will exchange acts of individuals result in fluctuating prices that integrate the economy" (1957:252). More than one type of integration may characterize any given empirical economy, and the three do not represent a series of stages. But for Polanyi, only when the third is dominant to an extent that excludes the other two does modern economics come into its own as a set of explanatory principles, and the "artificial identification of the economy with its market form" is what he calls the "economistic fallacy" (1957:270n). He thought it urgent to expose this fallacy on account of what he saw as the fall of market society in the twentieth century. In "the receding rule of the market in the modern world, shapes reminiscent of the economic organization of earlier times make their appearance" (1957:xviii) and hence one cannot understand the new situation without the help of this broader substantivist framework.

Having made these claims, the Polanyi group might have oriented their empirical research around a number of different elements, such as the actual extent of distribution of the profit motive, the perception by economic actors of scarcity of resources available for the achievement of alternative ends, or the extent to which norms that deflect unbridled individualism in favor of community responsibility to each member actually characterize tribal and peasant economic activity. Instead, most of the program of *Trade and Market in the Early Empires* revolved around demonstrating the absence of price-making markets in the ancient world, where economic life was said to be integrated instead by reciprocity and especially redistribution. At times in the work, it is literally argued that the absence of markets as a *physical* phenomenon in economic life proves that the economy was not *integrated* by markets—that if the most important trading was not actually conducted in one physical location by some process of auction or haggling, then prices could not have been made by markets and one should speak of "marketless trading" (Polanyi et al. 1957:Ch. 2). And this is taken to be a significant matter because nonmarket trade "is in all essentials different from market trade" (1957:19).

Thus, Arnold argues that for West Africa, trade was historically an affair of state, carried out in specially designated and organized ports of trade, unrelated to the physical markets that existed, but that served only to match common goods with ordinary people (in Polanyi et al. 1957:177 ff.). In general, the writers in the *Trade and Market* volume stress that international trade is a matter of state, and that prices in such trade are established through some combination of tradition and strong administration, rather than by any market process. They stress that traders were a small, elite group whose income derived not from price differentials but from commissions and from the comparative monopoly status conferred on them by civil authorities.

The other highly influential theoretical work in substantivist economic anthropology was Marshall Sahlins's *Stone Age Economics* (1972).[2] The

---

[2] I make no attempt to give a full historical account of economic anthropology, but discuss only some of the main disputes insofar as they provide background for my later treatment of particular issues in economic sociology. Thus, many important economic anthropologists are either omitted or given cursory treatment. One brief historical treatment, from the formalist viewpoint, is given in the introduction to LeClair and Schneider (1968), which also collects many of the most important theoretical and empirical articles up through

choice facing economic anthropologists, for Sahlins, is easy: it is "a choice between the perspective of Business, for the formalist method must consider the primitive economies as underdeveloped versions of our own, and a culturalist study that as a matter of principle does honor to different societies for what they are" (1972:xii). This comment signals that Sahlins will take up in much more detail the fundamental questions of culture and "human nature" that the Polanyi group adumbrate but do not flesh out. The first chapter, for example, which characterizes hunting and gathering groups as "the original affluent society," asserts that the fundamental orientation of members of such groups is alien to the "businesslike" mentality assumed by economics, in that wants are finite and satisfied. By contrast, modern microeconomics assumes that all actors face scarcity and tradeoffs: "Where production and distribution are arranged through the behavior of prices, and all livelihoods depend on getting and spending, insufficiency of material means becomes the explicit, calculable starting point of all economic activity. . . . every acquisition is simultaneously a deprivation, for every purchase of something is a foregoing of something else . . ." (1972:4). Sahlins goes on to describe the "domestic mode of production," where production is for use, within finite, well-defined customary needs, unlike capitalism, where the aim of production is wealth and is therefore unlimited (1972:Ch. 2). In fact, Sahlins characterizes the domestic mode of production as involving "underproduction," and argues that under many circumstances strong central political leadership is required to mobilize a more impressive economic performance (1972:Ch. 3). He goes on to argue that in trade relations in tribal societies, the ratios at which goods are traded or bartered are not fundamentally established by supply and demand, but are customary, a claim I discuss below.

I treat substantivist arguments in more detail than formalist ones because the latter consist mainly of assertions that the familiar neoclassical assumptions are indeed satisfied for tribal as well as modern societies. Many of the explicit claims of substantivists are simply denied, as in the typical formalist claim that individuals in many if not most tribes are in fact rational actors with well-defined needs, facing scarcity and acting as if they understood the relevant tradeoffs. (LeClair and Schneider 1968;

the mid-1960s. Another useful collection, with a more substantivist bias, is Dalton 1967. Orlove (1986) assesses the status of economic anthropology as of the mid-1980s, noting that the substantivist-formalist debate continues in attenuated form, with few participants willing to be associated with the older polemically tinged group categories, but nevertheless making arguments with a distinct family resemblance to them, and now joined in the fray by neo-Marxists, who had been no more in evidence in 1950s anthropology than in other social sciences of the period.

Schneider 1974). LeClair and Schneider point out that rational choice among tradeoffs in economic thought need not be limited to strictly economic goals. "An individual might readily give up a full belly in order to secure an added measure of social status, and indeed, the anthropological literature contains numerous cases of this sort of decision. Here the individual is not choosing something noneconomic over something economic. He is allocating his resources between nourishment and status, accepting somewhat less nourishment in the interest of having somewhat more social status" (1968:7).

Schneider charges that substantivism is allied to functionalism in anthropology, as both focus on how societies maintain themselves. "The economy, in Polanyi's terms, seems naturally to be 'embedded', i.e., to serve the maintenance of the system. When it does not it needs to be adjusted in order to avoid adverse effects on the social system" (1974:7). Substantivists are functionalists in part because, rejecting self-interest as a motive, they see "functional theory, with its emphasis on how actions serve the community rather than the self" (1974:20) as more appropriate. Here, Schneider points to the emphasis on interpreting individual action in terms of commonly held values in the community as undergirding substantivist arguments. I would argue that reliance on either undersocialized or oversocialized arguments produces a bias toward functional explanations because one cannot understand how institutions are constructed without seeing individual actors as embedded in social structure. In these terms we might recast the formalist charge against the substantivists as the recognition that an oversocialized view of action leads to functionalist emphasis, since there is always a ready end-in-view to which we can attribute all actions and institutions: the welfare of the community.

A related theme is that, in Cook's words, "the substantivists' intransigency concerning the cross-cultural applicability of formal economic theory is a by-product of a romantic ideology rooted in an antipathy toward the 'market economy' and an idealization of the 'primitive.'" And, he continues, "implicit in Polanyi's writings and inevitably adopted by other substantivist writers is a utopian model of primitive society which minimizes the role of conflict, coupled with a model of man which emphasizes innate altruistic and cooperative propensities while playing down self-interest, aggressiveness and competitiveness" (1968:209, 213). I will begin my assessment of the debate, and move toward the subject of how economic relationships are constituted, by examining the claims about human nature.

## "Human Nature" and Economic Relations in Tribal and Peasant Economies

The phrase "human nature" lends itself to both undersocialized and oversocialized conceptions of action. The undersocialized account implies the existence of some fundamental character of individual human beings apart from and independent of membership and interaction within a social group, the classic *Homo economicus*. But oversocialized (e.g., substantivist) accounts also have a story about human nature, only a different one, that plays down the motive of gain, a motive taken to be, in some unspecified sense, "unnatural," compared to devotion to one's social group.

Thus, substantivists argue that human nature in nonmarket societies is less oriented to profit and gain and to the insatiable pursuit of more and more economic goods than it is in market societies. But this assertion neglects the standard neoclassical observation that material goods (or the income required to purchase them) are typically traded off against leisure in the usual indifference curve analysis, where the shape of the curve and the marginal rate of substitution between income and leisure result from the preferences described by some utility function (e.g., Nicholson 1985:531–534). Thus, when Sahlins tells us that hunting and gathering groups have finite wants and stop when they achieve them, this poses no difficulty for the usual neoclassical analysis of labor supply; it only describes preferences that are possibly (but not necessarily) different from the typical ones in capitalist societies, with a higher value put on leisure than on material goods. The fundamental neoclassical argument that some economizing takes place in the tradeoff between labor and leisure seems reasonable enough given the ethnographic data. When hunting and gathering groups find, in their temporary camps, that they have depleted the supply of nearby flora and fauna, and the time and effort required to go farther afield to find them becomes too burdensome, they decide to disband their camp and move to a new location (e.g., the Mbuti as described in Turnbull, 1961). Only if such decisions appeared totally arbitrary from the point of view of economizing on effort could we suspect that no rational tradeoffs were being made. Sahlins is struck by the "underuse" of their environment by hunters and gatherers, by which he means that they do not collect the maximum amount of food possible in a given day. He cites approvingly an account suggesting that perhaps "unconsciously they weigh the benefit of greater supplies of food against the effort involved in collecting it, perhaps they judge what they consider to be enough, and when that is collected they stop" (McArthur 1960:92 cited in Sahlins 1972:18). But this is equivalent to arguing that they economize via labor/leisure tradeoffs; it shows that the idea of underuse is quite arbitrary; and it implicitly assumes a set of preferences different from the ones most likely in place.[3]

If the substantivist case for an entirely different set of motivations in tribal and peasant economies is thus overdrawn, we may wonder whether this is not also the case for their picture of human beings entirely captured by greed and avarice when in the thrall of societies dominated by the market. Strangely enough, it is Polanyi himself, in the midst of his assertions about the domination of market society by the motive of gain, who occasionally steps back and acknowledges that this could never have really been so. "In actual fact," he tells us, "man was never as selfish as the theory demanded. Though the market mechanism brought his dependence upon material goods to the fore, 'economic' motives never formed with him the sole incentive to work. In vain was he exhorted by economists and utilitarian moralists alike to discount in business all other motives than 'material' ones. On closer investigation, he was still found to be acting on remarkably 'mixed' motives, not excluding those of duty towards himself and others—and maybe, secretly, even enjoying work for its own sake" (1947:114). Indeed, much of the argument of *The Great Transformation* is that measures were taken by society to ensure that the dangers of a truly self-regulating market would never be fully in place; and that these dangers were so great and immediate that countermeasures occurred quickly and spontaneously that prevented the market from ever attaining the hold on society that Polanyi, in other parts of the book, describes it as having had (e.g., 1944:Ch. 11). So the self-regulating market plays the role only of an ideal type in Polanyi's historical work. "We are not dealing here, of course, with pictures of actuality, but with conceptual patterns used for the purposes of clarification. No market economy separated from the political sphere is possible . . ." (1944:196). Or "we are not concerned here with actual, but with assumed motives, not with the psychology, but with the ideology of business" (1947:114). All this amounts to an admission that Polanyi's assertions about the submergence of society by the economy when markets are in place must be taken as rhetorical, only a statement of tendency,

---

[3] The substantivist attack on the supposed neoclassical attribution to humans of an "insatiable" demand for goods may rest on the postulate, in axiomatic treatments of consumption, that "more is better"—in the sense that more of any commodity carries higher utility, independent of prices or income. But a more precise version of the required postulate is much more modest in its claim, which is one only of "local nonsatiation"—that is, that whatever bundle of commodities one considers for a given consumer, there always exists one that is a little better, in which one need not require that there is more of every commodity, only more of some, with no less of the others (e.g., Varian 1978:82).

rather than as historical fact. And this suggests that the substantivist view really does rest on a conception of human nature as fundamentally oriented to group rather than individual benefit, since not even the juggernaut of the self-regulating market can entirely submerge this human characteristic.

The empirical ethnographic literature shows, in fact, an immense range of attitudes toward economic activity, rather than a simple model of human nature. There are tribal economies populated by individuals with a surprising resemblance to *Homo economicus,* and other such economies whose participants think very little about individual advantage. The existence of the former groups must cast doubt on the most extreme version of any embeddedness argument. Writing of a small Guatemalan community circa 1940, Sol Tax noted that there was "probably no Panajachel Indian over the age of 10 who has not calculated a way to make money with his available resources. . . . I doubt that I know even one man in the region who is not interested in new ways of making money, who does not have, typically, an iron or two in the fire, and who does not make his living partly as a business enterpriser. . . . The ethic of the community seems admirably suited to such an economy. There is frank admission that wealth is good." Though there are only 800 some odd residents in the village, relations "appear extraordinarily impersonal. . . . for its size, the community is surprisingly 'atomized'; that is, individuals tend to be separate units, each related to others with respect to a single role. . . . most of the ties that bind tend . . . to unite many people lightly and ephemerally rather than to bind a few in tightly knit groups. The family group tends to break up as the children mature; neighborhood ties mean next to nothing" (1963:18–19). But perhaps we are looking in the wrong place for a "tribal" economic pattern. Guatemalan Indians are involved in a monetized economy where they must engage in some commercial agriculture to earn the money required for their daily needs (1963:12).

And in fact the substantivist might point out that, with the exception of Tax's Indians, most cases of such behavior, called on by formalists to show the value of formal economic analysis, occur in just one part of the world: the Melanesian region north of Australia, comprising New Guinea and numerous smaller islands. So, Pospisil tells us of the (New Guinea) Kapauku Papuans that, "unlike many primitive peoples, [they] are basically profit-motivated in most of their activities. They place a great emphasis on accumulation of personal wealth from which they derive, through extension of credit, the highest prestige and following" (1963:381). Indeed, there is here a "native obsession with quantification. . . . These people are so fascinated by numbers that they indulge in counting, in recalling precise [shell money] sums paid in specific exchange transactions, and in discussing these data at any opportunity that presents itself" (1963:14). Long before we had heard about "Type A" behavior, Pospisil described natives constantly tense from their business deals, one in particular being a "formidably rich and active headman" who "one day, apparently healthy and in the prime of his life, . . . simply dropped dead. Although the Kapauku claim that it was an obvious case of sorcery, I still ponder about the possibility of a business type of heart failure" (1963:388).

In the most extreme examples of groups that are calculative and profit oriented, the general social pattern is one that is rather atomized, and economic relationships are rather impersonal.[4] Thus, Pospisil describes the Kapauku as having an extreme form of individualism. All property is individually owned, and common ownership to a Kapauku is simply inconceivable. The Kapauku dislike working together, so that the work is highly individualized. Unlike virtually all tribal societies, they do not even share food within the village (population size = 181), so that some children from poor homes are severely undernourished, and "there is no collective action that would keep individuals from starving." Pospisil suggests that "Kapauku individualism appears, in some respects, to be more rugged than our present Western capitalistic form" (1963:144, 402, 404).

This case does seem extreme in the ethnographic record. In another New Guinea case cited approvingly by formalists, the Siane, Salisbury (1962) concludes that in this fiercely individualist group "there is allocation of scarce means, based on a rational calculation in terms of quantities of goods and services, and in which goods are produced, exchanged and consumed" (1962:4). The elementary family hardly functions, men and women living apart and husbands visiting their wives only at night. Yet, even here there is a feeling of mutual obligation within the village, and food is distributed so that all individuals obtain equal shares (1962:17, 37, 81). And though the sense of property rights is extremely strong ("if a man enters a garden on which there are growing crops, the personalty [i.e., property] of a woman, he must first obtain the permission of that woman, even though she be his wife"), there is also extensive mutual borrowing of property, which is considered very difficult to refuse (1962:63, 65). And even among the rugged Kapauku, when labor contracts are explicitly in money terms, with no expectation of future rec-

---

[4]The converse, however, does not follow. Some societies whose members are ruggedly individualistic are nevertheless among those where ethnographers describe the economy as being completely embedded in social obligations. An excellent example is the Nuer, described by Evans-Pritchard (1940).

iprocity, there is nevertheless a preference for making such contracts with patrilineal relatives (Pospisil 1963:154).

The Melanesian cases all partake of a cultural complex revolving around what Douglas Oliver (1955), in his classic description of the Siuai in the Solomon Islands, has called the activities of "big men." In all these societies there is no regularly constituted authority; what influence there is, is exercised by leaders who have achieved their position by acquiring a following that they have used to accumulate wealth and then dispersing it in huge feasts, the prestige acquired being proportional to the scale of the occasion. The Melanesian big-man, comments Sahlins, "seems so thoroughly bourgeois, so reminiscent of the free enterprising rugged individual of our own heritage. . . . His every public action is designed to make a competitive and invidious comparison with others, to show a standing above the masses that is product of his own personal manufacture" (Sahlins 1963:289). The sense of hierarchy and invidious comparison that is pervasive in these groups is perhaps best summarized by the catchall term for those at the bottom of the status hierarchy: "rubbishmen" (Strathern 1971:187–188).

Ambition is a common denominator in all these groups. Oliver tells us that the Siuai "consider ambition to be a positive attribute and probably an inborn one. It is the desire for renown . . . and for the power that renown brings" (1955:79; also see 83). Social bonds appear relatively weak. Displays of emotion are highly formalized (1955:232), and "there is probably less emphasis on friendship in Siuai than in most societies" (1955:333).

Yet, one wonders how much of the apparent calculation and impersonality results from a cultural ideal that supports the appearance of such behavior, and discourages shows of affection. Oliver observes, for example, that gift-giving "among close relatives over and beyond the normal expectations of sharing cannot entirely be reduced to conscious expectation of reciprocity. A father might rationalize the giving of tidbits to his son by explaining that he expected to be cared for by the latter in his old age, but I am convinced that some giving between, say, father and son does not involve any desire or expectation for reciprocation" (1955:230).

And the general picture of "big men" as prototypical bourgeois, especially forwarded by Sahlins (1963), has been attacked as a misleading stereotype (Lindstrom 1984). The emphasis on big-man status as achieved rather than ascribed neglects the crucial role in attaining that status of one's place in a kinship network and on simple inheritance. (See, e.g., Strathern 1971:Ch. 9.) In the competition for leadership, cooperative skills within the groups headed by each would-be big-man are of paramount importance. And numerous accounts depict in some detail the valuable services provided by big men to their communities, and the sacrifices they incurred in doing so.[5]

I have devoted some space to description of tribes whose residents' action resembles what the formalist or neoclassical model would predict because they are in fact somewhat anomalous in the ethnographic literature. Though these and some peasant groups (e.g., Tax 1963 and Beals 1975) can be cited as examples of relatively atomized economic actors, there are probably many more groups that fit the substantivist description of actors whose economic action is embedded in social structure (e.g., Malinowski 1961 [1922]; Evans-Pritchard 1940; Dalton 1967; and Sahlins 1972).

But how many groups of each kind there are is not a very interesting question, certainly not one with a meaningful answer that would say anything about what human nature is *really* like. For one thing, though it seems hard to imagine that a group such as the Kapauku would appear much different to a substantivist observer, there must be a broad range of groups whose economic action would be interpreted very differently by observers with different views. This is not to say that there is no possibility of saying anything systematic about such groups, only that, since in the ethnographic tradition there is almost never more than one detailed monograph on any one group, we have very little possibility of triangulation. But more to the point is that human nature is not isolated from the rest of social structures, interactions, and institutions, and so we need most to answer the two questions: under what circumstances do people conduct their economic activity in a certain way, be it embedded or atomized; and what difference does it make?

The first question is, of course, central, but the second is important as well, since an answer of "very little" would render the whole discussion a waste of time. I will suggest some of the consequences of the degree of embeddedness of economic action. But let me pause here to note that

[5]To the extent that the competitive big-man pattern does fit the Sahlins stereotype, it may be that its present form is by no means the ancient cultural Melanesian pattern but rather the outcome of modern intrusions. Thus, Oliver suggests that modern technology, along with the colonial prohibition against either warfare or interisland trade, combined to give the Siuai more leisure time and more reason to increase internal trade and "feasting, which became a substitute for fighting. This culminated in the present institution of social-climbing and its wide ramifications . . ." (Oliver 1955:471; see also Strathern 1971:54). In Oliver's account, the big-man pattern so beloved of formalist anthropologists may be no more than a century old, rather than the native pattern from time immemorial.

one especially important theme is that there is no simple relation between this degree and the efficiency of outcomes. There is an argument, implicit in most neoclassical or formalist accounts, that rational behavior of the *Homo economicus* variety will lead to efficient overall outcomes in economic activity. Something of the sort is certainly true in the general equilibrium argument of neoclassical economics (e.g., Arrow and Hahn 1971). But an analysis of the circumstances leading to trust and malfeasance in economic life (e.g., Granovetter 1985) already makes the point that purely impersonal and interest-oriented action eliminates the possibility of interpersonal trust and thus imposes heavy costs on economic activity.

A related problem is that in practice, a high level of individualism need not even be empirically linked to rational calculation. Oliver notes of the individualistically oriented Siuai that "throughout the day they nap whenever opportunity arises and make haste almost never at all" (1955:97). Perhaps this just reflects a high marginal rate of substitution between labor and leisure? But more is involved. The Siuai language makes few time-related distinctions, and Oliver suggests that either the language "cannot be made explicit with respect to time, or the Siuai have so little awareness of the passage of time, and place so little value on time regularity, that no amount of precise comprehension could make them punctual; I suspect that all three . . . enter in. . . . I noted many occasions of individuals setting out on enterprises without rational consideration of the time element involved" and thence making unwanted and costly errors (1955:98).

And as we know from the discussion of trust, an individualistic orientation may make cooperative activity more difficult than if economic action were more closely embedded in other social obligations and relations. Thus, the Siuai "display a picayune concern about property rights and in most of their transactions they are inclined to pettifogging. Along with all this there are wide areas of ambiguous allocation, with the result that much time is consumed and many hostilities aroused in quarrels over conflicting claims" (Oliver 1955:476). And the Siuai are "exceedingly uncoordinated. In such enterprises as clubhouse construction and gong-carrying they waste prodigious amounts of time and effort through indecision, duplication, querulous complaints, and lack of effective direction" (1955:475–476). Among Tax's atomized and economically rational Guatemalan Indians, there exist no firms, all production being carried out by households (Tax 1963:13); Geertz (1963) explicitly proposes, for his Javanese case, that a highly rational, individualized orientation makes it most difficult to assemble the kind of collective action required to construct firms out of individual economic actors.

## Exchange Relationships and their Consequences

The above discussion of human nature is really a preface to the main text, since it remains at an atomized level of argument. I move now to a more detailed look at the texture of trade, barter, and exchange relations, and to an analysis of the causes and consequences of that texture. One of the main claims of those opposed to formal economic analysis in tribal settings is that economic transactions do not take place between strangers, in an impersonal way, but are embedded in ongoing personal relations.

An apparent refutation of this claim is an institution perhaps first described by Herodotus: the "silent trade" (see, e.g., Herskovits 1952). In this trade, reported for Africa, traders bring their goods from some distance away, to an accustomed place of exchange, and deposit them there. Local traders then deposit their own goods and leave. The first traders return and take the local goods if the exchange is acceptable; if not, they adjust their own offering and go away to await another "silent response" from their trade partners.

But it now appears unlikely that this extreme level of impersonality in trade actually ever occurred. In his comprehensive account of cross-cultural trade, Curtin comments that the story of the silent trade "is interesting for its recognition of the special problems of cross-cultural trade" but that "the empirical evidence for any of these accounts is extremely weak. . . . To bargain with such elaborate avoidance, yet to assume that total strangers will act with honesty and good faith, calls for an unusual degree of cross-cultural understanding from both parties—and to believe it requires unusual credulity from the reader" (1984:13).

The kernel of truth in the story of the silent trade is that trade relations become less personalized and embedded in ongoing personal relations the greater the social, cultural, and geographic distance between the traders. But this does *not* mean that long-distance and/or cross-cultural trade is fundamentally impersonal. On the contrary: cultural differences create especially acute problems of trust that can be dealt with only by the existence of personal ties between the two groups, a situation that led, during most of human history, to what Curtin calls trade networks or "diasporas," in which commercial specialists from one culture went to live in important towns of the other culture, to serve as brokers. Such groups usually lived in their own quarter of the host town, or even in an entirely separate town. The host society was generally suspicious of these traders on two counts: being foreigners and being merchants. Moreover, groups that became too assimilated to the host society would no longer be useful as brokers, so that it was instrumental to preserve the cultural and social integrity of the visiting group (Curtin 1984:Ch. 3; cf. Landa

1981). But the ties to host traders also had to be maintained. The balance required in order to continue trade illustrates what I have called elsewhere the "strength of weak ties" in connecting separate, internally cohesive groups (Granovetter 1973; 1983; and 1986).

Thus, all continuing exchange, however great the cultural and physical distance between traders, appears to be mediated by personal ties. But there are significant differences depending on the social distance spanned by those ties. Within a small local group, the exchange process is stretched out over some period of time, and the level of specificity of what is expected in return is much lower than in more impersonal, economically oriented exchanges. The extreme is what Sahlins calls "generalized reciprocity"—where, as in voluntary food-sharing among kin, "the expectation of a direct material return is unseemly. At best it is implicit. The material side of the transaction is repressed by the social: reckoning of debts outstanding cannot be overt and is typically left out of account. . . . the expectation of reciprocity is indefinite" (Sahlins 1972:194). Malinowski, who referred to this category as that of "pure gifts," observed that this "is not a type of transaction frequently met in Trobriand tribal life" (1961 [1922]:177), since most gifts have a more definite social meaning within a well-defined network of obligations. More generally, exchanges within local groups involve an expectation of a fair return, but one whose exact timing or character is left somewhat open. This openness has to do with the importance of most such intragroup exchanges in sustaining social relations. The existence of obligation is itself a tie between people and, as La Rochefoucauld observed long ago, "excessive eagerness to discharge an obligation is a form of ingratitude" (cited in Blau 1964:99).

The expectation in pure economic theory that all voluntary exchanges serve to effect Pareto improvements in the bundles of commodities held by traders makes it difficult to understand the value, to individuals, of the exchange process itself and its effect on the relationship of the exchanging parties. This remains significant even in most modern transactions, in ways that have an important impact on prices and the structure of business.

That an enormous amount of exchange is of a formally nonutilitarian variety is easy to verify, given the vast literature on ceremonial gift-exchange (see, e.g., Belshaw 1965). Malinowski takes as a "fundamental fact of native usage and psychology: the love of give and take for its own sake. . . . The view that the native can live in a state of individual search for food, or catering for his own household only, in isolation from any interchange of goods [ignores] the deep tendency to create social ties through exchange of gifts. Apart from . . . whether the gifts are necessary or even useful, giving for the sake of giving is one of the most important features of Trobriand sociology, and, from its very general and fundamental nature, I submit that it is a universal feature of all primitive societies" (Malinowski 1961 [1922]:173, 175; cf. Firth 1965:358 for similar comments). There are two reasons for the lack of more "businesslike" barter or exchange relations within the local community: one is the web of obligations that surrounds each transaction; the other is the greater likelihood of complementarities *between* local areas than within them, in what is possessed. Thus, within most local communities, there are few systematic deficits in material wants that can be remedied without going outside that area to one with different ecological or cultural environment and production.

As we examine exchange between more distant partners, we find an attenuation of the strength of the personal tie and less vagueness in the expectations of the what and when of an appropriate return. The more tenuous the social relation, the more immediate must be the return (Sahlins 1972:280). Extremes of impersonality in these intergroup exchanges, however, be they for ceremonial or more straightforwardly material-utilitarian purposes, are rarely reached—in part because the need for trust and regularity is sufficiently acute beyond group boundaries that most trade is conducted not at random but by pairs of individuals, one from each group, who have ongoing trade partnerships.

The dyadic focus of this discussion does not give a full picture, for trade relations are themselves structurally embedded in a wider network of such relations. Thus, when I exchange with you, or confer on you a gift of some magnitude, this has repercussions on my relation with others of a sort of which I am typically well aware. Especially in those Melanesian systems where my attempt to outdo my trading partners in the extent of my gifts to them constitutes a quest for higher status, I do not expect that status to come only or mainly from the respect of my outdone partner, but from the observation by others of these events, and by the effect of this on the relations that I and he have with others. And where trade partnerships between members of different groups are many, they generate a network of such relations that facilitates and creates the specific form of trading and political relations between the groups.

### The Problem of Clientelization in Third-World Markets

Many of these same themes carry over with surprisingly little change to exchange relations in markets populated by peasants or by the inhabitants of Third-World cities—even though in these settings little of the exchange is purely ceremonial. In particular, there are now many descriptions of open-air markets where large numbers of sellers have a customary place to display their wares, sometimes in a rudimentary structure, but not in a closed, glass-fronted store of the sort found in Western countries or in the more Westernized sections of some of the cities where these markets take place.[6] Furthermore, it is typical that sellers of the same commodity are found in close proximity, and that these markets are crowded, noisy, exuberant, and, to the uninitiated observer, chaotic in the extreme. Geertz describes the bazaar in Sefrou (Morocco) as "a tumbling chaos: hundreds of men, this one in rags, that one in silken robe, the next in some outlandish mountain costume, jammed into alleyways, squatting in cubicles, milling in plazas, shouting in each others' faces, whispering in each others' ears, smothering each other in cascades of gestures, grimaces, glares—the whole enveloped in a smell of donkeys, a clatter of carts, and an accumulation of material objects God himself could not inventory, and some of which He could probably not even identify [It is] . . . sensory confusion brought to a majestic pitch" (1979:197).

How do participants make sense out of such a ruckus? One way is clientelization—the establishment of regular relations between buyers and sellers. Such relations have been identified as an important aspect of many such markets, and are usually identified by a distinct local name, which is often, but not always, roughly translatable as "customer," though used symmetrically between buyer and seller: *pratik* in Haiti (Mintz 1961); *suki* in the Philippines (Szanton 1972; Davis 1973); *onibara* in Nigeria (Trager 1981); *casera* in highland Peru (Orlove 1986:93); *sedaqa* in Morocco (Geertz 1979).[7] But clientelization is not universal: in markets that are apparently quite similar to those listed above, buying and selling are sometimes conducted in the more impersonal way that conventional economics would lead us to expect. Thus, Tax tells us that the Panajachel Indians he studied do not "attend to the personality of the vendor; the buyer will accept a commodity from a stranger in the market as readily as from his own brother, from a Ladino as from an Indian" (Tax 1963:17). Dewey reports that in the Javanese market she studied, "even among the regular traders, carriers, and customers many are only slightly acquainted and do not know each other's names" (Dewey 1962:68).

On closer examination, the absence of such ties is not so sharply dis-

---

[6] Though Geertz refers to the merchants in the Moroccan bazaar he describes as having "shops," (1979:126), on more detailed description these are similar to the arrangements found in other markets: "a small, usually wooden cubicle . . . a couple of meters wide, deep, and high in most cases, rarely more than 3 or 4 meters, where he [the seller] squats with his goods about him as market goers stream by in front of him" (1979:179–180).

[7] But *sedaqa*, unlike the other terms, is not a firmly established usage, and means "friendship" or "loyalty," rather than "customer" (Geertz 1979:260, n. 155).

tinguished from their presence because where the ties exist there is a wide range of variation in their strength and character, both within and across settings. In some places the ties, though personalized, are confined almost entirely to economic transactions, and do not develop noneconomic content (e.g., Geertz 1979:260, n. 155). But in most reports, there is considerable variation among ties within each place in the extent of economic services and concessions, the level of trust and (consequently) credit, and the development of the economic ties out of or into relationships with friendly, diffuse social content.

What accounts for these variations? In the absence of detailed social structural analysis, the temptation to tell functionalist stories is ruinously high. In such a story, the exact configuration of ties observed is accounted for by the kinds of economic problems that must be solved for the market in question to function efficiently. The main such stories revolve around the problems of information and trust. Thus, Posner, in his economic "theory of primitive society," takes Geertz's arguments about the functions of clientelization in lowering the costs of collecting market information in Sefrou as a general law for "primitive" (by which he means preliterate) societies,[8] arguing that "the costs of obtaining information are higher in primitive than in advanced societies," and that this "is also true of information concerning the probability that the other party to a contract will perform (there are no courts to coerce his performance) or that the quantity delivered in a sale is the quantity bargained for (there are no scales in primitive markets)" (Posner 1980:5).

This is the first of many claims I evaluate, to the effect that embedded or personalized economic activity may be efficient, but only insofar as it serves to substitute for properly developed institutions that would facilitate impersonal economic relations—in this case, courts and standardized measures. The personalized activity would then be only a *stage* in the development of more perfectly functioning markets, to be transcended in the course of modernization. I generally oppose such accounts on the dual grounds that the practices in question are not in fact functional substitutes for more impersonal institutions when they appear in less developed countries, and that one continues to see them operate side-by-side with the impersonal institutions that were to have obviated their purpose.

For the functionalist account of clientelization to be correct would require that variations in its extent and character correspond precisely to

---

[8]This is, however, oddly inappropriate as a categorization of the Moroccan context of Geertz's own study, which is by no means "primitive" in that sense.

variations in problems of information and trust that cannot be otherwise handled (e.g., by formal institutions of contract law or arbitration). I will show that such correspondence does not occur, and that more generally the functionalist argument fails here for three reasons quite typical in the failure of such arguments: 1) where problems such as those of information and trust are real and thus provide motivations for individuals to develop relations with steady customers, this "solution" is not always structurally possible for individuals to create; 2) if they are successful in doing so, the "solution" may introduce new problems of its own that are difficult to prevent or contain and that may create problems as serious as those apparently solved; and 3) even if each individual could solve his or her *own* problems of information and trust by clientelization, it does not follow that efficiency in the broader collective sense required for an argument about selection pressures to work would result from the sum total of individual solutions.[9]

Szanton's description of the Philippine *suki* relationship summarizes many of the typical features found the world over: "Buyers expect good prices, good quality, personal favors or services, and credit if possible or convenient. A vendor is supposed to ask his *suki* lower prices than those he asks from others. He is also supposed to anticipate his customers' wishes, suggest the best items, keep unusual or better goods aside for him, welcome him with particular friendliness, and offer small services (e.g., storing a package)" (Szanton 1972:98). As client relations progress, the haggling element in trading often diminishes, as haggling is a way for buyer and seller to feel one another out where each is somewhat

---

[9]However, nothing in my argument should be taken to suggest that no economic factors affect the extent and character of clientelization; I argue only that these factors do not go very far toward explaining this extent and character. There clearly are characteristics of economic transactions that make it more or less rewarding to individuals to maintain steady ties with suppliers and customers. Dealers in highly perishable products, for example, face higher costs from fluctuations in purchases, and thus benefit more from the assurance of a steady clientele; thus, it is common to see dealers in such perishables as tomatoes, onions, and fish making greater efforts to sustain such a clientele than dealers in nonperishables (e.g., Davis 1973:234). The seller of an item generally bought in very small lots benefits little from a steady clientele unless the purchases are very frequent; where purchases are large, however, there is more to be gained. Furthermore, the larger the purchases, the greater the need for credit on the part of customers, and the greater the payoff to the information and trust (in the form of lower rates of default) that come from cultivating personal relations with them (e.g., Trager 1981:138). Most of the literature on clientelization deals with very localized trading, but Trager (1981) points out the need for *onibara* ties for Nigerian traders who travel long distances, outside their home ethnic territory, lest they find themselves unable to consummate a purchase despite the time and money invested in the trip.

suspicious of the other (e.g., Davis 1973:165); among those with strong client ties, purchases may approximate a fixed-price situation, since the buyer can trust the seller to offer as his first selling price a number quite close to the one at which he or she is actually willing to sell.[10]

Nearly universal is the practice of giving one's favored customers a little "extra," which is, in effect, a form of price discrimination that does not require one to lower one's stated price. Blau, in his general argument about social exchange, notes that "social bonds are fortified by remaining obligated to others as well as by trusting them to discharge their obligations for considerable periods" (1964:99). Accordingly, when credit is extended in client relations, the situation is typically that described by Davis: "In practice the total obligation owed to the seller *suki* is rarely removed entirely, and is not expected to be. This perpetual debt is said to demonstrate the good will which exists between *suki* partners. . . . perpetuating the debt is treating the affair as an enduring connection, rather than as a series of short-run, discrete exchanges" (1973:225).[11]

To understand better the distribution of client ties we first have to get past the idea implicit in Posner (1980) that all "primitive" or peasant societies face just the same problems of information and social control. The value of client ties in guaranteeing fair dealing and smoothing credit relations depends in part on the local social structure. We have a particularly instructive comparison in two studies in the Philippines, carried out around the same time, in two different cities where *suki* relations have a rather different character. In one of the cities, credit "is the essence of the *suki* relation" (Davis 1973:218), and the majority of the transactions in the market take place among *suki*s. Davis makes an argument similar to Posner's, that this occurs because the banking and legal systems do not facilitate either the granting of credit or the enforcement of credit obligations. Thus the "personalistic relationships of the marketplace economy function as analogs to contractual legal systems. . . . in the absence of universalistic legal sanctions, and lacking widely dissemi-

---

[10] In Sefrou, Geertz reports intensive haggling along several dimensions: price, quality, quantity, and terms of credit and repayment. This may persist despite clientelization because the ties between buyers and sellers are in most cases narrowly economic, but Geertz does report that "strong clientship ties normally shorten bargaining time" (1979:221–229). Notice the irony that only when relations become more personal, thus less modern by some accounts, do pricing arrangements attain the "modern" character of being fixed rather than generated by haggling. Here, the trust inherent in the personal relation eliminates the cost in time and energy and opportunities taken up by haggling.

[11] Plattner (1985) summarizes considerable evidence on this point as indicating the presence of what he calls "equilibrating market relationships".

nated information concerning individual credit ratings, such as those on which Western credit systems depend, personalistic market relations are extremely useful" (1973:280–281).[12]

But Szanton found, in the city she studied, that although *suki* relations certainly exist and are significant, they make up a small proportion of all transactions. And only a minority of vendors have *suki* ties that involve credit. Yet credit is often given outside of *suki* relationships, on a more narrowly contractual basis. Enforcement is then based on "face-to-face sanctions. Failure to repay results in a compromised business reputation, often excludes the possibility of future credit, and among men may well lead to physical violence" (1972:106). Only occasionally do the authorities intervene.

What is going on here then? In both settings there is no well-developed credit market or system of contract law that regulates the granting of credit; yet in one, credit is given through highly personalized relations, and in the other, it is more narrowly contractual but is enforced by face-to-face sanctions. Why can such sanctions not come into play in the first case? A look at the two cities can provide clues. In Baguio City (Davis 1973) there are 50,000 people and more than 1,500 stalls in the public market.[13] Estancia (Szanton 1972) has a population of 14,000, with 240 vendors in the market. Szanton suggests that, compared to Baguio City, Estancia is a smaller town "where face-to-face interaction within the marketplace is supplemented by numerous outside contacts. In this setting *suki* relationships are extraneous to contract enforcement" (1972:115). That is, some vendors and customers already have a multi-stranded relationship: they see one another in other contexts—church, school, or family gatherings. But this alone does not explain the effectiveness of collective action against those who renege on legitimate debts. I think we are safe in guessing that the relatively smaller number of merchants in Estancia form a much more densely knit and cohesive network of relations than in Baguio City, with a consequently greater likelihood of learning about customers' and one anothers' malfeasance and a greater ability to mobilize against it. While we know less than we should about the extent of human cognitive and emotional capacity for friendship ties (see Granovetter 1976), it is worth noting that for a network of 240 merchants to be completely connected requires the presence of less than

[12] Davis's description of *suki* relations is similar to Landa's depiction of ethnically homogeneous middleman groups as an "institutional alternative to contract law" (1981).

[13] But the number of vendors is somewhat smaller than the number of stalls because some vendors incorporate several stalls into one operation (Davis 1973:132); Davis does not estimate the exact number of vendors.

30,000 pairwise relations; for one of 1,500, you need more than a million. And the 240 are, moreover, in a smaller setting to begin with, with far fewer other possible individuals with which to connect.

So the ironic outcome is that where the social structure is more connected and cohesive—the less modern pattern—economic action can be conducted in a more narrowly contractual way; where it is more dispersed and disconnected, there is less capacity for collective action in sanctioning malfeasance, and economic action must be conducted via highly personalized relations.[14] A similar result emerges from Trager's study of Nigerian yam traders. She notes that in "resale from one middleman to another there are credit transactions but no *onibara* ties in this context. In part this is because all yam traders have shops in the same area of the market and already know one another" (1981:137). Though the city of Ilesa, Nigeria (population 165,000) is much larger still than Baguio City, Trager refers here to credit relations among merchants, not between them and customers, and in that case there are still apparently few enough merchants in the trade of a single commodity for the network of relations to be connected and efficient.

These comparisons suggest that we need a careful inspection of the exact configuration of social relations in a market before we can understand the nature of pairwise ties. This should remind us that such ties cannot be examined in isolation from larger structures, as we may be tempted to do if unduly seduced by methodological individualist principles.

But the argument so far, though it improves on sweeping generalities about the necessity for personalized trading in "primitive" settings, still has the functionalist character of suggesting that such trading occurs just where it is needed, even if we need to be a little smarter about where that is. I now point out the inadequacy of this functionalist account by observing first that some social structures make it harder than others to construct this personalist solution to the problems encountered, and second that the solution, even when constructed, may not be a good solution at all.

---

[14]There is other evidence, from noneconomic contexts, that pairs of individuals in tightly knit social structures cannot themselves usually sustain very strong social ties. Quite apart from whether such ties are functionally "necessary," the involvement in the larger group subtracts some of the energy required for the dyadic tie, and if the group has a substantial corporate identity as a group, it may discourage pairs of individuals from developing too intimate a relation as this detracts from group solidarity. Slater (1963) thus interprets the universality of the marriage ceremony as the attempt of groups to insert themselves between partners who might otherwise withdraw their energies into the private realm; see also Granovetter (1971).

Most observers agree that personalized economic relations are not built in a day, but slowly over time. In his general argument about social (as opposed to purely economic) exchange, Blau observed that such relations "evolve in a slow process, starting with minor transactions in which little trust is required because little risk is involved. . . . Hence, processes of social exchange, which may originate in pure self-interest, generate trust in social relations through their recurrent and gradually expanding character (Blau 1964:94). Compare Mintz's account for Haiti: "*Pratik* relationships seem to have a characteristic way of taking shape. A bulking intermediary will call over a would-be buyer unfamiliar to her and invite her to buy. After some talk, if the seller likes the buyer's manner, she will make a very reasonable selling offer. As the sale is consummated, she will ask the buyer if she buys regularly on that day and at that place. If the answer is a friendly affirmative, she will say meaningly: 'Wait for me. I always come on this day. I come from such-and-such a town. I come here with the truck called so-and-so. I keep my stock here, at the depot of Madame X.' With more talk, an understanding begins to emerge. Each woman will carefully watch the other's behavior on subsequent occasions, until there is genuine mutual trust" (Mintz 1961:60–61. See also Szanton 1972:97, 100; and Davis 1973:218–222 on the slow emergence of *suki* relationships.)

Because personalized economic relations emerge slowly, in the context of recurrent mutual probing and testing, circumstances in which the same pairs of individuals are not in contact very often over a given period of time will be unfavorable for the development of these relations. This may help explain why Dewey (1962), studying a Javanese market similar in most ways to those described above, did not find any equivalent to the clientelization reported in other studies. The city of Modjokuto (a pseudonym) has only about 18,000 people, with about 500 full-time traders, 1,000 customers at any given moment in the market, and perhaps several thousand during the average day (Dewey 1962:75). But there are several differences between this Javanese setting and the others. One is that at the time of Dewey's study (1953–1954), the city was undergoing rapid population growth and there had been a very substantial influx of new traders since World War II, in part made up of those forced off their land (Dewey 1962:xix). Another is the extraordinary population density of Java, an island with about 49,000 square miles and more than 50,000,000 people at this time—more than 1,000 per square mile, and scattered fairly evenly mostly in rural villages and small towns. Thus, though the average village had only 2,000–3,000 inhabitants, it typically lay only a few hundred yards from the next (Dewey 1962:14).

The urban traders in Dewey's market have typically come from the rural regions surrounding Modjokuto, and in an area of lower population density that would make it highly likely that they would have previous acquaintance with one another, having come from the same one or two villages. But here, with such an enormous catchment area to draw on, anonymity seems far more likely (though Dewey gives no data on the provenance of the traders). Moreover, at this density, the number of markets in easy reach of Modjokuto traders is large, and being rational economic actors, they move around readily in search of every economic opportunity. They are thus often at other markets, and so stay away from their home village for days, weeks, or even longer, thus weakening local ties even further. Customers are no less eager for economic advantage, and so have some choice of markets. Dewey thus suggests that, because "of the extreme density of population and the comparatively wide area from which the market draws trade, even among the regular traders, carriers and customers many are only slightly acquainted and do not know each other's names" (Dewey 1962:68).

Thus, social structural conditions can make it difficult for actors to construct client ties. Yet, the Modjokuto market is similar to other peasant markets in the ineffectiveness of formalized institutions of credit and contract. Does not some other institution then "emerge," to use the word of optimistic functionalist accounts, to fill this functional gap? None seems to, and Dewey gives evidence that the resulting absence of trust has real economic costs. Compared to the more cohesive Chinese community of Modjokuto traders, Dewey notes that the difficulty of enforcing ethics and agreements among the Javanese increases their cost of doing business. "Chinese will buy goods on description or from a sample when dealing with other Chinese and feel relatively sure that the quality and amount ordered will be forthcoming on time. Javanese feel they must themselves inspect all goods being considered, and, when delivery is made, check the quality and quantity. No payment is made until then. Such a rationale makes it difficult to calculate future expenditures, and delays resale negotiations as well as adding to costs in time and money spent in personal supervision of even simple transactions." The absence of stable ties among the Javanese "makes it almost impossible for informal sanctions to be effective. . . . [When debtors default, the creditor] may refuse to deal further with the offender, but there are always others who will. Should a trader alienate too many people it is easier for him to escape them by changing to a different type of trade or moving to another area than it is for a Chinese" (Dewey 1962:48, 49).

Note the contrast between the argument that large numbers of small traders sweep malfeasance from the market (e.g., in Williamson 1975:27) and the reality indicated here, that atomization of many small traders *prevents* collective action against malfeasance and protects offenders.

Finally, consider again what happens in settings where people are able to develop client ties. Are they always an efficient way to control malfeasance and protect against credit default? One might imagine that if a little knowledge of one's clients is good that a lot is better; that the more you know about someone the better you can gauge the risk; and that the closer your personal relation with that person, the more trustworthy he will be. But the greater the trust you repose in someone, the greater the risk, and the greater the power that person has over you (cf. Granovetter 1985). This is not unknown to merchants the world over, and Geertz, in trying to explain why clientship in Sefrou is a wholly economic, functionally specific tie, cites studies suggesting that "diffuse ties are often consciously avoided in Middle Eastern bazaars because of the fear they will be used exploitatively—to delay delivery, pass off shoddy goods, pressure terms, etc." (Geertz 1979:260, n. 155). Indeed, the tenor of the relations Geertz describes is more negative than that in most of the literature. Clientelization, he tells us, "transforms a diffuse, anonymous mob into a reasonably stable collection of familiar antagonists" (1979:218). Perhaps one reason that such relations can in fact be kept at arms' length is that the bazaar in Sefrou is extremely heterogeneous in distinctions of language, religion, residence, race, kinship, birthplace, and ancestry; Geertz found no less than sixty-six ethnic-like categories among the owners of bazaar establishments (1979:142). It may well follow (though Geertz gives no information on this) that customers and vendors are quite likely to be of different ethnic backgrounds, which makes it less likely for social content to overlay the economic clientship relation.[15]

But where there is ethnic homogeneity, people who deal with one another frequently may not be able to help coming to like one another. One of the best-supported generalizations in social psychology, after all, is that interaction, when voluntary, leads to liking; see especially Homans (1950). This is especially likely when the vendor and client have other friends and interests in common. Thus, Trager describes a former primary school teacher who entered the cloth trade and came to form *onibara* ties with other school teachers she had not previously known. "In addition to engaging in regular economic transactions, the trader and this customer have become good friends. They visit each other at home

---

[15] Because there is ethnic homogeneity, however, within trades, one might expect to see ties of economic cooperation *among* vendors being stronger and more tinged with social overtones than those between vendors and customers. Geertz's discussion, however, concerns only the former.

frequently and if one is celebrating a special occasion such as the birth of a child she will invite the other" (Trager 1981:140). To the extent that some customers recommend others who become regulars, the likelihood of stronger social content increases as well.

In countries influenced by Catholic doctrine, a common way to reinforce a social relationship is to form a *compadre,* or coparent tie. At marriage or the baptism of a child, one or more godparents are chosen, and though the relation is in principle between godparent and child, in practice the significance is for the relation between godparent and parent. Both Davis (1973) and Szanton (1972) report for the Philippines that *suki* ties are often cemented with *compadre* relations. Davis observes that once one "identifies any seller's most important suppliers and customers, it may be predicted that he has also identified at least some of that seller's ritual coparents," and that this tie stabilizes the economic relationship. But he also observes that debtors are more likely to initiate the *compadre* tie than creditors, because it is "difficult, for cultural reasons, to approach a ritual kinsman to request repayment of loans" (Davis 1973:237, 238).

In the smaller-scale setting of Estancia, Szanton (1972) stresses much more the economic liabilities for vendors in strong social relations to customers. When *suki* ties become more social, the kinds of reciprocity expected come to range beyond the purely economic. Thus, economic advantages "may well be, and often are, repaid in social or political services, and this may easily occur when a close personal friendship develops between a vendor and a customer, especially if and when the latter has become a substantial debtor to the vendor. Although the exchange of noneconomic goods and services for economic goods received is often acceptable and even expected and desired, for a vendor attempting to make a living in the marketplace it can be highly disruptive to his business. Since personal reasons for delayed payments are supposed to be understood and accepted by friends, it may become extremely difficult for the vendor to collect what he is owed. . . . Thus social bonds superimposed on economic relationships frequently create ambiguous situations which may be diversely interpreted. . . . This becomes most obvious when *suki* relationships are reinforced by *compadrazgo* [ = *compadre*] ties" (1972:110). Those seeking *compadre* ties from vendors, of course, often have this in mind. Vendors are aware of the danger—why then do they not resist such overtures? Here, the customer is cleverly manipulating a cultural symbolic pattern to advantage: "Because of the prior relationship, refusing a request [to be a child's godparent] is difficult and rare, although it is always theoretically possible. A refusal would be status-demeaning for the person who is refused and would create bitter feelings between the two parties" (1972:112, 114).

From the point of view of creditors in such systems, then, it appears that there is some optimum level of intensity for the personalized relations they make use of to assure trust in customers. If all such relations could be kept to this optimum, moreover, one would have more social energies and time to invest in other such relations. The problem that arises is one that plagues all discussions of "investment" in social relations: that one cannot always control the level of one's interest in any particular relation, nor that of the partner. The purely instrumental aspect can only with difficulty be segregated from other rewarding features of relationships.[16] It does not follow from this that there is no systematic relation between social structure and the likelihood that personalized relations will successfully mediate credit and other aspects of business life. On the contrary, I have pointed to a number of important aspects of structure that are relevant—such as the degree of social heterogeneity and network overlap between those tied in economic relations and the existence or absence of cultural symbols and practices (such as ritual coparenthood) that make it difficult to decouple social from economic aspects of relations. These, together with the arguments above on the structural conditions under which personal ties are valuable in economic life, and those in which they can be built up, should help us to understand better the wide range of patterns we find in peasant and Third World markets.

### Clientelization and Prices: Does Embeddedness Matter?

Does the personalization of economic relations result in any detectable economic outcomes? I have argued that, under many circumstances, they reduce the cost of business by creating trust. There is also evidence that they often affect market prices of the products that are traded.

Substantivists take as a major distinction between markets and other

---

[16]This is a problem, for example, with models of "investment" in social contacts for the purpose of assuring a steady flow of information about jobs (as in Boorman 1975; Delany 1988). Though Boorman is able to show the technical advantage of a network of ties that are all "weak" rather than "strong," members of one's network who come to perceive that they are being "used" may have less sympathy with the analysis. Yet, it is hard to see how anyone with a consistent policy of "investing" in relations but keeping them weak could avoid giving such an impression. This is a grave shortcoming of much of the advice given in the so-called networking self-help literature. It relates closely to Blau's point that there are certain important rewards in social exchange that do not lend themselves to calculated barter—especially intrinsic attraction to a person, approval of his opinions and judgments, and respect for his abilities, because the significance of these rewards "rests on their being spontaneous reactions rather than calculated means of pleasing him. These evaluations of a person or his attributes reward him only if he has reason to assume that they are *not* primarily motivated by the explicit intention to reward him" (Blau 1964:99).

systems of allocation that only in the former are prices the result of supply and demand; the market is often referred to in Polanyi's work as the "price-making market"—though in an offhand comment that he took less seriously than it deserved, Polanyi did observe that even "under modern conditions it is often a delicate matter to ascertain whether at a definite time and place a supply-demand price mechanism for a definite good or service is in operation or not" (Polanyi et al. 1957:13). In systems driven by reciprocity, the ratios (in the case of barter) or the prices at which goods are exchanged are said to be the result of custom and the balance of reciprocal obligations between the traders or their groups; in those organized by redistribution, prices are set administratively.

Polanyi and his followers were determined to show that allocation by markets was qualitatively entirely different from other allocative systems, and were thus concerned to exclude the possibility that supply and demand had any influence whatever on exchange in earlier times; the other side of this argument was that in "self-regulating markets" there was no influence from social sources on exchange. In fact, neither claim stands scrutiny.

The empirical evidence is overwhelming that prices and exchange ratios in societies of all kinds are affected both by supply and demand and by a variety of social structural effects. Which is more important varies by setting and circumstance. Within many tribes, where the utilitarian content of exchanges is swamped by their ceremonial significance, and elaborate duties are specified to this or that class of relative, it is difficult to see much impact of supply or demand. In tribes that are more oriented to utilitarian exchange, such as the many Melanesian groups described above, prices are much more responsive to economic circumstance. But even in a group so extreme in this respect as the Kapauku Papuans, Pospisil tells us that though prices certainly respond to supply and demand, all articles of trade nevertheless have a "customary price." It is often not the price paid, but one can be sure that if it is, there will be no dispute over the transaction. And prices are often lowered in trade between close relatives and friends. Status matters as well: a man of high status may be offered commodities at below-normal prices "either because the seller expects future favors . . . or because he is afraid the rich man might ask payment of a debt" (1963:305, 309, 310).

Polanyi (1957) is at great pains to show that international trade in the ancient world was conducted under strict political control with prices set by local authorities rather than by a market. But he says little about the crucial question of how these prices were set, leaving open the possibility that administrators adjusted them to market forces; in fact, Benet's chapter in Polanyi et al. (1957), on Berber markets, shows exactly this (Benet 1957:208). Moreover, Polanyi's insistence on the centrality of price as against other terms of trade is an overly literalistic measure of the influence of supply and demand, which may affect these other terms even if not price. Polanyi himself notes that even when prices are administered, there is nevertheless haggling, "since to meet changing circumstances adjustments cannot be avoided, higgling-haggling is practiced only on other items than price, such as measures, quality, or means of payment. Endless arguments are possible about the quality of the foodstuffs, the capacity and weight of the units employed . . ." (Polanyi 1957:262). Again, Polanyi did not take this comment seriously enough, and so described as "marketless trading" situations where prices may indeed have remained unchanged for centuries on end, but where intense bargaining revolved around the exact assortment of goods to be traded (see, e.g., Curtin 1984:58–59, on "assortment bargaining" in West Africa).

Sahlins, another leading substantivist, declares the need for economic anthropology to develop a theory of exchange value apart from the influence of supply and demand. He points out that exchange rates are more stable between groups than within, because there are more social influences and less need for immediate reciprocity within groups, whereas the more tenuous the social relation, the more it can be sustained only by an immediate and balanced exchange (1972:280). But rather than showing the unimportance of supply and demand, this is a valuable clue to the circumstances that determine its relative importance. He goes on to note that in primitive trade, all trades are not interconnected because so much intergroup trade is handled through partnerships, and not just anyone can trade with anyone since "exactly who exchanges with whom is prescribed in advance. . . . Lacking a trade contact, a man may not be able to get what he wants at any price (1972:298).

To the extent one is engaged in a continuing relation, the observed exchange ratio need not reflect what the traders view as equivalent, since given the fragility and potential for explosion of such intergroup trading, partners are typically at pains to give a little more than what seems appropriate in exchange, as a sign of good faith. (Sahlins 1972:302–303. See also Curtin on West Africa, 1984:46–47.) This "extra," which has sometimes been interpreted as a form of interest, is more appropriately seen as a way of keeping the relationship open by not "closing the books" completely on the exchange.

Sahlins argues that supply and demand does not have an impact on price in traditional intergroup trade because such impact requires that all trades be interconnected in a competitive market. He observes that exchange ratios have moral force, and can thus, in the short run, remain stable whatever the supply-demand situation (1972:308); even in the longer run, within a given partnership relation, there is pressure to maintain the traditional rates. This means that an imbalance in supply and demand is resolved by pressure on trade partners rather than exchange rates. But this pressure is a real force, and it makes the trade partnership all the more vulnerable to a sustained discrepancy of supply-demand. The trade partner disadvantaged by the traditional rate, as compared to the rate that would emerge in an open market, is the one who feels the pressure; but given the usual difficulty of changing the exchange rate within an ongoing relation, the only alternative is to reduce the frequency of trade. Empirically, Sahlins notes that when a trade partner becomes reluctant to trade, the sanction is dissolution of the partnership. "The solution, thus, to a persistent disconfirmity between exchange values and supply/demand would be a social process by which old partnerships are terminated and new ones negotiated. Perhaps even the network of trade will have to be modified, geographically and ethnically. . . . a fresh start restores the correspondence between exchange value and supply/demand" (1972:311–313).

This leads Sahlins to a broad generalization of considerable importance:

> depending on the social qualities of the trade relation, the rates of exchange in differently organized trade systems are probably differentially sensitive to changes in supply/demand. The precise nature of the partnership becomes significant: it may be more or less sociable, so admitting of longer or shorter delays in reciprocation—trade-kinship, for example, probably longer than trade-friendship. The prevailing relation has a coefficient of economic fragility, and the entire system accordingly a certain responsiveness to variations of supply/demand. The simple matter of customary privacy or publicity may be similarly consequential; perhaps it is feasible . . . to secretly come to new terms with old partners. And what freedom is given within the system to recruit new partners? Aside from the difficulties of breaking paths into villages or ethnic groups previously outside the system, partnerships may be by custom inherited and the set of contacts thus closed, or perhaps more readily contracted and the exchange values thereby more susceptible to revision. In brief, the economic flexibility of the system depends on the social structure of the trade relation. [1972:313]

What Sahlins has done here, despite his substantivist intentions, is not at all to show the irrelevance of supply and demand to trade, but rather to open the door to systematic arguments about the relation between price-stickiness and the social structure of trade relations; rather than show the unbridgeable chasm between tribal and modern economies, he shows how to make the connection between the two. There are more clues in the literature on peasant markets, where the general consensus is that clientelization raises prices above their competitive level and generates price-stickiness. Belshaw comments on Haiti that, paradoxically, "although a *revendeuse* [trader] may reduce prices to a *pratik* buyer, the monopolistic element in the relationship may make it possible for her to work at a profit. For her as an individual it creates economies of scale, and in the market as a whole the weight of *pratik* probably raises prices slightly above the level which would otherwise be arrived at through pure competition" (Belshaw 1965:78). This is possible in part because the price concessions to the *pratik* buyer are hidden in quantity concessions: the same price is quoted as to any other buyer, but on consummating the transaction, an extra quantity is thrown in (Mintz 1961:60), thus avoiding the appearance of price discrimination. Sellers in the Philippines prefer to give concessions on quantity rather than price because to reduce the price "would suggest to the buyer that prices were too high in the first place, thereby disturbing the buyer's confidence in his seller *suki*" (Davis 1973:222).

In Sefrou, prices are often kept constant while negotiations center not only on quantity but also on quality and the "size of supposedly established units, something the imperfect standardization of weights and measures not only facilitates, but actually encourages. A pint may be a pound the world around, but a medd (the reigning grain measure) certainly is not" (Geertz 1979:222). At times the buyer will first offer a price and then bargain over what it will buy. (See also Davis 1973:166.) Geertz comments that such "bargaining modes as these give rise to what may be called 'fixed-price illusion' with respect to certain bazaars that sometimes appears in the literature. This is especially common with respect to perishables, where price negotiation is hidden beneath delicate manipulations, invisible to the innocent observer, of the great inhomogeneity of goods" (1979:261, n. 162). To the extent that dealers do substantial business with nonclients, this appearance of prices fixed at a level higher than they are, in practice, with clients, raises their rate of return and the overall price level.[17]

Attachments between clientelized buyers and sellers make them less responsive to changes in market conditions than they would otherwise be. In some cases this means that prices are held below their competitive

---

[17] It would be interesting to determine, but as far as I can tell the evidence is insufficient, whether the extent of nonprice bargaining is a function of the extent of sales to nonclients in partially clientelized markets. One should not expect to see a linear relation because where clients are hardly important at all, pricing in transactions with them will make little difference, and where the overwhelming proportion of transactions are with them, the price one can offer to nonclients will also matter little.

level, if an increase would otherwise have occurred. Thus traders, in periods of rising prices, may, for specially favored *suki,* "sometimes calculate their selling prices on actual wholesale costs rather than on the current market prices. In general, then, prices are not as elastic as they would be if such relations did not exist, for relations make both buyer and seller substantially less free to seek the best bargain of the moment" (Davis 1973:222). Overall, prices are probably higher because having steady clients reduces sellers' overstocking and having to sell under distress conditions. Buyers require the credit and other services provided by *suki* and are thus not responsive to lower prices elsewhere. Because one cannot break into such a market by underselling the current price, entry costs are high and new entrants who try to carve out a niche by underselling may be driven out of business (Davis 1973:247, 278–279).

A further variable in determining the impact of clientelization on prices is the level of cooperation among existing vendors. In Baguio City,

> adjacent sellers in the marketplace have longstanding associations of cooperation and restrained competition. The marketplace, like other enduring social associations, has become constrained by a system of norms, such as the . . . tacit proscription against any overt attempt to alienate another seller's *suki.* . . . Sanctions which may be applied for violation of these norms include the termination of all mutual services which neighbors usually provide one another, and various degrees of public scorn and verbal abuse. Furthermore, if an individual makes repeated attempts to alienate other sellers' *suki* in spite of warnings, his neighbors eventually will attempt "to convince him that he is wrong," a popular local euphemism for physical violence. [Davis 1973:245]

Failure to maintain price uniformity, by trying to undersell one's neighboring vendors, is similarly frowned on. Thus, as one might expect, the higher the level of cooperation—a kind of cartelization—the easier it is to keep prices above their probable competitive level.

The evidence makes clear, then, that both supply and demand *and* social structure affect prices and quantities in tribal and peasant markets. The impact of trade partnerships and clientelization is that changes in supply and demand may result in quantity or quality rather than price adjustments, as prices are sticky in both directions in these economies. Modern economies would differ fundamentally from this situation if they fit the idealized "price-making" auction model proposed by neoclassical economics and assumed by substantivist anthropologists. But, as macroeconomist Arthur Okun observed, most modern transactions do not take place in auction markets, but rather in "customer markets." The "hallmark of auction markets is the absence of price tags; sellers are price takers and not price makers. In fact, most products are sold with price tags set by the seller and through a process of shopping by the buyer. As long as there are costs associated with shopping . . . buyers do not find it worthwhile to incur all the costs required to find the seller offering the lowest price" (1981:138).

Given recurrent purchases, the situation is similar to what we saw in peasant markets: if shoppers "have a favorable assessment of the terms of their last supplier, and if they believe that the information obtained from the last purchase is still relevant—that is, that the supplier is still offering essentially the same terms—they are likely to return to that supplier as customers or at least as shoppers. . . . Once customers establish a relationship with a particular supplier, then, on each shopping trip, they essentially make a quit-or-stick decision analogous to that of the worker who has a job. . . . The firm comes to recognize its ability to discourage customers from shopping elsewhere by convincing them of the continuity of the firm's policy on pricing, services and the like." The importance of this continuity inhibits sellers from "exploiting increases in demand by raising the price," as customers may be less "antagonized by back orders than by jumps in the price." Even professional buyers prefer continuing relationships with suppliers (1981:140–141, 149, 151).

In such markets, prices "rarely, if ever, equal marginal costs . . . and generally exceed them by a significant margin . . ."; but the customer-supplier attachments also "save a huge volume of resources that consumers would otherwise devote to shopping (and trying out) products with every transaction. To firms, an established clientele increases the predictability of sales, permitting important savings in inventory costs and in production scheduling." In sum, "Society pays the costs of monopoly elements and collects the benefits of genuine economies of transactions. It is not clear whether the benefits exceed, or fall short of, the costs" (Okun 1981:155, 178).

This picture of customer-supplier attachments is essentially similar to that in tribal and peasant economies.[18] It follows that some of the same

[18]The only pattern Okun reports that does not appear in the literature on peasant markets is that, while prices in customer markets may not respond to demand, they do respond to cost, because customers believe the latter is fair and the former not. "In many industries, when firms raise their prices, they routinely issue announcements to their customers, insisting that higher costs have compelled them to do so. No price announcement has ever explained to customers that the supplier has moved into a new position to capture a larger share of the surplus in the relation as a result of a stronger market" (1981:153). Thus the pattern of setting prices as a markup over cost, even in competitive markets. There is nothing in this pattern that is inconsistent with peasant markets, and it may simply be that anthropologists have not paid attention to the issue.

factors that explain the extent of clientelization and of cohesion among vendors may not only explain these for modern economies as well, but insofar as modern economies vary along these dimensions, this may lead to differences in levels of price stickiness that then ultimately derive from specifiable social structural differences.[19]

## Summary

In this brief discussion, extracted from a larger set of materials (in Granovetter, forthcoming), I have drawn away from what I call the "strong" embeddedness position—an oversocialized assertion that modern economic analysis cannot help us understand behavior in tribal or peasant societies because economic motives are so thoroughly swamped by more social motives; but I have also avoided the undersocialized assertion of formalist anthropologists, that economic analysis is the royal road to understanding in such settings. The middle road I have traveled is more arduous than either of these, requiring, as it does, detailed analysis of social structure and of the complex way social and economic motives and actions are intertwined. I believe that it is only by such arduous analysis that we can move away from the neat formulations that defy falsifiability, to the more complex and contingent generalizations that allow us to relate social structure to economic outcomes.

This paper is drawn from draft chapters of my manuscript, *Society and Economy: The Social Construction of Economic Institutions*, to be published by Harvard University Press.

## References

ARROW, KENNETH, and FRANK HAHN. 1971. *General Competitive Analysis*. San Francisco: Holden-Day.

BEALS, RALPH. 1975. *The Peasant Marketing System of Oaxaca, Mexico*. Berkeley: University of California Press.

BELSHAW, CYRIL. 1965. *Traditional Exchange and Modern Markets*. Englewood Cliffs, NJ: Prentice-Hall.

BENET, FRANCISCO. 1957. "Explosive Markets: The Berber Highlands." In Karl Polanyi et al. eds., *Trade and Market in the Early Empires*. New York: Free Press, pp. 188–217.

[19] For a general assessment of the significance and explanation for price stickiness and quantity adjustment, see R. J. Gordon 1983. There can be substantial disagreements on the actual level of price stickiness because of nontrivial econometric difficulties in the measurement of the response of prices to changes in demand. See, e.g., Bosworth's (1983:121–124) comment on Gordon (1983).

BLAU, PETER. 1964. *Exchange and Power in Social Life*. New York: Wiley.

BLOCK, FRED, and MARGARET SOMERS. 1984. "Beyond the Economistic Fallacy: The Holistic Social Science of Karl Polanyi." In Theda Skocpol ed., *Vision and Method in Historical Sociology*. New York: Cambridge University Press, pp. 47–84.

BOORMAN, SCOTT. 1975. "A Combinatorial Optimization Model for the Transmission of Job Information Through Contact Networks." *Bell Journal of Economics* 6 (1):216–249.

BOSWORTH, BARRY. 1983. "Comment." In James Tobin ed., *Macroeconomics, Prices and Quantities: Essays in Memory of Arthur M. Okun*. Washington, D.C.: Brookings Institution, pp. 121–124.

COOK, SCOTT. 1968. "The Obsolete 'Anti-Market' Mentality: A Critique of the Substantive Approach to Economic Anthropology." In Edward LeClair and Harold Schneider eds., *Economic Anthropology: Readings in Theory and Analysis*. New York: Holt, Rinehart and Winston, pp. 208–228. Originally in *American Anthropologist* 1966, 68:323–345.

CURTIN, PHILIP. 1984. *Cross-Cultural Trade in World History*. New York: Cambridge University Press.

DALTON, GEORGE, ed. 1967. *Tribal and Peasant Economies: Readings in Economic Anthropology*. Garden City, NY: The Natural History Press.

DAVIS, WILLIAM G. 1973. *Social Relations in a Philippine Market: Self-Interest and Subjectivity*. Berkeley: University of California Press.

————. 1986. "Class, Political Constraints and Entrepreneurial Strategies: Elites and Petty Market Traders in Northern Luzon." In S. Greenfield and A. Strickon eds., *Entrepreneurship and Social Change*. Lanham, MD: University Press of America, pp. 166–194.

DELANY, JOHN. 1988. "Social Networks and Efficient Resource Allocation: Computer Models of Job Vacancy Allocation Through Contacts." In Barry Wellman and Stephen Berkowitz eds., *Social Structures: A Network Approach*. Cambridge, MA: Cambridge University Press, pp. 430–451.

DEWEY, ALICE. 1962. *Peasant Marketing in Java*. Glencoe, IL: Free Press.

EVANS-PRITCHARD, E. E. 1940. *The Nuer*. Oxford: Oxford University Press.

FIRTH, RAYMOND. 1965. *Primitive Polynesian Economy*. New York: W. W. Norton.

GEERTZ, CLIFFORD. 1963. *Peddlers and Princes*. Chicago: University of Chicago Press.

————. 1979. "Suq: The Bazaar Economy in Sefrou." In Clifford Geertz, Hildred Geertz, and Lawrence Rosen eds., *Meaning and Order in Moroccan Society*. New York: Cambridge University Press, pp. 123–224.

GORDON, ROBERT J. 1983. "A Century of Evidence on Wage and Price Stickiness in the United States, the United Kingdom and Japan." In James Tobin ed., *Macroeconomics, Prices and Quantities: Essays in Memory of Arthur M. Okun*. Washington, D.C.: Brookings Institution, pp. 85–121.

GRANOVETTER, MARK. 1971. "Child-Raising, Weak Ties and Socialism." Unpublished paper.

———. 1973. "The Strength of Weak Ties." *American Journal of Sociology* 78 (6):1360–1380.

———. 1976. "Network Sampling: Some First Steps." *American Journal of Sociology* 81(May):1287–1303.

———. 1983. "The Strength of Weak Ties: A Network Theory Revisited." *Sociological Theory* 1:201–233.

———. 1985. "Economic Action and Social Structure: The Problem of Embeddedness." *American Journal of Sociology* 91 (November):481–510.

———. 1986. "Labor Mobility, Internal Markets and Job-Matching: A Comparison of the Sociological and the Economic Approaches." *Research in Social Stratification and Mobility* 5:3–39.

———. Forthcoming. *Society and Economy: The Social Construction of Economic Institutions.* Cambridge, MA: Harvard University Press.

HERSKOVITS, MELVILLE. 1952. *Economic Anthropology.* New York: Alfred Knopf.

HOMANS, GEORGE. 1950. *The Human Group.* New York: Harcourt, Brace, World.

LANDA, JANET. 1981. "A Theory of the Ethnically Homogeneous Middleman Group: An Institutional Alternative to Contract Law." *Journal of Legal Studies* 10:349–362.

LECLAIR, EDWARD, and HAROLD SCHNEIDER, eds. 1968. *Economic Anthropology: Readings in Theory and Analysis.* New York: Holt, Rinehart and Winston.

LINDSTROM, LAMONT. 1984. "Doctor, Lawyer, Wise Man, Priest: Big-Men and Knowledge in Melanesia." *Man (N.S.)* 19(June):291–309.

MALINOWSKI, BRONISLAW. 1922 [1961]. *Argonauts of the Western Pacific.* New York: E. P. Dutton.

MINTZ, SIDNEY. 1961. "Pratik: Haitian Personal Economic Relationships." In Viola Garfield ed., *Proceedings of the 1961 Annual Spring Meeting of the American Ethnological Society.* Seattle, WA: University of Washington Press, pp. 54–63.

NICHOLSON, WALTER. 1985. *Microeconomic Theory: Basic Principles and Extensions.* Third Edition. New York: Dryden Press.

OKUN, ARTHUR. 1981. *Prices and Quantities.* Washington, D.C.: Brookings Institution.

OLIVER, DOUGLAS. 1955. *A Solomon Island Society.* Cambridge, MA: Harvard University Press.

ORLOVE, BENJAMIN. 1986. "Barter and Cash Sale on Lake Titicaca: A Test of Competing Approaches." *Current Anthropology* 27(2):85–106.

PEARSON, HARRY, ed. 1977. *Karl Polanyi's The Livelihood of Man.* New York: Academic Press.

PLATTNER, STUART. 1985. "Equilibrating Market Relationships." In Stuart Plattner ed., *Markets and Marketing.* Lanham, MD: University Press of America, pp. 133-152.

POLANYI, KARL. 1944. *The Great Transformation*. Boston: Beacon Press.

———. 1947. "Our Obsolete Market Mentality: Civilization Must Find a New Thought Pattern." *Commentary* 3:109–117.

POLANYI, KARL, CONRAD ARENSBERG, and HARRY PEARSON, eds. 1957. *Trade and Market in the Early Empires*. New York: Free Press.

POSNER, RICHARD. 1980. "A Theory of Primitive Society, with Special Reference to Law." *Journal of Law and Economics* 23:1–56.

POSPISIL, LEOPOLD. 1963. *Kapauku Papuan Economy*. Yale University Publications in Anthropology, Number 67. New Haven: Yale University Department of Anthropology.

SAHLINS, MARSHALL. 1963. "Poor Man, Rich Man, Big-Man Chief: Political Types in Melanesia and Polynesia." *Comparative Studies in Society and History* 5(April):285–303.

———. 1972. *Stone Age Economics*. New York: Aldine.

SALISBURY, RICHARD. 1962. *From Stone to Steel: Economic Consequences of a Technological Change in New Guinea*. New York: Cambridge University Press.

SCHNEIDER, HAROLD. 1974. *Economic Man: The Anthropology of Economics*. New York: Free Press.

SLATER, PHILIP. 1963. "On Social Regression." *American Sociological Review* 28.

STRATHERN, ANDREW. 1971. *The Rope of Moka: Big-Men and Ceremonial Exchange in Mount Hagen New Guinea*. Cambridge, MA: Cambridge University Press.

SZANTON, MARIA C. B. 1972. *A Right to Survive: Subsistence Marketing in a Lowland Philippine Town*. University Park, PA: Pennsylvania State University Press.

TAX, SOL. 1963. *Penny Capitalism: A Guatemalan Indian Economy*. Chicago: University of Chicago Press.

TRAGER, LILLIAN. 1981. "Customers and Creditors: Variations in Economic Personalism in a Nigerian Marketing System." *Ethnology* 20(April):133–146.

TURNBULL, COLIN. 1961. *The Forest People: A Study of the Pygmies of the Congo*. New York: Simon and Schuster.

VARIAN, HAL. 1978. *Microeconomic Analysis*. New York: W. W. Norton.

WILLIAMSON, OLIVER. 1975. *Markets and Hierarchies*. New York: Free Press.

# 2

# On the Relationship Between Economic Theory and Economic Sociology in the Work of Joseph Schumpeter

### RICHARD SWEDBERG

Throughout his career Schumpeter tried to develop a kind of broad general economic science, which he usually referred to as *Sozialökonomik*.* The most thorough exposition of what Schumpeter meant by this term (which he had borrowed from Max Weber), can be found in his posthumously published *History of Economic Analysis*. *Sozialökonomik*, we here read, consists of several different "fields": *"economic theory," "economic history," "economic sociology,"* and *"statistics"* (1954c:12–24). None of these fields or perspectives can by itself exhaust the economic phenomenon, Schumpeter emphasized; they all have to cooperate in analyzing it. Exactly how this cooperation would work, we are never told. When, for example, should you resort to economic theory rather than to economic sociology? And how do you link up one type of analysis to another? Few, if any, answers to this kind of question can be found in Schumpeter's theoretical works. All that he was prepared to say about the relationship between economic theory and economic sociology, for example, was that economic theory should deal with "economic mechanisms" (such as value and price), and economic sociology should be devoted to the study of "economic institutions" (such as property and inheritance).

This distinction between economic mechanisms and economic institutions can be criticized on various grounds. It is, for example, not always clear what constitutes an "institution" as opposed to a "mechanism." Schumpeter thus classified the market as a mechanism and tariff policy as an economic institution, but one could just as easily reverse the labels. And why is sociology inherently unsuitable for the study of mechanisms and economic theory unsuitable for dealing with institutions? Recent developments have shown that economic sociology can very well be used to analyze economic mechanisms (such as markets) and economic institutions (such as the firm).

But even if it is agreed that Schumpeter's distinction between mechanisms and institutions is unsatisfactory from a theoretical viewpoint, it should immediately be added that in his own studies—as opposed to in his more programmatic statements about *Sozialökonomik*—Schumpeter always displayed great ingenuity and creativity in trying to relate economic theory and economic sociology to one another. As are many social scientists, Schumpeter was, in other words, more original when it came to theory making in his concrete studies than in his programmatic statements. That this is indeed the case with Schumpeter's ideas about the relationship between economic theory and economic sociology is something I try to show in this chapter by looking at a few of Schumpeter's studies in sociology. The ones on which I have chosen to focus were all written while Schumpeter was in his mid-thirties to early forties: "The Crisis of the Tax State" (1918), "The Sociology of Imperialisms" (1918–1919), and "Social Classes in an Ethnically Homogeneous Environment" (1927). Schumpeter (1949) used to refer to these studies as his "excursions" in sociology, and before discussing them a few words need to be said about his relationship to sociology. Schumpeter was trained as an economist—he received his doctorate in law and economics in Vienna in 1906—and he always identified himself as an economist. From early on, however, his great interest in sociology was apparent.

## Schumpeter's Background in Sociology

Even though Schumpeter did not do any serious work in sociology until he was in his mid-thirties, it is clear that his interest in sociology went far back. As a young boy at Theresianum—the famous prep school in Vienna for the Austro-Hungarian upper class—Schumpeter began to read in sociology as well as philosophy (see Swedberg 1991:11). Exactly which sociological works he read during these years is not known, except that he came across Ludwig Gumplowicz's books with their "racial theory of classes" (Schumpeter 1955a:102). We do not know much more about Schumpeter's study of sociology while he was a student of economics at the University of Vienna. But it was in all likelihood here that, for the first time, he encountered the works of Max Weber, Karl Marx, and the

Austro-Marxists. After having gained his doctorate in 1906, Schumpeter spent about a year in England. Here he followed the lectures by, among others, the prominent Finnish sociologist Edward Westermarck (Schumpeter 1909). From Schumpeter's writings in the early 1900s, we know that he was also familiar with the sociological writings of such authors as Emile Durkheim, François Simiand, and Georg Simmel (e.g., Schumpeter 1914). When Schumpeter applied for his *Habilitation* at the University of Vienna in 1909, he suggested that, besides economics and statistics, he was also competent to teach sociology. The course that he proposed to teach was entitled "The Foundation and the Contemporary State of Sociology." The way Schumpeter described the course, one gets the impression that he was quite familiar with sociology:

1. How sociology emerged and why it is necessary
2. Its area and which facts belong to it
3. Its problems
4. Its methods and contemporary results
5. Main currents in sociology
6. Sociology of everyday life; the sociological knowledge of artists [Schumpeter 1909].

It is clear that the border lines between the different social sciences were not as sharp in Schumpeter's day as they are today. When Schumpeter, for example, taught economics at the University of Czernowitz in the early 1910s, he gave a course in "State and Society" that was mainly sociological in nature. And when he was exchange professor at Columbia University in 1913–1914, he taught a course on "The Theory of Social Classes." That Schumpeter himself had a broad interest in social science is also obvious from a fine little pamphlet that he wrote on the past and the future of the social sciences while in Czernowitz (1915a). At this point, it should perhaps be noted that by "sociology" Schumpeter did not mean social science in general, but a distinct approach with its own set of problems. This is, for example, one of the points that he made in his first book, *Das Wesen und der Hauptinhalt der theoretischen Nationalökonomie* (1908). Schumpeter here says that sociology "is not—and must not be—just a term for social science in general; it is its own science with its own goals and methods." Even though economics, in Schumpeter's mind, should be clearly distinct from sociology, he also stressed that "no one could be more convinced than the economist of the necessity of this young science" (1908:539).

Schumpeter never felt that it was particularly important to give exact definitions of the different social sciences, and during his early years he often emphasized different aspects of sociology. In his history of economic theory from 1914, for example, he defined sociology as "the theory of social institutions and principles of social organization" (1954b:103). And in an article from about the same time, sociology is described as "the doctrine about the interaction between individuals and groups of individuals within the social whole" (1915b/1952:556). Usually, however, when Schumpeter spoke of economic sociology, it was *institutions* that he had in mind. By this term he meant what is normally understood by the notion of institution, namely ways of doing things, as enforced by norms and sanctions. Schumpeter also insisted that, while it was necessary always to start with the individual in economic theory, this was unsuitable in sociology since its basic unit is the group (e.g., 1990b:286–287).

A special study would be needed to describe properly the relationship between Schumpeter and Max Weber (for a fine attempt in this direction, see Osterhammel 1987). When Schumpeter first heard of Weber and started to read his work is not known, but it was probably while he was a student at the University of Vienna. Perhaps the two met for the first time at one of the meetings of the *Verein für Sozialpolitik*, to which all the prominent German-speaking economists belonged, including Weber and Schumpeter. In any case, we know that Schumpeter backed Weber in the famous debate about value judgments in economics that took place in the *Verein* (see Schumpeter 1913). That Weber, for his part, early became aware of Schumpeter's work is clear from Weber's annotated copy of Schumpeter's *Theorie der wirtschaftlichen Entwicklung* (1911), which still can be inspected at the Max-Weber-Arbeitsstelle in Munich (Osterhammel 1987:106, 118). Weber also commissioned Schumpeter to write a history of economic theory for *Grundriss der Sozialökonomik* in the early 1910s. When Weber was asked in 1918 to make a statement about which candidate he considered to be the most suitable for a chair in economics at the University of Vienna, he wholeheartedly supported Schumpeter over a host of other names.[1] Both Weber and Schumpeter were editors together of the famous *Archiv für Sozialwissenschaft und Sozialpolitik* toward the end of the 1910s.

Although Schumpeter could not stand some of the other editors at

---

[1] Weber wrote to the Vienna Faculty that "It is my absolute duty to state that the Faculty would injure itself badly if it does not appoint Joseph Schumpeter, who is the most prominent theoretical talent and (as I have understood it from all the accounts of the students) also the most eminent teaching talent" (Weber 1918). I thank Dr. Dieter Krüeger for having told me about this document. (The person who was finally appointed to the chair in Vienna was Othmar Spann, a controversial and second-rate economist).

the *Archiv* (he particularly disliked Werner Sombart), he got along well with Weber. There exists, for example, an account of a pleasant meeting in 1919 between Max Weber, Marianne Weber, and Walther Tritsch (Tritsch 1985). But there were also differences between Weber and Schumpeter, as the following anecdote from about the same time makes clear.

> Both had met in a Vienna coffeehouse, in the presence of Ludo Moritz Hartmann and Somary. Schumpeter remarked how pleased he was with the Russian Revolution. Socialism was no longer a discussion on paper, but had to prove its viability. Max Weber responded in great agitation: Communism, at this stage in Russian development, was virtually a crime, the road would lead over unparalleled human misery and end in a terrible catastrophe. "Quite likely," Schumpeter answered, "but what a fine laboratory." "A laboratory filled with mounds of corpses," Weber answered heatedly. "The same can be said of every dissecting room," Schumpeter replied. Every attempt to divert them failed. Weber became increasingly violent and loud, Schumpeter increasingly sarcastic and muted. The other guests listened with curiosity, until Weber jumped up, shouting, "I can't stand any more of this," and rushed out, followed by Hartmann, who brought him his hat. Schumpeter, left behind, said with a smile: "How can a man shout like that in a coffeehouse?" [Jaspers 1964:222]

But this flare-up between Schumpeter and Weber did not mean that they did not appreciate each other. When Weber died in 1920, Schumpeter wrote a moving obituary for *Der Österreichische Volkswirt*. From this brief article it is clear that Schumpeter also "had fallen under Weber's spell," as Fritz Karl Mann (1970:xiii) has put it. In the article entitled "Max Weber's Work," Schumpeter describes Weber in a rather exalted manner: "he led [and] you submitted, whether you wanted to or not"; "above all he was loved"; "this Lohengrin with his silver moral armor"; and so on (1990a:220–227). In terms of Weber's intellectual production, we already know that Schumpeter had borrowed the notion of *Sozialökonomik* from Weber, and it can be added that Weber had also been instrumental in creating the field of economic sociology, in which Schumpeter later became interested as well (e.g., Schumpeter 1954c:21, 819). In the obituary Schumpeter spoke very highly of Weber's contribution to the philosophy of the social sciences; he was clearly awed by Weber's immense mastery of historical facts, and he singled out "The Protestant Ethic" and "The Social Psychology of the World Religions" as "the best sociological achievements of German science." But even if Schumpeter praised Weber as a sociologist, it should be noted that he did not have a high opinion of him as an economist: "Weber was a sociologist above all. Even though he was a sociologist with a penchant for things that are primarily concerned with economics, he was an economist only indirectly and secondarily. His interest in economics does not focus on the mechanism of economic life as described by economic theory, nor on the real historical phenomenon for its own sake, but rather on the sequence of historical types and their social-psychological profusion" (1990a:225). In other words, Weber might be a superb sociologist, but he had little to contribute to the economic theory part of *Sozialökonomik*.

### "The Crisis of the Tax State"

Of Schumpeter's three major essays in economic sociology, "The Crisis of the Tax State" is the one he wrote first, probably in late 1917 and early 1918. This essay contains, among other things, a sharp analysis of the difficult financial situation that was to be expected in Austria after the war. The main focus, however, is on the possibility of opening up a new field in sociology called "fiscal sociology" and what this new field might look like.

At this point it is necessary to pause for a moment and make one thing clear: in writing his essay on the tax state, Schumpeter was not interested in contributing to sociology per se, as, for instance, an expression of his general erudition in the social sciences. Instead, the essay was first and foremost part of Schumpeter's attempt to work out a broad economic science or *Sozialökonomik*. Schumpeter, in other words, saw his essay as part of his attempt to expand the domain of the theoretically oriented economist. In this sense, this essay is no different from Schumpeter's two others in sociology, which were also attempts to introduce new topics into economics within the conceptual framework of *Sozialökonomik*. But in order for this to be possible, Schumpeter stressed, the economist had to give up on his ambition to use always a purely analytical approach and to focus exclusively on so-called economic mechanisms. This was something you could do only when you were working on a small set of problems, such as various aspects of price formation. But in order to be able to analyze such things as taxes, classes, and imperialism, the economist must make use of another technique available to the *Sozialökonom*: viz., that of *economic sociology*.

One of the many things that an economic theorist in Schumpeter's day could not talk about was the state. This was simply because the state was not primarily an economic phenomenon: the political structure of a society belonged to those things that an economic theorist *presupposed,* not what he analyzed. In reality, of course, the state too is an economic actor. The state is not, to use Weber's terminology, an "economic organization" or an organization whose main purpose is economic; but it is still an "economically active organization," or an organization whose activities are not primarily economic, but which include economic ones (see Weber 1978:74–75). And one of the most important economic activities of the state is the handling of taxes: the collection of taxes and the spending of its revenue. Still, the economic theorist (especially in the late 1910s when Schumpeter's article was written) would not analyze fiscal activities since they were too closely related to the political function of the state and, by definition, did not follow economic logic. The sociologist, on the other hand, lacked these restrictions, and since he could look at any kind of "economic institution" he could also analyze fiscal phenomena. Through sociology, therefore, a whole new field of problems and facts could be opened up to the social economist *(Sozialökonom),* and it was this field that Schumpeter (following the Austrian sociologist Rudolf Goldscheid) called *Finanzsoziologie* or "fiscal sociology."

With the help of fiscal sociology the economic theorist could follow a series of interesting economic phenomena far into society. By its financial measures, the state often affected the whole economic development of a country, according to Schumpeter. "Fiscal measures have created and destroyed industries, industrial forms, and industrial regions even where this was not their intent, and have in this manner contributed directly to the construction (and distortion) of the edifice of the modern economy and, through it, of the modern spirit" (1954a:7). One could also get a very realistic view of the state by looking at its budget, and Schumpeter liked to cite Goldscheid's words, that "the budget is the skeleton of the state stripped free of all ideology" (1954a:6). The type of taxes that the state tried to enforce, and the way that the state went about collecting them, also influenced the various groups in society and their respective standing. A strong group might be able to resist the state; a weak group would be destroyed; and so on. "The spirit of a people, its cultural level, its social structure, the deeds its policy may prepare—all this and more is written into its fiscal history, if you remove all phrases" (1954a:6).

Schumpeter also presented two general theses in his essay. The first was that the modern state had been born out of its fiscal needs; the second that there exists an inherent tendency toward a fiscal crisis in the capitalist state. Again, to trace the history of the modern state was not something an economic theorist would do; this was clearly outside his competence. "The Crisis of the Tax State," however, contains an excellent, ten-page account of the emergence of the modern state. The reader should note that Schumpeter was interested only in tracing the typical development of the state, since his article was not intended as a study in history but in sociology. In broad strokes, therefore, he described how the modern state had emerged in Central Europe toward the end of the Middle Ages as a result of the financial needs of the prince. A prince desperately needed money during this period for the following three reasons: he had mismanaged his affairs; he had to maintain a costly court (to divert the aristocracy); and—most importantly—he had to raise huge amounts of money for war against the Turks. The prince realized that the only way to be able to dispose of huge enough sums would be to get the estates to assume responsibility for the war against the Turks. He therefore proposed that he alone should not be responsible for the expenses of the war; it was really a "common exigency" and the estates must shoulder their responsibility as well. The estates finally agreed, and "out of this 'common exigency' the state was born" (1954a:15).

Schumpeter's thesis about the birth of the modern state—that "without financial need the immediate cause for the creation of the modern state would have been absent," (1954a:16)—has been criticized for underplaying the role of the political element in this process. With an explicit reference to this passage, Rudolf Braun, for example, has argued that, as opposed to what Schumpeter says, "the financial needs [of the state] are symptoms and effects as well as causes of new political, social and economic needs and of a new quality of life, which is developing" (Braun 1975:245). Fritz Karl Mann concurs: "without political need the cause for the creation of the modern finance and tax system would have been absent" (Mann as cited in Braun 1975:245–246). There is, no doubt, something to this critique. Still, Schumpeter was not far off the mark in stressing the role of the fiscal needs of the prince in this process. It should also be noted that the distinction between "economic" and "political" causes can easily become scholastic in this case, since, after all, one is talking about the actions of the same political actor.

One may also say that the obvious criticism that can be directed against Schumpeter's second thesis in his essay—the idea that a fiscal crisis is an inevitable as well as an integral part of the decline of the capitalist system—should not be allowed to detract from the originality of his thought. Schumpeter was saying simply that there exists a definite limit to the fiscal capacity of the state, and that if this limit is transgressed, the state will collapse. Schumpeter drew up several scenarios for how this situation could come about, while repeatedly stressing that they were all unlikely to take place in postwar Austria. His theory about the collapse of the fiscal state implied, first of all, a long-term perspective. And in such a long-term perspective, it was clear to him that the tax state would fall apart, due to the general development of capitalism. At this point,

Schumpeter's argument fuses with his general feeling that the time was up for the capitalist system; and indeed "The Crisis of the Tax State" contains the germ of some of the ideas that were later to be more fully developed in *Capitalism, Socialism and Democracy* (1942). We thus read: "The hour has not yet struck [for capitalism]. Nevertheless, the hour will come" (1954a:38).

Compared to *Capitalism, Socialism and Democracy,* however, Schumpeter's article on the tax state pays much more attention to the role that fiscal policy can play in triggering the demise of capitalism. A severe crisis can actually be brought about in several different ways, all involving some kind of fiscal measure by the state. For one thing, the state can tax entrepreneurial profit in such a radical manner that economic development will simply come to a standstill. The individual's motive for working hard and being entrepreneurial would be so affected by this that capitalism would grind to a halt. There is also the possibility that the state would just keep increasing taxes until they are far too high: "The closer the tax state approaches these limits, the greater is the resistance and the loss of energy with which it works. A bigger and bigger army of bureaucrats is needed to enforce the tax laws, tax inquisition becomes more and more intrusive, tax chicanery more and more unbearable. The absurd waste of energy that this picture entails shows that the meaning of the organization of the tax state lies in the autonomy of the private economy, and that this meaning is lost when the state can no longer respect this autonomy" (1954a:24).

Finally, there is a third possible kind of fiscal crisis, which is reminiscent of the second type, but which contains an original twist. This is the crisis that is brought about because the tax revenues are not sufficient to cover the expenses for all the measures to which people feel entitled by the state:

> If the will of the people is to demand higher and higher public expenditures; if more and more means are used for purposes for which private individuals have not produced them; if more and more power stands behind this will; and if finally all parts of the people are gripped by entirely new ideas about private property—then the tax state will have run its course and society will have to depend on other motive forces for its economy than self-interest. This limit can certainly be reached and thereby also the crisis which the state could not survive" [1954a:24].

That Schumpeter's ideas on this topic are still pertinent is testified to, for example, by the success that James O'Connor had in the 1970s with *The Fiscal Crisis of the State*. The general argument of this neo-Marxist book is that there exists a general tendency for the expenditures of the capitalist state to increase faster than it can raise money to finance them, and that this may lead to a fiscal crisis. Or, to phrase it differently, that there exists a dangerous contradiction between the task of "accumulation" and the task of "legitimation" in the capitalist state, which may lead to a fiscal crisis. Though O'Connor does not acknowledge Schumpeter's role in framing this thesis—he actually downplays "The Crisis of the Tax State" and lamely asserts that "fiscal sociology has always been central to the Marxist tradition" (O'Connor 1973:10)—it is obvious enough that O'Connor's main idea comes straight from Schumpeter's essay.

### *"The Sociology of Imperialisms"*

Schumpeter's article on imperialism was written around the same time as his article on the tax state and was published in 1918–1919 in two installments in *Archiv für Sozialwissenschaft und Sozialpolitik*. Here too Schumpeter's main concern was to extend the science of economics to topics that were outside the competence of the economic theorist. And again, he did this with the help of economic sociology—that is, through the semianalytical, semiempirical kind of approach that he considered typical of economic sociology (see especially Schumpeter 1926, with its discussion of Gustav von Schmoller). That imperialism was not a phenomenon that could be handled with economic theory is clear enough from Schumpeter's famous definition: *"imperialism is the objectless disposition on the part of a state to unlimited forcible expansion"* (Schumpeter 1955a:6; italics added). More precisely, there are three elements to this definition that make imperialism fall outside the scope of analytical economic theory. First, it involves the behavior of a political actor, the state. Second, and to a certain extent connected to the first point, imperialistic behavior always involves force, which is a taboo topic in economic theory.[2] And third, imperialist behavior is not rational behavior, and economic theory only deals with rational behavior.

That imperialism is profoundly irrational in nature is somewhat hidden by the words "objectless disposition" in Schumpeter's definition. At

---

[2] See in this context Schumpeter's contribution, around the turn of the century, to the debate on whether prices are set through power or through economic laws. Schumpeter argued that power could, at the most, have a minor impact on the key problem in economics, which was to formulate economic laws. To illustrate his thought on this point he used the example of a card game. In a card game, he said, every player is dealt different cards at the beginning of the game; in a similar manner, power influences the way every individual starts out in society. But once the players have their cards—and this is the main point— they all have to play by the rules (see Schumpeter 1916:26).

other places in his essay, however, Schumpeter clarifies that there exist no "definite, utilitarian limits" to imperialist behavior. Instead, "non-rational and irrational" elements play a key role, and imperialist wars are often set off without any specific goal in mind (1955a:61). For imperialism to work effectively and to be able to mobilize support, it has to be able to arouse "the dark powers of the subconscious"; and to do this, it has to appeal to "the need to hate," "inchoate idealism," and the like. In brief, it has to appeal to a totally different set of motives than those referred to in conventional economic theory (1955a:11–12).

The difference between imperialism, as Schumpeter sees it, and the behavior on which economic theory focuses ("price-value-money") is further accentuated by his idea that capitalism is, by nature, absolutely antithetical to imperialism. Schumpeter's general idea was that in a capitalist society, people put all their energy into work and have little energy left over for martial activities, including imperialist adventures. "In a purely capitalist world, what was once energy for war becomes simply energy for labor of every kind," he writes (1955a:69). In a capitalist society people also think rationally, since the economic logic of capitalism is hammered into their minds on a daily basis. This makes them resistant to irrational phenomena such as imperialism. "Everything that is purely instinctual, everything insofar as it is purely instinctual, is driven into the background by this development" (1955a:68). Schumpeter summarizes his thesis about the relationship between capitalism and imperialism in one sentence: *"capitalism is by nature anti-imperialist"* (1955a:73; italics added).

From this quick overview of Schumpeter's theory of imperialism one might get the impression that this phenomenon, in Schumpeter's mind, has nothing to do with economics and is therefore of little interest to the economist. For two reasons, however, this is not the case. First, there already exists an attempt to account for imperialism on purely economic grounds. This is the Marxist theory of imperialism, and the economist needs to take a position vis-à-vis this argument. Second, imperialism can, in Schumpeter's mind, be explained from an economic viewpoint—but it has to be an explanation that draws primarily on economic sociology as opposed to theoretical economics. As to the first point, Schumpeter was mainly concerned to show that what he called the "neo-Marxist theory of imperialism" was wrong. By this he meant the works by Rudolf Hilferding and Otto Bauer (but not Lenin's theory of imperialism as the highest stage of capitalism, which was probably not available to Schumpeter when he wrote "The Sociology of Imperialisms"). There were several reasons for Schumpeter's sharp rejection of the Marxist theory of imperialism. For one thing, Hilferding et al. had nothing to say about imperialism in precapitalist societies, since they saw imperialism as closely connected to capitalism. This was a position that Schumpeter could not accept. The Marxist idea that capitalism would have some inherent tendency toward imperialism was equally unacceptable to Schumpeter, who felt that capitalism was inherently peaceful. And finally, Schumpeter thought that it was far too simplistic to say that imperialism was caused by the economic structure or the relations of production; this type of argument ruled out the kind of complexity that Schumpeter was convinced was involved.

What then did Schumpeter's own theory of imperialism look like, and, more precisely, how did he propose to link imperialism to economic behavior so that it would be of interest to the *Sozialökonom?* The answer is that just as Schumpeter felt that there exist several types of imperialism (the title to his essay explicitly refers to "imperialisms" in the plural), there also exist several types of explanations for this type of behavior. Early in his essay, for example, he discusses imperialism in antiquity and especially in Persia, Egypt, and Assyria. In all of these empires, he said, imperialism was built into society via the social structure; these were all warrior nations that would collapse if they did not expand. The particular way in which they would fall apart in the absence of expansion varied from case to case. But the main point was that such expansion was absolutely necessary. Imperialist behavior was linked to the social structure of the economy in such a way that certain social groups could not survive by their own labor; they therefore continuously had to conquer new areas. "In order to exhibit a continual trend toward imperialism, a people must not live on—or at least not be absorbed by—its own labor" (1955a:46).

Since imperialism is irrational in nature, Schumpeter argued, it is strengthened by age. Tradition, in other words, plays an important role in imperialism; and this is particularly clear in Schumpeter's analysis of the imperialism of the absolutist state. This type of state, which was common in Europe during the seventeenth and eighteenth centuries, was a kind of war machine and the king was primarily a warlord. Schumpeter does not say much more than this about the absolutist state, except that its ruling class was disposed to war and that the king saw war as a way of maintaining its prestige. Nevertheless, as we soon shall see, the absolutist state plays an extremely important role in Schumpeter's analysis of imperialism in the capitalist society.

As we already know, according to Schumpeter capitalism was "by nature anti-imperialist." This, however, only meant that there could be no imperialism in a *purely* capitalist society. In many contemporary capitalist states, however, there existed a tendency toward something he called "modern imperialism," which had to do with the fact that warlike elements from the absolutist state had survived and become part of capitalism. Schumpeter explains:

> Imperialism thus is atavistic in character. It falls into that large group of surviving features from earlier ages that play such an important part in every concrete social situation. In other words, it is an element that stems from the living conditions, not of the present, but of the past—or, to put it in terms of the economic interpretation of history, from past rather than present relations of productions [1955a:65].

Schumpeter's argument was therefore that modern imperialism was linked in an indirect way to economic factors; it was caused by "past rather than present relations of production." What this meant, in more detail, was that modern capitalism had inherited a tendency to rely on certain restrictive economic measures that had originally been instituted by the absolutist state. One example of this was trade regulations. These distorted the economic logic of the market and, in some cases, even made a country prone to imperialism.

Schumpeter singled out the role that tariffs especially have played in this whole process. Tariffs had originally been used by the monarchy to provide revenue, and they were clearly an example of "artificial" economic measures in the sense that they went directly counter to the logic of capitalism. Tariffs were instrumental in fostering imperialism in the following way. They prevented free trade and created protective walls around nations. This made it possible for cartels and trusts to reap monopoly profits in the domestic market, while they dumped the rest of their production abroad. And this led to "economic aggression" between countries, which often ended in various imperialistic ventures.

Schumpeter's article on imperialism has been criticized by a variety of authors. In the opinion of the Marxists, for example, Schumpeter's theory of imperialism is more or less useless since it denies that there is a link between capitalism and imperialism.[3] Given the fact that Schumpeter's theory is diametrically opposed to the Marxist thesis of imperialism as a creation of capitalism, this verdict is not surprising. The Marxist tendency to reject Schumpeter's analysis *in toto* is, however, much too radical and it fails to do justice to the wealth of ideas in Schumpeter's essay. The Marxists also miss the point that Schumpeter's theory of the inherent peacefulness of capitalism is little more than a modernized ver-

---

[3] See, for example, Winslow (1931) and Greene (1952). Greene makes the good point that since Schumpeter says that imperialism has to involve "forcible expansion," many forms of economic imperialism are automatically ruled out in this type of analysis.

sion of Montesquieu's idea of "commerce doux" and the thesis of Saint-Simon and Herbert Spencer that in an "industrial society," as opposed to a "military society," there will be peace and not war.[4] Today very few people believe that industrialism will lead to peace, especially after two world wars and multiple colonial wars. This notion, however, also exists in a revised and more sophisticated version, which is quite similar to Schumpeter's idea that "modern imperialism" is the result of a survival of absolutism. The notion, popularized among others by Barrington Moore in *The Social Origins of Dictatorship and Democracy* (1966), is that societies that industrialize and have a strong feudal past will have more difficulty in establishing a democratic regime. In his Auguste Comte Memorial Lecture from 1957, entitled "War and Industrial Society," Raymond Aron has also pointed out that "the facts which . . . Schumpeter can quote in support of [his] theory are not open to doubt. The survivals of the *ancien regime* were stronger in Germany and Japan than in Great Britain or France. In both countries there was this combination of a property-owning class and a militaristic caste which can be regarded as the chief cause of imperialism" (1958:19).

### *"Social Classes"*

Schumpeter's third major article in sociology, "Social Classes in an Ethnically Homogeneous Environment," was published in 1927 in *Archiv für Sozialwissenschaft und Sozialpolitik*. In the introduction Schumpeter says that the basic idea for his essay went back to 1910–1911, when he had taught a course on "State and Society" at the University of Czernowitz (1955b:101). This was also the time when he was putting the finishing touches to *Theorie der wirtschaftlichen Entwicklung*, and the parallels between the theory of entrepreneurship developed in this book and the basic thesis in his essay on social class are striking. In the 1910s Schumpeter continued to work on the concept of social class, but it was not until the mid-1920s that he sat down to write the essay on class, spurred on by the fact that he had to give a lecture in November 1926 on "Leadership and Class Formation" at the University of Heidelberg. But even at this late point Schumpeter emphasized that it would be "years" until he would be able to present a final version of his ideas on this topic (1955b:101). This final version, however, never appeared; in his later works, Schumpeter always referred to his 1927 article (1975:204).

---

[4] During the seventeenth and eighteenth century several thinkers argued that the expansion of *commerce* would lead to an end of war between the European states. During the nineteenth century this idea was extended to *industry*, especially by Saint-Simon and Herbert Spencer.

According to Schumpeter, the concept of class was extremely important and promised to solve a number of difficult problems in the social sciences. Schumpeter's description of the potentials of class analysis is nearly lyrical: "the subject [of class]—and this is what constitutes its fascination—poses a wealth of new questions, offers outlooks on untilled fields, foreshadows sciences of the future. Roaming it, one often has a strange feeling, as though the social sciences of today, almost on purpose were dealing with relative side-issues; as though some day—and perhaps soon—the things we now believe will be discounted" (1955b:103). In order to carry out this exciting type of analysis, however, it was necessary to use the sociological concept of class and not the one used in theoretical economics. This last point was crucial to Schumpeter, who argued that the economic concept of class was only to be used as an analytical tool, while its sociological counterpart denoted a distinct part of social reality. The economist, Schumpeter specified, used the notion of class to "classify different things according to certain chosen criteria"; and the economic concept of class was consequently "a creation of the researcher" (1955b:105). Schumpeter used the following example to bring out the difference between the economic and the sociological concepts of class. Take a lawyer and a manual worker. From the viewpoint of economic theory, it is clear that both receive a wage and therefore belong to the working class. From a sociological viewpoint, however, wage earners can belong to several different classes, and it would be absurd to put a lawyer and a manual worker in the same class.

Just as in his earlier sociological essays, Schumpeter emphasized that the only way that an economist could hope to deal with certain aspects of socioeconomic problems was to switch from economic theory to economic sociology. The concepts of economic theory were very useful for some tasks, but it was not possible to use them for all purposes. The temptation to do so was, however, there: "there is the fact that the economic theorist finds it exceedingly difficult to confine himself strictly to his problems, to resist the temptation to enliven his presentation with something [social and sociological] that fascinates most of his readers." But the only way to proceed for the *Sozialökonom* in this situation was to use the sociological concept of class, according to which class was a concrete entity, "a special social organism, living, acting, and suffering" (1955b:105, 106). A social class, he continued, typically had "its own life and characteristic spirit." People preferred to interact with people from the same social class: "class members behave toward one another in a fashion characteristically different from their conduct toward members of other classes. They are in closer association with one another; they understand one another better; they work more readily in concert; they close ranks and erect barriers against the outside; they look out into the same segment of the world, with the same eyes, from the same viewpoint, in the same direction" (1955b:107).

The most important consequence of this tendency to interact with members from the same social class was that most people also married within their own class. This last point was very important to Schumpeter, who saw the family as absolutely central to class cohesion: "The family, not the individual," he wrote, "is the true unit of class and class theory" (1955b:113). This focus on the family, as opposed to the individual, was finally a further reason why conventional economic theory could not be used to analyze social classes. Methodological individualism had a place—but not in sociology.

The huge number of questions that could be addressed through a class analysis, Schumpeter said, made it imperative for him to limit himself to one topic. The one he chose was that of "class formation," which he defined in the following manner: "the question of why the social whole, as far as our eye can reach, has never been homogenous, always revealing a particular, obviously organic stratification" (1955b:107). The problems that he wanted to deal with, in other words, were fundamental to the very concept of class. A close reading of his article also makes it clear that he thought that the existing literature in class theory—by Schmoller, Durkheim, Spann, Simmel, and so on—was deficient in some fundamental manner. Though Schumpeter does not say so explicitly, he seems to have felt that an acceptable theory of social class did not exist and the task that he set for himself was to construct such a theory. He proposed to do this by linking the phenomenon of class to his own theory of economic change.

The main part of Schumpeter's article is devoted to an analysis of three phenomena: intraclass mobility, interclass mobility, and the rise and decline of whole classes. The kind of intraclass mobility that Schumpeter had in mind was that of families. It is typical for classes, Schumpeter said, that even though their basic structures remain the same, at different times they contain different individuals. Or, in the famous formulation: "Each class resembles a hotel, . . . always full, but always of different people" (1955b:126). The turnover process, however, was slow and usually took several decades. The basic reason the turnovers took place at all had to do with the fact that certain individual families could successfully adapt to new situations while others could not. If we look at the industrial bourgeoisie, for example, it is clear that the leading families in the 1920s are not the same as those in the middle of the nineteenth century. In a capitalist society, Schumpeter said, a bourgeois family had to be innovative or it would automatically decline. The reason for this was that new profit was continuously needed to maintain a prominent position, and this profit could only be gained through innovative business practice. At this point Schumpeter explicitly referred to his own theory of entrepreneurial profit, as he had presented it in *Theorie der wirtschaftlichen Entwicklung* (1911). The link between his economic theory and his sociological analysis is obvious: "This decline [of bourgeois families] *is* automatic, for it is not a matter of omission or commission, but flows instead from the self-actuating logic of the competitive system, by the simple fact of profits running dry. As to the question why this is so, it is answered by [my] theory of entrepreneurial profit" (1955b:120).

In his analysis of interclass mobility, Schumpeter was first of all concerned with showing that, contrary to what was often asserted, there did indeed exist quite a bit of movement from one class to another. Schumpeter stressed that this process, just like intraclass mobility, became visible only from a long-term perspective. And again, Schumpeter sought the explanation among the factors that he had highlighted in his theory of the entrepreneur: "Those factors that account for shifts in family position within a class are the same that account for the crossing of class barriers" (1955b:134).

The most impressive and imaginative part of Schumpeter's whole essay is his analysis of why whole classes rise and fall. Here, as elsewhere, he focused mainly on ruling classes and in particular on the fate of the feudal class. Every ruling class fulfills a specific function, Schumpeter said, and the function of the feudal class was military in nature. During the Middle Ages, the feudal lord had taken care of this function himself ("the lord would mount his horse and defend himself, sword in hand, against dangers from above or below"—1955b:146). From the fourteenth century onward, however, the feudal class was in a slow decline. One reason for this was the gradual emergence of commercial society and the slow demilitarization that accompanied this process. But there was more to the decline of the feudal class than this objective development. The aristocracy had also begun to lose interest in its military function. It increasingly preferred to hire mercenaries and to work in the administration of the state rather than in its army. The situation was soon such, Schumpeter said, that the lord "was likely to don armor only when his portrait was to be painted." He was clearly fascinated by the self-destructive element in this process, which was "turning the nobility against its basic function, causing it to undermine the very foundations of its own military importance" (1955b:149, 150). The similarity between this analysis and the main thesis about the decline of the capitalist system in *Capitalism, Socialism and Democracy* is obvious.

Toward the end of the essay, Schumpeter summarized his findings and presented his own theory about why social classes exist. The aptitude for innovative behavior, Schumpeter said, is evenly distributed throughout a population or nation. But once a successful innovation is established, the innovator is surrounded, as it were, by an aura of success. This aura exerts a lasting effect on the surroundings and has a life of its own: "It does not necessarily disappear when its basis disappears—nor, for that matter, does its basis readily disappear. *This is the very heart and soul of the independent existence of 'class'* " (1955b:166). The prestige and success, however, does not only attach to the innovator, but also to the family of the innovator. Several families soon cluster together: "Coordinate families then merge into a social class, welded together by a bond, the substance and effect of which we now understand. This relationship assumes a life of its own and is then able to grant protection and confer prestige" (1955b:167).

## Concluding Remarks

We have now come to the end of Schumpeter's excursions into sociology and are in a position to summarize their importance for the problem we raised in the introduction to this chapter, namely: how does Schumpeter conceive of the links between the different parts of *Sozialökonomik?* It is clear that in each of the three studies in sociology we have considered, Schumpeter was trying out different solutions to the problem of how to join economic theory and economic sociology to one another. In one of his studies he experimented with the idea of introducing his own theory of the entrepreneur directly into the sociological analysis—this is the basic idea behind "Social Classes." In another study, Schumpeter tried to make sociology of the economists' old idea that economic activity is apolitical and peaceful by nature—this is the core argument of "The Sociology of Imperialism." And in his third essay, Schumpeter was wise enough to follow Schmoller and rely more on historical data than on pure economic theory—this is how "The Crisis of the Tax State" was constructed. This last strategy—linking economic sociology to a historically grounded type of economic theory—was probably the most successful. In any case, it was this strategy that Schumpeter would follow during the rest of his career.

It should finally be said that it could be useful to revive Schumpeter's (and Weber's) idea of *Sozialökonomik* today, on the ground that it represents a reasonable strategy for analyzing economic phenomena. Radical economists and radical sociologists will no doubt disagree, since they think that they can handle all economic phenomena on their own. But this is little other than an illusion as things stand today; neither economic theorists nor sociologists have the conceptual tools that would entitle them to an intellectual monopoly on economic phenomena. *Sozialöko-nomik* represents a much more sensible alternative, and here Schumpeter's recipe is simply to approach any economic problem with an open mind plus a combination of economic theory, economic sociology, and economic history.

    This essay draws on the author's *Schumpeter—A Biography* (Princeton University Press, 1991).

# References

ARON, RAYMOND. 1958. *War and Industrial Society*. London: Oxford University Press.

BRAUN, RUDOLF. 1975. "Taxation, Sociopolitical Structure, and State Building: Great Britain and Brandenburg-Prussia." In Charles Tilly ed., *The Formation of National States in Western Europe*. Princeton: Princeton University Press, pp. 243–327.

GREENE, MURRAY. 1952. "Schumpeter's Imperialism—A Critical Note." *Social Forces* 19:453–463.

JASPERS, KARL. 1964. *Three Essays: Leonardo, Descartes, Weber*. New York: Harcourt, Brace & World.

MANN, FRITZ KARL. 1970. "Einführung des Herausgeber". In *Das Wesen des Geldes* by Joseph A. Schumpeter. Göttingen: Vandenhoeck & Ruprecht, pp. i–xxvii.

MOORE, BARRINGTON. 1966. *The Social Origins of Dictatorship and Democracy*. Boston: Beacon Press.

O'CONNOR, JAMES. 1973. *The Fiscal Crisis of the State*. New York: St. Martin's Press.

OSTERHAMMEL, JÜERGEN. 1987. "Varieties of Social Economics: Joseph A. Schumpeter and Max Weber." In Wolfgang J. Mommsen and Jüergen Osterhammel eds., *Max Weber and His Contemporaries*. London: The German Historical Institute, pp. 106–120.

SCHUMPETER, JOSEPH A. 1908. *Das Wesen und der Hauptinhalt der theoretischen Nationalökonomie*. Leipzig: Duncker & Humblot.

———. 1909. Vita in Akt. Nr. 9501 vom 8 März 1909 des k.k. Ministeriums für Kultus und Unterricht, Dep. Nr. VII. Vienna: Allgemeines Verwaltungsarchiv.

———. 1911. *Theorie der wirtschaftlichen Entwicklung*. Leipzig: Duncker & Humblot.

———. 1913. "Meinungsäusserung zur Frage des Werturteils". In *Äusserungen zur Werturteildiskussion im Ausschuss des Vereins für Sozialpolitik*. Privately printed, pp. 49–50.

————. 1914. "Die 'positive' Methode in der Nationalökonomie." *Deutsche Literaturzeitung* 35:2101–2108.

————. 1915a. *Vergangenheit und Zukunft der Sozialwissenschaften.* Leipzig: Duncker & Humblot.

————. 1915b/1952. "Wie studiert man Sozialwissenschaft?" In Joseph A. Schumpeter, *Aufsätze zur ökonomischen Theorie.* Tübingen: J.C.B. Mohr, pp. 555–565.

————. 1916. "Das Grundprinzip der Verteilungstheorie." *Archiv für Sozialwissenschaft und Sozialpolitik* 42:1–88.

————. 1926. "Gustav v. Schmoller und die Probleme von heute." *Schmollers Jahrbuch für Gesetzgebung, Verwaltung und Volkswirtschaft* 50:337–388.

————. 1942. *Capitalism, Socialism and Democracy.* New York: Harper & Brothers.

————. 1949. Schumpeter to Lewis H. Haney, April 22. Harvard University Archives.

————. 1954a. "The Crisis of the Tax State." *International Economic Papers* 4:5–38.

————. 1954b. *Economic Doctrine and Method.* London: George Allen & Unwin. Originally published in 1914.

————. 1954c. *History of Economic Analysis.* New York: Oxford University Press.

————. 1955a. "The Sociology of Imperialisms." In Joseph A. Schumpeter, *Imperialism and Social Classes.* New York: Meridian Books, pp. 1–130.

————. 1955b. "Social Classes in an Ethnically Homogeneous Environment." In Joseph A. Schumpeter, *Imperialism and Social Classes.* New York: Meridian Books, pp. 131–182.

————. 1975. *Capitalism, Socialism and Democracy.* New York: Harper & Row.

————. 1990a. "Max Weber's Work." In Joseph A. Schumpeter, *The Economics and Sociology of Capitalism.* Princeton: Princeton University Press, pp. 220–229.

————. 1990b. "Recent Developments of Political Economy." In Joseph A. Schumpeter, *The Economics and Sociology of Capitalism.* Princeton: Princeton University Press, pp. 284–297.

SWEDBERG, RICHARD. 1991. *Schumpeter—A Biography.* Princeton: Princeton University Press.

TRITSCH, WALTHER. 1985. "A Conversation between Joseph Schumpeter and Max Weber." *History of Sociology* 6:167–172.

WEBER, MAX. 1918. "Gutachen." Rep. 92, Nr. 30, Bd. 13 of the Max Weber Collection. Merseburg: Zentrales Staatsarchiv.

————. 1978. *Economy and Society: An Outline of Interpretive Sociology.* Berkeley: University of California Press.

WINSLOW, E. M. 1931. "Marxian, Liberal, and Sociological Theories of Imperialism." *Journal of Political Economy* 39:713–758.

# II

# TRUST, COOPERATION, AND COMPETITION

# 3

# The Social Structure of Competition

## RONALD S. BURT

My starting point is this: a player brings capital to the competitive arena and walks away with profit determined by the rate of return where the capital was invested. The market-production equation predicts profit: invested capital, multiplied by the going rate of return, equals the profit to be expected from the investment. Investments create an ability to produce a competitive product. For example, capital is invested to build and operate a factory. Rate of return is an opportunity to profit from the investment.

Rate of return is keyed to the social structure of the competitive arena and is the focus here. Each player has a network of contacts in the arena. Certain players are connected to certain others, trust certain others, are obligated to support certain others, and are dependent on exchange with certain others. Something about the structure of the player's network and the location of the player's contacts in the social structure of the arena provide a competitive advantage in getting higher rates of return on investment. This chapter is about that advantage. It is a description of the way in which social structure renders competition imperfect by creating entrepreneurial opportunities for certain players and not for others.

## Opportunity and Social Capital

A player brings three kinds of capital to the competitive arena. There are more, but three are sufficient here. First, the player has financial capital—

**65**

cash in hand, reserves in the bank, investments coming due, lines of credit. Second, the player has human capital. Natural abilities—charm, health, intelligence, and looks—combined with skills acquired in formal education and job experience give you abilities to excel at certain tasks. Third, the player's relationships with other players are social capital. You have friends, colleagues, and contacts more generally through whom you receive opportunities to use your financial and human capital. I refer to opportunities broadly, but I certainly mean to include the obvious examples of job promotions, participation in significant projects, influential access to important decisions, and so on. The social capital of people aggregates into the social capital of organizations. In a firm providing services—for example, advertising, brokerage, or consulting—there are people valued for their ability to deliver a quality product. Then there are the "rainmakers," valued for their ability to deliver clients. The former do the work and the latter make it possible for all to profit from the work. The former represent the financial and human capital of the firm; the latter represent its social capital. More generally, property and human assets define the firm's production capabilities. Relations within and beyond the firm are social capital.

### Distinguishing Social Capital

Financial and human capital are distinct in two ways from social capital. First, they are the property of individuals. They are owned in whole or in part by a single individual defined in law as capable of ownership, typically a person or corporation. Second, they concern the investment term in the market production equation. Whether held by an actual person or the fictive person of a firm, financial and human capital gets invested to create production capabilities. Investments in supplies, facilities, and people serve to build and operate a factory. Investments of money, time, and energy produce a skilled manager. Financial capital is needed for raw materials and production facilities. Human capital is needed to craft the raw materials into a competitive product.

Social capital is different on both counts. First, it is a thing owned jointly by the parties to a relationship. No one player has exclusive ownership rights to social capital. If you or your partner in a relationship withdraws, the connection dissolves with whatever social capital it contained. If a firm treats a cluster of customers poorly and they leave, the social capital represented by the firm-cluster relationship is lost. Second, social capital concerns rate of return in the market production equation. Through relations with colleagues, friends, and clients come the opportunities to transform financial and human capital into profit.

Social capital is the final arbiter of competitive success. The capital invested to bring your organization to the point of producing a superb product is as rewarding as the opportunities to sell the product at a profit. The investment to make you a skilled manager is as valuable as the opportunities and the leadership positions to which you get to apply your managerial skills. The investment to make you a skilled scientist with state-of-the-art research facilities is as valuable as the opportunities and the projects to which you get to apply those skills and facilities.

More accurately, social capital is as important as competition is imperfect and investment capital is abundant. Under perfect competition, social capital is a constant in the production equation. There is a single rate of return because capital moves freely from low-yield to high-yield investments until rates of return are homogeneous across alternative investments. Where competition is imperfect, capital is less mobile and plays a more complex role in the production equation. There are financial, social, and legal impediments to moving cash between investments. There are impediments to reallocating human capital, both in terms of changing the people to whom you have a commitment and in terms of replacing those people with new. Rate of return depends on the relations in which capital is invested. Social capital is a critical variable. This is all the more true where financial and human capital are abundant—which in essence reduces the investment term in the production equation to an unproblematic constant.

These conditions are generic to the competitive arena, making social capital a factor as routinely critical as financial and human capital. Competition is never perfect. The rules of trade are ambiguous in the aggregate and everywhere negotiable in the particular. The allocation of opportunities is rarely made with respect to a single dimension of abilities needed for a task. Within an acceptable range of needed abilities, there are many people with financial and human capital comparable to your own. Whatever you bring to a production task, there are other people who could do the same job; perhaps not as well in every detail, but probably as well within the tolerances of the people for whom the job is done. Criteria other than financial and human capital are used to narrow the pool down to the individual who gets the opportunity. Those other criteria are social capital. New life is given to the proverb of success being determined less by what you know than by who you know. As a senior colleague once remarked, "Publishing high-quality work is important for getting university resources, but friends are essential." Only a select few of equally qualified people get the most rewarding opportunities. Only some of comparably high-quality products come to dominate their markets. So, the question is how.

## The Who and the How

The competitive arena has a social structure; players trust certain others, are obligated to support certain others, are dependent on exchange with certain others, and so on. Against this backdrop, each player has a network of contacts: everyone you now know, everyone you have ever known, and everyone who knows you even though you don't know them. Something about the structure of the player's network and the location of the player's contacts in the social structure of the arena form a competitive advantage in getting higher rates of return on investment.

There are two routes into the social capital question. The first describes a network as your access to people with specific resources, creating a correlation between theirs and yours; the second describes social structure as capital in its own right. The idea for the first approach has circulated as power, prestige, social resources, and more recently, social capital. Nan Lin and his colleagues provide an exemplar for this line of work, showing how the occupational prestige of a person's job is contingent on the occupational prestige of a personal contact leading to the job (Lin 1982; Lin, Ensel, and Vaughn 1981; Lin and Dumin 1986). Related empirical results appear in Campbell, Marsden, and Hurlbert (1986); De Graaf and Flap (1988); Flap and De Graaf (1989); and Marsden and Hurlbert (1988). Coleman (1988) discusses the transmission of human capital across generations. Flap and Tazelaar (1989) provide a thorough review with special attention to social network analysis.

Empirical questions in this line of approach concern the magnitude of association between contact resources and your own resources, and variation in the association across kinds of relationships. Granovetter's (1973) weak-tie metaphor, discussed in detail shortly, is often invoked to distinguish kinds of relationships.

Network analysts will recognize this as an example of social contagion analysis. Network structure does not predict attitudes or behaviors directly. It predicts similarity between attitudes and behaviors. The research tradition is tied to the Columbia Sociology survey studies of social influence conducted during the 1940s and 1950s. In one of the first well-known studies, for example, Lazarsfeld, Berelson, and Gaudet (1944) show how a person's vote is associated with the party affiliations of friends. Persons claiming to have voted for the presidential candidate of a specific political party tend to have friends affiliated with that party. Social capital theory developed from this approach describes the manner in which resources available to any one person in a population are contingent on the resources available to individuals socially proximate to that person.

Empirical evidence is readily available. People develop relations with people like themselves (see, for example, Fischer 1982; Marsden 1987; Burt 1990). Wealthy people develop ties with other wealthy people. Educated people develop ties with one another. Young people develop ties with one another. There are reasons for this. Socially similar people, even in the pursuit of independent interests, spend time in the same places. Relationships emerge. Socially similar people have more shared interests. Relationships are maintained. Further, we are sufficiently egocentric to find people with similar tastes attractive. Whatever the etiology for strong relations between socially similar people, it is to be expected that the resources and opinions of any one individual will be correlated with the resources and opinions of their close contacts.

A second line of approach describes social structure as capital in its own right. Where the first line describes the network as a conduit, the second line describes how networks are themselves a form of social capital. This approach is much less developed than the first. Indeed, it is little developed beyond intuitions in empirical research on social capital. Network range, indicated by size, is the primary measure. For example, Boxman, De Graaf, and Flap (1991) show that people with larger contact networks obtain higher paying positions than people with small networks. A similar finding in social support research shows that persons with larger networks tend to live longer (Berkman and Syme 1979).

Both lines of approach are essential to a general definition of social capital. Social capital is at once the structure of contacts in a network and resources they each hold. The first term describes *how* you reach. The second describes *who* you reach.

For two reasons, however, I ignore the question of "who" to concentrate on "how." The first is generality. The question of "who" elicits a more idiographic class of answers. Predicting rate of return depends on knowing the resources of a player's contacts. There will be interesting empirical variation from one kind of activity to another, say job searches versus mobilizing support for a charity, but the empirical generalization is obvious: doing business with wealthy clients, however wealth is defined, has a higher margin than doing business with poor clients. I want to identify parameters of social capital that generalize beyond the specific individuals connected by a relationship.

The second reason is correlation. The two components in social capital should be so strongly correlated that I could reconstruct much of the phenomenon from whichever component more easily yields a general explanation. To the extent that people play an active role in shaping their relationships, a player who knows how to structure a network to provide high opportunity knows who to include in the network. Even if networks are passively inherited, the manner in which a player is connected within social structure says much about contact resources. I will show that *players with well-structured networks obtain higher rates of return*. Resources accumulate in their hands. People develop relations with people like themselves. Therefore, how a player is connected in social structure indicates the volume of resources held by the player and the volume to which the player is connected.

The nub of the matter is to describe network benefits in competition so as to be able to describe how certain structures enhance those benefits. The benefits are of two kinds, information and control. I describe information benefits first because they are more familiar; then control benefits, showing how both kinds of benefits are enhanced by the same element of social structure.

# Information

Opportunities spring up everywhere: new institutions and projects that need leadership, new funding initiatives looking for proposals, new jobs for which you know of a good candidate, valuable items entering the market for which you know interested buyers. The information benefits of a network define who knows about these opportunities, when they know, and who gets to participate in them. Players with a network optimally structured to provide these benefits enjoy higher rates of return to their investments because such players know about, and have a hand in, more rewarding opportunities.

### Access, Timing, and Referrals

Information benefits occur in three forms: access, timing, and referrals. Access refers to receiving a valuable piece of information and knowing who can use it. Information does not spread evenly through the competitive arena. It is not that players are secretive, although that too can be an issue. The issue is that players are unevenly connected with one another, are attentive to the information pertinent to themselves and their friends, and are all overwhelmed by the flow of information. There are limits to the volume of information you can use intelligently. You can only keep up with so many books, articles, memos, and news services. Given a limit to the volume of information that anyone can process, the network becomes an important screening device. It is an army of people processing information who can call your attention to key bits—keeping you up to date on developing opportunities, warning you of impending disasters. This secondhand information is often fuzzy or inaccurate, but it serves to signal something to be looked into more carefully.

Related to knowing about an opportunity is knowing who to bring into it. Given a limit to the financing and skills that we possess individually, most complex projects will require coordination with other people as staff, colleagues, or clients. The manager asks, "Who do I know with the skills to do a good job with that part of the project?" The capitalist asks, "Who do I know who would be interested in acquiring this product or a piece of the project?" The department head asks, "Who are the key players needed to strengthen the department's position?" Add to each of these the more common question, "Who do I know who is most likely to know the kind of person I need?"

Timing is a significant feature of the information received by a network. Beyond making sure that you are informed, personal contacts can make you one of the people informed early. It is one thing to find out that the stock market is crashing today. It is another to discover that the price of your stocks will plummet tomorrow. It is one thing to learn the names of the two people referred to the board for the new vice-presidency. It is another to discover that the job will be created and your credentials could make you a serious candidate for the position. Personal contacts get significant information to you before the average person receives it. That early warning is an opportunity to act on the information yourself or invest it back into the network by passing it on to a friend who could benefit from it.

These benefits involve information flowing from contacts. There are also benefits in the opposite flow. The network that filters information coming to you also directs, concentrates, and legitimates information about you going to others.

In part, this does no more than alleviate a logistics problem. You can only be in a limited number of places within a limited amount of time. Personal contacts get your name mentioned at the right time in the right place so that opportunities are presented to you. Their referrals are a positive force for future opportunities. They are the motor expanding the third category of people in your network, the players you do not know who are aware of you. I am thinking of that remark so often heard in recruitment deliberations: "I don't know her personally, but several people whose opinion I trust have spoken well of her."

Beyond logistics, there is an issue of legitimacy. Even if you know about an opportunity and could present a solid case for why you should get it, you are a suspect source of information. The same information has more legitimacy when it comes from someone inside the decision-making process who can speak to your virtues. Speaking about my own line of work, which I expect in this regard is typical, candidates offered the university positions with the greatest opportunity are people who have a strong personal advocate in the decision-making process, a person in touch with the candidate to ensure that all favorable information, and responses to any negative information, get distributed during the decision.

### Benefit-Rich Networks

A player with a network rich in information benefits has: 1) contacts established in the places where useful bits of information are likely to air, and 2) a reliable flow of information to and from those places.

The second criterion is as ambiguous as it is critical. It is a matter of trust, of confidence in the information passed and in the care with which contacts look out for your interests. Trust is critical precisely because competition is imperfect. The question is not whether to trust, but who to trust. In a perfectly competitive arena, you can trust the system to provide a fair return on your investments. In the imperfectly competitive arena, you have only your personal contacts. The matter comes down to a question of interpersonal debt. If I do for her, will she for me? There is no general answer. The answer lies in the match between specific people. If a contact feels that he is somehow better than you—a sexist male dealing with a woman, a racist white dealing with a black, an old-money matron dealing with an upwardly mobile ethnic—your investment in the relationship will be taken as your proper obeisance to a superior. No debt is incurred. We use whatever cues can be found for a continuing evaluation of the trust in a relation, but really don't know it until the trusted person helps when you need it. With this kind of uncertainty, players are cautious about extending themselves for people whose reputation for honoring interpersonal debt is unknown. The importance of this point is illustrated by the political boundary that exists around senior management for outsider managers trying to break through the boundary (Burt 1992: Ch. 4).

We know from social science research that strong relations and mutual relations tend to develop between people with similar social attributes such as education, income, occupation, and age (e.g. Fischer 1982; Burt 1986, 1990; and Marsden 1987).

This point is significant because it contradicts the natural growth of contact networks. Left to the natural course of events, a network will accumulate redundant contacts. Friends introduce you to their friends and expect you to like them. Business contacts introduce you to their colleagues. You will like the people you meet in this way. The factors that make your friends attractive make their friends attractive because like seeks out like. Your network grows to include more and more people.

These relations come easily, they are comfortable, and they are easy to maintain. But these easily accumulated contacts do not expand the network so much as they fatten it, weakening its efficiency and effectiveness by increasing contact redundancy and tying up time. The process is amplified by spending time in a single place; in your family, or neighborhood, or in the office. The more time you spend with any specific primary contact, the more likely you will be introduced to their friends. Evidence of these processes can be found in studies of balance and transitivity in social relations (see Burt 1982:55–60, for review), and in studies of the tendency for redundant relations to develop among physically proximate people (e.g., the suggestively detailed work of Festinger, Schachter, and Back 1950; or the work with more definitive data by Fischer 1982, on social contexts; and Feld 1981, 1982, on social foci).

Whether egocentrism, cues from presumed shared background and interests, or confidence in mutual acquaintances to enforce interpersonal debt, the operational guide to the formation of close, trusting relationships seems to be that a person more like me is less likely to betray me. For the purposes here, I put the whole issue to one side as person-specific and presumed resolved by the able player.

That leaves the first criterion, establishing contacts where useful bits of information are likely to air. Everything else constant, a large, diverse network is the best guarantee of having a contact present where useful information is aired.

Size is the more familiar criterion. Bigger is better. Acting on this understanding, a person can expand their network by adding more and more contacts. They make more cold calls, affiliate with more clubs, attend more social functions. Numerous books and self-help groups can assist you in "networking" your way to success by putting you in contact with a large number of potentially useful, or helpful, or like-minded people. The process is illustrated by the networks at the top of Figure 3.1. The four-contact network at the left expands to sixteen contacts at the right. Relations are developed with a friend of each contact in network A, doubling the contacts to eight in network B. Snowballing through friends of friends, there are sixteen contacts in network C, and so on.

Size is a mixed blessing. More contacts can mean more exposure to valuable information, more likely early exposure, and more referrals. But increasing network size without considering diversity can cripple the network in significant ways. What matters is the number of nonredundant contacts. Contacts are redundant to the extent that they lead to the same people, and so provide the same information benefits.

Consider two four-contact networks, one sparse the other dense. There are no relations between the contacts in the sparse network, and strong

**Figure 3.1   Network Expansion**

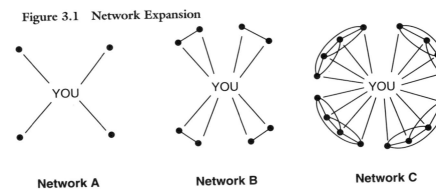

| Network A | Network B | Network C |

relations between every contact in the dense network. Both networks cost whatever time and energy is required to maintain four relationships. The sparse network provides four nonredundant contacts, one for each relationship. No one of the contacts gets you to the same people reached by the other contacts. In the dense network, each relationship puts you in contact with the same people you reach through the other relationships. The dense network contains only one nonredundant contact. Any three are redundant with the fourth.

The sparse network provides more information benefits. It reaches information in four separate areas of social activity. The dense network is a virtually worthless monitoring device because the strong relations between people in the network means that each person knows what the other people know, so they will discover the same opportunities at the same time.

The issue is opportunity costs. At minimum, the dense network is inefficient in the sense that it returns less diverse information for the same cost as the sparse network. A solution is to put more time and energy into adding nonredundant contacts to the dense network. But time and energy are limited, which means that inefficiency translates into opportunity costs. Taking four relationships has an illustrative limit on the number of strong relations that a player can maintain, the player in the dense network is cut off from three-fourths of the information provided by the sparse network.

## Structural Holes

It is convenient to have a term for the separation between nonredundant contacts. I use the term *structural hole*. Nonredundant contacts are connected by a structural hole—a structural hole is a relationship of nonre-

**Figure 3.2    Structural Indicators of Redundancy**

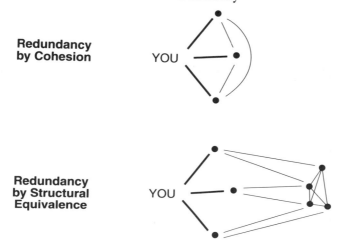

dundancy between two contacts. The hole is a buffer, like an insulator in an electric circuit. As a result of the hole between them, the two contacts provide network benefits that are in some degree additive rather than overlapping.

### Empirical Indicators

Nonredundant contacts are disconnected in some way—either directly in the sense that there is no direct contact between them or indirectly in the sense that one has contacts that exclude the others. The respective empirical conditions that indicate a structural hole are *cohesion* and *structural equivalence*. Both conditions define holes by indicating where they are absent.

Under the cohesion criterion, two contacts are redundant to the extent that they are connected to each other by a strong relationship. A strong relationship indicates the absence of a structural hole. Examples would be father and son, brother and sister, husband and wife, close friends, people who have been partners for a long time, people who frequently get together for social occasions, and so on. You have easy access to both people if either is a contact. Redundancy by cohesion is illustrated at the top of Figure 3.2. The three contacts are connected to one another, and so provide the same network benefits. The presumption here—routine in network analysis since Festinger, Schachter, and Back's (1950) analysis of information flowing through personal relations and

Homans' (1950) theory of social groups—is that the likelihood of information moving from one person to another is proportional to the strength of their relationship. Empirically, strength has two independent dimensions: frequent contact and emotional closeness (see Marsden and Hurlbert 1988; Burt 1990).

Structural equivalence is a useful second indicator for detecting structural holes. Two people are structurally equivalent to the extent that they have the same contacts. Regardless of the relation between structurally equivalent people, they lead to the same sources of information and so are redundant. Where cohesion concerns direct connection, structural equivalence concerns indirect connection by mutual contact. Redundancy by structural equivalence is illustrated at the bottom of Figure 3.2. The three contacts have no direct ties with one another—they are nonredundant by cohesion. But each leads you to the same cluster of more distant players. The information that comes to them, and the people to whom they send information, are redundant. Both networks in Figure 3.2 provide one nonredundant contact at a cost of maintaining three.

The indicators are neither absolute nor independent. Relations deemed strong are only strong relative to others. They are our strongest relations. Structural equivalence rarely reaches the extreme of complete equivalence. People are more or less structurally equivalent. Also, the criteria are correlated. People who spend a lot of time with the same other people often get to know one another. The mutual contacts responsible for structural equivalence set the stage for the direct connection of cohesion. The empirical conditions between two players will be a messy combination of cohesion and structural equivalence, present to varying degrees, at varying levels of correlation.

Cohesion is the more certain indicator. If two people are connected with the same people in a player's network (making them redundant by structural equivalence), they can still be connected with different people beyond the network (making them nonredundant). But if they meet frequently and feel close to one another, then they are likely to communicate and probably have contacts in common. More generally, and especially for fieldwork informed by attention to network benefits, the general guide is the definition of a structural hole. There is a structural hole between two people who provide nonredundant network benefits. Taking the cohesion and structural equivalence conditions together, redundancy is most likely between structurally equivalent people connected by a strong relationship. Redundancy is unlikely, indicating a structural hole, between total strangers in distant groups. I return to this issue again, to discuss the depth of a hole, after control benefits have been introduced.

## The Efficient-Effective Network

Balancing network size and diversity is a question of optimizing structural holes. The number of structural holes can be expected to increase with network size, but the holes are the key to information benefits. The optimized network has two design principles: efficiency and effectiveness.

EFFICIENCY. The first principle concerns efficiency, and it says that you should maximize the number of nonredundant contacts in the network to maximize the yield in structural holes per contact. Given two networks of equal size, the one with more nonredundant contacts provides more benefits. There is little gain from a new contact redundant with existing contacts. Time and energy would be better spent cultivating a new contact among previously unreached people.[1] Maximizing the nonredundancy of contacts maximizes the structural holes obtained per contact.[2]

Efficiency is illustrated by the networks in Figure 3.3. These reach the same people reached by the networks in Figure 3.1, but in a different way. What expands in Figure 3.1 is not the benefits, but the cost of maintaining the network. Network A provides four nonredundant contacts. Network B provides the same number. The information benefits provided by the initial four contacts are redundant with benefits provided by their close friends. All that has changed is the doubled number of relationships maintained in the network. The situation deteriorates even further with the sixteen contacts in network C. There are still only four nonredundant contacts in the network, but their benefits are now obtained at a cost of maintaining sixteen relationships.

With a little network surgery, the sixteen contacts can be maintained at a fourth of the cost. As illustrated in Figure 3.3, select one contact in each cluster to be a primary link to the cluster. Concentrate on maintaining the primary contact, and allow direct relationships with others in the

[1] For the purposes here, I ignore the many day-to-day tactical issues critical to maintaining a network. Thorough treatment requires considerable discussion and didactic devices. This is the function of the seminars offered by the Denver firm, Strategic Connections. I discuss tactical issues in a short book, *The Network Entrepreneur,* written in 1987 for distribution from the firm.

[2] The number of structural holes is not increased directly, but is likely to increase. The presumption through all this is that the time and energy to maintain relationships is limited and the constant pressure to include new contacts will use all time and energy available (as in the preceding footnote). Although structural holes are not increased directly by maximizing nonredundant contacts, they can be expected to increase indirectly from the reallocation of time and energy from maintaining redundant contacts to acquiring new nonredundant contacts (as illustrated in Figure 3.4).

**Figure 3.3   Strategic Network Expansion**

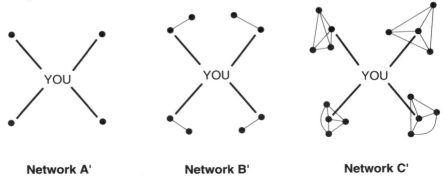

| Network A' | Network B' | Network C' |

cluster to weaken into indirect relations through the primary contact. Those players reached indirectly are secondary contacts. Among the redundant contacts in a cluster, the primary contact should be the one most easily maintained and most likely to honor an interpersonal debt to you in particular. The secondary contacts are less easily maintained or less likely to work well for you (even if they might work well for someone else). The critical decision obviously lies in selecting the right person to be a primary contact. That is the subject of trust discussed above. With a good primary contact, there is little loss in information benefits from the cluster and a gain in the reduced effort needed to maintain the cluster in the network.

Repeating this operation for each cluster in the network recovers effort that would otherwise be spent maintaining redundant contacts. By reinvesting that saved time and effort in developing primary contacts to new clusters, the network expands to include an exponentially larger number of contacts while expanding contact diversity. The sixteen contacts in network C of Figure 3.1, for example, are maintained at a cost of four primary contacts in network C' of Figure 3.3. Some portion of the time spent maintaining the redundant other twelve contacts can be reallocated to expanding the network to include new clusters.

EFFECTIVENESS.   The second principle for the optimized network requires a further shift in perspective. Distinguish primary from secondary contacts and focus resources on preserving the primary contacts. Here contacts are not people on the other end of your relations; they are ports of access to clusters of people beyond. Guided by the first principle, these ports should be nonredundant so as to reach separate, and therefore more diverse, social worlds of network benefits. Instead of maintaining relations with all contacts, the task of maintaining the total network is delegated to primary contacts. The player at the center of the network is then free to focus on properly supporting relations with primary contacts, and expanding the network to include new clusters. Where the first principle concerns the average number of people reached with a primary contact, the second concerns the total number of people reached with all primary contacts. The first principle concerns the yield per primary contact. The second concerns the total yield of the network. More concretely, the first principle moves from the networks in Figure 3.1 to the corresponding networks in Figure 3.3. The second principle moves from left to right in Figure 3.3. The target is network C' in Figure 3.3; a network of few primary contacts, each a port of access to a cluster of many secondary contacts.

Figure 3.4 illustrates some complexities inherent in unpacking a network to maximize structural holes. The BEFORE network contains five primary contacts and reaches a total of fifteen people. However, there are only two clusters of nonredundant contacts in the network. Contacts 2 and 3 are redundant in the sense of being connected with each other and reaching the same people (cohesion and structural equivalence criteria). The same is true of contacts 4 and 5. Contact 1 is not connected directly to contact 2 but he reaches the same secondary contacts, so contacts 1 and 2 provide redundant network benefits (structural equivalence criterion). Illustrating the other extreme, contacts 3 and 5 are connected directly, but they are nonredundant because they reach separate clusters of secondary contacts (structural equivalence criterion). In the AFTER network, contact 2 is used to reach the first cluster in the BEFORE network, and contact 4 is used to reach the second cluster. The time and energy saved by withdrawing from relations with the other three primary contacts is reallocated to primary contacts in new clusters. The BEFORE and AFTER networks are both maintained at a cost of five primary relationships, but the AFTER network is dramatically richer in structural holes, and so the network benefits.

Network benefits are enhanced in several ways. There is a higher volume of benefits because more contacts are included in the network. Beyond volume, diversity enhances the quality of benefits. Nonredundant contacts ensure exposure to diverse sources of information. Each cluster of contacts is an independent source of information. One cluster, no matter how numerous its members, is one source of information because people connected to one another tend to know about the same things at about the same time. The information screen provided by multiple clusters of contacts is broader, providing better assurance of the player being informed of opportunities and impending disasters. Further, since non-

**Figure 3.4   Optimizing for Structural Holes**

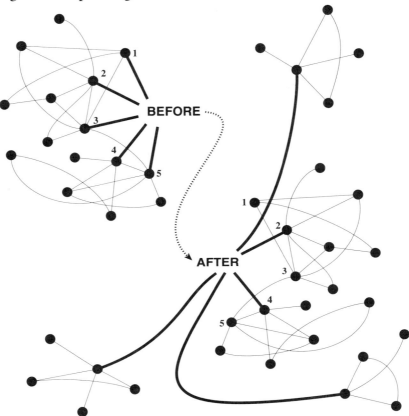

redundant contacts are only linked through the central player, you are assured of being the first to see new opportunities created by needs in one group that could be served by skills in another group. You become the person who first brings people together, giving you the opportunity to coordinate their activities. These benefits are compounded by the fact that having a network that yields such benefits makes you even more attractive as a network contact to other people, easing the task of expanding the network to serve your interests best.

GROWTH PATTERNS.   A general sense of efficiency and effectiveness is illustrated with network growth. In Figure 3.5, the number of contacts in a player's network increases from left to right on the horizontal axis. The number who are nonredundant increases up the vertical axis. Ob-

**Figure 3.5 Efficiency and Effectiveness**

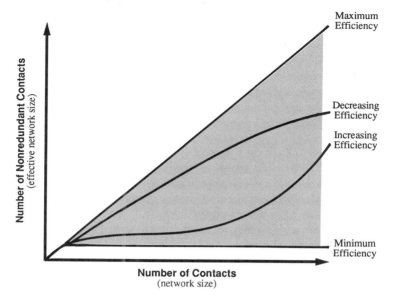

served network size is indicated on the horizontal axis; effective size on the vertical axis. Networks can be anywhere in the gray area. The maximum efficiency line describes networks in which each new contact is completely nonredundant with other contacts, where effective size equals actual size. Efficient-effective networks are in the upper-right of the graph. The minimum efficiency line describes networks in which each new contact is completely redundant with other contacts; effective size equals one regardless of multiple contacts in the network.

The two lines between the extremes illustrate more probable growth patterns. The decreasing efficiency line shows players building good information benefits into their initial network, then relaxing to allow increasing redundancy as the network gets large. Friends of friends begin to be included. Comparisons across networks of different sizes suggest that this is the growth pattern among senior managers (Burt 1992: Ch. 4).

The increasing efficiency line illustrates a different growth pattern. Initial contacts are redundant with one another. A foundation is established with multiple contacts in the same cluster. After the foundation is established, the player's network expands to include contacts in other clusters and effective size begins to increase. There are two kinds of clusters in which optimizing for saturation is wiser than optimizing for efficiency.

The first is obvious. Leisure and domestic clusters are a congenial environment of low maintenance, redundant contacts. Efficiency mixes poorly with friendship. Judging friends for efficiency is an interpersonal flatulence from which friends will flee. The second exception is a cluster of contacts where resources are dense. For the CEO, the board of directors would be such a cluster. The university provost is similarly tied to the board of trustees. For the more typical manager, the immediate work group is such a cluster, especially with respect to funding authority within the group. These clusters are so important to the vitality of the rest of the network that it is worth treating each person in them as a primary contact regardless of redundancy. Saturation minimizes the risk of losing effective contact with the cluster and also minimizes the risk of missing an important opportunity anywhere in the cluster.

The more general point is that the probability of receiving network benefits from a cluster has two components: the probability that a contact will transmit information to you, and the probability that it will be transmitted to the contact. I count on dense ties within a cluster to set the second probability to one. The probability of having a benefit transmitted to you, therefore, depends only on the strength of your relationship with a contact in the cluster. However, where the density of ties in an opportunity-rich cluster lowers the probability of your contact knowing about an opportunity, there is value in increasing the number, and so redundancy, of contacts in the cluster so that total coverage of the cluster compensates for imperfect transmission within it.

### Structural Holes and Weak Ties

In 1973, Mark Granovetter published his now-famous article "The Strength of Weak Ties." The weak-tie argument is elegantly simple. The stage is set with results familiar from the social psychology of Festinger and Homans circa 1950, the results discussed above with respect to cohesion indicators of structural holes. People live in a cluster of others with whom they have strong relations. Information circulates at a high velocity within these clusters. Each person tends to know what the other people know. Therefore, and this is the insight of the argument, the spread of information on new ideas and opportunities must come through the weak ties that connect people in separate clusters. The weak ties so often ignored by social scientists are in fact a critical element of social structure. Hence the strength of weak ties. Weak ties are essential to the flow of information that integrates otherwise disconnected social clusters into a broader society.

The idea and its connection with structural holes is illustrated in Fig-

**Figure 3.6  Structural Holes and Weak Ties**

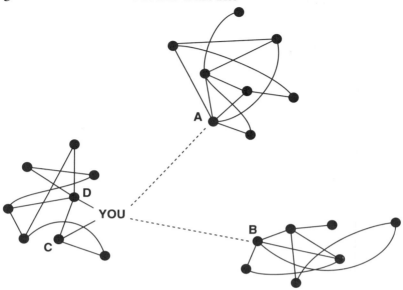

ure 3.6. There are three clusters of players. Strong ties, indicated by solid lines, connect players within clusters. Dashed lines indicate two weak ties between players in separate clusters. One of the players, you, has a unique pattern of four ties: two strong ties within your cluster and a weak tie to a contact in each of the other clusters. There are three classes of structural holes in your network: 1) holes between the cluster around contact A and everyone in your own cluster, for example, the hole between contacts A and C; 2) holes between the cluster around contact B and everyone in your own cluster, for example, the hole between contacts B and C; and 3) the hole between contacts A and B.

Weak ties and structural holes seem to describe the same phenomenon. In Figure 3.6, for example, they predict the same ranking of information benefits. You are best positioned for information benefits, contacts A and B are next, followed by everyone else. You have two weak ties, contacts A and B have one each, and everyone else has none. You have the largest volume of structural holes between your contacts, contacts A and B have fewer, and everyone else has few or none.

The weak-tie argument is simpler than my argument and is already well known. Why complicate the situation with the structural-hole argument?

There are two reasons. First, the causal agent in the phenomenon is not the weakness of a tie but the structural hole it spans. Tie weakness is a correlate, not a cause. The structural hole argument captures the causal agent directly, providing a stronger foundation for theory and a clearer guide for empirical research. Second, by shifting attention away from the structural hole responsible for information benefits to the strength of the tie providing them, the weak-tie argument obscures the control benefits of structural holes. Control benefits augment, and in some ways are more important than, the information benefits of structural holes. Building both benefits into the argument more clearly speaks to the generality of the phenomenon under study. I will elaborate the first point, then move to the second in the next section.

The weak-tie argument is about the strength of relationships at the same time that it is about their location. The two dashed lines in Figure 3.6 are bridges. They are the only connection between two otherwise separate clusters of strongly interconnected players (compare Granovetter 1973:1365 on weak ties as bridges). A bridge is at once two things: it is a chasm spanned and the span itself. By title and subsequent application, the weak-tie argument is about the strength of relationships that span the chasm between two social clusters. The structural-hole argument is about the chasm spanned. It is the latter that generates information benefits. Whether a relationship is strong or weak, it generates information benefits when it is a bridge over a structural hole.

Consider a cross-tabulation of ties by their strength and location. Relationships can be sorted into two categories of strength. Strong ties are the most frequent and close contacts. Weak ties are the less frequent, less close contacts. Between these two categories, there are a few strong ties and many weak ties.

Now sort by location, separating the redundant ties within your social cluster from the nonredundant ties to people in other clusters. The nonredundant ties are your bridges to other clusters. From what we know about the natural etiology of relationships, bridges are less likely to develop than ties within clusters. The category of redundant ties includes your strong ties to often-met, close friends and colleagues, but it also includes their friends, and friends of friends, whom you meet only occasionally if at all. As you expand your inventory from your closest, most frequent contacts to your more distant, contacts tend to be people like yourself before you reach a sufficiently low level of relationship to include people from completely separate social worlds. This tendency varies from one person to the next, but it is in the aggregate the substance of the well-documented tendency already discussed of relations to develop between socially similar people. In the illustration in Figure 3.6, you are one of nine people in your social cluster. You have strong ties to two people. Through those two, you have weak ties to the other six people

**Table 3.1   The Natural Distribution of Relationships**

| | Location in Social Structure | | |
| --- | --- | --- | --- |
| | Redundant Tie Within Cluster | Nonredundant Tie Beyond Cluster | TOTAL |
| Strength | | | |
| Weak Tie | many | some | MORE |
| Strong Tie | some | rare | LESS |
| TOTAL | MORE | LESS | |

in the cluster. To keep the sociogram simple, I deleted the dashed lines for those ties and their equivalent inside the other clusters. The other six people in your cluster are friends of friends, people you know and sometimes meet but have neither the time nor energy to include among your closest contacts. The cluster is clearly held together by strong ties. Everyone has two to five strong ties to others within the cluster. All nine people are likely to know about the same opportunities, as expected in a cohesive cluster. Of the thirty-six possible connections among the nine people in the cluster, however, only twelve are solid line strong ties. The remaining two-thirds are weak ties between redundant friends of friends.

Now cross-tabulate the two classifications and take expected values. The result is given in Table 3.1. Information benefits vary across the columns of the table, higher through nonredundant ties. This is accurately represented in both the weak-tie and the structural-hole argument. But quick reading of the weak-tie argument, with its emphasis on the strength of a relationship, has led some to test the idea that information benefits covary inversely with the strength of ties. This is a correlation between the rows and columns of Table 3.1, which is no correlation at all. In fact, the typical tie in Table 3.1 is weak and provides redundant information. The correlation in a study population depends on the distribution of ties in the table, but there is no theoretical reason to expect a strong correlation between the strength of a relationship and the information benefits it provides.

The weak-tie argument is about the two cells in the second column of the table. It predicts that nonredundant ties, the bridges that provide information benefits, are more likely weak than strong. In the second column of Table 3.1, weak-tie bridges are more likely than strong-tie bridges. To simplify his argument, Granovetter makes this tendency absolute by ruling out strong-tie bridges (the "rare" cell in Table 3.1, the "forbidden triad" in Granovetter's argument 1973:1363). As Granovetter puts it, "A strong tie can be a bridge, therefore, only if neither party to it has any other strong ties, unlikely in a social network of any size (though possible in a small group). Weak ties suffer no such restriction, though they are certainly not automatically bridges. What is important, rather, is that all bridges are weak ties" (Granovetter 1973:1364).

Bridge strength is an aside in the structural-hole argument. Information benefits are expected to travel over all bridges, strong or weak. Benefits vary between redundant and nonredundant ties, the columns of Table 3.1. Thus, structural holes capture the condition directly responsible for the above-described information benefits. The task for a strategic player building an efficient-effective network is to focus resources on the maintenance of bridge ties. Otherwise, and this is the correlative substance of the weak-tie argument, bridges will fall into their natural state of being weak ties.

## Control and the Tertius Gaudens

I have described how structural holes can determine who knows about opportunities, when they know, and who gets to participate in them. Players with a network optimized for structural holes enjoy higher rates of return on their investments because they know about, and have a hand in, more rewarding opportunities.

They are also more likely to secure favorable terms in the opportunities they choose to pursue. The structural holes that generate information benefits also generate control benefits, giving certain players an advantage in negotiating their relationships. To describe how this is so, I break the negotiation into structural, motivational, and outcome components. The social structure of the competitive arena defines opportunities, a player decides to pursue an opportunity, and is sometimes successful.

### Tertius Gaudens

Beginning with the outcome, sometimes you will emerge successful from negotiation as the *tertius gaudens*. Taken from the work of Georg Simmel, the *tertius* role is useful here because it defines successful negotiation in terms of the social structure of the situation in which negotiation is successful. The role is the heart of Simmel's later (1922) analysis of the freedom an individual derives from conflicting group affiliations (see Coser 1975 for elaboration).[3] The *tertius gaudens* is "the third who benefits"

---

[3] This theme is often grouped with Durkheim's (1893) argument for the liberating effect of a division of labor, but it is useful to distinguish the two arguments for the purposes here. Simmel focuses on the liberating quality of competition between multiple affiliations,

(Simmel 1923:154, 232).[4] The phrase survives in what I am told is a well-known Italian proverb: *Fra i due litiganti, il terzo gode* (Between two fighters, the third benefits), and it has moved north to a more jovial Dutch phrase; *de lachende derde* (the laughing third).[5] *Tertius, terzo,* or *derde*—the phrase describes an individual who profits from the disunion of others.

There are two *tertius* strategies: being the third between two or more players after the same relationship, and being the third between players in two or more relations with conflicting demands. The first, and simpler, strategy is the familiar economic bargaining between buyer and seller. Where two or more players want to buy something, the seller can play their bids against one another to get a higher price. The strategy extends directly to social commodities: a woman with multiple suitors, or a professor with simultaneous offers of positions in rival institutions.

The control benefits of having a choice between players after the same relationship extends directly to choice between the simultaneous demands of players in separate relationships. The strategy can be seen between hierarchical statuses in the enterprising subordinate under the authority of two or more superiors: for example, the student who strikes her own balance between the simultaneous demands of imperious faculty advisors.[6] The bargaining is not limited to situations of explicit competition. In some situations, emerging as the *tertius* depends on creating

which is the concern here. Durkheim focuses on the liberating quality of interdependent affiliations. Integration, rather than competition, is Durkheim's theme. That theme continues in Blau's (1977) analysis of cross-cutting social circles, in which he argues that conflict between strata becomes increasingly difficult as affiliations provide people with alternative stratification hierarchies. Flap (1988) provides a network-oriented review of such work, building from anthropology and political science, to study the "crisscross" effect inhibiting violence.

[4] Georg Simmel introduced this phrase in papers on the importance of group size, translated and published by Albion Small in the *American Journal of Sociology* (Simmel 1896:393–394; 1902:174–189). A later version was translated by Wolff (Simmel 1923:154–169; 232–234).

[5] I am grateful to Anna Di Lellio for calling my attention to the Italian proverb and to Hein Schreuder for calling my attention to the Dutch expression. The idea of exploiting a structural hole is viscerally familiar to all audiences, but interestingly varied across cultures in phrasing the profit obtained (an interesting site for a Zelizer 1989 kind of analysis).

[6] This point is nicely exemplified in Simmel's discussion of subordination comparing the freedom of two medieval subordinate positions, the bondsman ("unfree") and the vassal: "An essential difference between the mediaeval 'unfree' men and the vassals consisted in the fact that the former had and could have only one master, while the latter could accept land from different lords and could take the oath of fealty to each. By reason of the possibility of placing themselves in the feudal relation to several persons the vassals won strong security and independence against the individual lords. The inferiority of the position of vassalage was thereby to a considerable degree equalized" (1896:394).

competition. In proposing the concept of a role-set, for example, Merton (1957:393–394) identifies this as a strategy designed to resolve conflicting role demands. Make simultaneous, contradictory demands explicit to the people posing them, and ask them to resolve their—now explicit—conflict. Even where it does not exist, competition can be produced by defining issues in a way that contact demands become contradictory and must be resolved before you can meet their requests. Failure is possible. You might provide too little incentive for the contacts to resolve their differences. Contacts drawn from different social strata need not perceive one another's demands as carrying equal weight. Or you might provide too much incentive. Now aware of one another, the contacts could discover sufficient reason to cooperate in forcing you to meet their mutually agreed upon demands (Simmel 1902:176, 180–181, calls attention to such failures). But if the strategy is successful, the pressure on you is alleviated and replaced with an element of control over the negotiation. Merton states the situation succinctly: the player at the center of the network ". . . originally at the focus of the conflict, virtually becomes a more or less influential bystander whose function it is to high-light the conflicting demands by members of his role-set and to make it a problem for them, rather than for him, to resolve *their* contradictory demands" (1957:430).

The strategy holds equally well with large groups. Under the rubric "divide and rule," Simmel (1902:185–186) describes institutional mechanisms by which the Incan and Venetian governments obtained advantage by creating conflict between subjects. The same point is illustrated more richly in Barkey's (1990) comparative description of state control in early seventeenth-century France and Turkey. After establishing the similar conditions in the two states at the time, Barkey asks why peasant-noble alliances developed in France against the central state while no analogous or substitutable alliances developed in Turkey. The two empires were comparable in many respects that scholars have cited to account for peasant revolt. They differed in one significant respect correlated with revolt—not in the structure of centralized state control, but in control strategy. In France, the king sent trusted representatives as agents to collect taxes and affect military decisions in provincial populations. The intrusion by these outside agents, *intendants,* affecting fundamental local decisions was resented by the established local nobility. Local nobility formed alliances with the peasantry against the central state. In Turkey, the sultan capitalized on conflict between leaders in the provinces. When a bandit became a serious threat to the recognized governor, a deal was struck with the bandit making him the legitimate governor. As Barkey puts it, "At its most extreme, the state could render a dangerous rebel legitimate overnight. This was accomplished by the striking of a bargain which ensured new sources of revenue for the rebel and momentary relief from internal warfare and perhaps, an army or two for the state" (1990:18). The two empires differed in their use of structural holes. The French king ignored them, assuming he had absolute authority. The Turkish sultan strategically exploited them, promoting competition between alternative leaders. Conflict within the Turkish empire remained in the province, rather than being directed against the central state. As is characteristic of the control obtained via structural holes, the resulting Turkish control was more negotiated than the absolute control exercised in France. It was also more effective.

### The Essential Tension

There is a presumption of tension here. Control emerges from *tertius* brokering tension between other players. No tension, no *tertius*.

It is easy to infer that the tension presumed is one of combatants. There is certainly a *tertius*-rich tension between combatants. Governors and bandits in the Turkish game played for life-or-death stakes. Illustrating this inference, a corporate executive listening to my argument expressed skepticism. Her colleagues, she explained, took pride in working together in a spirit of partnership and goodwill. The *tertius* imagery rang true to her knowledge of many firms, but not her own.

The reasoning is good. But the conclusion is wrong. I referred the skeptical executive to an analysis of hole effects that by coincidence was an analysis of managers at her level, in her firm (Burt 1992:Ch. 4). Promotions are strongly correlated, illuminatingly so for women, with the structural holes in a manager's network.

The tension essential to the *tertius* is merely uncertainty. Separate the uncertainty of control from its consequences. The consequences of the control negotiation can be life or death in the extreme situation of combatants, or merely a question of embarrassment. Everyone knows you made an effort to get that job, but it went to someone else. The *tertius* strategies can be applied to control with severe consequences or to control of little consequence. What is essential is that control is uncertain, that no one can act as if they have absolute authority. Where there is any uncertainty about whose preferences should dominate a relationship, there is an opportunity for the *tertius* to broker the negotiation for control by playing demands against one another. There is no long-term contract that keeps a relationship strong, no legal binding that can secure the trust necessary to a productive relationship. Your network is a pulsing swirl of mixed, conflicting demands. Each contact wants your exclusive attention, your immediate response when a concern arises. Each, to warrant their continued confidence in you, wants to see you measure up to the values against which they judge themselves. Within this preference web, where no demands have absolute authority, the *tertius* negotiates for favorable terms.

### The Connection with Information Benefits

The negotiating of the *tertius* brings me back to information benefits. Structural holes are the setting for *tertius* strategies. Information is the substance. Accurate, ambiguous, or distorted information is moved between contacts by the *tertius*. One bidder is informed of a competitive offer in the first *tertius* strategy. A player in one relationship is informed of demands from other relationships in the second *tertius* strategy.

The two kinds of benefits augment and depend on one another. Application of the *tertius* strategies elicits additional information from contacts interested in resolving the negotiation in favor of their own preferences. The information benefits of access, timing, and referrals enhance the application of strategy. Successful application of the *tertius* strategies involves bringing together players who are willing to negotiate, have sufficiently comparable resources to view one another's preferences as valid, but will not negotiate with one another directly to the exclusion of the *tertius*. Having access to information means being able to identify where there is an advantage to bringing contacts together and is the key to understanding the resources and preferences being played against one another. Having that information early is the difference between being the one who brings together contacts versus being just another person who hears about the negotiation. Referrals further enhance strategy. It is one thing to distribute information between two contacts during negotiation. It is another thing to have people close to each contact endorsing the legitimacy of the information you distribute.

# Entrepreneurs[7]

Behavior of a specific kind converts opportunity into higher rates of return. Information benefits of structural holes might come to a passive player, but control benefits require an active hand in the distribution of information. Motivation is now an issue. The *tertius* plays conflicting

---

[7] In the interests of saving space, a substantial block of material was deleted between here and the next section, on: 1) the literal meaning of entrepreneurs, 2) the importance of structural holes within the clusters of secondary contacts, 3) market boundaries, and 4) a more thorough discussion of holes defined by cohesion versus structural equivalence. If the leap to structural autonomy seems awkward here, consider looking at the full discussion (Burt 1992: Ch. 1).

demands and preferences against one another, building value from their disunion. You enter the structural hole between two players to broker the relationship between them. Such behavior is not to everyone's taste. A player can respond in ways ranging from fully developing the opportunity to ignoring it. When you take the opportunity to be the *tertius,* you are an entrepreneur in the literal sense of the word—a person who generates profit from being between others. Both terms will be useful in these precise meanings: *entrepreneur* refers to a kind of behavior, the *tertius* is a successful entrepreneur.

Motivation is often traced to cultural beliefs and psychological need. For example, in *The Protestant Ethic and the Spirit of Capitalism,* Weber (1905:especially 166 ff) describes the seventeenth-century bourgeois Protestant as an individual seeking—in his religious duty, his Calvinist "calling"—the profit of sober, thrifty, diligent exploitation of opportunities for usury and trade. Psychological need is another motive. McClelland (1961) describes the formation of a need to achieve in childhood as critical to later entrepreneurial behavior (a need that can be cultivated later if desired—McClelland 1975). Schumpeter stresses nonutilitarian motives: "First of all, there is the dream and the will to found a private kingdom, usually, though not necessarily, also a dynasty. . . . Then there is the will to conquer: the impulse to fight, to prove oneself superior to others, to succeed for the sake, not of the fruits of success, but of the success itself. . . . Finally, there is the joy of creating, of getting things done, or simply of exercising one's energy and ingenuity" (Schumpeter 1912:93).[8]

### Opportunity and Motivation

These are powerful frameworks for understanding competition, but I do not wish to detour into the beliefs behind entrepreneurial behavior. I propose to leap over the motivation issue by taking, for three reasons, a player's network as simultaneously an indicator of entrepreneurial opportunity and motivation.

First, there is the clarity of an opportunity. Players can be pulled to entrepreneurial action by the promise of success. I do not mean that players are rational creatures expected to calculate accurately and act in their own interest. Nor do I mean to limit the scope of the argument to

[8]I am grateful to Richard Swedberg for giving me the benefit of his careful study of Schumpeter in calling my attention to these passages. Their broader scope and context are engagingly laid out in his biography of Schumpeter (Swedberg 1991). The passages can also be found in the Schumpeter selection included in Parsons et al.'s *Theories of Society* (1961:513). See also Chapter 2 by Swedberg in this volume.

situations in which players act as if they were rational in that way. I mean simply that between two opportunities, any player is more likely to act on the one with the clearer path to success. The clarity of opportunity is its own motivation. As the number of entrepreneurial opportunities in a network increases, the odds of some being clearly defined by deep structural holes increases, so the odds of entrepreneurial behavior increase. To be sure, a person whose abilities or values proscribe entrepreneurial behavior is unlikely to act, and someone inclined to entrepreneurial behavior is more likely to act, even taking the initiative to create opportunities. Regardless of ability or values, however, within the broad range of acceptable behaviors, a person is unlikely to take entrepreneurial action if the probability of success is low. You might question the propriety of a scholar negotiating between universities offering a position, but the question is not an issue for the player with one offer.

There are also network analogues to the psychological and cultural explanations of motive. Beginning with psychological need, a person with a taste for entrepreneurial behavior is prone to building a network configured around such behavior. If I find a player with a network rich in the structural holes that make entrepreneurial behavior possible, I have a player willing and able to act entrepreneurially. But it is the rare person who is the sole author of his or her network. Networks are more often built in the course of doing something else. Your work, for example, involves meeting people from very different walks of life, so your network ends up composed of contacts who, without you, have no contact with one another. Even so, the network is its own explanation of motive. As the volume of structural holes in a player's network increases—regardless of the process that created them—the entrepreneurial behavior of making and negotiating relations between others becomes a way of life. This is a network analogue to the cultural explanation of motive. If all you know is entrepreneurial relationships, the motivation question is a nonissue. Being willing and able to act entrepreneurially is how you understand social life.

I will treat motivation and opportunity as one and the same. Because of a clear path to success, or the tastes of the player as the network's author, or the nature of the player's environment as author of the network, a network rich in entrepreneurial opportunity surrounds a player motivated to be entrepreneurial. At the other extreme, a player innocent of entrepreneurial motive lives in a network devoid of entrepreneurial opportunity.

**Figure 3.7    Rate of Return and Structural Holes**

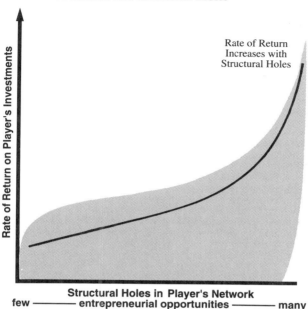

*Measurement Implications*

Entrepreneurial motivation highlights a complexity that might otherwise obscure the association between structural holes and rates of return. Consider the graph in Figure 3.7. Players are defined by their rate of return on investments (vertical axis) and the entrepreneurial opportunities of structural holes in their networks (horizontal axis).

The sloping line in the graph describes the hole effect of players rich in structural holes (horizontal axis) getting higher rates of return on investments (vertical axis). The increasingly positive slope of the line captures the increasing likelihood of *tertius* profit. A player invests in certain relationships. They need not all be high-yield relationships. The higher the proportion of relationships enhanced by structural holes, the more likely the player is an able entrepreneur, and so the more likely that the player's investments are in high-yield relationships. The result is a higher aggregate rate of return on investments.

I have shaded the area in the graph to indicate how I expect data to be distributed around the line of association. There is no imperative that says players have to take advantage of the benefits provided by structural holes. Players rich in entrepreneurial opportunity may choose to develop opportunities (and so appear in the upper-right corner of the graph) or ignore them (and so appear in the lower-right corner of the graph). Some players in Figure 3.7 are above the line. Some are below. If players were perfectly rational, observations would be clustered around the line. Players would take advantage of any entrepreneurial opportunity presented to them. A control for differences in player motivation, such as a Mc-Clelland measure of need for achievement, would have the same effect. The point is not the degree of deviation from the line of association; it is the greater deviation below the line. Variable motivation creates deviations below the true hole effect on rate of return.

This emphasizes the relative importance for empirical research of deviations above and below the line of association. Observations in the lower-right corner of the graph, players under-utilizing their entrepreneurial opportunities, might be due to variation in motivation. Observations in the upper-left corner are a severe test of the argument. Players who have opportunities can choose whether to develop them. Players without opportunities do not have that choice. Within the limits of measurement error, there should be no observations in the upper-left corner of the graph.

## Structural Autonomy

I can now summarize the argument with a concept defining the extent to which a player's network is rich in structural holes, and so entrepreneurial opportunity, and so information and control benefits. That concept is structural autonomy. I present the concept in a general way here (see Burt 1992, Ch. 2, for formal details).

I began with a generic production equation: profit equals an investment multiplied by a rate of return. The benefits of a relationship can be expressed in an analogous form: time and energy invested to reach a contact multiplied by a rate of return. A player's entrepreneurial opportunities are enhanced by a relationship to the extent that: 1) the player has invested substantial time and energy to secure a connection with the contact, and 2) there are many structural holes around the contact ensuring a high rate of return on the investment. More specifically, rate of return concerns how and who you reach with the relationship. Time and energy invested to reach a player with more resources generates more social capital. For the sake of argument, as explained in the discussion of social capital, I assume that a player with a network optimized for structural holes can identify suitably endowed contacts such that I do not have to carry the issue of *who* as another variable in the analysis. My concern is the *how* of a relationship, defined by the structure of a network and its connection with the social structure of the competitive arena. Thus, the rate of return keyed to structural holes is a product of the extent to which there are: 1) many primary structural holes between the contact and others in the player's network, and 2) many secondary structural holes between the contact and others outside the network who could replace the contact.

There is also the issue of structural holes around the player. As the holes around contacts provide information and control benefits to the player, holes around the player can be developed by contacts for their benefit. Developing entrepreneurial opportunities depends on having numerous structural holes around your contacts and none attached to yourself.

These considerations come together in the concept of structural autonomy. Players with relationships free of structural holes at their own end and rich in structural holes at the other end are structurally autonomous. These are the players best positioned for the information and control benefits that a network can provide. These are the players to the far right of the graph in Figure 3.7. Structural autonomy summarizes the action potential of the *tertius*'s network. The budget equation for optimizing structural autonomy has an upper limit set by *tertius*'s time and energy, and a trade-off between the structural holes a new contact provides and the time and energy required to maintain a productive relationship with the contact.[9] The conclusion is that players with networks op-

---

[9]This sentence is the starting point for an optimization model in which the benefits of a contact are weighed against the cost of maintaining a relation with the contact, subject to a time and energy budget constraint on the aggregate of contacts in a network. The work is beyond the scope of this discussion, but I want to remove an ostensible barrier to such work, and in the process highlight a scope limitation to my argument. Marks (1977) provides a cogent argument against the energy scarcity metaphor so often used to justify discussions of role negotiations. Instead of viewing roles as energy debilitating, Marks argues for an "expansion" view in which energy is created by performing roles (compare Sieber 1974). Marks and Sieber discuss the advantages of performing multiple roles. Both are responding to the energy scarcity arguments used to motivate discussions of mechanisms by which people manage role strain (most notably, Merton 1957; Goode 1960). To quote Goode, a person ". . . cannot meet all these demands to the satisfaction of all the persons who are part of his total role network. Role strain—difficulty in meeting given role demands—is therefore normal. In general, the person's total role obligations are overdemanding" ( 1960:485). I have borrowed the theme of overdemanding role obligations. The *tertius* budget constraint concerns both the time and energy cost of maintaining existing relations and the opportunity costs of contacts lost because of redundancy. However, my argument concerns only negotiations within a single role. The mechanisms used to manage role strain, such as segregating role relations in time and space, could also be used by the *tertius* to manage conflict to his or her own advantage. I am, however, ignoring that

timized for structural holes—that is to say, players with networks providing high structural autonomy—enjoy higher rates of return on their investments because they know about, have a hand in, and exercise control over, more rewarding opportunities.

## The Broader Context

The structural-hole argument has four signature qualities:

1. Competition is a matter of relations, not player attributes
2. Competition is a relation emergent, not observed
3. Competition is a process, not just a result
4. Imperfect competition is a matter of freedom, not just power

These qualities are not individually unique to the structural-hole argument—they are jointly characteristic of it.

First, competition is a matter of relationships, not player attributes. The structural-hole argument escapes the debilitating social science practice of using player attributes for explanation. The unit of analysis in which structural holes have their causal effect is the network of relations that intersect in a player. The intersection is known by various names as a role, a market, or a position in social structure. The players in which relations intersect are physical and legal entities: a person, an organization, or a broader aggregation of physical and legal entities. The attributes of the players in whom the relations intersect—black, white, female, male, old, young, rich, poor—are an empirical curiosity irrelevant to the explanation. Competition is not about being a player with certain physical attributes; it is about securing productive relationships. Physical attributes are a correlate, not a cause, of competitive success. Causation resides in the intersection of relations. Holes can have different effects for people with different attributes or for organizations of different kinds, but that is because the attributes and organization forms are correlated with different positions in social structure. The manner in which a structural hole is an entrepreneurial opportunity for information and control benefits is the bedrock explanation that carries across player attributes, populations, and time. The task for the analyst is to cut past the spurious correlation between attributes and outcomes to reach the underlying social structural factors that cause the outcome. This point is developed at length elsewhere (Burt 1992:Ch. 5).

possibility, and so limiting the scope of my argument, to focus on the situation in which *tertius* negotiates conflicting demands that have to be met simultaneously.

Second, competition is a relation emergent, not observed. The structural holes in which competition develops are invisible relations of nonredundancy, relations visible only by their absence. Consider the atavistic driver experiment. You're on the freeway. There is a car ahead of you going 65 mph. Pull up so your front wheels are parallel to his. Stay there. This won't take long. If he speeds up, speed up. If he slows down, slow down. You feel the tension in yourself as you know it's building in the next car. He looks over. Is this a sexual come-on or a threat? Deciding against sex, he may slow down, hoping you'll go away. If that doesn't work, and he doesn't feel that his car can escape yours, his anger will only be apparent on his face. If he is more confident, he'll accelerate to get away from you. Let him.

For the moment when you two stood in common time and place, you were competitors. Break the parallelism, and the competition is gone. There is no behavioral relationship between the drivers that is competition. Competition is an intense, intimate, transitory, invisible relationship created between players by their visible relations with others. It is the cheek by jowl with respect to the passing environment that makes the drivers competitors.

The task of analyzing competition is made more difficult by the fact that the structural holes in which competition thrives do not connect the players we see. They connect invisible pieces of players, the pieces we see in any one of the many roles and markets in which the person or firm is a player. I see one piece of you in the office, another on the street, another at home. Each piece has an attendant network of relations with relevant others. The causal force of structural holes resides in the pattern of relations that intersect in each network. That intersection happens in players, but where it occurs is distinct from the causal force released by its occurrence. This is another view of my first point, that people and organizations are not the source of action so much as they are the vehicles for structurally induced action.

These qualities make it very difficult to capture competition without having the conceptual and research tools to represent the social structure of the competitive arena. Understanding competition will be one of the important returns from the work invested during the 1970s and 1980s in network analysis. The social structure of competition is not about the structure of competitive relations. It is about the social structure of the relations for which players compete. The structural-hole argument is not a theory about competitive relationships. It is a theory about competition for the benefits of relationships. To explain variation in competitive success, I have to look beyond the competitors themselves to the circumstances of the relations for which they compete. The terrain on which competition plays out lies beyond the competitors themselves. It lies in their efforts to negotiate relations with other players. Where those relations are positioned in social structure such that there is little room to negotiate, the margin between success and failure is slim. The social structure of competition is about the negotiability of the relationships on which competitors survive. That is the essence of the structural autonomy concept.

Third, competition is a process, not just a result. With important exceptions, most competition theories are about what is left when competition is over. They are an aside in efforts to answer the practical question of how to maximize producer profit. Answering the question requires a definition of how price varies with output. It is convenient to assume that there is a condition of "competition" such that price is constant with output. The presumed competition exists when: 1) there are an infinite number of buyers and sellers known to one another, 2) goods can be divided for sale to any number of buyers, and 3) buyers and sellers are free to exchange without interference from third parties. When goods are exchanged under these conditions, conditions of "perfect" competition, equilibrium prices can be derived that will clear the market. An architecture of powerful economic theory about price and production follows.[10]

The alternative to this kind of competition is to start with the process of competition and work toward its results. This is a less elegant route for theory, but one that veers closer to the reality of competition as we experience it. The structural-hole argument is not about the flow of goods. No mechanism is proposed to define the prices that "clear" the imperfectly competitive market. Such a mechanism could be proposed, but not here. This chapter is about the competitive process by which the price and occurrence of transactions is decided. If you will, it is about the players who form the deal, not the lawyers who write the contracts. The

---

[10]This paragraph owes much to Stigler's (1957) review of the evolution of competition in economic theory. He provides the simple profit question that calls for an assumption of competition. The three conditions for perfect competition are adapted from Edgeworth (1881:17–19), but I only appreciated their evolutionary significance in the context of alternatives laid out in Stigler's review. Beyond providing context, the clarity of Stigler's presentation, here and with respect to Edgeworth on marginal utility, offers a great improvement over the original. At the same time, as always, the original has value. Edgeworth's characterization of free choice in terms of no intrusive third parties is the key to the social structure of competition. Structural holes are the variable determining the extent to which there are no intrusive third parties to a relationship. Stigler's recoding of that to be the "complete absence of limitations upon individual self-seeking behavior" (1957:247) states the original thought in terms more compatible with subsequent developments in economic theory, but obscures the social structural insight in the original.

social structure of competition is about negotiating the relationships on which competitors survive. Structural holes determine the extent to which, and the manner in which, certain players have a competitive advantage in that negotiation.

Fourth, imperfect competition is a matter of freedom, not just power. The structural-hole argument is a theory of competition made imperfect by the freedom of individuals to be entrepreneurs. In this, the theory cuts across the usual axis of imperfect competition.

In the perfectly competitive arena, any party to a transaction has unlimited choice between alternative partners. Numerous alternatives exist and players are free to choose. The fact of that choice drives price to a minimum. The significance of any one player as an entrepreneur is zero. The structural image is one of relational chaos. Players are free to withdraw from existing relations to join with anyone who better serves their interests. Obligation stops with the execution of the transaction.

Deviations from this image measure imperfect competition, usually defined by the extent to which choice is concentrated in the hands of the strongest player. As Stigler concludes his historical review, "If we were free to redefine competition at this late date, a persuasive case could be made that it should be restricted to meaning the absence of monopoly power in a market" (1957:262). At the extreme of perfect competition, every player has unlimited choice between alternative relationships. At the other extreme, choice is concentrated in the hands of a dominant player. Everyone else is assigned to relations by the dominant player. Familiar images are monopoly, cults, village kinship systems, political machines, fascist bureaucracies. The structural image is one of a completely and rigidly interconnected system of people and establishments within a market. High-obligation relations, with obligation enforced by authority or convention, allow neither negotiation nor the strategic replacement of partners.

Observed behavior lies between these extremes. Control is never absolute; it is negotiated—whether exercised through competitive price, bureaucratic authority, or some other social norm. In the most regulated arena, there are special relationships through which certain players get around the dicta of the governing mechanism. In the most competitive of arenas, there are relations between certain players that provide them special advantages. Competition is omnipresent and everywhere imperfect.

The extremes of perfect and regulated competition are more similar on a critical point than either is to the reality of observed behavior between them. They are both images of dominance. Players are homogeneously trivial under competitive market pricing and, at the other extreme, homogeneously trivial under the dicta of the dominant player. The dominant player defines fair exchange in the regulated market. Buyer and seller are locked into exchange relations by the dicta of the dominant player. The press of numbers defines fair exchange in the perfectly competitive market. Competition between countless buyers and sellers involves negotiation between alternative relations, not within a relationship. Any one partner in a relationship is a faceless cog, readily replaced with someone else. At either extreme, the lack of negotiation within a relationship denies the individuality of buyer and seller.

But their individuality is the key to understanding competition. The substantive richness of competition lies in its imperfections, the jostling of specific players against one another looking for a way to make a difference. In the substantive details of imperfect competition lie the defining parameters of competition. They are the parameters of player individuality. Competition is imperfect to the extent that any player can affect the terms of any particular relationship. Oligopoly, the extent to which multiple players together constitute a monopoly, is insufficient answer. The central question for imperfect competition is how players escape domination, domination by the market or domination by another player.

That is the focus of the structural-hole argument—a theory of freedom instead of power, of negotiated control instead of absolute control. It is a description of the extent to which the social structure of a competitive arena contains entrepreneurial opportunities for individual players to affect the terms of their relationships.

This chapter is about two-thirds of a chapter by the same name in a book, *Structural Holes,* published in 1992 by Harvard University Press. Permission to reproduce the material is gratefully acknowledged. Professor Richard Swedberg skillfully condensed the original material for the purposes of this anthology. This was yet another occasion where Professor Swedberg made me aware of an assumption implicit in my argument. I refer to people and organizations in the competitive arena as players. Professor Swedberg felt I used the term to denote a very active actor, seeking out contacts and opportunities. He gently suggested that the term had a touch of frivolity that I might do well to eliminate with a more neutral term like actor. I have used the more neutral term for more general discussion (Burt 1982), but for the topic of competition, I prefer the term *player*. It better fits my felt reality of the phenomenon. More than implying activity, it is a term of peer recognition: "Yes, he's a player." He's a presence in the game. If you have the motivation, resources, and skills to compete, you're a player; otherwise, you're scenery. Everyone is a player in some arenas, scenery in most. This chapter is about the social structural conditions that give certain players a competitive advantage.

# References

BARKEY, KAREN. 1990. "Rebellious Alliances; The State and Peasant Unrest in Early Seventeenth Century: France and the Ottoman Empire." Paper presented at the 1989 annual meeting of the American Sociological Association.

BERKMAN, LISA F., and S. LEONARD SYME. 1979. "Social Networks, Host Resistance, and Mortality: A Nine-Year Follow-Up Study of Alameda County Residents." *American Journal of Epidemiology* 109:186–204.

BLAU, PETER M. 1977. *Heterogeneity and Inequality*. New York: Free Press.

BOXMAN, ED A. W., PAUL M. DE GRAAF, and HENDRIK D. FLAP. 1991. "The Impact of Social and Human Capital on the Income Attainment of Dutch Managers." *Social Networks* 13:51–73.

BURT, RONALD S. 1982. *Toward a Structural Theory of Action*. New York: Academic Press.

———. 1986. "A Note on Sociometric Order in the General Social Survey Network Data." *Social Networks* 8:149–174.

———. 1990. "Kinds of Relations in American Discussion Networks." In C. Calhoun, M. W. Meyer, and W. Scott eds., *Structures of Power and Constraint*. New York: Cambridge University Press, pp. 411–451.

———. 1992. *Structural Holes*. Cambridge, MA: Harvard University Press.

CAMPBELL, KAREN E., PETER V. MARSDEN, and JEANNE S. HURLBERT. 1986. "Social Resources and Socioeconomic Status." *Social Networks* 8:97–117.

COLEMAN, JAMES S. 1988. "Social Capital in the Creation of Human Capital." *American Journal of Sociology* 94:S95–120.

COSER, ROSE LAUB. 1975. "The Complexity of Roles as a Seedbed of Individual Autonomy." In L. A. Coser ed., *The Idea of Social Structure*. New York: Harcourt, Brace, Jovanovich, pp. 237–263.

DE GRAAF, NAN D., and HENDRIK D. FLAP. 1988. "With a Little Help from My Friends." *Social Forces* 67:453–472.

DURKHEIM, ÉMILE (1893) 1933. *The Division of Labor in Society*. Translated by G. Simpson. New York: Free Press.

EDGEWORTH, F. Y. 1881. *Mathematical Psychics*. London: C. Kegan Paul.

FELD, SCOTT. L. 1981. "The Focused Organization of Social Ties." *American Journal of Sociology* 86:1015–1035.

———. 1982. "Social Structural Determinants of Similarity." *American Sociological Review* 47:797–801.

FESTINGER, LEON, STANLEY SCHACHTER, and KURT W. BACK. 1950. *Social Pressures in Informal Groups*. Stanford: Stanford University Press.

FISCHER, CLAUDE S. 1982. *To Dwell Among Friends*. Chicago: University of Chicago Press.

FLAP, HENDRIK D. 1988. *Conflict, Loyalty, and Violence*. New York: Verlag Peter Lang.

FLAP, HENDRIK D., and NAN D. DE GRAAF. 1989. "Social Capital and Attained Occupational Status." *Netherlands' Journal of Sociology* 22:145–161.

FLAP, HENDRIK D., and F. TAZELAAR. 1989. "The Role of Informal Social Networks on the Labor Market: Flexibilization and Closure." In H. Flap ed., *Flexibilization of the Labor Market*. Utrecht, Holland: ISOR, University of Utrecht, pp. 99–118.

GOODE, WILLIAM J. 1960. "A Theory of Role Strain." *American Sociological Review* 25:483–496.

GRANOVETTER, MARK S. 1973. "The Strength of Weak Ties." *American Journal of Sociology* 78:1360–1380.

HOMANS, GEORGE C. 1950. *The Human Group*. New York: Harcourt, Brace and World.

LAZARSFELD, PAUL F., BERNARD BERELSON, and HAZEL GAUDET. 1944. *The People's Choice*. New York: Columbia University Press.

LIN, NAN. 1982. "Social Resources and Instrumental Action." In P. V. Marsden and Nan Lin eds., *Social Structure and Network Analysis*. Beverly Hills, CA: Sage, pp. 131–145.

LIN, NAN, and MARY DUMIN. 1986. "Access to Occupations Through Social Ties." *Social Networks* 8:365–385.

LIN, NAN, WALTER M. ENSEL, and JOHN C. VAUGHN. 1981. "Social Resources and Strength of Ties." *American Sociological Review* 46:393–405.

MARKS, STEPHEN R. 1977. "Multiple Roles and Role Strain: Some Notes on Human Energy, Time and Commitment." *American Sociological Review* 42:921–936.

MARSDEN, PETER V. 1987. "Core Discussion Networks of Americans." *American Sociological Review* 52:122–131.

MARSDEN, PETER V., and JEANNE S. HURLBERT. 1988. "Social Resources and Mobility Outcomes: A Replication and Extension." *Social Forces* 67:1038–1059.

MCCLELLAND, DAVID C. 1961. *The Achieving Society*. Princeton: Van Nostrand.

———. 1975. *Power*. New York: Irvington.

MERTON, ROBERT K. (1957) 1968. "Continuities in the Theory of Reference Group Behavior." In *Social Theory and Social Structure*. New York: Free Press, pp. 335–440.

PARSONS, TALCOTT, EDWARD SHILS, KASPAR D. NAEGELE, and JESSE R. PITTS. 1961. *Theories of Society*. New York: Free Press.

SCHUMPETER, JOSEPH A. (1912) 1961. *The Theory of Economic Development*. Translated by R. Opie. Cambridge, MA: Harvard University Press.

SIEBER, SAM D. 1974. "Toward a Theory of Role Accumulation." *American Sociological Review* 39:567–578.

SIMMEL, GEORG. 1896. "Superiority and Subordination as Subject-Matter of Sociology, II." Translated by A. Small. *American Journal of Sociology* 2:392–415.

————. 1902. "The Number of Members as Determining the Sociological Form of the Group, II." Translated by A. Small. *American Journal of Sociology* 8:158–196.

————. (1922) 1955. *Conflict and Web of Group Affiliations*. Translated by K. H. Wolff and R. Bendix. New York: Free Press.

————. (1923) 1950. *The Sociology of Georg Simmel*. Translated by K. H. Wolff. New York: Free Press.

STIGLER, GEORGE J. (1957) 1965. "Perfect Competition, Historically Contemplated." In George J. Stigler ed., *Essays in the History of Economics*. Chicago: University of Chicago Press, pp. 234–267.

SWEDBERG, RICHARD. 1991. *Schumpeter—A Biography*. Princeton: Princeton University Press.

WEBER, MAX. (1904–1905) 1930. *The Protestant Ethic and the Spirit of Capitalism*. Translated by T. Parsons. New York: Charles Scribner's Sons.

ZELIZER, VIVIANA A. 1989. "The Social Meaning of Money: 'Special Monies'." *American Journal of Sociology* 95:342–377.

# 4

# Studied Trust: Building New Forms of Cooperation in a Volatile Economy

## CHARLES F. SABEL

## Trust in a Volatile Economy

Trust, the mutual confidence that no party to an exchange will exploit the others' vulnerability, is today widely regarded as a precondition for competitive success. As markets become more volatile and fragmented, technological change more rapid, and product life cycles correspondingly shorter, it is too costly and time-consuming to perfect the design of new products and translate those designs into simply executed steps. Those formerly charged with the execution of plans—technicians, blue-collar workers, outside suppliers—must now elaborate indicative instructions, transforming the final design in the very act of executing it. But in a world of half-formed plans to collaborate in the production of highly specialized goods or services, any party can hold up the others—most ruthlessly by simply enticing a collaborator into dedicating resources to a joint project, and then refusing to dedicate the necessary complementary resources until the terms of trade are renegotiated in its favor. Absent trust, no one will risk moving first, and all will sacrifice the gains of cooperation to the safe, if less remunerative, autonomous pursuit of self-interest.

It is frequently noted in practice and concluded in theory that collective appreciation of this dilemma does not resolve it. Indeed, the burden of experience and reflection is that trust can be found, but never created. In declining or threatened economic areas, for example, firm owners and trade-union officials very often agree that labor and capital would both benefit if firms cooperated more with one another and with labor, yet despair of ever doing so. In each case, the outsider is given to understand, the industry has developed an unalterable tradition of universal suspicion. This tradition, exacerbated by the struggle to survive in hard times, precludes the cooperation necessary to reverse developments. In those areas that do prosper because of the collaboration that trust makes possible, on the other hand, these same actors regard their mutual confidence as a natural fact, as much an expression of their way of life as their language, and no less resistant to political direction. Here I am thinking in particular of the many small- and medium-sized-firm industrial districts in Western Europe and Japan. Each district tells a different story of how trust became for it a fact of life; the only common feature of these stories is that none could be reproduced elsewhere precisely because each depended on an improbable chain of fortuitous local circumstances.[1]

This fatalism is echoed, and subtly if indirectly reinforced, by disheartening theoretical conclusions. The theoretical arguments ring the changes on the hold-up theme. If there is a sufficiently high probability of a sufficiently costly breach of trust in the last of many exchanges, the argument runs, each economic agent will want to cease dealing at the last-but-one exchange. Repeated application of this logic of backward induction leads the parties to refrain from all exchanges, and thereby excludes experiences that might dispose them to be more trusting and trustworthy.

From this perspective, cooperation is likely in two contrary and unusual circumstances. First, when the exchanges are many and the gains from future dealings highly valued in relation to current ones, then it can well be more advantageous to risk betrayal in the end than to forego the profits to be made in the meantime. Second, for reasons rooted in a common history—belief in the same god, dedication to the same political ends, or a common ethnic or cultural heritage—the parties may come to see themselves as members of a community of fate whose implicit (and sometimes explicit) conditions of membership exclude exploitation of the economic vulnerabilities of their fellows.

Neither circumstance, of course, justifies the hope that trust can be created where it is needed. In the first case, in fact, it would be wrong to associate cooperation with trust at all, because cooperation results from continuous calculation of self-interest rather than a mutually recognized

---

[1] For a good discussion of one such origin myth, see the analysis of local accounts of the introduction of injection moulding industry in Oyonnax, a town northeast of Lyon, in Saglio (1991).

suspension, however circumscribed, of such calculation. Here it would surely be more accurate to speak of a *modus vivendi* than of trust.[2] In the second case, trust is a by-product of events which, to the extent they are planned at all, did not have the creation of trust as their goal. Seen this way, trust is one of those states, like drowsiness, spontaneity, or—archetypically—having no thoughts, that cannot be produced directly by willing them and hence at first blush are inaccessible to individual or collective acts of volition. Surely, in this view, it is as self-defeating to try to cease continuous calculation of economic advantage because of the (calculating) conviction that it would be beneficial to do so as to concentrate on the thought of thinking nothing.[3]

The dominant theories of the role of politics and the state, moreover, reinforce these conclusions. These theories assume that politics sets the rules for and mediates the conflicts among groups in civil society with distinct interests. But those interests are as they are, and the state would overburden its rule-making and mediating capabilities, as well as abuse the citizens' mandate, were it to attempt to alter the definition of those interests—for example, by encouraging the creation of trust relations. The success of mercantile states that do arguably reshape interests to meet new circumstances is regarded as just as anomalous as the existence of real trust among firms. It is also explained the same way: by reference to a community of fate whose very definition includes the subordination of particular to general interests.[4] The expression "Japan Inc." expresses the bewilderment, anger, and envy of a world that recognizes the apparently inimitable efficacy of the (alleged) historical fusion of a collective national identity and particular economic ambitions.

These observations lead naturally to a paralyzing acceptance of history as destiny. Those rare clusters of firms or national economies in which trust is second nature will reap the benefits of their loyal dispositions in a world in which loyalty increasingly pays. Those who reasonably protect their self-interest will actually shortchange themselves. Politics will spontaneously abet the coordination of the former and the self-destructive defensiveness of the latter. Those firms and policies that cannot bear the burden of this passivity will, like wavering Puritans, make fitful efforts at cooperation—hoping that they will find themselves among the elect, knowing that many are called, but few are chosen.

[2] For a recent general statement of the distinction between calculating cooperation and cooperation framed by a moral order, see Rawls (1985).

[3] Elster has written extensively on such paradoxes. See, for example, Elster 1983:43–52.

[4] For a nuanced discussion of the role of culture in Japan's economic success, see Dore 1986:244–252.

This pessimism is, I think, unwarranted. In what follows I first argue that the theoretical views discussed so far mischaracterize human nature and, as a correlate, the malleability of trust. I know that many are skeptical of these theories and can readily cite one counter-example or another. I address the theories nonetheless because I believe that in times of crisis even many of the skeptics act on deep intuitions still shaped by the very ideas they dispute.

To escape the grasp of these refractory intuitions it is necessary to provide an alternative conception. The starting point for an alternative, I argue in the next section, is the idea that trust is a precondition of social life. Hence the proper question is not how trust can be created from mistrust, but whether particular persons or relations come to be seen as trustworthy and if so, how. I claim further that the extension of trust in any particular setting depends in part on the actors' reinterpreting their collective past, and especially their conflicts, in such a way that trusting cooperation comes to seem a natural feature, at once accidental and ineluctable, of their common heritage.

But if these two claims are sustained, the prima facie case for the futility of creating trust collapses, and it is no longer reasonable to dismiss as futile efforts by economic agents and public officials to improve economic performance in mistrustful environments. Thus in the bulk of the chapter I take up the case of current and arguably successful efforts to revitalize segments of the garment, foundry, injection-molding, and machine-tool industries in certain areas of the Commonwealth of Pennsylvania. The argument is that it depends on just the sort of redefinition of the actors' identity that the actors and many observers regarded—and may still, in the abstract, continue to regard—as contrary to the nature of economic exchange and political mediation. My aim is to show by these examples how a new understanding of trust can lead to a new understanding of the role of government in economic development. A brief conclusion reaffirms the central theme of the essay while cautioning against making too much of those arguable successes.

## Negotiated Loyalty

Given what has already been said, the heading of this section is an oxymoron, because parties to a negotiation do not spontaneously share the very standards of fairness in all circumstances that the notion of loyalty supposes. Nonetheless, I argue that the oxymoron expresses the practical truth that the line between trust and mistrust is much more blurred and easier to cross than our theories suggest. This practical truth finds partial expression in such ambiguous phrases as "blind trust" and "undying loyalty," which frequently suggest abdication of responsible judgment more than respect for duty. We (particularly in the Anglo-American world) often fail to register this disjuncture between our idea of trust and our practice of it because of deep-seated ideas of personhood and human motivation. It is to these, their defects, and a communitarian understanding of individuality as an alternative to them that I now turn.

The notions of trust discussed so far rest on two complementary and widespread views of human nature. The first is the idea, familiar from neoclassical economics and rational-choice social theory, that individuals act to maximize satisfaction of their current desires, where these desires are given as the results of an unexplained and theoretically irrelevant process of individual development. Where this is so, cooperation is the result of an accidental complementarity of maximizing strategies, and its culmination can only be a *modus vivendi,* never trust. The second is that, under rare circumstances—notably those associated with archaic or premodern societies, or modern communities that have retained key features of these earlier ones—many persons have compatible preferences. Hence they not only have compatible motives, but they also know that they do, know that they know they do, and know that in their simple worlds the cost of obtaining all this knowledge and verifying its implications is not prohibitive. Consequently they trust one another. On this view a miss is again as good as a mile, because anything short of a synchronization of preferences and motives so perfect as to be self-evident (and thus easily assimilated to the preconditions of collective life) sets in motion the backward inductions that transform the second case into the first.[5]

To this view of personhood and human nature I want to counterpoise a lawyer's list of alternatives, all of which blur the distinction between trust and mistrust and suggest passages from one to the other in ways that I shall spell out in a moment. By a "lawyer's list" I mean a catalog of arguments that could be simultaneously true, although it is unlikely that they are, and any one of which, if true, would discredit the claim to which all are opposed. A familiar American illustration would be the lawyer who defends a client accused of stealing a bucket by arguing that the accuser is not the rightful owner, that the bucket was in any case borrowed with his or her consent, worthless because it leaked, and returned in improved condition.

[5] For discussions of the fragility of trustlike relations from the point of view of methodological individualism by writers who adopt the point of view but are disconcerted by its implications, see Williams 1988:3–13 and Elster 1990:51, who concludes: "Why . . . are we not in a state of nature? There is no general answer to this question. Altruism, codes of honor, and long-term self-interest all enter into the explanation. What seems clear is that self-interest cannot be the whole story."

I prefer this form of criticism of the liberal or neoclassical view to exposition of a single alternative for two reasons. First, those readers who already have doubts about the liberal picture are likely to have different reasons for doing so; and within the wide limits of the catalog I am about to supply it is immaterial to the subsequent argument which these are. Following Rawls's (1985:231) principle of avoidance, I do not want to pick any fights to whose outcome I am for present purposes indifferent. Second, the variety of alternatives may itself sow some doubt where none currently exists, although after more than a century of explicit and inconclusive debate on these matters, I am aware that this seed takes root only under extra-ordinary and unpredictable circumstances.

For ease of exposition I will initially draw a crude distinction between criticisms that have grown out of sociological theories whose suppositions are antithetic to the methodological individualism of liberalism, and views that have emerged as the result of liberalism's own critical self-examination. This distinction carries less and less weight in current debate, and ideas from one source are more and more often combined with those from the other. Subsequently I will treat conclusions drawn from both sometimes as complementary, sometimes as equivalent formulations.

The core of the sociological view of personhood is simply the idea that persons are constituted, or can constitute themselves, only in society. Individuality can only be expressed and appreciated as individual application of a complex body of common norms that define a shared universe of meanings and expectations: a community. Because it supposes this community, the only spontaneity there is, is coordinated, the only originality is collectivized. Just as acquisition of a style, or even the creation of a new one (which after all only changes some of the prior constraints), simultaneously subordinates the artist to a common culture and enables expression of his or her otherwise ineffable individuality, so specialization requires individuals to define themselves by means that, in many ways, reinforce the common culture within which and by whose lights they seek distinction.[6]

Notice, however, that this view does not require that all beliefs be completely shared, or all behavior harmonious or even pacific. Individuals in this world define their individuality, and their place in the social ranking of honor, in part by struggling to outdo one another in doing just what ought to be done in their society: for example, by giving magnificent gifts or accumulating vast wealth. In part, and relatedly, they achieve the same ends by struggling for social validation of practices once

---

[6] An elegant development of this view is Bourdieu (1977).

viewed as discrediting variations of orthodox ways. In either case, the community can be shaken by the conflicts that ultimately honor it.[7] But even if it is shaken to pieces, individuals will maintain the same relationships with the fragments as they did with the whole, and nothing about the constitution of individuality will have changed.

In this perspective, of course, trust in the sense of shared expectations (and confidence that the expectations are and will continue to be shared) is the constitutive fact of social life. What needs to be explained here is how the boundaries of a particular community are drawn, or, collaterally, how mistrust arises. One way it can arise is through disputes that begin as disagreements (prompted, say, by the struggle for honor) over the interpretations of common norms, and end as the articulation of irreconcilable views of the world. Another way would be through the clashes of different cultural worlds that were, so to speak, irreconcilable from the first. But whatever the answer to this question, so long as social life is possible, the realm of trusting behavior can always in principle be enlarged by extending to new realms the shared understandings that make sociability possible in the first place. The contentious interpretations can be reinterpreted to reestablish consensus; two alien cultures can discover—each in its own way but prompted and provoked by the other—the grounds for a common self-definition. Put another way, every *modus vivendi* can be made a trust relation simply by assimilating it to the kinds of exchanges regarded as just by the common culture—a culture whose very existence is denied in the liberal characterization of the modern world.

There are, moreover, variants of this view that connect the social constitution of individuality to specific spheres of social life. In the spirit of lawyerly listing I mention two of these. One is the idea, central to certain strands of Marxism, that work is the collective activity—the artistry of material survival—that simultaneously subordinates the individual or groups of individuals to common constraints, yet thereby provides the material means for self-development upon which the emancipation of humankind from these and subsequent constraints depends.[8] Another is the notion, central to much of late twentieth-century philosophy, that we constitute ourselves and our humanity by trying to make ourselves intelligible and

---

[7]To put the point more generally: under some circumstances, the exchange of gifts according to norms of reciprocity can lead to violence just as, conversely, the competitive pursuit of individual advantage can, under other circumstances, lead to harmony. Disagreements about the constitution of the self are not by nature connected to views about the sources of and threats to social stability. On the dangerously "agonistic" character of gift exchanges, see Mauss (1967:4–5). On the mollifying effects of commercial exchange, see Hirschman (1977).

[8]The fullest treatment is Lukács (1984–1986).

by understanding others' efforts to do the same: in short, by speech acts. With all its ambiguities and lacunae constantly revealed by application in social situations (whose central issue is precisely the struggle to impose or agree on meanings), language here becomes the medium of socialization and individuation.

Because language is so imperfect, and mutual intelligibility so dependent on hard-fought collaboration, shared understandings and hence trust are always extensible in this view too. Unless individuals constantly assumed that others, like themselves, were seeking common meanings—the assumption that Donald Davidson (1985:129–144) calls the "act of charity" necessary and sufficient to produce mutual intelligibility—there could be no communication at all. But these same acts of charity constantly create (without necessarily realizing) the possibility for the substantive agreements that are the foundations of trust. A world in which all know that no one can think his or her own thoughts without conversing with the others—a world, that is, in which one's thoughts only become one's own in conversation—is a world that is constantly reminded how much it has to lose from the selfish exploitation of ambiguity. In this world it is literally impossible to discuss how trust is possible, because if trust as the willingness to make mutually intelligible sense of the ambiguous were not a primitive characteristic of human nature, it would not be possible to talk about anything at all. Rather, the question here, too, is how boundaries between communities are formed, and under what conditions they may be revised.

Conclusions that overlap these can be reached through criticism of liberalism's core idea. The characteristic claim of this critique is that the notion of an individual maximizing satisfaction of an arbitrary bundle of current desires simply cannot capture crucial aspects of our intuitions of what it is to be a person, especially our capacity for prudential action and even our capacity to understand and draw moral conclusions from what it means to be a person.

Take first the problem of prudence.[9] To act prudentially is to do something for which there is no current motivation, but that one will want to have done at some time in the future. But unless the notion of current desires is implausibly stretched to include the desire to do things that, in the future, one would regret not having done, it is unclear why the desires of my future self should influence my current behavior at all. Indeed, why should I care for the satisfaction of the bundle of desires that, by accident, will define my future self any more than the satisfaction of the desires that define any one of my immediate contemporaries? If

---

[9]The argument here follows Nagel 1970:33–76.

persons are capable of, and in part defined by, the capacity for prudential action, as I take them to be, then they must have a view of their personalities as extended in time. Because of this extension, present desires lose their absolute motivational priority; *now* is a particular time, one among many in the life of a being aware of its continuous existence, and not the locus where identity forms.

An analogous argument connects the ability to grasp others as persons—and hence to achieve some conception of personality that is not an extrapolation of one's own unique experiences—with the need to view the self as one among many: a someone. To understand someone else as a person, it is necessary to fix what they have in common with you. But to do that, it is necessary to ask how the other, posing the same question, would view you. Thus to imagine someone else as a person it is necessary to view oneself impersonally as a someone. Just as the capacity for prudential action supposes the existence of a personality that encompasses the present in an extended lifetime, so the capacity to grasp the very idea of a person supposes a personality that can understand itself as one self among many. By demonstrating that the self is not hostage to its own selfish present, and indeed by its very nature entertains thoughts about what would be good for persons in general (of which it is one) or itself in the future, this criticism of liberalism creates the preconditions for a psychology or even metaphysics of the person in which the question, What would happen if everyone did *that?* can always be asked, and hence trust is always an arguable proposition.

These critical arguments directly suggest the common theme of all the entries in my lawyer's list of objections to the neoclassical picture of the person and to the pessimism about the possibility of trust which follows from it. The theme is that the self is always a virtual or reflexive self. Its defining capacity is the ability to choose through reflection which possible self will actually motivate action. The choices express and elaborate a personal identity that is shaped by consideration of the future and other possible selves, and that can in principle be more and more shaped by them. Writers in the tradition of self-critical liberalism will refer to this self-creation as the ordering of preference orderings, or, as Sen puts it, "rankings of rankings" (1979:317–344). Writers in the sociological tradition may prefer to speak of self-creation hermeneutically, as the definition of an individual personality through the struggle to make sense of one's self in relation to one's own (constantly redefined) community of shared but ambiguous norms.

Either way we have a conception of personality, and by extension of community, that escapes the liberal's dismaying oscillation between a conception of the self and the group that can perceive the benefits of trust but cannot act to obtain them (because of a paralyzing belief that present preferences inevitably rule), and a conception of the self and the group that benefits from trust but cannot conceive how others might similarly benefit (because, as an accident of history, they share values whose commonality is taken to be irreproducibly accidental). The reflexive self, which on this account is the one we actually have, can entertain and act on the idea of creating or extending common values regarding loyalty and forbearance in the face of vulnerability precisely because it knows that other selves can entertain and act on the same idea.

Whether and under what conditions such a change is likely to occur is an empirical question the answer to which depends, among other things, on the prevailing economic conditions and their history, as well as on the agents' skill in reinterpreting these. The crucial point is that there is in this view nothing in principle mysterious about the creation of trust in economic affairs. Mutual dependence is the precondition of both individuality and sociability, and it is in some sense known to be such. What precise bearing this mutual dependence has for economic exchanges is another open question, to which one might expect a wide range of answers, depending on circumstances. The answer one would *not* expect is precisely the one liberalism, in the sense intended here, has taught us to count on: that by our nature we cannot discuss the question as though the discussion could be consequential.[10]

Notice, finally, that from this viewpoint trust in economic affairs becomes much less of an all-or-nothing psychological gamble on the reliability and verifiability of guesses about the harmony of our motives and those of others. A community of reflexive selves is by definition both prudent and other-regarding. It can imagine a trusting world and imagine others imagining the same. It can also devise stratagems for testing and encouraging these beliefs. These stratagems, moreover, will appear to be part of the continuous and inevitable process of individual and collective self-definition in a mutually dependent world, rather than leaps of faith hedged by various fallback strategies.

Seen this way trust is both a thick and thin human relation. It is thick

---

[10] In presenting the laundry list of alternatives to the liberal view of self I do not, to repeat, mean to suggest that there is any single positive formulation of the alternative view that is widely regarded as established doctrine by proponents of this class of conception. The struggle to capture the balance between the constraining powers of institutions, habits, and beliefs, on the one hand, and the capacity of individuals or groups to transcend these limits, on the other, rages on amongst those who believe the right form of words can be found. Often, indeed, the struggle rages within a single breast; see, for example, Bourdieu's most recent efforts to keep the books straight on this (1990:106–123). For an exemplary exegetic discussion of the general problem, see Aboulafia (1986).

in that each party must suppose, as I have argued that they should, that the others have at least an intuitive understanding of what it means to make oneself vulnerable to others and are capable—because there is no other choice—of sometimes doing so. But it is thin in that it supposes that each party might decide, after due and prudential deliberation, and well understanding the gravity of the act, to put its trust elsewhere. Trust in this sense is like a constitutional, democratic compact that requires of the citizens only that they agree to resolve disputes in ways that do not violate their autonomy, and roots this agreement in the citizens' recognition of the connection between the assertion of one's own autonomy and respect for that of the others.[11]

In such a world, loyalty could be negotiated and trust vigilant without fomenting disloyalty and mistrust precisely because the elaboration of norms of collective behavior as a concomitant and precondition of the elaboration of one's own or group personality is what the exercise of autonomy is all about. Blind trust and undying loyalty are here regarded as deformations, at once admirable and deplorable, because they bespeak a suspicious renunciation of the self's or the group's powers of self-creation. By the same token, it would be possible for individuals and groups to outwit themselves and achieve, by indirect means, changes that could neither be willed directly nor made accessible to a single act of collective volition.

This view of trust relations as makable and breakable because more "political" or "prudential" than commonly thought is corroborated by both ethnographic accounts of trust-based dealings and the sociology of organizations. Dore's account of subcontracting relations in the Japanese textile industry and Lorenz's account of subcontracting among metalworking firms in Lyon both emphasize that trust obligates partners to behave loyally in the present, but does not obligate them to refrain from asking—out loud—whether and under what conditions they should continue to do so in the future. Nor is it regarded as a breach of trust to make provisions—for example, by recourse to a second supplier—for the possibility that trust could be breached. Conversely, the absence of trust does not prohibit joint discussion of the conditions under which it might exist. No wonder, then, that Lorenz characterizes the partners' views of each other by exclusion: vendor and customer are "neither friends nor strangers" for one another.[12]

The sociology of organizations emphasizes the ways in which elements of systems not built on trust can be used to construct ones that are and

---

[11] See for the conditions of such a compact, Rawls (1985).

[12] See Dore (1983) and Lorenz (1988).

hence, by extension, the surprising facility with which an organization of one type can pass from one side of an apparently unbreachable barrier to another. Stinchcombe, for example, demonstrates in his study of the Norwegian oil-drilling industry how contracts—the symbol and instrument of market relations—can be used to construct complex dispute-resolution regimes of the kind usually associated with communities of (trusting) firms. He argues as well that trust relations can emerge from a series of exchanges whose initial intent was the achievement of short-term advantage (Stinchcombe 1985:121–171). Bradach and Eccles (1989) extend the argument by showing how elements of the market system such as prices can be used to facilitate nonmarket exchanges precisely by setting standards and thus removing potential sources of dispute that might threaten such exchanges.

The more one looks, in sum, the harder it becomes to draw a clear line between states of mind or kinds of organizations that are trusting or mistrustful. But if that is so, why do the agents themselves seem so sure that such lines can be drawn? In the following section I return to the broad-brush characterization of the agents' view of trust to see whether, on closer examination, their experience lends support to the views arrived at here.

## Reconciliation and Genesis Amnesia: The Politics of Trust

The views of the economic agents, it seems, confirms neoclassical expectations on two central points. Those who suffer the costs of mistrust can imagine the benefits of trust, but despair of obtaining them given the motivations of persons such as themselves; those who profit from trust think it an historical accident that they and the (few) others in similar situations do so. Here I want to focus on this second perception, although at the end I touch briefly on the first perception. I discuss it again at length in connection with the analysis of the case of Pennsylvania.

In reexamining the reports of trust as historical good luck I do not, of course, mean to challenge the existence of such reports or the good faith of those who repeat them. I myself have heard or read different variants of this tale, each emphasizing the particularities of local circumstance, in at least a baker's dozen industrial districts in Italy, West Germany, Austria, France, and Denmark. For what it is worth, all strike me as sincere and guileless in the sense of concentrating on themes and events that everyone in a particular locale regards as important to their collective self-definition. Indeed, once you have come across one of these stories about how misery in a particular place was turned to prosperity through the cooperative exploitation of folk ingenuity galvanized by the genius of a few widely traveled native sons (daughters in these tellings tend to stick to their knitting, quite literally; but that is another story), you can be sure of two things: so long as you keep the conversation on that place, you will hear almost exactly the same story again and again; and what you hear will be different in many details—for instance, whether the setting is in the city or the country—from similar stories about similar places. But it is precisely these two regularities—that accounts of the same place are always the same and those of different places always different—that, I think, ought to arouse the suspicion that the story you are getting is not the whole story.

What is suspicious or at least curious about the similar stories is that they sound similar enough to have been, if not rehearsed, then at least repeated with proverbial frequency. But rehearsal or repeated for whom, and why? Surely they do not circulate for the benefit of outsiders. As a rule the stories themselves explain why the local society is different from, morally superior to (because capable of greater solidarity), and hence in some profound sense inaccessible to outsiders. On this point the story does seem to be the whole story. There is nothing put on, so far as I can tell, in either the self-effacement or the pride contained in the remark periodically heard in the Italian metalworking district of Emilia-Romagna: "America is here!"

But why should the insiders, the members of the local society, tell themselves these homilies so often that they sound rehearsed? In the most austerely liberal account of psychology in these societies, everyone simply has the same or compatible motivations, and there is no need for anyone to advertise that fact. In less austere versions, there might be room for a little sociological folklore in which the common knowledge is ritually publicized to reassure everyone that their assumptions about shared expectations still hold. Even taking account of that possibility, however, it is hard to see why people who do rely on one another, and allegedly believe that it is a matter of (cheerfully accepted) historical inevitability that they do, spend so much time getting straight what they all are supposed to take for granted.

The obvious alternative explanation, in the light of the preceding discussion of the reflexive construction of self and community, turns the liberal account on its head. It is that the stories are articulated when persons or groups that once had incompatible stories agree on a common history that resolves or renders irrelevant those differences. The stories continue to circulate because they set bounds on subsequent disagreements. Instead of expressing a consensus, the stories in this view are part of the process of creating it. They create a past in which the prior conflicts resulted from mistakes and misunderstandings rather than fundamental differences, and suggest a future in which all subsequent conflicts will be limited by virtue of being defined in advance as family fights. Seen this way it is not us outsiders but themselves that the tellers of these stories aim to fool; and it is no fault but our own if their efforts to induce a kind of genesis amnesia in themselves lead us to believe that their history was actually without conflict.

A deliberately shocking example from the practices of the Ilongot headhunters of Northern Luzon in the Philippines will illustrate the process I have in mind. The Ilongot bear grudges, and bear them hard. Offenses to certain classes of their kin produce in the young males of the society a resentful anger that can only be relieved by severing the head of someone appropriately related to the offender and hurling it joyously in the air. In this way feuds start and ramify, with the result that in time the very survival of the society is jeopardized. When they believe things reach this point, the feuding groups meet and—here is the crucial point— try to reinterpret kin relations in such a way that the original offense need not have obligated a revenge killing, nor, because of the understandable error, the revenge killing a feud (see Rosaldo 1980). If this sounds far-fetched as a description of a dispute-resolution mechanism that might apply in any way to advanced industrial societies, consider how insistent formerly hostile nations are that, as an indispensable part of their reconciliation, the textbook history of their hostility be rewritten in a mutually recognizable way as a series of tragic misunderstandings. A nineteenth-century example is the United States and Great Britain; twentieth-century examples include France and West Germany, the United States and Japan, and currently Japan and China and South Korea. Letting bygones be bygones requires a collective act of self-redefinition, not simple forgetting.

Let me add, to avoid any suggestions that these mechanisms are self-activating, that nothing *requires* that bygones be bygones.[13] If they always were, disputes would never proceed far enough for the issue to become explicit, and there would never be cases, which there manifestly are, of mutually destructive conflicts. The point is merely that when so-

---

[13] Historians have become attentive to the cases where traditions are created deliberately, for, as a rule, politically manipulative ends. The more self-effacing, less-documented cases in which new traditions are discovered rather than invented received, so far as I know, less notice. On the invention of tradition, see the collection of essays by that title edited by Eric Hobsbawm and Terence Ranger (1983).

cial cohesion is threatened domestically or internationally, the parties generally know it, and efforts to reinterpret the past or recreate a new collective identity are indispensable to resolution of the problem.

As I do not want to break stride to introduce the historical evidence that would buttress my argument about the creation of trust relations in particular economic settings, I will merely mention a few prima facie cases in favor of my interpretation and indicate several well-documented instances of the "discovery" of historical conflict in industrial districts that once did or do today tell stories about themselves that exclude such possibilities. The prima facie cases are the twentieth-century experiences of countries such as West Germany, Italy, Austria, and Japan. All of these came to the brink of or actually fought civil wars in the 1920s or 1930s. Yet all today enjoy, reasonably, in the light of their economic performance, a reputation for putting to productive use a national culture of cooperation that is itself a source of national pride and identity. The power of current success to blind nationals and foreigners alike to the obvious fact that these "cooperative" cultures did not exclude the possibility of fratricide cannot be overestimated. I recall, for instance, once being told by a group of AFL-CIO trade-union leaders that certain West German institutions of labor-management cooperation were unsuited to U.S. conditions because German employers could never *think* of doing to German unions what American managers did to organized labor here.

The historical "discoveries" I have in mind concern industrial districts such as the modern woolens center at Prato, near Florence; the Sheffield cutlery industry, which saw its heyday in the late nineteenth century; and the center of injection molding in Oyonnax, near Lyon.[14] One common feature of all these districts—and every other one of which I have knowledge—is a history of complex struggles between shifting alliances of merchant factors or converters, high-volume producers of semifinished goods, artisans making highly differentiated finished products and working independently or in large factories, and less-skilled workers employed directly or as nominally independent subcontractors by the independent artisans or the large firms. A second common feature is that, whenever the parties to these conflicts regulate their disputes through arbitration boards or councils that police quality or set and monitor wage schedules, the districts flourish; when not, then not. The third common feature, and the reason "discoveries" is set in quotation marks, is that the preceding two are immediately obvious in historical retrospect, but almost completely invisible (because taken for granted and obscured by tales of a

---

[14]On Prato, see Trigilia (1989); on Sheffield, Lloyd (1913); on Oyonnax, Ravèyre and Saglio (1984) and Saglio (1991).

cooperative culture) to contemporaries so long as the districts are prospering. A visitor to Prato today, for example, will hear a great deal about how trade unions and employers' associations are working (as they apparently always have) to solve the problems of industrial adjustment, but nothing about the fact that for almost a decade after a wave of decentralization in the late 1940s, the unions and manufacturers were unable to sign a single collective bargaining agreement.

This view that conflict and an almost mythologically extolled consensus co-exist in high-trust systems is, moreover, supported by the few ethnologically sophisticated studies of such systems in action. "Negotiated Loyalty" is the title of an oral history of labor-management relations in a U.S. shoe firm in the 1920s (Zahavi 1983). In Dore's (1989) account of subcontracting by large Japanese firms, "cooperative pursuit of common goals" and "vigilant monitoring of the distribution of the costs and benefits of cooperation" are two sides of the same coin. Surely these characterizations evoke worlds that mistrust blind trust without, for all that, being mistrustful.

Consider next the diversity of (unique) stories about the history of particular districts. A few diverse histories support the liberal assumption that trust is a rare accident. Many diverse histories, on the other hand, suggest that there are many paths that end in the creation of trust relations. To connect the point to the earlier discussion of the reflexive self and community, many diverse histories suggest that many groups of producers can reinterpret themselves and their history in such a way as to make trust the natural outcome of their common experiences. Whether there were few or many, or—above all—an increasing number of industrial districts and other trust-based economic systems, is, of course, a matter of considerable debate. To caricature the positions: those who see many claim any instance of cooperation as a case of trust. Those who claim few claim any instance of conflict as a proof that it does not and cannot exist.

From the foregoing, it should be clear that this way of framing the question makes it impossible to answer. Cooperation that is not more or less institutionalized in a system that enlists public sanctions in the defense of shared values may be no more than a *modus vivendi*. But it should also be clear that conflicts can lead to the creation of trust and persist, transmogrified and limited, after it has been established. How many production systems have crossed or are crossing the *modus vivendi* threshold and institutionalizing conflict in a way that does not obstruct flexibility I cannot say. But my strong suspicion, watching developments in Western Europe, Japan, and the United States, is that the number is growing. If that turns out to be true, then the history of the contemporary period will treat the switch to high-trust systems much as history has treated the whole process of industrialization beginning with Great Britain: apparently impossible for any country to do until it does it, and dependent on some short list of rare preconditions that is successively extended as new cohorts of nations or regions prove that it is in fact possible to industrialize under conditions different from those of their predecessors.

Finally I return to the first of the two confirmatory reports of economic experience: the complaints of those in declining or threatened regions that they are incapable of the trust they require. Again it would be foolish to deny the prevalence of such complaints or impugn their sincerity. Taken at face value, they suggest that the agents themselves recognize the force of the theoretical conclusion that it is impossible to create trust by an act of will. And in this, the theoreticians and the actors may be right. But the interesting question, we saw, is not whether trust can be created at will. If the reflexive view of self and society is correct, then the real problem is how trust can be built in particular circumstances through a circuitous redefinition of collective values. In the next section I provide an example of one way this can be done by reporting on recent developments in the Commonwealth of Pennsylvania, a large industrial state just south of New York whose declining mass-production industries and efforts at economic revitalization mirror the dilemmas and possibilities of industrial America as a whole.

## Studied Consensus: Learning to Cooperate in Fragmented Industries

This section tells a tale within a tale about the revitalization of the foundry industry near Pittsburgh in the southwest part of the state, plastics firms in the northwest on the Lake Erie shore, apparel firms in the Lehigh Valley in the northeast, and four scattered clusters of tool-and-die firms. The larger narrative concerns the reorientation of economic development policy both nationally and in Pennsylvania. In the last fifteen years, that policy has shifted from a strategy aimed at providing individual firms with the services needed to increase their innovative capacity to one aimed at helping the actors in particular industries and locales—firms, trade associations, trade unions, educational institutions, and local governments—define collectively which services they need severally and collectively. Put in a way that resonates with the language of the preceding discussion, the consensus is drifting from the view that individual actors know their interests, and that government's role is to remove obstacles to realizing them, to the view that it is only by recognizing their mutual dependence that the actors can define their distinct interests, and that government's role is to encourage the recognition of a collectivity and the definition of particularity.

The smaller, interior story, and the one on which I concentrate, concerns this twofold process of identity formation. The aim here is to show how, in coming to a common and generally surprising view of an economic situation that each thought it had understood fully, mutually suspicious groups can redefine their relations and (prudently) begin to construct communities of interest—yet another practicable oxymoron— where none had seemed possible. These beginnings are no more than that, and I will underscore their fragility later. They are nonetheless worth discussing because they have already gone beyond the limits of what the conventional liberal view of the wellsprings of cooperation suggest is probable. Should they in fact revitalize their respective local industries, the projects will have demonstrated that it is possible to create vigilant trust in settings—such as declining industries in the heart of mass-production, unrepentantly individualistic America—where theory and practice should rule it out entirely. If economic community can be discovered in Erie or the Lehigh Valley or the environs of Pittsburgh, then it can certainly be discovered in many other places. Not least for this reason, those concerned with economic development in the United States are following developments in Pennsylvania with increasing attention.

In retrospect, of course, it is easy to trace the changing direction of economic development policy in the United States. For ease of exposition, I distinguish three successive models, although they in fact overlap and the seeds of the later ones are contained in the earlier experiences.[15]

By the second half of the 1970s, traditional mass-production industries in the leading manufacturing states came under increasing domestic and, particularly, foreign competition. As the federal government proved less able and less willing to cushion, much less reverse the changes, state governments were forced to articulate new strategies of economic development. To Republicans on the right and Democrats on the left two points seemed clear. First, "smokestack chasing"—the use of tax incentives to attract branch plants of large, typically mass-production corporations—did not work. Study after study showed that firms' locational decisions were rarely influenced by the universal (and hence self-defeating)

---

[15] For a comprehensive survey of changes in economic-development policy, particularly at the state level, and further description of the programs and institutions referred to in the following account, see Osborne (1988). A succinct presentation of recent developments is Herbers (1990). Interpretations of the political appeal of the various policies, however, reflect my own discussions with administrators, legislators, managers, and trade unionists in the relevant states during the last five years.

offers of tax breaks; and when they were, the kinds of firms that were attracted by such means tended to close up shop at the first sign of economic trouble. Second, it was therefore necessary to foster the state's existing economy, particularly by encouraging the foundation and growth of firms in new industries such as computers, semiconductors, or test equipment, where competition depended on the ability to innovate rather than to reduce manufacturing costs. Both convictions seemed well founded in the product-life-cycle theory of industrial development: the view that new products and industries are born in the most sophisticated and technologically advanced economies, and then diffuse to less-advanced and lower-cost settings as the products and production processes become standardized and hence easier to master and transfer. From this perspective, the only plausible strategy was to stop chasing smokestacks—the "mature" industries—and encourage the transition to youthful, technologically dynamic ones.

The upshot was the first new strategy of growth, which might, for want of a generally accepted name, be called the *development-bank model*. Given the assumptions about the self-directing powers of the market and its close relation to technological development on which the product-life-cycle view rested, the problem for policy was simply to reduce the barriers to innovation for firms. These were seen to be of two kinds. One was access to capital: banks were very reluctant to accept new ideas as collateral for loans, and hence it was difficult to finance their translation into commercial products. The other was access to technology: somehow the ideas developed in university laboratories had to be brought within the reach of the economy.

State-funded development banks in various guises could solve both problems. By providing grants or guaranteeing or matching private-sector loans to firms with innovative projects, the banks could address the capital problems. Use of similar instruments would encourage joint industry-university research efforts in areas of benefit first to individual firms, but, by extension, to whole sectors of the state economy. Massachusetts, pushed by the decline of its textile and shoe industries and pulled by the prospect of distributing the treasure trove of ideas accumulated (and in part already commercialized) at MIT and Harvard, led the way. But it was followed in the early 1980s by Pennsylvania, which created the Ben Franklin Partnership (BFP) to fund joint research-and-development projects, and Michigan, which passed legislation allowing a portion of the state employees' pension funds to be invested in uncollateralized ventures. The idea was attractive because, beyond its resonance with deep-seated conceptions of economic growth, it promised a lot for a little and appealed to a wide spectrum of political interests.

As was widely noted, the development banks affected the economy beyond their immediate radius of action. By demonstrating the viability of certain kinds of investments, they drew private and semiprivate capital such as pension funds into previously avoided areas, thereby vastly multiplying the effect of the state's own lending activity. For those on the free-market right of American politics, moreover, all this could be seen as a remedy for clearly limited market failures, and hence a way of reinforcing the broader appeal of a market economy. For those on the New Deal left, it could be seen as a form of French-style indicative planning or a publicly controlled variant of the coordination of private firms exercised through long-term loans by German universal banks. The ambiguity of these viewpoints and the coalitions they permitted recalls the Progressives' efforts to establish social welfare programs in the United States in the first decades of this century by creating public insurance schemes that were meant to serve as both an alternative and a compelling model to private insurers.

By the mid-1980s, a second, extension-service model began to take root in the undergrowth of the first one. One cause was the discovery that even firms in the new, high-tech sectors of the economy needed a longer list of services than originally imagined. If access to capital and technology were problems, so too were access to managerial expertise in areas ranging from marketing to manufacturing, as well as training of technicians and workers. A second cause was the realization that often, indeed typically, the solution to industry's problems lay not in abandoning current markets for new ones (the recommendation of the product-life-cycle theory), but rather in introducing high technologies into the products and production processes of the mature industries (the strategy at firms in such advanced economies as those of West Germany, Japan, Italy, Sweden, and Switzerland, which were outcompeting their U.S. counterparts). To do that as well, new services were needed, particularly for those small- and medium-sized firms. Their modernization was indispensable to the success of their larger clients because the reintegration of conception and execution requires increasing reliance on collaboration with sophisticated suppliers. But the latter had been so weakened by the crisis that they could not afford the necessary help. In the United States, the Agricultural Extension Service of the Department of Agriculture had successfully provided general consulting services to family farms since the Great Depression. It was therefore a convenient model—or, rather, analogy, as few agricultural institutions were actually transferred to the industrial sector—for state governments moving from provision of resources that firms combined as they saw fit, to provision, through consulting services, of knowledge about how best to combine resources.

Examples are the Technology Deployment Service in Michigan (later part of the Michigan Modernization Service), which serves primarily the automotive parts suppliers; the Cooperative Regional Industrial Laboratories in Massachusetts (now called Action Projects), which serve the Springfield machine-tool industry (Machine Tool Action Project, or MTAP) and the New Bedford-Fall River garment industry (the Needle Trades Action Project, or NTAP); and the nine Industrial Resource Centers (IRCs) spread through Pennsylvania.

In this case, too, the model was palatable in part because it was consistent with politically divergent interpretations of its underlying motivations. For the right, the extension services could be seen as an elaboration of the preceding, market-perfecting activities: marginal interventions needed in order to make further, and consequential, state intervention unnecessary. For the left, the new activities could be seen as part of a comprehensive effort to reshape markets through politics: to establish, by new institutional means, new boundary conditions appropriate to the current conditions of competition, as the New Deal had done by the then-appropriate use of regulatory agencies and the like.

Once again, however, a new model has begun to grow in the underbrush of the old. This third, incipient model of economic development also has twin roots. One root is the discovery by those immediately involved with economic development that what makes the successful extension services and development banks work is that their operation creates more or less informal networks of business persons, trade unionists, local government officials, bankers, and educators who together discover ways to bring resources to bear efficiently to the problems at hand. These resources include, but are hardly limited to, those provided by the state or local authority. Indeed, the original program, redefined to serve ends only distantly connected to the intent of its originators, often comes to play a subordinate part in a package of resources that could not have been assembled without the efforts of the network—whose own formation would in turn have been unlikely but for authorization of the now-marginal program. Thus programs such as the Springfield machine-tool project worked only at one remove, and for reasons not anticipated at the time of their conception.[16] The second root is the growing realization that the systems of West German, Italian, or Swedish firms whose success had played an important role in casting doubt on the product-life-cycle theory and in suggesting the plausibility of the extension-service model themselves depended on (often highly formalized) networks of a similar type (see Katzenstein 1985).

[16] Discussions in 1990–1991 with Robert Forrant, director of MTAP.

In short, the more carefully U.S. observers studied domestic or foreign industrial structures well adapted to current economic conditions, the clearer it became that what mattered was the social system by which packages of programs were defined and administered rather than the precise definition of any single program or service. But if that were so, then instead of trying to define programs directly—extend the extension services—state governments should try to design programs that encourage the actors to define their own needs. Insofar as the definition of needs depends on the creation of certain types of local cooperative networks, this means programs that encourage creation of the appropriate forms of cooperation among the actors in particular industries in particular locales.

I call the new model, amorphously, "associative" or "cooperative" because characterizations with more definition have misleading theoretical echoes. One candidate would be autopoietic (literally: self-creating) or reflexive systems. These are systems in which the logic governing the development of each of the elements is constantly reshaped by the development of all the others: the parts reflect the whole and vice versa. It is easy to see affinities between this logic of reciprocal institutional influence and the kind of mutual adjustment of identities under discussion. The difficulty is that the idea of autopoiesis is typically embedded in theories of social evolution in which epochal institutional change is connected to increasing organizational complexity. Increased efficiency at first requires increased differentiation of spheres of activity and tasks within those spheres. Law becomes separated from religion and morality, agriculture becomes distinct from industry, and production within each is decomposed into more and more specialized operations. As society becomes still more complex, however, the costs of specialization exceed the gains. The solution is de-differentiation, the costless, automatic, and—above all—self-adjusting form of coordination called autopoiesis or institutional reflexivity.

One general problem with this view is that there is no convincing metric of social complexity, and without one it is impossible to make sense of, let alone evaluate, the theory's evolutionary core. A more particular historical difficulty, which corroborates the first problem, concerns the role of autopoiesis in American constitutional thought. As I will argue in depth, shortly, the New Deal idea of law making by private groups can be interpreted as an argument for the legalization of reflexive institutions. That the collective bargaining institutions built in part on the basis of those ideas did not prove adaptive or self-reforming shows either that the ideas did not capture the essence of autopoiesis, or—more plausibly—that the autopoietic character of institutions is always limited by the historical circumstances under which they come into being. If the latter, then strictly speaking, there can be no unqualifiedly autopoietic institutions at all. In any case, given the New Deal precedents, it would be necessary in the United States to speak of neo-autopoiesis—a word that is hard to mouth even as a neologism and harder to swallow as a concept.[17]

A second way to characterize the new development model would be as neo-corporatist. In the late 1970s and early 1980s neo-corporatism referred to a system of interest representation in which the national state and the peak organizations of labor and capital established policies that ideally minimized inflation and unemployment and maximized growth. Since then, national economic performance has come to depend less on national, macroeconomic policy, however coordinated, and more on co-operation at the plant, regional, and sectorial levels, as suggested above. Neo-corporatism has been accordingly qualified and extended to include micro(-neo)-corporatism, meaning plant-level cooperation, and meso(-neo)-corporatism, meaning regional or sectorial cooperation. But if the con-cept is thus extended to cover any form of economically advantageous cooperation, or even any institutionally mediated form of such coopera-tion, why not speak directly of cooperative or associative institutions? Better a place-holder that reveals the outline of the terminological gap clearly than a stop-gap term with blurry contours.[18]

One of the first, and certainly the most comprehensive of these asso-ciative programs, is the Manufacturing Innovation Networks (MAIN) project announced by the Commonwealth of Pennsylvania in the spring of 1989.[19] The program's sponsors, all in their thirties and early forties, held responsible staff or line positions in the commonwealth's Depart-ments of Commerce and Labor and Industry, or worked directly for the governor. All had come of age in government in the late 1980s, just as ideas of economic development were changing most rapidly. One, Jacques Koppel, had helped found the commonwealth's industrial-extension ser-

[17] For an exemplary formulation of the autopoietic view of the development of law and state structures, see Teubner (1983).

[18] For an elaboration of neo-corporatism as the system of precontractual institutions that makes possible not only contingent claims contracting but "production coalitions" between labor and management of, presumably, any kind, see Streeck (1987:241–246, esp. p. 244).

[19] The following is based on numerous meetings and telephone discussions with partic-ipants in the MAIN project. Here is the place to disclose that I have acted as a consultant to MAIN since its inception; in addition, I serve on the Strategic Investment Committee of the Ben Franklin Partnership (BFP), whose purpose is to review the performance of that institution and recommend ways of improving it.

vice, the Industrial Resource Centers (IRCs). Another, Robert Coy, who was chiefly responsible for organizing MAIN and currently directs the program, had served as executive director of a committee to foster labor, management, and government cooperation on a range of statewide economic development issues. All were familiar with the related efforts of other states, and Coy was particularly knowledgeable about the situation in Western Europe. All were aware of the shortcomings of discrete services, no matter how appropriately designed, and sensed the possibility of improving the performance of all the pieces of the already extensive economic development program by integrating them first locally, and perhaps later at the state level as well. No one, however, had a clear idea of how to do this, and the MAIN program was in large measure an experiment to see whether, as current fashion had it, the actors themselves could play a decisive role in solving the problem.

The program itself was straightforward and fiscally modest enough to be almost negligible. In the spring of 1989 the commonwealth invited groups of firms in a particular locale and serving common markets to submit, together with trade associations, unions, and any relevant public entities, plans for assessing the strategic situation of their industry and the utility, if any, of more cooperative arrangements among themselves. Small- and medium-sized firms were to have preference, for reasons having to do with the general shift in policy toward the weakest part of the traditional industrial base. But plans contemplating increased cooperation between large and small firms were also encouraged. The proposals also had to stipulate the membership of a steering committee, composed of representatives of all these groups, whose task would be to oversee administration of the project. The applications were due less than two months after the commonwealth's Request for Proposals was announced, and the four submissions judged best by a committee of the program's originators were to be funded for one year in amounts of not more than $100,000 (see Departments of Commerce and Labor and Industry, Commonwealth of Pennsylvania 1989).

By giving the applicants little time, the commonwealth could be sure that only industrial agglomerations already toying with the idea of new forms of association would be likely to enter the competition. The kind of collective "strategic audit" (a consultants' term of art for an assessment of a firm's competitive possibilities) that the Request for Proposals called for would seem worthwhile only to assemblies of distinct groups that had begun to see themselves as collectivities. By making the grants small, the commonwealth ensured that no group of firms already cooperating in the way envisioned would bother submitting a proposal: the bother was simply more trouble than it was worth for a going concern. By forcing the applicants to present a single steering committee of the "relevant" groups, the commonwealth brought to the surface submerged conflicts that might have thwarted subsequent efforts had they remained hidden. In fact, in several cases, different groups claiming to represent the same industry in the same area did submit or consider submitting competing proposals. Only Coy's mediation composed the differences.

Given these constraints, then, it was no surprise that the projects selected came from industrial agglomerations whose situation makes it nearly impossible, in the liberal view, to establish trust. On the one hand, all had long traditions of entrepreneurial independence; and competition among firms, generally considered a fact of business life, had turned cutthroat in the late 1970s and early 1980s. The Pittsburgh-area foundries, to begin with, went into crisis with their traditional customers, the steel industry. The Erie plastics firms came on hard times as their customers in the automobile industry were battered by imports, and as foreign injection-molding firms began to compete in the United States. For firms in Erie, often the only way to survive was to shoot and ship plastic cups and other low-value-added products, where relentless price competition increasingly pitted local firms against one another.

The situation was similar for the apparel firms in the Lehigh Valley. In the 1950s and 1960s, these firms had prospered as subcontractors (or simply contractors, in the industry's language) for the large New York manufacturers who essentially dictated fashions and provided the corresponding piece goods to the giant department-store chains that dominate retailing in the United States. In the 1970s and 1980s, however, most of the traditional manufacturers were pushed aside as the retailers began to design garments themselves and subcontract production to new, usually foreign firms (private labels), or to a new more flexible kind of manufacturer able to keep abreast of more rapidly changing fashions—in large measure by also using foreign production sites (as with Liz Claiborne). Men's wear, women's wear, and sportswear firms in the Lehigh Valley were left chasing the business for reorders of those items that proved more successful than anticipated. Given the relatively high price they commanded, these reorders could be resupplied on short notice by relatively high-cost local producers.

For the tool-and-die producers from Pittsburgh, Philadelphia, Erie, and the Pennsylvania Dutch area in the center of the commonwealth, the decline of domestic industry and the rise of imports had also apparently led to an intensification of local competition. Although it is impossible to get strictly comparable figures for the clusters of firms concerned, several summary statistics indicate the extent of the economic trauma. Between 1979 and 1988, some 262,381 jobs were lost in the apparel industry in the United States. In Pennsylvania 47,551 jobs were lost in the same period (a decline of 35 percent). Of these, 8,484 were in the two counties of the Lehigh Valley area (a decline of 43 percent). In the same period, the Pennsylvania foundry industry lost 13,027 jobs (a decline of 58 percent, as against a decline of 48 percent for the industry in the United States as a whole). Nineteen of 134 foundries closed, a drop of 15 percent. In the greater Pittsburgh area, including Allegheny, Washington, and Montgomery counties, the number of firms declined by just under 28 percent, from 28 to 20, and the number of jobs in the industry by 60 percent, from 2,601 to 1,037.[20] The Erie plastics industry was the only case in which employment grew through the 1970s and 1980s, but this was widely perceived to be the result of an explosive growth in demand for plastic goods of all kinds, rather than a sign of the technological prowess of the local firms. During this period, firms grew in number without strengthening their competitive position.[21]

On the other hand, all four industry groups had had in the more or less recent past some experience of inter-firm or labor-management cooperation that, together with their increasing awareness of the organizational basis of their foreign competitors' success, made it plausible to think that each could benefit from rethinking its current forms of association. The most extreme case was apparel, where unions had long played a role in stabilizing the industry. Unions put a floor under wages by controlling the flow of work from unionized manufacturers to unionized contractors; they even provided industrial-engineering services to small shops to help the latter operate efficiently enough to pay the higher union-scale wages. But Erie, which billed itself in the 1920s as the "plastics capital of the world," was evidently for a time an industrial district. The plastics industry there grew out of the activities of two resistor manufacturers (which accumulated experience with the new materials) and a zipper maker (which trained several generations of highly skilled tool-and-die makers, who turned their knowledge to mold making). Most firms in the area still trace their lineage back to one of these three companies. Awareness of this common heritage, and many of the friendships and associations on which it is based, seems to have survived the increased competition of the 1970s and 1980s. In the foundry and tool-and-die

[20] All figures are drawn from the U.S. Department of Commerce, County Business Patterns, appropriate years.

[21] In Erie county, for example, employment in firms producing plastic products increased by 106 percent between 1972 and 1987, from 1,726 to 3,562 persons. See U.S. Department of Commerce, County Business Patterns, appropriate years.

industries, an analogous role is played by craft pride and the cognate sense of membership in a community where everyone has something to learn from the others.

Thus the situation of the four project groups could, at first glance, be assimilated by either of the two views of trust presented earlier. They were balanced, as the liberal view suggests they would be, between the view that efforts to organize cooperation would founder on calculations of current self-interest, and a longing for the benefits of cooperation that would prove futile precisely because it was too imprecise to evaluate. But they were also balanced, as the sociological view suggests would be the case, between two possible identities, each with its own referents in recollected experience. In a very loose sense, then, the changing self-conception of the groups constitutes a kind of primitive demonstration of the greater explanatory power of this latter perspective.

The ability of the MAIN project to tip the balance in favor of trust depended, as almost all the participants seemed to realize, on the utility of a simple device. By "studying" their industries jointly, it was hoped, the parties would at best discover new sources of vitality that could serve as models for collective reorganization. At worst, it was further hoped, they would discover a reality different enough from the one they expected to force reconsideration of their traditional assumptions. This reconsideration would, in turn, lead to the formulation of new ideas of best practice. Just as insomniacs can be led to forget their insomniacal thoughts and fall asleep by the request that they write down the symptoms of their insomnia, so the industry groups were invited, or invited themselves, to connive in a form of self-distraction that would allow them to catch sight of new possibilities. I call the kind of consensus and the associated forms of economic transactions that theoretically result from such a process *studied trust*.[22]

---

[22] Students of weakness of the will or *akrasia* may want to distinguish the strategy of self-transformation described here from the strategy associated with Pascal's wager. Pascal argued that if there was any chance that a god capable of granting infinite satisfaction existed, then it was reasonable for any self-interested person to believe in the existence of that god. Because there are reasons to believe god exists, belief is reasonable. But, the argument continues, a conclusion founded on such reason has nothing to do with the unreflective affirmation of the existence of a supreme being that we commonly understand as belief in god. To believe unthinkingly what we have reasonably concluded to believe, therefore, we act *as if* we believed that way, practicing all the religious ceremonies that express unconditional faith. Because the ceremonies become habitual and habits are by definition unthinking, calculated belief finally becomes true faith.

The situation described here is like Pascal's wager in that the actors in some sense choose what they eventually want to believe. It is also like Pascal's wager in that actions occasioned by their choices are self-reinforcing. But the situation is crucially different in

The "trick" seems to be producing such studied trust—because the groups are capable of redefining their community interests, as the previous discussion has suggested they could, and because they have reason to do so given the results of their investigations. Most generally, all have found that they overestimated the costs and underestimated the benefits of cooperation. This was because the estimations were typically based on the experience of the crisis years of the early 1980s, when the firms were truly competing head-to-head and cooperation would have been meaningless. But the firms that survived that period did so largely by specializing in mastery of a particular production process or manufacture of a particular product. Hence, many had become more and more dependent on the provision of complementary products or processes by local companies, without, however, grasping the cumulative significance of the incremental changes. Even as it was becoming more pervasive and mutually beneficial, cooperation among specialists was still generally regarded as an exception to the old rule of cutthroat competition, and in any case, assimilated to traditional forms of neighborliness or craft solidarity.

These findings were not self-evident. Entrenched views and interests of the trade associations, firms, and unions drew attention away from those situations that might have alerted them to emergent changes in the environment. The commonwealth's role was to bring these limiting assumptions to light, either by bringing in consultants to suggest alternative ways of looking at the situation or by using the surprises encountered by one project to jog the others. It was this process, of course, that created the possibility for redefining collective identities and cleared the way for studied trust. Had it been otherwise, the groups would have solved their coordination problems long before they were identified as such.

Some examples will clarify the sorts of barriers that obstructed joint efforts, and will clarify too how the groups have begun to dismantle those barriers in the name of a new collective self-definition. The Lehigh Valley project was initially conceived as an effort to improve relations between the unions and the unionized contractors. The initial participants were aware that there was a growing nonunion sector of recent Vietnamese, Lebanese, and Syrian immigrants. But to the Italians and

that this self-reinforcement leads rarely, if ever, to suspension of self-reflective, and hence in some sense calculating, evaluation of one's current situation. If the self-reinforcement of initial choices *did* have this effect, the world could consist of nothing but trusting zones like Japan and mistrustful ones like Sicily. But, as the preceding discussion has suggested and the subsequent argument will reaffirm, such cases are the exceptions. The rule is that persons define and experience trust in a way that allows them to distinguish that condition from both distrust and unquestioning faith. For an excellent discussion of Pascal's wager, see Elster (1984:47ff).

Jews who dominated the firms and unions in the organized sector, the new firms were essentially sweatshops, and the problem—to be addressed in part by the project—was how to make operations there conform to union standards, whether the workers themselves were organized or not. From the point of view of the new immigrants, a number of whom had adopted best-practice technologies and were paying wages well over minimum union rates, the established groups and the unions in particular were simply taxing them. Firms that subcontracted work to nonunion shops were forced to pay an amount into the union social welfare funds equal to the contribution that a unionized subcontractor would have made, regardless of the level of wages and benefits actually paid by the nonunion firm.

To the extent that the nonunion firms absorbed the penalties paid by their unionized clients they were subsidizing union members at the expense of their own employees and profits. But through meetings and shop visits, employers from unionized shops and union officials became more aware of the dynamism of parts of the nonunion sector. Conversely, representatives of the latter began to similarly distinguish a dynamic part of the unionized sector that was prepared to trade services with them and a stagnant sector that counted on enforcement of old rules and practices to assure its flow of work. As this happened, the problem became less one of regularizing sweatshops (the original union view) or outwitting an out-dated but still powerful monopolist (the new-immigrant view), and more a question of rethinking the collective needs of the new specialist firms in the Valley, their relation to one another, and ultimately their relation to the manufacturers and retailers in New York.

The Pittsburgh foundries provide a second example. Their trade association is the Pennsylvania Foundrymen's Association, a for-profit organization that sells its services to individual foundries. The principal service is workmen's compensation insurance, which the association, through one of its entities, can provide at advantageous rates because it has identified and taught its members to eliminate the chief hazards in foundries. Because the association is run by persons who do not come out of the industry and who think of themselves as providing discrete services, they do not have a detailed grasp of changes in foundry technology or the structure of the industry. For example, they are unaware of the customers' growing insistence that foundries provide design services and furnish products that require little if any further machining. Nor did they learn of these changes from their current members, because these latter tend to be the oldest, most traditional, and often economically most desperate of the surviving firms. Again, shop visits, organized by outside consultants with little prior knowledge of the industry, turned up facts that surprised the more traditional shop owners and trade associations alike.

The first surprise was that many foundries were in fact selling foundry-related services, or rather providing customers with services that went far beyond the simple pouring of metal according to the client's specifications. Of the 42 (out of 45) foundries in the area that responded to a questionnaire, 20 provided just-in-time delivery; 29, machining services; 20, welding services; 20, drafting services; and 15, engineering services. Plant visits revealed, moreover, that the firms had begun to cooperate systematically in the provision of complementary services. Some went so far as to bid jointly on jobs; many were enthusiastic about advertising the region as a foundry center. The industry, finally, was attracting a surprising amount of investment. Eight of the firms, or nearly 20 percent, had either been purchased by new owners, sold to management, merged into joint ventures, or started from scratch. All of those, domestic or foreign, who entered the business were foundrymen, and all brought knowledge of the latest technologies (see Pennsylvania Foundrymen's Association 1990).

The strategic audits also uncovered less surprising surprises, such as situations that confirmed widely held views about common problems, but that cast those views in a new light and led to unexpected conclusions regarding their implications for the organization of particular industries. Training is the chief example. It is banal to remark that U.S. workers have not been trained for the tasks that the new competitive conditions require of them. All four project groups observed in their applications to the commonwealth that collective provision of training was a crucial area in which they expected gains from cooperation, and none were disappointed.

What was surprising was the precise relation in each case of training to other problems of workplace organization. In apparel, for example, training was crucial to the flexible use of new garment-routing technologies: unless sewing operators mastered several tasks, there was no point in introducing conveyance systems that allowed managers rapidly to reconfigure the shop for new products. In the tool-and-die industry, shop owners and managers were compensating for skill deficits by programming machines and organizing work themselves. As a result they had little time to manage, and considerations of long-term strategy were sacrificed to the daily struggle for survival. Increased training in this industry is thus literally the precondition to thinking through other changes. As foundries expand into foundry services, to take a final example, they discover that the need for broad training in metalworking overlaps with the needs of the mold makers in plastics and the tool-and-die industry.

Hence cooperation in training soon came to include the idea of cooperation across industry lines, and raised the possibility of collaboration well beyond what had been imagined by each group in isolation.

All of these discoveries, surprising or not, reacted in turn on the orientation of the parties to each project and ultimately on the commonwealth as well. The dynamic firms are gently emarginating the more traditional ones in the Foundrymen's Association, and the association's leaders see the possibilities of leading an expanding sector rather than administering the decline of a moribund one. Nonunion firms are playing an increasing role in the apparel project, particularly in the important committee that has been established to investigate the full range of new technologies appropriate to producers in Lehigh Valley. These changes have just begun, but everyone concerned with the projects remarks on the new and more numerous faces that appear at meetings. This shift of public is itself a strong hint that the institutional identities of these industries are in flux.

The commonwealth's role has changed in at least two ways. First, whatever the outcome of these projects, the commonwealth is now part of the social system within which firms in these industries decide their future. In this sense it has become an unobtrusive participant rather than an intrusive spectator. Information about the economy flows to the commonwealth because the commonwealth has helped create the system by which that information is generated. The better informed the commonwealth is, the better it is, presumably, at making decisions of all kinds regarding the economy.

Second, as the projects learn to coordinate the efforts of their member groups and the latter to define the services they need, the commonwealth has begun to learn how to define and coordinate the provision of public services. To make the extension-service IRCs and the community colleges more responsive to the needs of the MAIN groups means to change the administrative structure of both, and raises the question of their relation to the development bank, the BFP. Just what this will require is still unclear, but even a cursory backward glance at the unruly profusion of economic-development institutions in Pennsylvania shows that something must be done.

Consider the following administrative tangle.[23] At present the Part-

[23] For the BFP's administrative structure and the composition of its budget, see Board of the Ben Franklin Partnership Fund (1988). The following was written before the first meeting of the BFP's Strategic Investment Committee on October 24, 1990, and therefore reflects the views of persons closely associated with and responsible for the BFP before that date. Information brought to light by that committee has changed those views, to the surprise of many, myself included, for the better. I plan to report on these findings on

nership disburses about $25 million a year to fund its various projects. The bulk of the projects are proposed to the BFP's governing board and, upon approval, administered by four technology centers. These are non-profit corporations, governed themselves by boards of officers of universities and private firms. The technology centers may use BFP funds to support technology transfer (including research and development), operation of existing university centers of excellence, development of entrepreneurial skills, training for the workforce, and incubation of small businesses. In addition, the BFP has created forty-five centers of excellence at educational institutions in the commonwealth. These are to acquire expertise in particular technologies selected in consultation with the companies that serve on or can be attracted to their governing boards. The vast majority of the Partnership's projects involve one or a very small number of firms. Although some undoubtedly demand a level of technological sophistication beyond that of the IRCs, many apparently do not. Many consulting services that are or could be offered by the BFP also overlap those currently or potentially offered by the IRCs. There is, therefore, no clear line distinguishing the jurisdiction of one organization from the other. More important, there is no consensus regarding the most effective relation between projects aimed at influencing the behavior of whole sectors and local economies through encouragement of inter-firm cooperation—the associative model—and projects aimed at influencing the behavior of individual firms—the extension-services model.

With the commonwealth's help, ideally the actors will be able to define the public services they require, as well as the balance between services provided to collectives of firms as against services provided to single enterprises. But arriving at such a definition will be hard, and institutionalizing it harder still, in the face of the entrenched opposition of those who find the current situation acceptable. The commonwealth's ability to reshape indirectly the economic actors' identity and change their interests will thus be indispensable to its own reorganization. Coy's promotion from Director of the MAIN project to Director of the Office of Technology Development in the Department of Commerce, with responsibility for, among other things, the BFP, the IRCs, and MAIN, assures that this will be on the agenda.

The project is also likely to have repercussions on local and state politics. In the much longer term, it may even lead to a reordering of national institutions. You do not have to be a Marxist to recognize that economic crises discredit the political classes responsible for averting them, whereas economic successes accredit their political sponsors. It is too early

another occasion in a broader analysis of changes in the commonwealth's internal governance structure and relation to the private sector.

to tell what effects the continued revitalization of Pennsylvania's industry will have on the political composition of the relevant communities and the commonwealth as a whole. But an analogous process in the French town of Annonay and the more strictly comparable experience of MTAP in Springfield, Massachusetts show the new trust relations established through the reorganization of production do tend to create a new group of local notables.[24] What unites the group is the sense that the reorganization of production in the plant depends on collaboration among firms and between them and the private sector.

The first political ramifications of the Springfield project, which began in 1986, are already apparent. The mayor of the city ran successfully for a seat in the U.S. House of Representatives on a platform that promised the extension of the cooperation between the groups of firms, government, and educational institutions. The last president of the Western Massachusetts chapter of the National Tooling and Machine Association (NTMA) was closely associated with the project. He has become the head of the NTMA's model technical school in Rochester, New York. Meanwhile, his place in Springfield has been filled by one of the machine-shop owners who was one of the founding members of MTAP's governing board. The head of the local community college is beginning to make a career as a reformer in the commonwealth's educational system; and the director of MTAP, Robert Forrant, not only sits on the boards of several technical schools, but also participates in the Commonwealth of Massachusetts' certification of particular training facilities as degree-granting institutions. The trade unionist (from an electrician's union) who followed the development of MTAP most closely and encouragingly has become president of the Greater Springfield Central Labor Council.

It may be, of course, that all of these persons took an interest in the project because they are interested in everything that is novel, and that it is their energy and curiosity rather than anything learned by affiliation with MTAP that explains their subsequent progress. But by all accounts they have been influenced by the project. If the latter continues to succeed, it seems reasonable to expect that they will try to extend and apply what they take to be its lessons elsewhere in Massachusetts. The MAIN project could in time have similar results in Pennsylvania.

Finally, the project may have national repercussions as well. Reinvigorating and systematizing a technique of political innovation that cul-

---

[24]On the relation between changes in factory organization and the recomposition of social groups in Annonay, see Ganne (1983, 1989). The discussion of developments in Springfield is based on conversations with Robert Forrant.

minated in the New Deal, the governors of the U.S. states have taken the initiative in experimenting with new policies on their home ground, and then orchestrating national implementation of their successes.[25] The recent reform of the welfare system was elaborated by the National Governors' Association before being presented to and enacted by Congress; a reform of the educational system is being prepared in the same way. The governors have also expressed interest in economic development, especially of the sort undertaken in Pennsylvania: the working group that prepared the governors' deliberations in this area in 1990 discussed an analysis of economic development that draws on the experience of the MAIN project.[26]

There is thus likely to be a public and political airing of the obvious question, What might be done nationally to encourage the creation of new relations of trust in local economies? While it is hard to say what, if anything, will come of such deliberations, it is possible to focus consideration of possible outcomes by indicating both an important continuity and an important discontinuity between efforts to draw out the national implications of the new economic-development localism and New Deal experience. The continuity concerns the constitutional interpretation of the powers of self-governance of groups engaged in productive activities—an issue that has been at the heart of constitutional disputes in the advanced capitalist countries throughout this century. Earlier I referred to a regulatory tradition in which expert administrative boards create a framework of rules for whole industries.[27] But there is a second, sometimes competing, sometimes complimentary New Deal tradition of regulation through economic self-government. This tradition emphasizes the right of groups, in a society formed of groups, to create by mutual agreement and with a minimum of administrative supervision, legal regimes that suit their needs. In this view, associated with the work of Louis Jaffe, if groups acknowledge mutual economic dependence and hence the need for trust in the sense used here, they are constitutionally entitled to devise institutions for policing behaviors that, uncontrolled, might undermine the possibility of collaboration (see Jaffe 1937).

Under the New Deal, the crucial instance of such law making and such groups was collective bargaining between unions and management.

[25] The actual policies of the New Deal depended, of course, on a complex interplay between state-level innovations, the outcome of fights within the federal bureaucracy, and the balance of power between Congress and the executive branch. See generally on these themes, Weir, Orloff, and Skocpol (1988).

[26] For the comprehensive document that framed the governors' discussion of economic development in 1990, see Bosworth (1991).

[27] The classic statement of this position is Landis (1938).

The unions were granted exclusive jurisdiction in the company or plant bargaining units whenever they represented a majority of nonsupervisory employees. The managers were obligated by law to bargain in good faith with labor. Until recent decades these bargaining regimes were analogized to miniature democracies in which the citizens reconciled the differences using collective bargaining contract in place of the constitution that governed disputes in the larger polity (see Stone 1981).

But as originally articulated, the argument for self-governance was not meant to empower particular groups to the exclusion of others. Many of the most persuasive constitutional glosses validating collective bargaining assimilated such contracting to the broader category of what Jaffe called "law-making by private groups." A paradigmatic case, which recalls many of the economic-development activities considered above, would be the creation, with governmental approval, of special tax districts to finance improvement of local infrastructure (see Jaffe 1937).

Seen this way, the MAIN project is simply returning to these first principles by sanctioning the participation of educational institutions, trade associations, and government entities in the kind of bargaining about the conditions of economic development that were in the post–World War II period the privileged reserve of trade unions and employers. Those on the right will see a broadening of such encouragement, especially when disassociated from "preferential" treatment for labor and capital, as a means of enabling entrepreneurs or those who want to become entrepreneurs to realize their ends. This is community capitalism in which the stronger the economic community, the more numerous the capitalists. Indeed, it is noteworthy that a number of leaders of the trade associations participating in the MAIN project and the consultants with whom they are working hold such Ripon Republican views.[28] Those on the left, on the other hand, will stress the government's responsibility to ensure that public sanction of more extensive and effective forms of group cooperation does not reinforce, and if possible reduces, disparities of power between the participants. But what unites left and right is the realization that to secure for the economic actors the legal autonomy needed for the collaborative pursuit of their respective interests, it is necessary to set, or allow *them* to set, rules that redefine and even blur the distinctions between their identities. Were it indeed to flourish in the law, this view would give authoritative expression to the claim that groups engaged in production constantly redefine those they trust by redefining their own self-conceptions and redirecting—not abandoning—their vigilance. In short,

---

[28] See, for example, Krauss (1990). Krauss conducted the survey of foundries referred to above.

the view developed earlier of trust as a local constitution would itself become constitutional doctrine.

The discontinuity between efforts to draw national implications from the Pennsylvania projects and the New Deal experience goes to a paradoxical ambiguity in the very idea of state or local government as, in the famous phrase, laboratories of democracy—the sites where new plans of governance are proven before being extended to the national polity. This notion is self-explanatory as long as it makes sense to think of applying experimental programs in something like their local form to national problems. Obvious cases where such a transfer does make sense are social insurance programs, where coverage can be extended without changing the principles governing eligibility, contributions, and distributions of benefits. Thus the influence of state-level experiments with unemployment insurance on the corresponding New Deal program is the standard illustration of the role of the states as laboratories of democracy.

Although standard, however, the illustration is inaccurate in a way that casts doubt on the tenability of at least the garden-variety version of the laboratories-of-democracy view. The Federal Unemployment Tax Act financed federal unemployment benefits by a 3 percent tax on payrolls. Employers could deduct contributions to state unemployment insurance programs from their federal tax liability up to a limit of 2.7 percent of their payrolls. But the law also provided that monies that firms were excused from paying into state funds because of superior records of employment stability or because of compensation paid to unemployed workers could be included in the sum offset from the federal tax. The intent was to reward employers who organized production to provide stable jobs, and to encourage others to emulate them. But different states rated firms' employment experience and credited payments by firms to the unemployed in vastly different ways. The result was that firms in many states were soon meeting much of their federal tax payroll obligations with state tax credits that would not have been granted in the other states; not surprisingly, where states were most generous in excusing firms from tax liabilities, benefits for the unemployed were the most meager. A general lesson might be that at least in the federal systems that are the most likely to see localities as laboratories of government there can almost never be a direct transfer of local experiences to the national level: the very success of the local model program argues for allowing other localities to choose between some version of it (thus permitting further experimentation) and the national program it inspires. To do otherwise—say through the imposition of uniform national rules—would invite the accusation that the central government was destroying the preconditions of its own self-improvement. But freedom to choose between national and local plans, in combination with the subsequent exercises of local discretion in the elaboration of the program, means that the national system creates a framework within which different local variants proliferate, rather than generalizing a particular local situation.[29]

But what if, as in the case of Pennsylvania, the lesson of the local experiment is precisely that programs of a certain type must *remain* local if they are to function at all? In that case the only sense in which the national government could generalize a local experience would be by creating conditions under which other localities could, *mutatis mutandis,* emulate it. The national program in such instances would thus complement rather than duplicate, and it would extend the laboratory experiment as in the stylized account of the origins of the New Deal.

Besides a permissive legal environment of the kind just described, the obvious national complement to MAIN-type projects would be a system of grants-in-aid to distressed localities. The monies would be spent, at the discretion of the local economic actors, to formulate and begin execution of an adjustment strategy. The transfers could be organized as a national or supranational re-insurance system (in, for example, the European Economic Community): prosperous regions would pay into the fund in the expectation of drawing on it when they themselves needed to restructure. At the least such a system would encourage rationalization of the current hodgepodge of subsidies to distressed areas, sectors, groups of workers, and the unemployed, which in many countries amounts to a badly coordinated, inefficient analogue to such a system. At the most it would bring into the open and encourage public recognition of the economic locales' mutual dependence, giving each a stake in the others' prosperity as an ultimate guarantee of its own, and extending, perhaps, local trust relations beyond local boundaries.[30]

## Some Pessimism of the Intellect

But here the strains of what the Germans call future music are drowning out current concerns. At the outset I said I would conclude by reaffirming the central theme of the essay and cautioning against overly enthusiastic conclusions, and I intend to do just that. I have argued that liberal pessimism about the possibility of creating trust is theoretically untenable, and that the actors' echo of it can be reconciled with the alternative view that trust is a constitutive—hence in principle extensible—feature

---

[29] On unemployment insurance in the United States, see Altmeyer (1963). See also the discussions in Weir, Orloff, and Skocpol (1988).

[30] For a discussion of this kind of reinsurance system, see Sabel (1989).

of social life. The example of Pennsylvania, I think, supports this skepticism about neoclassical claims. But it does not prove that there is even one sure—let alone Pennsylvanian—way actually to extend trust when the actors believe it is in their interest to do so. Many economic-development projects, as everyone knows, are either well-intentioned failures or publicity-minded frauds. The Pennsylvania example is indubitably neither. But it is only a year old, and it would be foolishly premature to celebrate its success. The most that can be said, and I think it is enough, is that it has done well enough to strengthen confidence that something like it will succeed if it does not—and that such success will further loosen the hold of ideas that undermine trust where trust is possible.

Research for this chapter was funded in part by the International Institute for Labor Studies of the International Labor Organization, Geneva. In writing this essay, I profited greatly from discussions with Joshua Cohen, Robert W. Coy, Robert Forrant, Richard Locke, Edward Lorenz, and, as usual, Michael J. Piore. Earlier drafts were discussed at seminars organized by the Nihon Fukushu University, Nagoya, and the TEP Conference, Paris, both in June 1990. I wish to thank participants in both seminars for their helpful comments as well. The usual exculpations apply.

# References

ABOULAFIA, MITCHEL. 1986. *The Mediating Self: Mead, Sartre, and Self-Determination*. New Haven: Yale University Press.

ALTMEYER, ARTHUR J. 1963. "The Development and Status of Social Security in America." In Gerald G. Somers ed., *Labor, Management, and Social Policy*. Madison: University of Wisconsin Press, pp. 123–159.

BOARD OF THE BEN FRANKLIN PARTNERSHIP FUND. 1988. "Challenge Grant Program for Technological Innovation, Five Year Report, March 1, 1983–February 29, 1988." Harrisburg: Pennsylvania Department of Commerce.

BOSWORTH, BRIAN. 1991. "State Strategies for Manufacturing Modernization." Washington, D.C.: National Governors' Association.

BOURDIEU, PIERRE. 1977. *Outline of a Theory of Practice*. Richard Nice, trans. Cambridge, MA: Cambridge University Press.

———. ed., 1990. "A Reply to Some Objections." In *In Other Words*. Matthew Adamson, trans. Stanford: Stanford University Press, pp. 106–110.

BRADACH, JEFFREY L., and ROBERT G. ECCLES. 1989. "Price, Authority, and Trust: From Ideal Types to Plural Forms." *Annual Review of Sociology* 15:97–118.

DAVIDSON, DONALD. 1985. "On the Very Idea of a Conceptual Scheme." Presidential address delivered to the Seventieth Annual Eastern Meeting of the American Philosophical Association, Atlanta, December 28, 1973. Reprinted in John Rajchman and Cornel West eds., *Post-Analytic Philosophy.* New York: Columbia University Press, pp. 129–144.

DEPARTMENTS OF COMMERCE and LABOR and INDUSTRY, COMMONWEALTH OF PENNSYLVANIA. 1989. "Request for Proposal for Industry-Specific Development Plan Initiative." Harrisburg, PA, April 15.

DORE, RONALD. 1983. "Goodwill and the Spirit of Market Capitalism." *British Journal of Sociology* 34(4):459–482.

———. 1986. *Flexible Rigidities: Industrial Policy and Structural Adjustment in the Japanese Economy, 1970–1980.* Stanford: Stanford University Press.

———. 1989. "The Management of Hierarchy." Paper presented to the NOMISMA Conference, Industrial Policy: New Issues and New Models, the Regional Experience. Mimeography. Bologna, November 16–17.

ELSTER, JON. 1983. *Sour Grapes: Studies in the Subversion of Rationality.* Cambridge, MA: Cambridge University Press.

———. 1984. *Ulysses and the Sirens.* Revised Edition. Cambridge, MA: Cambridge University Press.

———. 1990. "Selfishness and Altruism." In Jane J. Mansbridge ed., *Beyond Self-Interest.* Chicago: University of Chicago Press, pp. 44–52.

GANNE, BERNARD. 1983. "Conflit du travail et changement urbain: transformation d'un rapport local." *Sociologie du Travail* 25(2)(April–June):127–146.

———. 1989. "PME et districts industriels: quelques réflexions critiques à propos 'du modèle italien'." *P.M.E., Revue Internationale* 2–3:273–285.

HERBERS, JOHN. 1990. "A Third Wave of Economic Development." *Governing* (June):43–50.

HIRSCHMAN, ALBERT. 1977. *The Passions and the Interests: Political Arguments for Capitalism before its Triumph.* Princeton: Princeton University Press.

HOBSBAWM, ERIC, and TERENCE RANGER. 1983. *The Invention of Tradition.* Cambridge, MA: Cambridge University Press.

JAFFE, LOUIS. 1937. "Law Making by Private Groups." *Harvard Law Review* 51(2)(December):201–253.

KATZENSTEIN, PETER J. 1985. *Small States in World Markets.* Ithaca: Cornell University Press.

KRAUSS, JORDAN P. 1990. "Producing Growth: Infrastructure Improvement, Enterprise Zones and Sound Economic Policy." In Don E. Eberly ed., *Leading Pennsylvania into the 21st Century: Policy Strategies for the Future.* Harrisburg, PA: The Commonwealth Foundation for Public Policy Alternatives, pp. 230–239.

LANDIS, JAMES M. 1938. *The Administrative Process.* New Haven: Yale University Press.

LLOYD, G.I.H. 1913. *The Cutlery Trades.* London: Longmans, Green and Co.

LORENZ, EDWARD H. 1988. "Neither Friends nor Strangers: Informal Networks of Subcontracting in French Industry." In Diego Gambetta ed., *Trust: Making and Breaking Cooperative Relations.* New York: Basil Blackwell, pp. 194–210.

LUKÁCS, GEORG. 1986. *Zur Ontologie des gesellschaftlichen Seins.* Two volumes. Frank Benseles ed. Darmstadt: Luchterhand.

MAUSS, MARCEL. 1967. *The Gift.* Ian Cunnison, trans. New York: W. W. Norton.

NAGEL, THOMAS. 1970. *The Possibility of Altruism.* Oxford: Clarendon Press.

OSBORNE, DAVID. 1988. *Laboratories of Democracy.* Boston: Harvard Business School Press.

PENNSYLVANIA FOUNDRYMEN'S ASSOCIATION. 1990. "Quarterly Report, March 31, 1990 to July 1, 1990, Southwest Pennsylvania Foundry Industry, MAIN Project." April 20, 1990, on file at the Department of Labor and Industry, Commonwealth of Pennsylvania, Harrisburg.

RAVÈYRE, MARIE-FRANÇOISE, and JEAN SAGLIO. 1984. "Les systèmes industriels localisés: éléments pour une analyse sociologique des ensembles de P.M.E. industriels." *Sociologie du Travail* 2:157–177.

RAWLS, JOHN. 1985. "Justice as Fairness: Political not Metaphysical." *Philosophy and Public Affairs* 14(3):223–251.

ROSALDO, RENATO. 1980. *Ilongot Headhunting, 1883–1974: A Study in Society and History.* Stanford: Stanford University Press.

SABEL, CHARLES F. 1989. "Flexible Specialisation and the Re-emergence of Regional Economies." In Paul Hirst and Jonathan Zeitlin eds., *Reversing Industrial Decline?* New York: St. Martin's Press, pp. 17–70.

SAGLIO, JEAN. 1991. "*Industrie locale et stratégie des acteurs: Du Peigne à la plasturgie dans la zone d'Oyonnax.*" Manuscript. Groupe Lyonnais de la Sociologie Industrielle, Lyon.

SEN, AMARTYA K. 1979. "Rational Fools: A Critique of the Behavioral Foundations of Economic Theory." In Henry Harris ed., *Scientific Models and Man.* New York: Oxford University Press, pp. 317–344.

STINCHCOMBE, ARTHUR L. 1985. "Contracts as Hierarchical Documents." In Arthur L. Stinchcombe and Carol A. Heimer eds., *Organization Theory and Project Management.* Oslo: Norwegian University Press, pp. 121–171.

STONE, KATHERINE VAN WEZEL. 1981. "The Post-War Paradigm in American Labor Law." *Yale Law Journal* 90(7)(June):1509–1580.

STREECK, WOLFGANG. 1987. "Industrielle Beziehungen, soziale Ordnung und Beschäftigung: Ein Kommentar." In Egon Matzner, Jan Kriegel, and Allessandro Roncaglia eds., *Über ökonomische und institutionelle Bedingungen erfolgreicher Beschäftiguns- und Arbeitsmarktpolitik.* Berlin: Edition Sigma, pp. 241–246.

TEUBNER, GUENTHER. 1983. "Substantive and Reflexive Elements in Modern Law." *Law and Society Review* 17(2):239–285.

TRIGILIA, CARLO. 1989. "Il distretto industriale di Prato." In Marino Regini and Charles F. Sabel eds., *Strategie di riaggiustamento industriale.* Bologna: Il Mulino, pp. 283–333.

U.S. DEPARTMENT OF COMMERCE, "County Business Patterns." Ann Arbor: Inter-University Consortium for Political and Social Research.

WEIR, MARGARET, ANN SHOLA ORLOFF, and THEDA SKOCPOL, eds. 1988. *The Politics of Social Policy in the United States*. Princeton: Princeton University Press.

WILLIAMS, BERNARD. 1988. "Formal Structures and Social Reality." In Diego Gambetta ed., *Trust: Making and Breaking Cooperative Relations*. New York: Basil Blackwell, pp. 3–13.

ZAHAVI, GERALD. 1983. "Negotiated Loyalty: Welfare Capitalism and the Shoeworkers of Endicott Johnson, 1920–1940." *The Journal of American History* 71(3)(December):602–620.

# 5

# Undoing the Managerial Revolution?
# Needed Research on the Decline
# of Middle Management
# and Internal Labor Markets

## PAUL M. HIRSCH

From William Whyte's *The Organization Man* (1956) through Rosabeth Kanter's *Men and Women of the Corporation* (1977), the portrayal of the large successful American corporation in social sciences and the business press closely followed Doeringer and Piore's (1971) description of an internal labor market (Hirsch 1985). Successful managers at many of the most visible and admired firms entered early, climbed up the rungs of the company job ladder, and played out their careers as "company men," embodying organizational memory and firm-specific skills of particular value to their companies. From 1950 to 1985, this mobility model socialized corporate managers and formed the basis for innovative scholarship delineating such mechanisms as vacancy chains (White 1970), tournaments (Rosenbaum 1979), and selection multipliers (Stewman and Konda 1983). The employment relationship portrayed in internal labor market (ILM) models assumes long-term reciprocal commitments, careers within companies, attractive wages, and job security. With few exceptions, it is seen as a win-win situation for both parties.[1]

Since 1985, this idealized recipe for success has come under vociferous attack from opinion leaders in both academe and the business press. An

[1] Within the "primary" sector, a number of different types of internal labor markets have been specified, by Althauser and Kalleberg (1981), Fligstein and Fernandez (1988), Granovetter (1988), and others. All of them share these core characteristics, however, and are encompassed in the above statement.

increasingly heard economic perspective attacks companies with ILMs for wasteful misappropriations by management (agents) of funds better distributed to their rightful owners (principals). ILM attributes such as slack, previously praised as prudent investments, become pejoratively redefined as "corporate fat." While tolerable during the post-war years when U.S. industry had market power and could afford to act like a "corporate family" paying above-market wages, the realities of global competition and deregulation put an end to such artificial advantages. And the economy is far better off without these wasteful, inefficient props.

This neoclassical "revisionist" view holds that American industry succeeded *in spite of* its attachment to ILMs, not because of them. The proper corrective solution, which it believes came not a moment too soon during the Reagan years, is the downsizing ("rightsizing") of the Fortune 500. This encourages greater reliance on the spot labor market to purchase the services of managers on an as-needed basis, rather than paying high overhead costs to stockpile and hold them in place even when there is no work for them. The same prescription is echoed loudly in today's business press. For example, *Fortune* magazine's cover story of June 17, 1991, lauds "Bureaucracy Busters." Its text (Dumaine 1991) attacked orderly job ladders, with added pictures of Chief Executive Officers placing red X's over, and swinging baseball bats at, their corporations' traditional organization charts. The alternative organization form endorsed is that of continuously changing project teams, staffed by whichever organization members have the skills needed for the moment, who are assigned to participate for (only) as long as their particular mix of skills remains useful.

While empirical reality may lie between these two ideological poles, their conflicting perspectives—on the proper policies and interpretations for structuring labor markets and the employment relationship—are competing head to head in the 1990s for legitimacy and adoption (Hirsch et al. 1987 and Hirsch 1990). Even though dual labor theory's "secondary labor market" descriptively encompasses the neoclassical libertarian free market ideal, it is not normatively espoused by dual labor-oriented theorists, nor is it assumed to be universally preferable to its more people-centered alternatives. At this writing (1992), it is fair to say neither camp has much empirical support: critical data have not been collected and much research remains to be done. Although the ideological momentum of the economic view is presently stronger, the idealization of ILMs and their benefits still underlies the process of determining compensation in large companies,[2] and continues to dominate management

---

[2]The Hay system and its variants provide the most widely used formulas in setting compensation for large-scale organizations. Its fundamental tenet is to key salaries to internal job ladders and considerations of equity in relation to the pay scales of other jobs within the same organization.

education, where textbooks continue espousing early ports of entry with clearly defined job ladders and internal mobility via promotions. The American court system also is caught between the arguments of these two perspectives. In numerous "wrongful termination" suits, this competition takes the form of the plaintiff's claim of an (ILM-like) implicit contract violation versus the defendant's (neoclassical) counterclaim of its right to enforce "employment at will." State laws vary widely in their guidance here. In Arizona, for example, the economic view prevails; in California, juries and judges are treating employment as virtually tenured once a minimum probationary period has been passed.

While the debate flourishes within academe, an incredibly rich social laboratory has emerged, enhancing opportunities to test out, explore, and compare the strengths and weaknesses of these perspectives. Events over the past six years, from major corporate downsizings through redesigning corporate hierarchies (via flattening and "delayering") to (simultaneously) seeking to build teams and increase the (remaining) employees' "buy-in," provide enormous field-based research opportunities to assess and rethink each field's most basic propositions. These opportunities include: 1) reexamining the employment relationship's content and assumptions about mutual definitions, motives, and trust; 2) reexamining the changing cultures and ideologies required by each; and 3) exploring and researching the implications of the new employment situation for defining and modeling upward and downward mobility and, more generally, the sociology of work. The opportunity to interrelate these areas—rather than reduce the study of labor to any of their single, more traditionally narrow components—is necessary, exciting, and overdue.

## The Employment Relationship and Mutual Trust

In sociological terms, the U.S. labor force has exhibited signs of alienation since ILM-like attributes of worklife began their steep decline in the 1980s. Widely publicized downsizings, workforce reductions, and organizational restructurings in primary sector industries such as oil, airlines, electronics, and steel and automobile manufacturing (whose decline began in the 1970s) signaled clear shifts away from the earlier provision of job security and career ladders. Job cuts, starting with blue-collar workers, soon extended up to white-collar and management personnel. As educated baby boomers came on-stream for their anticipated promotions, many found the tournament was canceled.

Not only were there fewer slots for more candidates; the route was further clogged by superiors taking demotions to stay in the company. Additionally, new needs for midlevel managers were now met through short-term contracts with outside suppliers, or through outsourcing for temporary employees. Kelly Services, for instance, now offers companies male accountants just as readily as female secretaries on a daily basis. Temporary employment agencies were one of America's fastest growing industries during this period (Carey and Hazelbaker 1986). A wave of voluntary and forced early retirements further reduced the long career time frame traditionally associated with tenure in ILMs. Some companies even proposed ending their pension plans, based on their projection that few of their current employees would remain with the firm long enough to reach retirement age there.

During this period, the long-term trend of Fortune 500 companies to shrink in the size of the workforce employed accelerated. As companies also shed divisions and reversed movements towards vertical integration, Chandler's (1977) and Williamson's (1975) frameworks asserting the triumph of hierarchies over markets became empirically suspect—a possibility that was anticipated in Perrow's (1981; 1986) critiques of their frameworks. Rather than following the growth-oriented logic of organization theory, these cutbacks were more in line with prescriptions from the neoclassical economic perspective. In keeping with Fama's (1980) powerful metaphor, the firm is increasingly conceived as a "bundle of contracts," none of which requires elaborate headquarters, overhead, staff, hierarchy, slack, or much in the way of organizational memory. These organizational attributes are seen as irrelevant, if not unnecessary and wasteful. Managers are conceived of as interchangeable; specialized skills, if not already available in house, can be purchased from outside at market prices, like any other factor of production.

The weight of this change in employment philosophy was soon felt by white-collar managers. While line and staff managers in ILMs earlier were treated as if they had nothing in common with their ("inferior") blue-collar subordinates, they now inhabit an increasingly similar job world.[3] The paradigm shift that managers experienced was immediate. By 1985, headlines, with long accompanying articles, prominently chronicled these changes in the business press (also making its own contribution to consciousness-raising). These include:

1985: "Job Loyalty: Not the Virtue It Seems." *The New York Times* (March 3)

1986: "More Executives Finding . . . a Limited Future . . . in Traditional Job Ladders." *The Wall Street Journal* (November 14)

---

[3] Dahrendorf (1959) foresaw this over twenty years ago, in his classic *Class and Class Conflict in Industrial Society*.

1987: "Pushed Out at 45—Now What?" *Fortune* (cover story, March 2)

"Growing Small: As Big Firms Continue to Trim Their Staffs, 2-Tier Setup Emerges. 'Outside' Workforce Does Many Former Inside Jobs, Without All the Benefits. Requiem for Paternalism." *The Wall Street Journal* (May 4)

1988: "Caught in the Middle: Six Managers Speak Out on Corporate Life." *Business Week* (cover story, September 12)

1990: "Is Your Company Asking Too Much?" *Fortune* (cover story, March 12)

1990: "White Collar Blues: This Time Layoffs are Hitting Professionals and Young Employees Especially Hard." *The Wall Street Journal* (October 4)

1991: "The New Executive Unemployed." *Fortune* (cover story, April 8)

In academic and public discussions of these changes, the managerial class also soon found itself perceived as the *cause* of its own falling star. Its legitimacy as a highly valued player in the running of the biggest U.S. corporations collapsed almost overnight. Echoing assumptions from agency theory, for example, financier Carl Ichan describes executives as opportunists and self-serving "gardeners," warranting dismissal from the owner's estate. Popular prescriptions (noted earlier) for straightening out the mess they created became "flattening (unneeded) hierarchies" by "delayering" bureaucracies and eliminating the "corporate fat." Appropriately "lean and mean" companies would also discourage or remove "treehuggers"—employees with seniority who often get awards for loyal long service, but who must be unqualified for good outside offers (or else, being "rational," they would have left long ago).

These shifts in employment practice and philosophy have hardly gone unnoticed by American workers and managers. Surveys commissioned and reported by the business press (university-based researchers have not been active in tracking these developments) show consistent drops, at all levels, in employees' trust and confidence in their employment relationships. A 1989 *Time* magazine report (September 11), appropriately entitled "Where Did the Gung-Ho Go," found that 50 percent of American employees thought it "likely they will change jobs within five years." *Fortune*'s conclusion, based on an Opinion Research Corporation survey of 100,000 employees of Fortune 500 companies, was summarized in its cover headline "The Trust Gap" (December 4, 1989). And *Business Week,* in the first major survey report on employee reactions to the shifts under way (August 4, 1986), simply headlined its cover story "The End of Corporate Loyalty."

The actual probabilities of switching (or losing) one's job, or personally experiencing (another) downsizing are lower than the estimates provided by respondents in these polls. As people encounter trouble themselves or see others experiencing trouble in the workplace, prospect theory and other psychological research suggest they will overestimate the extent of danger lying ahead (Einhorn and Hogarth 1985).

If the American workforce feels increasingly cynical, shortchanged, and alienated, what differences does it make? This poses a host of additional empirical questions. If the managerial class is losing its variation of welfare capitalism, which was until recently taken for granted, we should anticipate finding correlates in both the economic and social sides of work and community. Long- and short-term indirect effects may include increases in white-collar crime, more refusals to relocate for one's employer, a rise in interfirm mobility, and more generalized transformations of long-term relationships into short-term transactions.

With perceived risk/reward ratios so redefined, the economist's assumption of opportunistic, self-regarding behavior as universal may increase in its plausibility. If the neoclassical view prevails, for example, we should expect to encounter a much more Hobbesian job world. Embeddedness should decrease. Even if we assume people are, first and foremost, opportunistic and rational, it still *paid off* in an ILM to work cooperatively to contribute to an employer's future value when an employee knew he or she had a clear stake in the outcome. If widespread organizational restructurings discourage cooperative behavior, which then declines (as people act rationally), economic theorists will be confirmed in their belief they were right all along. Sociologists will likely counter that the increase in self-regarding behavior is a self-fulfilling prophecy, that people's tastes are very subject to change, especially when the structure of rewards and incentives is so transformed. As Sabel (p. 104) phrased it, "Absent trust, no one will risk moving first and all will sacrifice gains of cooperation to the [safer] . . . autonomous pursuit of self interest."

How ironic, then, in the midst of conditions mitigating against trust, to find greater cooperation and teamwork widely proclaimed as the new decade's solution to the economic need for raising productivity in the new era of global competition. Along with increasing *dis*incentives to invest in commitments to any one company and equate one's career with mobility on its job ladder, managers are being exhorted to delegate their evaluations to the performance of the ad hoc groups and teams to which they are assigned, and to accept lateral transfers taking them outside their specialties. Although such a suspension of short-term careerist behavior is more characteristic of (and rewarded by) the ILMs it attacks, this doctrine also runs counter to the rational separation of self from organization that is supported by the neoclassical perspective.

In an era of "one minute contracts," with the job ladders and security of ILMs under such strong attack, it seems fanciful seriously to expect a skeptical workforce to place their performance assessments willingly in the hands of unstable teams whose members may turn over before the project is completed. Team results transfer poorly to resumes needing to stress individual accomplishments. In their paper predicting increased resistance by managers to relocating for their companies, Stroh, Reilly, and Brett (1990) quote one respondent whose representative views are instructive:

> Five years ago I started (at this company) with 45 other employees. It cost $30,000 per employee to train us. Today only two of those employees are still with the company. This high rate of turnover and other problems associated with potential takeovers are forcing more employees to say no to company moves. A company no longer protects your job. While you used to be guaranteed that if you performed well you would have a job, now other factors come into play. These factors affect what you will do for the company. [p. 44]

Orientations such as this do not support the belief that one can simultaneously advocate dismantling ILMs and rely on workers and managers to gamble on long-term projects or the performance of transitory teams and workgroups. As Stroh, Reilly, and Brett conclude, "employees will think hard before agreeing to move to a subsidiary that the corporation might decide to sell the next day. Why move to a (team or) division that just might be folded into another, and 50% of the managers folded out?"

## Implications for Sociological Research and Theory

The sociological study of labor markets has close ties to demography and often presents interesting findings about inequality and occupational structures drawn from highly aggregated datasets. Despite its strengths, this approach provides very limited answers to questions raised by the issues and problems highlighted here. These questions require more micro data that enable us to link the jobs and mobility of individuals to the firms and industries in which they are located. In their classic article, "Bringing the Firm Back In: Stratification, Segmentation, and the Organization of Work," Baron and Bielby (1980) critiqued sociology for leaving these gaps wide open. And, in laying the groundwork for the innovative stream of research generated by the vacancy chain concept, White also criticized the field for: 1) ignoring the sequence of jobs and moves made by individuals over the course of a career; 2) failing to consider the impact of downward or upward mobility on the consciousness, thoughts, and emotions of the individuals affected; and 3) neglecting to mount the large surveys of mobility "necessary to establish the actual numbers of moves as well as to permit assessments of their consequences and antecedents in attitudes" (1970:5).

The flags raised by Baron and Bielby and White become all the more pressing if, as suggested here, internal labor markets are in a steep decline. If, indeed, they are, we need to assess whether the management layers being eliminated are an important organizational infrastructure that should be maintained, or whether, as the neoclassical perspective argues, the high value accorded ILMs previously was in error and, when articulated by self-serving agents, takes on the appearance of an ideological hoax.

A far more basic question for the field at this time lies in a) ascertaining whether ILMs are in fact declining, and b) if so, at what rate, and to what degree? With ILMs in place, research on job mobility is able to assume, model, and examine a closed system, largely ignoring much of the noisy action in the external labor markets outside the system. But if, in fact, they are declining, mobility of personnel *across* firms should increase, as much impressionistic evidence suggests has already occurred. *Instead of following orderly sequential patterns, more individuals' career patterns may be becoming stochastic.*

Impeding progress here is the virtual absence of systematic data that could contribute and help clarify the answers to these questions. Underlying official reports of unemployment is a great deal of employee turnover for which there is no information. Missing from the unemployment statistics are: job-switchers who quit and moved to another company (but did not miss a day of employment); people who quit and did not have another position waiting but did not report being unemployed; employees who were fired but quickly found another position; and employees who were fired but did not report it. While unofficial estimates of the number of white-collar managers "laid off" to become out of work since 1985 converge around five million, this number remains hazy because the managers involved would only show up in government statistics if they were counted as "unemployed." Also subject to guesswork (Granovetter 1988) are the related questions of whether job exiters left voluntarily (for advancement) or were forced out, as well as where they went, and whether their salaries rose or fell from their previous level.

Interestingly, the field of compensation consulting has no answer to these questions either. While expert in pricing the dollar amounts each position is worth, companies like Hay and Hewitt Associates do not keep track of the extent of (or reasons for) turnover in any of them. Althauser and Kalleberg's (1981) proposed research agenda for the field emphasized disaggregating national surveys of employment that do not connect employees to their organizations or industry. To develop a systematic database to learn more about job changes and mobility in today's changing labor markets, it is time to develop consortia to undertake the data collection that they (as well as White, Baron and Bielby, and others) have long advocated.

To document shifts under way, in the meantime, a variety of more unobtrusive, less systematic, and/or more qualitative measures can be utilized. For example, classified ads for positions available show a clear trend away from emphasizing job training in company-specific skills and the resulting implied promise of a long-term employment relationship. Which types of positions, and at what level, are being filled from inside instead of outside labor pools? Interviews I have held with human resource executives at large companies suggest far more attention to external labor markets, both to recruit new employees and to preempt or bid against them for the continued services of highly valued employees; until recently, this latter practice was categorically rejected by companies with strong internal labor markets, and with compensation formulas built on the presumption that these employees would wait patiently in line while ascending the firm's job ladder. How widely the practice of bidding against the external market has diffused is an interesting, unanswered question. Recruiters ("headhunters") report being deluged with resumes from managers eager to "jump ship" from large firms that are restructuring, underscoring survey findings of drops in trust, commitment, and loyalty to a single employer. These resources, as well as "outplacement" firms— a growth industry since the 1980s—provide an enormous reservoir of expert observers familiar with the strategies and experience of both downsizing corporations and the managers being sent out for "repackaging." The time is also ripe for a new generation of Melville Daltons (1959), to provide insightful and updated ethnographic knowledge of management practice and culture in companies without ILMs today.

The issues on which these types of generally accessible resources shed further light are, I think, both timely and important. All of these informal information sources suggest a ferment and churning in the labor market that the aggregate demographic/unemployment datasets from which we derive so much information have so far failed to reflect. The aggregate data will continue to mask these types of changes unless the number of blue- and white-collar employees dismissed skyrockets further and these employees do not find jobs waiting.

## Further Implications: An Expanded Working Class?[4]

Although supporting numbers are not precise, it seems clear that recent job loss in the white-collar sector is far higher than historical averages. Flatter organizations, sophisticated information technology, and larger spans of control have also altered the work content of jobs for middle managers. As work loads have increased and job security diminished, this segment of the labor force is showing signs of disillusionment and alienation. Historically, the alienation of middle managers is a novel development, quite possibly analogous to the experience ("deskilling") of the productive workforce during earlier periods of industrialization. This industrial labor class became distinct only as the product was separated from its production, and execution separated from conceptualization. Thus the alienated worker continued to perform on a contractual basis but had no vested interest in the status of the firm, so long as the firm continued to exist and pay wages.

The alienation of the managerial class may be parallel. If managers identified with the firm in part because they saw themselves as distinct from the wage class—that is, if they viewed careers as creating a vested interest in the performance of the firm—and that distinction becomes blurred or disappears, the managerial class begins to look much more like labor. This seems to have already taken place at the lowest levels of management, where first-line supervisors have long identified more with their crew—the wage labor—than with other layers of management, or else experienced the stress of being marginal to both groups but stranded between them.

This alienation, or at least confusion, may move up the levels of the organization. Related to this is the nature of the reduction in levels and manpower. To the extent that the reduction in management is a) proportional across levels, and b) relatively anonymous, its impact on career and opportunity may not be obvious. However, to the extent that this impact is noticed, and perhaps even more important, to the extent that it is personalized in some nontrivial way (the elimination of jobs of friends, relatives, or simply direct supervisors), the implicit contract between the

---

[4]This section is co-written with Tom Vonk.

organization and employee comes under closer scrutiny. Here, the employee may question its continued existence.

Presumably two of the benefits of career stability for the individual are promotional opportunities and job security. The relative importance of the two may, and probably does, vary with factors such as age, gender, and family status. Nevertheless, noticeable shifts in the ILM are likely to influence both factors. Independent of economic effects, changes in the implicit contract also suggest changes in the nature of work.

The nature of the change is not obvious and may depend on firm-level differences or even individual differences; however, one might anticipate that differences will be manifested in shifts in the managerial class. Decreasing promotional opportunities might encourage greater or lesser risk taking, depending on what the remaining managers see as the behavior likely to lead to scarce promotions. Decreases in security would imply a focus on not making mistakes. Lifestyle considerations will affect the extent to which predictable financial rewards (salary plus raises rather than the variable bonuses that are coming to replace them) drive individuals' behaviors and definitions of what is desirable. These all affect the extent to which the remaining managers conceive their careers as rooted in their employing organization or in the marketplace of many possible employers.

Alienation may also influence work relationships independently of, or at least quasi-independently of, the work activity itself. As alienation increases, loyalty shifts to those who share the same experience. That might be horizontal—to other managers stuck in the same boat—or it might be downward in the organization. In either respect, I am less likely than before to equate my interests with those articulated by the levels above me.

White-collar alienation leads to the possibility of a realignment of class identities. If middle managers have served as the link between capitalists and labor, mediating between them and serving as a mobility model for those below, the extent to which job ladders crash has larger societal implications. While managers have not been closely aligned with either group, they often have connections and social ties to both. To the extent that friends and relatives cross social groupings, the potential differences between groups are reduced. As the management class begins to see itself as more like labor and less like capital, the polarization of society may increase. Indeed, that is one interpretation of the rise of coalitions opposing corporate takeovers. While the motivations of management may be very distinct from labor's, the practical overlap of interests in opposing raiders (today's finance capitalists) may serve to realign interests as both groups see historical concerns potentially coopted to pursue more immediate interests.

If, over time, middle managers' performance and organizational commitment become more critical to the success of their employers, the incentive structure will have to be reconfigured once again. There are already signs of some movement in this direction. With more pensions becoming portable and job tenure at any one firm decreasing, salaries and bonus arrangements for valued employees are likely to increase disproportionately. Relatedly, as women and minorities become more indispensable throughout the organizational hierarchy, new benefits—such as more flexible hours and day care—will diffuse and seem far less exceptional. Efforts to restore some of the worker-friendly attributes of the "old" ILM will have to go hand in hand with the unfolding of the more hostile neoclassical economic perspective on managing complex organizations.

Special thanks to Roberto Fernandez, Christopher Jencks, Wayne Kriemelmeyer, Marshall Meyer, Art Stinchcombe, Richard Swedberg, David Tansik, Tom Vonk, and Michael Useem for helpful suggestions in conversations which influenced my thinking on these topics. And to Northwestern University's Newspaper Management Center for generously funding the research from which this paper is drawn.

# References

ALTHAUSER, R. P., and A. KALLEBERG. 1981. "Firms, Occupations, and the Structure of Labor Markets: A Conceptual Analysis." *Sociological Perspectives on Labor Markets* 8:119–149.

BARON, J. N., and W. T. BIELBY. 1980. "Bringing the Firm Back In: Stratification, Segmentation, and the Organization of Work." *American Sociological Review* 45:737–765.

CAREY, M., and K. HAZELBAKER. 1986. "Employment Growth in the Temporary Help Industry." *Monthly Labor Review* (April) 109(4):37–44.

CHANDLER, A. 1977. *The Visible Hand: The Managerial Revolution in American Business.* Cambridge, MA: Harvard University Press.

DAHRENDORF, R. 1959. *Class and Class Conflict in Industrial Society.* Stanford, CA: Stanford University Press.

DALTON, M. 1959. *Men Who Manage.* New York: John Wiley.

DOERINGER, P. B., and M. D. PIORE. 1971. *Internal Labor Markets and Manpower Analysis.* Lexington, MA: Heath Lexington Books.

DUMAINE, B. 1991. "The Bureaucracy Busters." *Fortune* June 17:36–50.

EINHORN, H., and R. M. HOGARTH. 1985. "Ambiguity and Uncertainty in Probabilistic Inference." *Psychological Review* 92:433–461.

FAMA, E. 1980. "Agency Problems and the Theory of the Firm." *Journal of Political Economy* 88:288–307.

FLIGSTEIN, N., and R. FERNANDEZ. 1988. "Worker Power, Firm Power, and the Structure of Labor Markets." *Sociological Quarterly* 29:5–28.

GRANOVETTER, M. 1988. "The Sociological and Economic Approaches to Labor Market Analysis: A Social Structural View." In G. Farkas and P. England eds., *Industries, Firms, and Jobs: Sociological and Economic Approaches.* New York: Plenum Press, pp. 187–216.

HIRSCH, P. M. 1985. "The Study of Industries." In S. Bachrach ed., *Research in the Sociology of Organizations,* Volume 4. Greenwich, CT: JAI Press, pp. 271–309.

HIRSCH, P. M. ed. 1990. "Rational Choice Models for Sociology: Pro and Con." *Rationality and Society* 2:2.

HIRSCH, P. M., S. MICHAELS, and R. FRIEDMAN. 1987. " 'Dirty Hands' versus 'Clean Models': Is Sociology in Danger of Being Seduced by Economics?" *Theory and Society* 16:317–336.

KANTER, R. M. 1977. *Men and Women of the Corporation.* New York: Basic Books.

PERROW, C. 1981. "Markets, Hierarchies and Hegemony: A Critique of Chandler and Williamson." In A. Van de Ven and W. Joyce eds., *Perspectives on Organization Design and Change.* Interscience. New York: Wiley, pp. 371–386 and 403–404.

———. 1986. *Complex Organizations.* Third Edition. New York: Random House.

ROSENBAUM, J. 1979. "Tournament Mobility: Career Patterns in a Corporation." *Administrative Science Quarterly* 24:200–241.

STEWMAN, S., and S. KONDA. 1983. "Careers and Organizational Labor Markets: Demographic Models of Organizational Behavior." *American Journal of Sociology* 88:637–685.

STROH, L. K., A. H. REILLY, and J. M. BRETT. 1990. "New Trends in Relocation." *HRMagazine* 35(February):42–44.

WHITE, H. 1970. *Chains of Opportunity: System Models of Mobility in Organizations.* Cambridge, MA: Harvard University Press.

WHYTE, W. H. 1956. *The Organization Man.* New York: Simon and Schuster.

WILLIAMSON, O. 1975. *Markets and Hierarchies.* New York: Free Press.

# III

# THE SOCIAL CONSTRUCTION OF ECONOMIC INSTITUTIONS: MONEY, MARKETS, AND INDUSTRIES

# 6

# Markets in Production Networks

## HARRISON C. WHITE

In this chapter I consider markets in Western production economies. Each market operates itself and reproduces itself without external planning or tangible auctioneer. It ties to other markets in a production network via the actions of specialized firms. Western economics texts (e.g., Mansfield 1975) conceive of each market separately in terms of price schedules of aggregate supply and demand, for a product specified abstractly, and with little attempt to specify mechanisms. These aggregate schedules are unobservable either by participants or by observers.[1] And what is a product? Each actual market emerged amid some network of other existing production markets. When, in this context, some set of differentiated producers manages to establish itself as a set vis-à-vis an "other side," the amalgam of the outputs from this set becomes established as a product through concurrent cultural and technological rationalizations. Thus, different production economies can have distinct networks of markets for products. These networks are subject, however, to pressures from trade between themselves.[2]

I begin from the individual positions of production firms within mar-

[1] This textbook conception grew up after the fact as a rationalization and easy description of the observed industrial scene: it is no help for understanding how to construct or radically change a production economy. It does not, I claim, account for major observed features of our production economy, such as those I identify subsequently. I am not aware of any empirical verifications of predictive power for this conception as a theoretical model.

[2] Recent surveys of social network analysis, with applications to business, can be found in Wellman and Berkowitz (1988) and Mizruchi and Schwartz (1988).

kets, and of markets within networks. For example, in a market for rubber used to manufacture tires, one firm becomes known for producing lower quality but cheap rubber, another for higher-cost rubber of high durability but low flexibility, and so on.[3] Within each such market, producers become specialized, and so each is committed to that particular market for a substantial period with a view to maximum net return given the constraints of the structure of competition imposed as that market.

The result of such an evolution is that each producer has established a position on a schedule of terms of trade, in some space perceived to have dimensions for producers' volumes and revenues. This schedule is observable from information available to every producer, and it is reproduced by the actions of the "other side" of the market.[4] The producers here do not bounce in and out of a market, as they can in the exchange market of economic theory. Each producer is also a consumer of inputs from other markets, so that each market presupposes a continuing network of flow from and among specific other markets (cf. Leontief 1966). The production economy consists of overlapping networks of procurement and supply among firms in markets (e.g., Corey 1978).

My view contrasts with the pure exchange market of economic theory (Newman 1965), which leads to a General Equilibrium theory, which is very abstract (Arrow and Hahn 1975). Producers' basic concerns are to hold on to distinctive positions in their markets. They adapt their current outputs to fluctuations in the economy by layoffs and the like without necessarily experiencing change in market positions as producers. Discussions of supply and demand recede into the background, along with discussions of money supply and other macroinstitutional features.

Each production economy is the result of an historical evolution in which market and firm and network and product change together, usually slowly, from a base system of markets in long-distance trade and exchange. The process began several times independently in Europe, as putting-out systems evolved in tandem with production networks.[5] Slow

---

[3] It depends in part on incident and chance whether the market boundaries are of all tires, or only auto tires, or only in a region, or whether, for example, a separate market develops, permanently or temporarily, around a technological innovation such as radial tires. It is also possible that rubber markets may not partition according to end use in vehicles at all.

[4] For simplicity, I treat the "other side" as consisting of all *buyers,* but a dual form of the same model holds when the other side consists of *suppliers* of a dominant input, such as skilled labor.

[5] In Florence and other Italian cities of the early Renaissance, cloth production induced networks for putting-out aspects of producing a product, each of which aspects could itself become established as product of separate market (see Lachmann and Peltersen 1988).

change on the surface, however, does not contradict intense social pressures of competition for and to sustain a distinct position in putting-out systems and their modern descendants.

There are levels in network economies, but they are not discrete hierarchical levels. A given firm may have a position in several distinct production markets, and the total size of the firm may exceed each of the markets it is in. Although there must be at least several firms to provide a structure for any given market mechanism, this mechanism usually cannot sustain participation by more than, say, ten or twelve producers. One can, by contrast, distinguish hundreds or more distinct markets in a production network.[6]

Terms of trade establish themselves as an interface within a given market very differently than do terms of trade between markets in a production network. New and surprising features emerge in the latter, where social discipline from competitive pressures is less structured. Efforts at control are as important as strivings for profit. Profit margins themselves depend on network possibilities for autonomy and constraint. Autonomy is possible to the extent that there are alternative market sources and destinations for a given producer, whereas constraint comes via the producer's lack of alternatives within the established network of markets.

I have embodied my view of the single market in an explicit model, the mathematical formulas and equations for which I have supplied in Wellman and Berkowitz (1988). The main conclusion to be drawn is that the average price in a production market is arbitrary; only relative prices among producers matter in the market's construction. The conception behind this model derives from Chamberlin (1933),[7] but its implementation is developed from the mechanism proposed by Spence (1974) for market signaling.

To aid comprehension, I demonstrate how the western production market, in its particular institutional dress, is an example of a very wide-

There were similar developments into *verlager* and *kaufman* systems (Kriedte, Medick, and Shlumbohm 1981), in the hinterlands of medieval networks of German cities, as early entrepreneurs "put out" raw materials and/or tools to cottagers and then "marketed" the resulting product that they collected. The process was elaborated further in subsequent periods and locales (see Bythell 1978).

[6] The assertions of my model, like assertions in microeconomic textbooks, to obtain useable predictions and insights require the imposition of sharp boundaries on blurry situations. For example, producers may string out geographically in such a way that the buyers from one overlap but do not coincide with buyers of even the nearest neighboring producers. Thus the vision of a neat partition among separate markets is an idealization.

[7] His seminal analysis of monopolistic competition and Joan Robinson's parallel discovery (1933), each of which brought into focus the vision offered by Marshall (1891), subsequent microeconomics has proved unable to assimilate.

spread social formation (cf. White 1992). This demonstration leads to a formulation of networks of such markets as special cases of social networks in general. To this end, I draw upon models of control interactions from Burt (1990), which he applies to systems of other actors as well as of markets, in order to explain aggregate volumes and payments in markets from a production network.

## A Production Market

In a given market, each producer firm will have a position that is entirely relative to the positions of other producers in that market, as perceived by and across all of those whom they jointly supply. So this production market can be conceived as an interface, or terms of trade, which comprise a schedule of, say, volume versus price. This is a schedule in which each producer firm has a distinctive position. The schedule will not reproduce itself in successive periods unless the specialized product varieties from the various producer firms come to seem to the other side to be trade-offs of quality for price at observed total volumes. A handful of producers is sufficient to sustain a market, which cannot support the very large number of producers envisioned in the pure competition markets of microeconomics texts.

The key point here is that the terms of trade and the choices of position within this schedule can be estimated by businesspeople using ordinary calculations made from the tangible signals that each can garner in the course of business, together with the practical knowledge of one's own cost-of-production schedule. No auctioneer need be hypothesized; instead, the practical activities generate the signals needed. Thus the concrete market composes itself as some definite mesh between an array of use values and an array of costs; without such meshing it does not reproduce itself in the continuing actions of producers and buyers.

I show that market stability comes from having *unequal* shares held by the different producers, while, sadly for them, cash flows—price less cost—tend to be larger the more nearly equal are the market shares. Increasing returns to scale, which in microeconomics textbooks bar market formation, can be accommodated by the market mechanism as I model it.

## Economic Analysis and Social Structure

I have a disciplinary goal that I now wish to make explicit. It is time to show how economic analysis can and should be fitted in as a special case of more general analysis of social structure.[8] At a time when attempts are being made in many socialist societies to change whole economies to a form closer to those in the West, it is especially useful to be explicit about how capitalist forms can be understood as particular cases of more general social processes.

To promote clearer understanding, the aura of magic that at present surrounds "the market" in discussions within state socialist societies should be dissipated. Here I present component processes of markets as examples of more general processes that have other embodiments more familiar in both socialist and democratic societies. Western economic institutions are robust and effective, but the academic economic analysis of them that is on offer corresponds poorly to their realities, as evidenced by the disdain of business executives for academic microeconomics. The abstract and hypothetical nature of modern microeconomic theory unfortunately contributes to the view of Western economics as magical by inexperienced reformers in the Eastern bloc.

The focus here is how separate actors combine into a joint formation and thus induce a new joint identity. A set of actors can become comparable peers by jostling to join in production on comparable terms. They commit by joining together to pump downstream versions of a common product, which versions are subjected by both themselves and downstream actors to invidious comparison. Children competing in hopscotch or reciting for a teacher, mathematicians in a test for a prize, actors in a play—and manufacturers of recreational aircraft for the U.S. market—are all examples of this basic social formation. The production market is a special case of this social formation, which I term the *interface*.

Material production generally comes from interfaces. Here the receivers are a distinct set, and the context need not be relaxed and social. The hunting or gathering groups described for tribal contexts (Firth 1957; Lee 1979; Rose 1960; Udy 1959) are early realizations that have analogues today in sports teams (Leifer 1989) and in children's games (Fine 1983; Opie and Opie 1969). The basic mechanism does not require or presuppose distinct roles among the producers along with explicit cues and assignments. Rather, a spread on quality is induced by attention of producers to differing preferences by the other side, who can turn off their attention (or more tangible payments for production).

Interfaces do not build from a concern with ecology. In shaping structures of importance, it is control projects that compete, and they only

---

[8] In my opinion, microeconomics began to lose its way around the 1940s when it ceased to be concerned with social phenomenology, as Chamberlin still was, and instead retreated behind the excuse that one can get valid predictions even if one's models make no attempt to be realistic.

peripherally attend to effectiveness of physical work. Social life is about actors' importance within social settings, so these settings cannot be shaped primarily to effective joint operations on physical settings. As Udy (1970) first said explicitly, production in the ordinary sense of practical work is difficult to reconcile with the universal tendencies to elaboration or embedding that come with the ongoing process of social structuring.[9]

Asymmetry underlies all the variations of the commit interface. Embedding is built into the form. On one side, individual flows are being induced amid jockeying for relative position, or niche; on the other side are (possibly disparate) receivers appropriating the aggregate flow. The flow is always from one disaggregate side to the other. The social perceptions that discipline produces come from both sides, but behavioral cues to specific niches are on one side only. Producers are choosing what flows to offer. The interface presupposes and requires unremitting attention to the flows and the interface by the producers.

Underlying this mechanism is a matching of variances. Producers differ by having various combinations of abilities, and so are differentially attractive to receivers. The interface discipline will not continue unless relative recognition of producers can be matched to their range of actual productivity. This matching must emerge and reproduce itself, which happens only when the producer set is arrayed in reward in the same order in which their productions are discriminated. Only if there is variance in abilities across producers, correlated with variance in their receptions, can the interface reproduce itself.

Reference group theory long ago came to the view that it was dispersions among actors in rewards, not averages, that drove any organized system. The classic formulation came from the Stouffer (1948) study of World War II military: anticipation over time was equally as important as dispersion. Recently, Tversky and Kahneman (Kahneman, Slovic, and Tversky 1982), among others (Lindenberg, 1989), have revived this notion. Through the study of production markets, I have come to a clipped version of the same general view: species of interfaces disciplined by quality orderings survive or not according to, and only according to, matchings of variances among the constituent actors.

[9] Udy worked out his argument from an extensive cross-cultural investigation of detailed forms of hunting, gathering, agriculture, craft, manufacturing, and other contexts for work. Succession is one major exemplification of this tension between work and social life. Performance in a work team can be seen as dependent on succession, day by day, to tasks of work. The same issue recurs at larger scopes and periods. Solutions of social equations of balance are what deliver the successors and thereby impinge on technical equations of physical production. Udy's theorem is that the longer and more fully developed the social context of production, the less effective and efficient the work process. Hunting and gathering, he argues, exceeds settled agriculture in efficiency.

This social formation recurs with many scopes and under many institutional guises. I turn now to results from a particular mathematical formulation of the production market, before returning to further discussion of the interface in general.

## Mathematical Formulation of the Production Market

Industrial production markets of this century are exemplars of interfaces. A production market must induce distinctive flows, at the same time as it renders them comparable, from a to-be-determined set of producers and into the hands of an array of buyers becoming accustomed and committed to that market. Valuations can provide a scaffolding for dispersions in social formations that then prove able to reproduce themselves. "Quality" captures the connotations of the invidious transitive order induced to form this mechanism of commitment. This is the market as an interface, which was induced from quality valuation. Valuations need not find their source in the induction and routing of average flows.[10]

The producer firms can be seen as pumps expensively committed to spouting continuing flows of products. The set of pumps acting together forms the market as super pump in interaction with, and with confidence in, provision of an orderly and continuing social setting with buyers. This social process is what induces a definition of product from the common properties of the flows.

Gossip can supply to each producer an estimate of most of the terms achieved by peers. The production market consists, in the observable spread, of terms of trade being achieved by various producers with their distinctive flows. At their simplest, these terms are revenue for volume shipped.[11] For the market to reproduce itself, each producer must continue to see its pair, revenue and volume, as its optimal choice from the menu of observed terms of trade; only this menu is known to be sustainable by the buyers, who themselves are comparison shopping. Terms of trade are a commonly observable shape that cues actors into niches by their own preferences, which yet are agreeable across the interface.

The market mechanism operates through the terms-of-trade schedule. This is an interpolation across revenue and volume pairs observed for the various producers. (For illustration see Figures 3.1, 3.2, and 3.3 in Leifer and White [1988].) The mathematical model identifies each shape of

[10] This is just as the economist Frank Knight long ago intuited (1921).

[11] Leave aside for more detailed modeling the line of related products that any given producer may supply.

schedule that can sustain itself.[12] A schedule can reproduce itself as firms confirm their distinctive choices of volume from the schedule, given their costs, and as buyers confirm their acceptances of the quality judgments that are implicit in the schedule.[13]

The terms of trade must be accepted by the embedding side, which is the arbiter of the competition or relative performance. The ironic implication is that production markets, whether at a micro level or the level of manufacturing firms, generate only the relative sizes of differentiated flows, not the aggregate size of flow. The aggregate size is a byproduct of accident—so that aggregate "demand," so to speak, is also an induced and arbitrary byproduct.[14]

I characterize possible market contexts as a Shepard plane: see Figure 6.1. The abscissa in Figure 6.1 indicates the ratio between, in the numerator, spread $b$ across different firms' products in buyers' valuations, and in the denominator, spread $d$ across the firms in their respective difficulties of producing as measured by costs. This realizes a differentiation of products.

In Figure 6.1, the vertical, ordinate dimension indicates a different sort of spread ratio. The ordinate is a ratio of sensitivities across different volumes of operation. This is a realization of dependence across the commit interface. When the numerator, $a$, is small, the embedding buyers are much more desirous of some initial small flow than of any subsequent increment in flow volume of a particular product. When the denominator, $c$, is large, each producer runs into accelerating costs for larger volumes, and so on.

Each single point in the plane of Figure 6.1 will characterize a family of embedding contexts as matched with a family of decoupled profiles of participation. I claim that all these particular combinations fit into essentially the same outcome in the workings of the market mechanism. Here producing firms are the actors supplying streams of their differentiated products to the buyers who embed the flows into supplies to other markets and/or consumers.

Viable schedules yield comparability to peers in aspects crucial to market members, such as profits for firms and consumer surplus for buyers, as well as comparability as seen by the other side.[15] Comparability can mean being similar, or close together. Comparability also can mean being

---

[12] Equations 9.5 and 9.6 in the mathematical formulation, Chapter 9 in Wellman and Berkowitz, eds. (1988).

[13] Ibid., equations 9.1 and 9.2, respectively. More discussion and empirical illustration is found in the first paper (White 1981).

[14] Ibid., equations 9.14 and 9.15.

[15] Ibid., equation 9.4.

**Figure 6.1   Shepard Plane for an Interface: Market Realization**

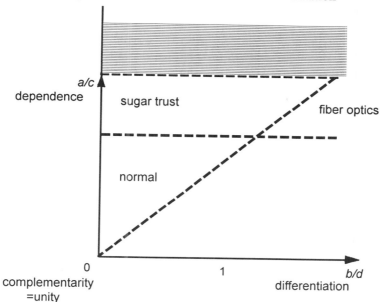

Notes   *a/c* = the ratio of dispersions over volume for evaluation and cost
*b/d* = parallel ratio over quality-index *n*

spread apart in a pattern predictable from known measures of historical circumstance that can affect performance of the mechanism. The upper shaded region in Figure 6.1 indicates packages of embedding and decoupling that cannot sustain a mechanism under any circumstances. In the lower right, at each package point a trade schedule can be sustained but only under some historical starting point, and then the schedule remains vulnerable to manipulation by likely new entrants to the market.

A great deal about the market is not included in the parameters forming the two ratios defining the Shepard plane of Figure 6.1. The number of firms, as well as how they are spaced out on quality, are not specified. Nor is the initial scale in volume and money at which terms of trade started sorting themselves out. The specific model cited for the mechanism incorporates these arbitrary descriptive features as baselines in the predictions of total outcomes, but these features do not affect the structure of outcomes, the viability of the market.[16]

The operation of a production market may continue indefinitely and still be identified by a particular point on the Shepard plane, minor changes

[16] Ibid., inequalities 9.7 and 9.8.

in descriptive features not moving it away. Social mechanisms are, however, unlikely to continue very long without sustaining impact from above, that is, from the embedding situation. Embedding here is to a network of other markets and purchasers. Also there is impact from below, that is, from the decoupling situation, in which distinct actors may merge or come into the arena with new facilities or other change in identity.

Industrial interpretations of different regions in the plane are indicated in Figure 6.1. To the upper right are contexts where typically are found markets in exciting new products, say color television in the early 1960s or fiber optics today. Toward the upper left are the sort of contexts in which trusts have emerged, such as the Havemeyer sugar trust of the early 1900s. Both of these upper regions presuppose increasing returns to scale, which violate microeconomics textbook assumptions.[17] In the lower left are more typical everyday markets. Only their immediate neighborhood in the Shepard plane is of much interest to participants in some of these commit interfaces, since there are massive inertias both in the distribution of context and of members' internal characteristics, which underlie both ratios and make big changes difficult.

The production market mechanism implies gradients in outcomes—that is, gradients in dependent variables of interest to participants. Of particular interest are special cases where, as in the pure competition discussed in textbooks, the gradient disappears. For example, market shares tend to become more equal the closer an interface is to the 45-degree line, and in particular to the point (1,1), in Figure 6.1. Profit rates for all producers tend to go up under these circumstances, but, at the same time, the market becomes more vulnerable to chance unraveling.

Supply and demand are not concepts through which the participants can operate. "Supply equals demand" is a tautology, each time after the fact. It is the variation in quality among producers, and the difficulties each confronts in production, that shape the interface that motivates and sets the terms of trade that reproduce themselves. But actors ordinarily do not conceive and relate to higher-order measures such as variances, and they may tell stories in stylized terms of supply and demand. The production market mechanism, like any other interface, must be realized through forms that are perceived and estimated directly in everyday terms.

## Star Systems

The interface comes in many other varieties and other institutional embodiments. "Star" systems, in entertainment and elsewhere, grow out of

---

[17] But see, for example, Dehez and Dreze 1987 for microeconomic theory of increasing returns.

interfaces where embedding induces perceptions of events that are greatly exaggerated by the view of actors producing them (Faulkner, 1983). Even where the differentiation or dependence is limited, as among starlets in entertainment, there is the same pressure to generate events that are sufficient to embed them with a skewed distribution of fame despite indetectable differences as judged within the interface. These star systems can be seen as analogous to the industrial markets.

Competition in any interface is about the importance of doing slightly better than the peers who, in the larger context, are so very similar to the competitor. What is not necessarily signified explicitly is the strength of the new joint identity created by the competition. Attempts at control by manipulations from within through assembling peers or receivers find hard going. The equivalency in peer positions subjects insiders to very strong discipline by the comparable others. Effective discipline comes from those similarly located, and thus conversant with the information and perspective held by the subject of discipline. Interjections by outsiders also find the interface difficult to disrupt. The interface is robust to both external and internal control projects.

Interfaces, by their construction, do not control for averages and cannot be programmed to yield pre-specified flows. Instead, interfaces build their dynamics around the spread of contributions across the comparable set. The interface is best portrayed as a curvature or response across the variation in members' properties. Mutual attention of peers is directed toward jockeying for relative positions that yield each a distinctive niche.

It follows that the interface can become a control profile that depends on skill in manipulation of multiple rhetorics. Only variances and their ratios constrain the shape and positioning of the interface when it is operating autonomously. But rewards, severally and in aggregate, depend upon means so that there is latent the motivation to try to shift interface in concert. The shift can be accomplished only if the acceptable shapes of profile are retained so that they are envelopes for achieved control profiles. Participants can make systematic use of these facts (see Eccles and White [1986] for how chief executive officers use these interfaces to achieve control over leading subordinates). The managerial perspective on markets is to use markets to enhance control within the firm.[18]

## Network of Market Flows

Struggles for control and autonomy accompany every tie between markets in the network of a production economy. A market's terms-of-trade

---

[18] Tendencies toward this have been observed in large Soviet as well as American firms in a recent comparative field study by Vlachoutsicos and Lawrence (1990).

schedule can be pushed up or down in these struggles, although the relative positions of producers within the market need not change. The preceding model for a single market leaves arbitrary its overall size—in physical volume and in cash flow, characterized by the parameter theta. The model also shows how the sizes of buyer surplus and producer profit, the respective aggregate payoffs for the two sides, follow exactly from the aggregate size, and move in opposite directions with respect to it.

Location in the network determines how much autonomy can accrue to a given market through efforts of producers in it vis-à-vis other markets located upstream, downstream, and parallel—how much choice it has among other markets for supplying and being supplied with components. Burt has systematically developed this thesis and applied it to interrelations among industries in the United States. He shows (1983; 1990; Ch. 4) that profit margins correlate with network measures of autonomy. If entrepreneurs within a market exploit autonomy and constraint, they increase control and can obtain higher average returns.

I propose to link Burt's theory to my model of individual production markets. Two parameters in my model, theta (defined by Equation 9.4) and $k$ (defined by Equation 9.5), provide the bridge:

> The constant $k$ in the equilibrium form of the schedule in Equation 9.5 reflects the fact that there is no authoritative planner and organizer of a production market. Since Walras, economic theorists have postulated a counter-factual auctioneer who receives and collates bids so as to clear the market without recourse to actual actors in actual networks. In reality, the market schedule is an affair of circumstance: It is the trace, in equilibrium form, of jockeying by firms and other actors at risk. The value $k$ reflects in particular the actions of those producers who end up contributing smaller amounts to the market . . .
>
> Aggregation presupposes another feedback loop: The average size of the payment schedule . . . The second 'wild card' constant now appears: the level of theta. The buyers' side can insist on equally good deals from every firm, and so a sharp numerical value is given for theta. But buyers have no mechanisms . . . Like $k$, theta is a value that emerges in equilibrium after a period of backing and filling." [Chapter 9 by White in Wellman and Berkowitz 1988:249, 250, 251]

Profits of producers in different markets can be expected to correlate with the objective measures of autonomy in production networks that constrain action for control by executives. Substitution is the key in the network of markets. It follows that autonomies and constraints suffered by neighbor markets also should be taken into account, since they will indirectly influence the autonomy achievable in a given market. Average price levels, and thus profits, come from ties between whole markets and not from relative positions of producer firms within a market, which can shape only relative prices.

Control struggles in the network of production markets account for the form for any particular market with which I began. No firm (and no market) likes to depend on a single supplier or a single customer firm or market. So it is hard for firms to survive as isolated entities, against the pressures from others' desires to have multiple partners for trade. Firms find it necessary to push into a niche among peers in a market. This profile of evolution in Western production markets, and their network economies, may suggest leads for conversion of Soviet ones (Podolny 1990).

Thus a combination of control struggles combine over time to generate the production market as a social category. The evolution of markets has continued further, as large firms diversify by buying positions in production markets for other products, in an effort to enhance their overall autonomy (Eccles and White 1986). But the production market remains the social construction for what "a product" is, overriding engineering and cultural preconceptions.

An earlier version of this paper was given at the U.S.-Soviet Seminar on the Market as an Economic, Social, Cultural, Political and Psychological Institution, Moscow, USSR, October 29–November 2, 1990.

# References

ARROW, KENNETH J., and FRANK H. HAHN. 1971. *General Competitive Analysis*. San Francisco: Holden-Day.

BURT, RONALD S. 1983. *Corporate Profits and Cooptation: Networks of Market Constraints and Directorate Ties in the American Economy*. New York: Academic Press.

———. 1990. *Structural Holes. The Social Structure of Competition*. New York: Department of Sociology, Columbia University, November.

BYTHELL, DUNCAN. 1978. *The Sweated Trades: Outwork in Nineteenth Century Britain*. London: St. Martin's.

CHAMBERLIN, EDWIN. 1933. *The Theory of Monopolistic Competition*. Cambridge, MA: Harvard University Press.

COREY, E. RAYMOND. 1978. *Procurement Management*. Boston: CBI.

DEHEZ, PIERRE, and JACQUES DREZE. 1987. "Competitive Equilibria with Increasing Returns." Florence: European University Institute, Working Paper No. 86/243.

ECCLES, ROBERT G., and HARRISON C. WHITE. 1986. "Firm and Market Interfaces of Profit Center Control." In Siegwart Lindenberg et al. eds., *Approaches to Social Theory*. New York: Russell Sage Foundation, pp. 203–220.

FAULKNER, ROBERT R. 1983. *Music on Demand: Composers and Careers in the Hollywood Film Industry*. New Brunswick: Transaction Books.

FINE, GARY A. 1983. *Shared Fantasies: Role Play Games as Social Worlds*. Chicago: University of Chicago Press.

FIRTH, RAYMOND. 1957. *We. The Tikopia*. London: Allen & Unwin.

KAHNEMAN, DANIEL, P. SLOVIC, and AMOS TVERSKY, eds. 1982. *Judgment under Uncertainty: Heuristics and Decisions*. Cambridge: Cambridge University Press.

KNIGHT, FRANK. 1921. *Risk, Uncertainty and Profit*. Boston: Houghton Mifflin.

KRIEDTE, PETER, HANS MEDICK, and JURGEN SHLUMBOHM. 1981. *Industrialization before Industrialisation*. Cambridge: Cambridge University Press.

LACHMANN, RICHARD, and STEPHEN PELTERSEN. 1988. "Rationality and Structure in the 'Failed' Capitalism of Renaissance Italy." Memorandum. Department of Sociology, University of Wisconsin-Madison.

LEE, RICHARD B. 1979. *The !Kung San*. Cambridge: Cambridge University Press.

LEIFER, ERIC M. 1989. "Inequality among Equals: Performance Inequalities in League Sports." Manuscript. Department of Sociology, Columbia University.

LEIFER, ERIC M., and HARRISON C. WHITE. 1988. "A Structural Approach to Markets." In Mark Mizruchi and Michael Schwartz eds., *Intercorporate Relations: The Structural Analysis of Business*. Cambridge: Cambridge University Press, pp. 85–107.

LEONTIEF, WASSILY W. 1966. *Input-Output Economics*. New York: Oxford University Press.

LINDENBERG, SIEGWART. 1989. "Choice and Culture: the Behavioral Basis of Cultural Impact on Transactions." In Hans Haferkamp ed., *Social Structure and Culture*. Berlin: DeGruyter, pp. 175–200.

LINDENBERG, SIEGWART, JAMES S. COLEMAN, and STEFAN NOWAK, eds. 1986. *Approaches to Social Theory*. New York: Russell Sage Foundation.

MANSFIELD, EDWIN. 1975. *Microeconomics: Theory and Applications*, 2d ed. New York: Norton.

MARSHALL, ALFRED. 1891. *Principles of Economics*. London.

MIZRUCHI, MARK S. and MICHAEL SCHWARTZ, eds. 1988. *Intercorporate Relations: the Structural Analysis of Business*. Cambridge: Cambridge University Press.

NEWMAN, PETER. 1965. *The Theory of Exchange*. Englewood Cliffs, NJ: Prentice-Hall.

OPIE, PETER, and IONA OPIE. 1969. *Children's Games in Street and Playground: Chasing, Catching, Seeking, Hunting, Racing, Duelling, Exerting, Daring, Guessing, Acting, Pretending*. Oxford: Clarendon Press.

PODOLNY, JOEL. 1990. "A Sociologically Informed View of the Market." Memorandum, Sociology Department, Harvard University.

ROBINSON, JOAN. 1933. *The Economics of Imperfect Competition*. London: Macmillan.

ROSE, F. G. G. 1960. *Classification of Kin, Age Structure, and Marriage amongst the Groote Eylandt Aborigines*. Berlin: Akademie-Verlag.

SPENCE, A. MICHAEL. 1974. *Market Signalling*. Cambridge, MA: Harvard University Press.

STOUFFER, SAMUEL A. 1948. *The American Soldier*. Princeton, NJ: Princeton University Press.

UDY, STANLEY. 1959. *Organization of Work*. Human Relations Area Files.

———. 1970. *Work in Traditional and Modern Society*. Englewood Cliffs, NJ: Prentice-Hall.

VLACHOUTSICOS, C., and PAUL LAWRENCE. 1990. "What We Don't Know about Soviet Management." *Harvard Business Review* (November–December):50–66.

WELLMAN, BARRY, and STEVEN D. BERKOWITZ, eds. 1988. *Social Structures: A Network Approach*. New York: Cambridge University Press.

———. 1981. "Where do Markets Come From?" *American Journal of Sociology* 87:517–547.

WHITE, HARRISON C. 1988. "Varieties of Markets." In Barry Wellman and Steven D. Berkowitz eds., *Social Structures: A Network Approach*. New York: Cambridge University Press.

———. 1992. *Identity and Control*. Princeton: Princeton University Press.

# 7

# Auctions: From Walras to the Real World

## CHARLES W. SMITH

For over ten years, I have been engaged in a study of real-world auctions, including fish, cattle, tobacco, stock, bond, real estate, fine art, antique furniture, gun, horse, book, manuscript, and automobile auctions, to name just a representative sample (C. Smith 1989). During these ten years I have not only collected a tremendous amount of data and information, but also deepened my understanding of a number of social practices. Perhaps most importantly, I was forced to reexamine the very conception of an auction. This has necessitated not only generating a new classification system for grouping auctions, but also fashioning a conception of auctions that is fundamentally different from the one promulgated by most economists.

Since I firmly believe that nearly all data lends itself to multiple interpretations, I shall not categorically assert that the neoclassical model is wrong—but I will suggest that it has little to do with real-world auctions. What makes this situation particularly troubling is the fact that real-world auctions reveal a great deal about various facets of socioeconomic processes and behaviors that the neoclassical model obfuscates. More specifically, real auctions—rather than being ideal examples of the individual, rational, maximizing behavior of the neoclassical paradigm (Becker 1976)—highlight the extent to which most "economic" transactions are both embedded in complex social situations and subject to collective, nonrational, expressive factors.

Although there are a number of different ways to proceed, because so much of my argument is based on what actually occurs in real auctions,

176

I first give the reader a sense of what happens at various auctions by presenting some auction vignettes drawn from my fieldwork. I then attempt to extrapolate a number of general social features bearing on various auction practices. In this context, I am particularly interested in examining how fairness and participation are defined and how they function within real auctions as compared with the theoretical auctions of economics. Before presenting these accounts, however, a few general comments on auctions are in order.

As just suggested and as will become clearer later, the apparently simple act of specifying what constitutes an auction in the real world is not that simple. While there is a general consensus of what constitutes a theoretical auction for most economists (V. Smith 1987), there is considerably more ambiguity among those engaged in ethnographic research.[1] Fortunately, all is not chaos. There is, for example, fairly widespread acceptance of Cassady's (1967) taxonomy of fixed-price transactions, private treaty transactions, and auctions, where auctions are distinct from fixed-price and private-treaty transactions insofar as auction prices are typically determined in a competitive and public manner. While both the fixed-price and private-treaty forms of pricing and exchange allow for price adjustments in response to market conditions, they lack the public competition and social interaction characteristic of most auctions.

While all auctions exhibit this public competitive character, there are significant differences among auctions in the way bids are actually made and accepted. Auction bidding can be categorized in terms of two major features: 1) the form in which bids are made, and 2) the sequence rules for bidding. More specifically, bids may be made in written, visual, or oral form. In each case, such bids may be made privately[2] or publicly. Sequencing, in turn, tends to be governed either by a principle of bid increases or bid decreases; there are also auctions, however, where bids are made simultaneously. Taken together, these variables generate a number of different types. The most commonly used and discussed are:

---

[1] Cassady's *Auctions and Auctioneers* (1967) and my *Auctions: The Social Construction of Value* (1989) are the only two books of which I am aware that attempt to give a general overview of real world auctions. There do exist, however, a number of ethnographic pieces, including three unpublished Ph.D. theses: Roger G. Branch, *The Structure of the Tobacco Auction: A Sociological Analysis* (1970); Robert E. Clark, *On the Block: An Ethnography of Auctions* (1973); and George Albert Boeck, Jr., *The Market Report: A Folklife Ethnography of a Texas Livestock Auction* (1983). Another unpublished thesis, Susan Gray's *Power in the Auction Setting* (1976), though based on participant observation, is much more focused in its concern and significantly less rich ethnographically. I have included a number of other articles in the Reference section.

[2] Although the maker of a bid may be able to retain his or her privacy, the bid itself is public, maintaining the public character of the auction process.

1. *English auctions,* where bids are made openly in ascending order with the highest bidder winning;

2. *Dutch auctions,* where bids are made openly in descending order with the first—and usually only—bid winning;

3. *Japanese auctions* (less common), where simultaneous bids are made openly and the auctioneer pulls the highest bids he hears from the bidders;

4. *Sealed-bid auctions,* where bidders submit written bids that are opened at one time with the highest bidder winning; and

5. *Second-price auctions,* which are a variation on number 4, but where the highest bidder wins at the price bid by the second highest bidder.

While there exists a number of other types of auctions (C. Smith 1989),[3] most concrete auctions can be categorized in terms of one of the major types just noted.

Real auctions also differ in the types of goods they allot, the multiples of goods traded, and the rules governing access for both buyers and sellers. Goods commonly auctioned include agricultural products, economic instruments, old and used items, and other goods where value is ambiguous. While these variables generate literally scores of different types of auctions, most can be categorized either as exchange/commodity auctions, dealer/collector auctions, or one-of-a-kind/sale auctions (C. Smith 1989).

While real auctions of various types have existed for quite some time— Cassady notes that Herodotus refers to auctions of potential wives in Babylonia in 500 B.C., and that Roman soldiers auctioned war booty— auctions are significantly more common in modern market economies than in more traditional societies. This fact would seem to support some

---

[3] One of the most interesting of these other types is the *English Knockout* used by dealers to auction goods among themselves that they have bought as part of a buying ring when there is a feeling that some of the dealers may be attempting to catch a free ride (C. Smith 1989:70–72). Each member of the ring is allowed to make a single bid that is submitted in writing without the others seeing it. All the bids are then opened and the highest bid wins; the way the difference between the price paid in the first auction and this high bid is divided, however, is much more complex than in the more commonly used *Round Robin Knockouts,* where the surplus is divided among the members of the ring. In an English Knockout, the lowest bidder drops out first, receiving the difference between the price paid for the item in the first auction and his low bid, divided by the number of pool members still in, which in the case of the lowest bidder would be all the members. The next highest bidder is paid off in a similar manner, with the cost being adjusted to make up for the money paid to pool members who have dropped out, until only the highest bidder is left.

of the basic assumptions built into the economic auction model regarding individual preferences, rationality of actors, and noncollusion. In point of fact, however, while clearly part of the modern world, real auctions seldom reflect these characteristics. This has not impeded most economists, who have been content to examine the theoretical implications of their various theoretical models, including the equivalency of various forms. Moreover, the assumptions regarding individual preferences, self-interest and rationality hold whether one attributes to the auctioneer independent status as in Walras's famous "auctioneer tatônnement" idea [4] or prefers the more popular game theoretic approach influenced by Vickrey's (1961) seminal piece. [5]

Although the different theoretical models used by economists display certain surface similarities with real auctions, they fail to grasp their essential character. As I attempt to show, where participants in real auctions are generally uncertain as to what things are worth, most economists assume that auction participants have predetermined preferences and act rationally. In this respect, the economists follow not only in the neoclassical tradition and the assumption's of Walras's "tatônnement," but also in that of Vickrey (1961). As the stories that follow reveal, however, the economists do not reflect what actually goes on in real auctions.

### Four Auction Stories

STORY 1.   The first story is about an auction that occurred over fifty years ago, run by the father of Tom Caldwell, [6] who himself runs the leading thoroughbred auction company in the country.

One day Tom's father received a call from a judge he knew. The judge had been presiding over a divorce case involving one of the richest men in town, who was married to a woman of considerable wealth in her own right. They had been married for over forty years and were in their seventies. Since both wanted the divorce and there were no children at

---

[4] For an excellent discussion of the Walras tatônnement, see F. Hahn (1987).

[5] In both cases, the auction, or in the case of Walras's tatônnement, the auctioneer's action, is conceived as the means for revealing equilibrium through a step-by-step process. In Walras's view, the auctioneer is central in this process. In Vickrey's model, participants react directly to each other. In this context, I should note that nearly all laboratory empirical research by economists has adopted the latter paradigm. For an excellent recent review of these materials see Vernon L. Smith (1987).

[6] Tom Caldwell runs one of the, if not *the*, premier auction companies specializing in livestock in the world. He is perhaps most famous, however, as the chief auctioneer of the Keeneland Thoroughbred horse sales.

home, the divorce proceedings moved ahead quite easily until it came to the division of the joint property. It had been agreed to divide the property evenly, but all attempts to work out an equitable division had failed. The judge brought in a range of experts to value their various and sundry possessions, but sooner or later both husband and wife refused to accept the evaluations offered by the experts. The husband and wife felt that only they knew the true value of what they owned and they couldn't agree. The judge couldn't even get them to indicate what they thought most things were worth.

The judge proposed that Tom's father hold a two-person auction at which he would auction off everything they jointly owned, and when it was over they could settle up the difference. The idea was that the husband and wife would bid against each other on everything, and when it was over the cash would be divided to ensure that each received equal shares. Everyone agreed to this plan. The next week, after going through all the items, grouping them, and making initial evaluations as he would have in a normal sale, Tom's father set up his stand in the courtroom and proceeded to auction off their joint property. It took close to three full days. Both husband and wife seemed satisfied, despite the fact that the prices set for most everything were, in Tom's father's words, "bizarre." Expensive silver went for nothing, whereas pieces of junk went for thousands of dollars.[7]

It might be argued that the participants are not relying on a communal judgment. In the auction described, they are acting as individuals. This is the argument that auctions really are made up of individuals seeking their own self-interests. This example further shows how misleading that model can be. Neither the husband nor wife were interested in simply getting what they wanted. They were equally, if not more, interested in making sure that the other paid for what he or she wanted. More specifically, what this auction did was to reveal their collective judgment of the value of these items to the two of them. In the case of some items, in fact, one or the other drove the price up even though they had no interest in the item. They did so knowing that the other really wanted it. In other cases, items went for a tenth of what they were worth. What is

[7] I might just note here that the similarity between auctions and juries runs deeper than might initially appear. In both cases there is the sense that a properly constituted group has the ability to establish communal guidelines. Here, as in many other cases, an auction is used to establish fair prices when other, more-established means for assigning value prove unacceptable. What is of specific interest in this particular case and what makes it noteworthy is the fact that the "normal" way of making such decisions has somehow been turned upside down. This gives us a unique, if not better, perspective on the whole process, much as turning over an object at an auction can prove informative.

important to realize about this process is that, while it was clearly influenced by the preference of the parties involved, the prices reached in no way reflect these preferences in any logical way. The prices rather reflected the rather complex joint values of the items in question. In short, the example is noteworthy because the prices are clearly determined by their collective evaluation, which is not a simple composite of their individual evaluations, but a unique product of their respective evaluations, influenced by the evaluation of the other. Though this language may appear unnecessarily complex, it is meant to underscore the fact that the joint evaluation is not an aggregate phenomenon but a product of interaction.

STORY 2.   The second story concerns two auctions I attended a few years ago within the space of a few blocks and a few hours of each other. One auction was an estate jewelry auction located in a hotel suite in upper Manhattan attended by approximately twelve buyers, all but one of whom were dealers who knew each other quite well. The other was an auction from the estate of Rock Hudson, the actor, and was held at Doyle's to a standing-room-only crowd of over a hundred people, most of whom seemed to know no one except perhaps the other person they had come with.

In the jewelry auction, 117 lots were sold in a period of approximately 90 minutes. Prices ranged from $1,000 to $10,000 per lot. The average number of bids per item was 1.2. There was continual chatter among the buyers, most of which took the form of such comments as "Thanks, you can have the next one." "That looks like the piece you got last week." From the auctioneer, "Hey come on now, who is going to take this?" On a number of occasions more than one buyer indicated an interest in a particular piece. In nearly all cases, however, what could be described as a generally accepted hierarchy exerted itself, with the dominant player's bid taking precedent, or with the dominant player quite explicitly announcing his or her willingness to forgo a particular piece.

In contrast, at the Doyle's auction during the two hours I was present, 55 lots were sold for between $100 and many thousands. There were multiple bids—15 to 20—on most every item. The most excitement, however, was over a simple wooden footstool that Elizabeth Taylor had left for Hudson after using his apartment for a week, which was sold for $1,200 after heated bidding among four bidders. The stool had been put together by the janitor in the building from a single $1 \times 8$ six-foot piece of ordinary pine in approximately 30 minutes. When the auctioneer finally said "Sold," the crowd burst into applause that lasted for a full minute.

STORY 3.   The third story covers two auctions, a year apart, that occurred at the Select Yearling sale at Keeneland in Lexington, Kentucky. In 1985, the all-time record for a thoroughbred yearling was set at the Keeneland sale in July: $13,100,000 for one horse, which was close to five million dollars higher than the high of the previous year, and three million higher than the previous record set two years earlier. What had caused this enormous jump? The answer is something that economists would label irrational, namely, a head-to-head confrontation between two major buyers: Robert Sangster, a self-made English multimillionaire whose fortune was based on bookmaking parlors, and Sheik Maktoum of Dubai.

The dynamics governing this confrontation are not open to direct observation, but anyone with some knowledge of the Arab/English relationships regarding thoroughbred racing at the time has little difficulty in imagining what thoughts raced through their respective heads. Sangster won in 1985. The next year, the excitement in the room became intense as the bid passed $3,000,000 for a Northern Dancer colt and the crowd realized that Sangster and Maktoum were at it again. At $3,500,000, however, Sangster moved from the back of the auditorium to sit beside Maktoum. The horse was sold at $3,600,000 to the partnership of Maktoum and Sangster. No yearling, incidently, has sold for over $3,700,000 since.

STORY 4.   After more than a year of observing various auctions of repossessed automobiles, I became convinced that most cars went for less than they could be sold for privately.[8] This was true both of marshal and bank sales.[9] I began to ask various insiders why. The response of one major garage/towing operator connected to a number of city marshals was very revealing.

> Sure, the city would probably end up with 10 to 15 percent more if the cars were sold one on one. [By private treaty rather than by auction.] But

[8] Most automobiles are auctioned at regularly scheduled auctions in which from 20 to 100 cars will be auctioned in a given session that can run from thirty minutes to a few hours. It is only the very rare automobile, such as John Lennon's "psychedelic" Rolls Royce (C. Smith 1989:25, 97, 201) that is sold individually.

[9] Nearly all automobile auctions, like other auctions, are conducted by a licensed auctioneer. The distinction between bank and marshal auctions reflects the two major "sellers" of used automobiles in auctions: banks, which sell repossessed cars and marshals who sell cars confiscated for unpaid tickets and abandoned cars. Automobile dealers and private sellers also regularly sell cars through auctions. In any given auction on a given day, cars from all of these sources may be sold. Most regular automobile auctions, however, tend to sell cars put up for sale either by banks or marshals, hence the common habit of describing automobile auctions in this way.

you couldn't do it. There'd be too many problems. There are a lot of regulars here. If I sold a car to one guy, another guy might come in the next day and say "Hey, I hear you've got an 1983 red caddie." I'd answer "No more. Vinnie bought it yesterday." Right away he would start to bitch. "What did you sell it to him for?" "A grand." "A grand?" he'd answer, "Hell, I would have given you twelve hundred easy. You and Vinnie must be having a thing or something."

It is just not worth it. The next thing, someone from downtown would be calling to find out why there was monkey business going on and why I sold a car for less than it was worth.

A response from an auctioneer who handles bank repossessions was quite similar:

The banks could probably get more money for their cars if they sold them privately through a dealer, but then they would be exposing themselves to all sorts of trouble. Here they pick up a year-old buick with an outstanding loan of seven thousand bucks. The blue-book value on the car is eleven thousand, but that is a retail price. There is no way that a dealer will give more than eight-and-a-half grand for that car. At auction it may bring only seven-and-a-half. If the bank takes the eight-and-a-half, however, the guy who they took the car from will start to bitch that the bank did him out of two-and-a-half grand because the blue-book value of the car is eleven-thousand dollars. If he takes the bank to court, they may have a hell of a time convincing the judge that they really got the best price, especially if they have regular dealing with this dealer. If they auction it, they have no problems. They simply tell the judge that they put the car up for auction with a recognized auctioneer who advertized the auction and that is the price that the car brought.

## Discussion: Fairness and Participation

These stories are rich in detail and lend themselves to a range of interpretations. I could tell an equal number of similar stories drawn from a variety of other types of auctions. I think, however, these are sufficient to support the following propositions—namely that, in contrast to the neoclassical paradigm:

1. buyers in most auctions do not have anything like clearly defined preferences;
2. in most cases, in fact, price is quite secondary to allocation—put differently, price is more often the result of allocative decisions rather than vice versa;

3. in most auctions there is an explicit interest in establishing what will be considered a legitimate price, where the notion of legitimacy is tied to the consensual/social character of the auction;

4. in pursuit of this legitimacy, auctions differ significantly in the manner in which collusion, signaling, and other strategies are accepted and built into the auction—though all are a part of most auctions;

5. participants in most auctions have clearly defined roles that endow them with both specific rights and specific responsibilities;

6. auctions tend to be highly emotional processes with instrumental rationality at best secondary—what rationality there is tends to be due to structural factors built into the auction, and finally,

7. real-world auctions, rather than revealing how competitive individual preferences are resolved through self-interested market behavior, underscore the consensual and even cooperative character of most economic exchange. More specifically, they highlight the need for communal legitimation of both price and allocation. They do this by revealing how price and allocation are socially determined in situations of uncertainty. Real-world auctions are nearly always more concerned with establishing consensual definitions of the situation than with the particular transactions.

In summary, auctions are not so much a paradigm for the exchange of material goods among rational, knowing, self-interested actors as they are for a collective, highly emotional, groping process of assigning values and attributes to material goods.[10]

It is not my intention to deny the value of the neoclassical model in modeling various restricted situations, some of which may actually approximate certain real-world auctions such as those of oil leases. My intention is rather to suggest that real-world auctions raise a number of questions, which deserve attention, about economic transactions. This is clearly the case with what could be considered the most simple question: Who deserves to acquire the item being auctioned?

In the dominant economic paradigm, the item should go to the person who bids the highest amount. In most cases, it is further assumed that the various participants enter the auction with defined preferences. In most real-world auctions, however, we discover that determining who

---

[10] While no economists that I am aware of have embraced the seven points just listed, a good number are aware of various anomalies inherent in the neoclassical paradigm. See for example Hirschman (1985), Sen (1977), and Thurow (1983). Others (Simon 1957, 1972; Williamson 1975) have offered different but similar critiques.

is seen as entitled to a particular object is considerably more complex. The fact that a given person ends up bidding the highest price is a result of an allocative process of which the actual bidding is only a small part. Moreover, this allocative process is usually governed by collective decisions that are highly sensitive to the various social positions of the participants.

The emphasis of allocation raises a number of interesting questions and puts a number of issues in a different light. This is especially the case with fairness and access, earlier referred to as participation.

Auctions are widely seen as mechanisms for generating a "fair" price. The price is considered fair in most economic models because it is the Pareto optimal, that is, it allocates the item to the buyer who values it most highly. No one is able to get a thing for less than it is worth in dollars to someone else. What the above stories reveal, however—in this respect the stories told are quite representative of auctions in general—is that buyers seldom have such pre-existing preferences. They may have hunches and ideas regarding what they think an item will sell for, but seldom do they have a firmly determined evaluation. This is because normally any such evaluation is likely to be meaningless.

In most commodity auctions, the wholesale buyers do not concern themselves with the price paid per se. They are only concerned with the difference between the price paid and the price for which they can resell the goods. They can resell the goods for a "normal, commonly accepted" markup. The only thing that need concern them is that they pay no more than their competitors. Since this is the concern of all the wholesale buyers, they have a collective interest of ensuring that everyone pays the same price for the same goods. This is what commodity/exchange auctions are structured to do.[11] As such, the participants in these auctions tend to accept the last price as a fair indicator of the next price. When there are regular and frequent auctions—which is often the case in commodity auctions, be the commodities agricultural goods or financial instruments—there is a sense in which the price is "known," and, therefore, it is often not an issue of disagreement.

The fairness question in exchange auctions is, in fact, seldom framed in terms of price. The fairness issue has rather to do with allocation: Who will get what? This, in turn, is not decided in terms of individual

---

[11] It can be legitimately argued that the situation described here appears to be consistent with what economists would predict in situations of "perfect competition." In the perfect competition model, however, the particular demands of a single buyer are irrelevant to the common price. Buyers can take as much or as little as they want at the given price specifically because each individual buyer is irrelevant to the overall supply/demand situation. This is clearly not the case in most commodity auctions.

preferences, but in terms of particular positions within the auction community. The specific dynamics vary from auction to auction.

Tobacco buyers—generally the large cigarette companies—have their own individual relationships with the various tobacco warehouses from whom they buy. Each buyer is "entitled" to a different percentage of daily sales from the different warehouse owners based on the nature of that particular relationship (C. Smith 1989:42–44). In fish auctions, on the other hand, different buyers have different rights in times of scarcity based on their responsibilities in times of surplus. This is not to deny that such privileges cannot be challenged by others; they do so by bidding more. In nearly all cases, however, when such a challenge is offered, it is recognized and responded to for what it is. The challengers are likely to be asked directly whether they simply need more for a specific reason or whether they want more as a general rule. If it is the former, a side deal will often be made. If it is the latter, then a real confrontation may occur. Moreover, other players will offer advice, encouragement, and criticism to both parties. What is of particular interest is the fact that such comments seldom have anything to do with the quality of, or market for, the goods in question. They nearly always deal rather with the social positions of the participants.

In most commodity/exchange auctions social rank entails both rights and responsibilities. Those with a high ranking may be entitled to larger shares when supplies are tight, but they are also expected to absorb surpluses when they exist. Given that items in commodity/exchange auctions are often sold to all at the same price, it is the willingness to accept more than one wants that entitles specific buyers to a larger share in times of scarcity.

Social rank is also significant in allocating goods in collectible/dealer auctions, but there are differences in the way social rank is determined. While the equitable distribution of goods tends to be the most important task of most commodity auctions, maintaining a definitional consensus among insiders is the prime objective of most collectible/dealer auctions. As there are significant status differences among exchange members, so there are significant differences among collectors and dealers since they are not equally important in maintaining and modifying the consensus. Where the key differences in most commodity auctions are the resources and willingness to absorb goods, the key differences among dealers and collectors are reputation and networks.

Although it is impossible for an outsider to disrupt the established hierarchies of most exchange auctions—they simply are not allowed to participate—outsiders can disrupt the hierarchy of most collectible/dealer auctions. To do so, however, they must be willing to pay more than the object is worth according to the insiders. While this price may be more than the insiders are willing to pay, it may still be a good price compared to what the buyer would have to pay in a shop. On the other hand, dealers have been known to run prices up to "stick" outsiders who refuse to show them the respect they believe they deserve. This is most commonly the case in auctions that are formally open but normally restricted to dealers such as various jewelry auctions. Although it is difficult to predict when dealers are apt to turn on a private buyer, it is most likely to occur when a private buyer challenges the professionals either by buying too much or acting as if he knows more than the professionals. Most dealers consider it legitimate for private buyers to purchase items they want for themselves at prices slightly more than the dealer is willing to pay. They are not willing, however, for an outsider to attempt to build a collection on their expertise by simply watching them and then bidding slightly more.

It should be noted that in collectible auctions, there seldom exist either the automatic resale of goods or the continuity of the auction process itself that characterize most commodity auctions. Price, consequently, is more uncertain. Value, however, is again a collective, not an individual judgment. Moreover, since the items that are being auctioned are by definition particulars belonging to various categories of collectibles, the price is seen as having an impact on other items. The price of fish today has relatively little relationship to the price of fish sold last year or next year, since it is not exchangeable. A piece of Depression glass sold today has a direct impact on all Depression glass. As a consequence, dealers and collectors owning significant amounts of Depression glass have an interest in all Depression glass sales.

There are a number of exceptions to the general impact principle described above. A particular item may be sold for considerably more or less than the expected price if it is being purchased for a particular buyer or if it is seen as somehow unique. In such situations the item is, in effect, reclassified. What is again of importance here is that such decisions are not only nearly always collective, but that the collective is a *recognized* collective. Exceptions that do not fall under this rubric are the true exceptions and are quite rare.

Although rules governing participation and fairness apply to all in collectible/dealer auctions, what is seen as fair for some is not fair for others. This is a highly complex issue that involves attitudes toward reserves, pools, and buy-backs. To sum up a lot of complicated practices, professional buyers are normally "allowed" to do a number of things to set a limit on prices, provided they also are willing to provide a price base. Professionals and auctioneers do not expect a lay buyer to step in and buy an item at a particular price simply because he or she bought a similar item at a slightly higher price the week before; but they do expect a professional to do so. It is because the professional has such a responsibility that he also has certain rights.

It is primarily in what I have called the one-of-a-kind/sales auction, where buyers function more as individuals, that allocation appears to be determined primarily by who is willing to pay more. It is also primarily in such auctions that what is considered a fair price is the price bid. This clearly seemed to be so in the Sangster/Maktoum case of the third story noted earlier. On the other hand, such a price tends to have little impact on other prices since, by definition, the item sold is considered unique. It is equally meaningless to talk of the economic value of the item to the new owner, since economic value is seldom the dominant issue. Most one-of-a-kind items have no value outside of the auction room, insofar as there is no reasonable way to determine the value without the auction. The items auctioned, such as artistic masterpieces, cultural icons, and rare manuscripts, often cannot be used for anything except to be "valued." Even when they can be used, as is the case with livestock that can be used for breeding and resale, the prime value of the good is tied to future auctions of offspring.

Although one-of-a-kind/sales auctions are often dominated by individual and even idiosyncratic decisions, they are also embedded within a collective context. The Sangster/Maktoum confrontations, the Rock Hudson footstool auction, and other such sales nearly always have meaning for the participants only insofar as there is an audience present to acknowledge the performance. In short, while it is true that such auctions are characterized less by existing auction hierarchies than are the other two types of auctions, participants in these auctions are often able to enhance their social status through the social visibility that such participation brings. The high bid in many of these auctions does not so much represent the winner's valuation of the item bought as much as it does his or her commitment to being the highest bidder. There is a sense, in fact, in which price often proves irrelevant in such auctions. Personal egos are normally a much more significant factor. This is clearly central in the divorce auction described earlier. Even when there is no formal or even informal collective definition of value, the process for determining value is collective. The husband and wife placed their own value on each object in response to the value placed on the objects by the other.

The importance given a bidder's willingness to make a personal statement touches on another chimera of the neoclassical paradigm, namely the rationality of auction behavior. It is seldom, if ever, the rationality of the performance that earns applause. Quite the opposite. It is nearly always the exercise of noneconomic—even anti-economic—preferences, or better yet passions, which have been spurred on by matching the passions of other bidders and enhanced by an appreciative audience, that receives the greatest applause.

## Concluding Remarks

It is, of course, possible to dismiss all of what has been said in this chapter by simply asserting that these are not examples of the "true" auctions that concern economics, upon which so much of neoclassical economic theory is supposedly built. I would suggest, however, that a more productive approach would be to use real-world auctions to rethink some key aspects of what is generally considered to be economic behavior. Auctions do more than promote the idea that most economic transactions are subject to various collective definitions. They suggest that these collective definitions are differentially subject to a range of nonideational contextual factors, as evidenced in the differences noted among commodity/exchange auctions, dealer/collectible auctions, and one-of-a-kind/sales auctions. Put slightly differently, real-world auctions not only underscore the importance of the social construction of value; they also reveal a good deal about the complexities of this process.

Despite the neoclassical ideal, real-world auctions also suggest that economic transactions seldom, if ever, occur on a "level playing field." Moreover, they generally serve to reinforce status and political inequalities. These inequalities, of course, are usually considered fair within the context of the auction.

Finally, real-world auctions raise serious questions about economic motivation. Auction participants generally seem more interested in participating in the determination of a desired price—though what makes a price desirable varies from auction to auction—than in acquiring an item. If I had to select one phrase to describe what motivates most auction activity, it would be "a desire for agency." In many of the most glamorous sales auctions, this striving for self-assertion is highly evident. It clearly plays a governing role in both exchange and collectible auctions as well. In exchange auctions, self-assertion takes the form of establishing, maintaining, and/or improving one's status within the group. In collectible auctions, it takes the form of having one's views taken seriously. In nearly all cases, however, there is a strong desire for social recognition. Admittedly, there are exceptions. Whatever exceptions there are, however, they are considerably fewer than the exceptions to be found to the self-interested, maximizing motivation featured by the as-of-yet reigning economic paradigm.

# References

APPADURAI, ARJUN, ed. 1986. *The Social Life of Things: Commodities in Cultural Perspective.* New York: Cambridge University Press.

BAZERMAN, MAX, and WILLIAM SAMUELSON. 1983. "The Winner's Curse: An Empirical Investigation." In Reinhard Teitz ed., *Aspiration Levels in Bargaining and Economic Decision Making.* Berlin: Springer-Verlag, pp. 186–200.

BECKER, GARY. 1976. *The Economic Approach to Human Behavior.* Chicago: Chicago University Press.

BERGER, PETER L., and THOMAS LUCKMANN. 1966. *The Social Construction of Reality.* Garden City, NY: Doubleday and Company.

BOECK, GEORGE ALBERT, JR. 1983. *The Market Report: A Folklife Ethnography of a Texas Livestock Auction.* Unpublished Ph.D. dissertation, University of Michigan, Ann Arbor.

BRANCH, ROGER G. 1970. *The Structure of the Tobacco Auction: A Sociological Analysis.* Unpublished Ph.D. dissertation, University of Georgia.

CARTER, ROBERT A. 1986. "Auctions Now." *Publishers Weekly* 17 (October):20–25.

CASSADY, RALPH, JR. 1967. *Auctions and Auctioneering.* Berkeley and Los Angeles: University of California Press.

CLARK, ROBERT E. 1973. *On the Block: An Ethnography of Auctions.* Unpublished Ph.D. dissertation, University of Montana.

CLARK, ROBERT E. and LARRY J. HALFORD. 1978. "Going . . . Going . . . Gone: Preliminary Observations on 'Deals' at Auctions." *Urban Life* 7(3)(October):285–307.

COX, JAMES C., VERNON L. SMITH, and JAMES M. WALKER. 1985. "Experimental Development of Sealed-Bid Auction Theory: Calibrating Controls for Risk Aversion." *American Economic Review* 75:2(May):160–165.

GRANOVETTER, MARK. 1985. "Economic Action and Social Structure: A Theory of Embeddedness." *American Journal of Sociology* (November):481–510.

GRAY, SUSAN. 1976. *Power in the Auction Setting.* Unpublished Ph.D. dissertation, City University of New York.

HAHN, FRANK. 1987. "Auctioneer." In John Eatwell et al. eds., *The New Palgrave.* London: Macmillan, pp. 136–138.

HANSEN, ROBERT G. 1985. "Empirical Testing of Auction Theory." *American Economic Review* 75:2(May):156–159.

HERMANN, FRANK. 1981. *Sotheby's: Portrait of an Auction House.* New York and London: W. W. Norton.

HIRSCHMAN, ALBERT O. 1985. "Against Parsimony." *Economics and Philosophy* 1:7–21.

HOFFMAN, ELIZABETH, and MATHEW L. SPITZER. 1985. "Entitlements, Rights, and Fairness: An Experimental Examination of Subjects' Concepts of Distributive Justice." *Journal of Legal Studies* 14(June):259–297.

*Insight.* 1986. Special Issue "Art for Profit." (March 31):6–17.

MASKIN, ERIC S., and JOHN RILEY. 1984. "Optimal Auctions with Risk Averse Buyers." *Econometrica* 52(November):1473–1518.

——. 1985. "Auction Theory with Private Values." *American Economic Review* 75(May):150–155.

MCAFEE, R. PRESTON, and JOHN MCMILLAN. 1987. "Auctions and Bidding." *The Journal of Economic Literature* XXV:2(June):699–738.

MILGROM, PAUL, and ROBERT J. WEBER. 1982. "A Theory of Auctions and Competitive Bidding." *Econometrica* 50(September):1089–1122.

OLMSTED, ALFRED D. 1986. "What Will You Give Me?: Buying and Selling at Public Auction." Unpublished paper presented in May at the *Qualitative Research Conference:* University of Waterloo.

PLATTNER, STUART MARK. 1969. *Peddlers, Pigs, and Profit: Itinerant Trading in Southeast Mexico.* Ann Arbor, MI: University Microfilms, Inc.

PLOTT, CHARLES. 1982. "Industrial Organization Theory and Experimental Economics." *Journal of Economic Literature* 20:4(December):1485–1527.

REITLINGER, GERALD. 1961. *The Economics of Taste.* Volume 1. London: Barrie and Jenkins.

——. 1963. *The Economics of Taste.* Volume 2. London: Barrie and Jenkins.

——. 1970. *The Economics of Taste.* Volume 3. London: Barrie and Jenkins.

RILEY, JOHN G., and WILLIAM SAMUELSON. 1981. "Optimal Auctions." *American Economic Review* 71(June):381–392.

SEN, AMARTYA K. 1977. "Rational Fools: A Critique of the Behavioral Foundations of Economic Theory." *Philosophy and Public Affairs* 6:317–344.

SIMON, HERBERT A. 1957. *Models of Man.* New York: John Wiley.

——. 1972. *Human Problem Solving.* Englewood Cliffs, NJ: Prentice-Hall.

SMITH, CHARLES W. 1981. *The Mind of the Market.* Totowa: Rowman and Littlefield.

——. 1989. *Auctions: The Social Construction of Value.* New York: Free Press.

SMITH, VERNON L. 1967. "Experimental Studies of Discrimination Versus Competition in Sealed-Bid Auction Markets." *Journal of Business* 40:1 (January):56–84.

——. 1982. "Microeconomic Systems as an Experimental Science." *American Economic Review* 72:5(December):923–955.

——. 1986. "Experimental Methods in the Political Economy of Exchange." *Science* 234(October 10):167–173.

——. 1987. "Auctions." In John Eatwell, Murray Milgate, and Peter Newman eds. *The New Palgrave,* London: Macmillan, pp. 139–144.

THUROW, LESTER C. 1983. *Dangerous Currents.* New York: Random House.

TOMKINS, CALVIN. 1988. "A Reporter at Large: Irises." *The New Yorker* (April 4):37–67.

TURNER, RONNY E., and KENNETH STEWART. 1974. "The Negotiation of Role Conflict: A Study of Sales Behavior at the Auction." *Rocky Mountain Social Science Journal* 11:2(April):85–96.

VICKREY, WILLIAM. 1961. "Counterspeculation, Auctions and Competitive Sealed Tenders." *Journal of Finance* 16(March):8–37.

VON NEUMAN, JOHN, and OSKAR MORGENSTERN. 1944. *Theory of Games and Economic Behavior.* New York: John Wiley and Sons.

WILLIAMSON, OLIVER E. 1975. *Markets and Hierarchies: Analysis and Antitrust Implications.* New York: The Free Press.

ZUKIN, SHARON, and PAUL DIMAGGIO, eds. 1986. "Special Issue on Economy and Society." *Theory and Society* 15.

# 8

# Making Multiple Monies

## VIVIANA A. ZELIZER

In his study of the development of sociology, Bruce Mazlish reminds us that sociologists have had a longstanding "obsessive concern" with the cash nexus, with the vision of an ever-expanding market inevitably dissolving all social relations and corrupting cultural and personal values (1989:9). But, paradoxically, it has remained a remarkably unsociological obsession. Mesmerized by this vision of inexorable force, sociologists implicitly adopted an extremely simple conception of the process, making it resemble the sweeping away of landmarks by a giant flood. That left unaddressed the crucial question: How do real markets work? Markets were seldom studied as social and cultural arrangements. For if indeed the modern market neutralized social relations and homogenized cultural distinctions, there was nothing much left for sociologists to study. Thus the market was surrendered to economists.

That is why the study of markets poses a theoretical challenge to social scientists. To deal effectively with the market, analysts must break the economists' intellectual monopoly of this elusive phenomenon. How do we go about dismantling the illusory yet pervasive assumption that market exchange and, more generally, economic phenomena, are free from cultural or social constraints? More specifically, how can we convincingly demonstrate that the market is one special category of social relations and cultural values, much as kinship or religion?

In recent years a growing number of critics have taken up the challenge, determined to treat market activity as a social phenomenon. This sociological rethinking of the market is part of a broader resurgence of economic sociology in the United States (on the "new economic sociology," see Swedberg 1987). Paradoxically, even as the rational-choice model seems to dominate sociological headlines, economic sociology is undercutting its premises at the core: showing how even the market is a created set of meanings and social relations.

There are two ways this has been done. One common approach is the "add-social-context-and-stir" method: correcting the economic model of a "free" market by uncovering noneconomic constraints of economic life. That was the strategy of economic sociology in the 1950s and 1960s. For instance, in a suggestive discussion of variation in market structures, Parsons and Smelser show how markets differ in "sociological type" and not "merely along some dimension of competitiveness." The focus, however, is on how noneconomic factors *constrain* the economy, enforcing "qualitatively different limitations on the respective market conditions" (1956:3, 173). Thus, in this model, the autonomy of the market is disturbed externally by a variety of noneconomic constraints. There are some dangers in this strategy. The add-on corrective technique in fact allows economics to define the terms of the discourse. The result is not just a matter of rhetorical advantage, but an approach that perpetuates a basic conceptual flaw.

The market should not be set in opposition to extra-economic sociocultural factors, but understood as one special category of social relations and cultural values; or, as Harrison White puts it, as "intensely social— as social as kinship networks or feudal armies" (1988:232). This is the second, more constructive approach to the study of markets. It breaks down an artificial market–nonmarket dichotomy. And it redefines the market. In contrast to the neoclassical assumption of the market as a universal, autonomous, and exclusive form of economic arrangement, market revisionists treat the market as one type of social relations that involve consumption, production, and exchange under a variety of cultural and social settings. The puzzle then turns on determining the historical variation of multiple markets.

This model of socially variable markets intersects with my own long-term inquiry into the ways social relations and culture inform people's economic life (Zelizer 1979; 1987); first with an analysis of the life insurance market, then with a study of changes in the market for children in the United States between the 1870s and 1930s, and now with a study of the social meaning of money: an exploration of the remarkably different ways in which people identify, classify, organize, and use money.

My general approach to economic phenomena, however, differs significantly from current mainstream economic sociology, including the work of most contributors to this volume. For the most part, sociologists have tried to outwit economists in their own terrain—that is, in domains that economists already recognize and claim as their own, such as the structure of corporations or other economic institutions. And they speak economists' "language", using, for instance, the same formal modeling techniques that economists use to contest and refine economists' assumptions. Although I am sympathetic to these alternatives to the economic model, I am more concerned with the substance of personal relations: how people experience and actively shape economic processes, including the use of money.

This chapter considers two dimensions of my ongoing project. The first is a new sociological model of multiple monies as an alternative to standard views of a single rationalizing modern currency. The second is a research agenda designed to identify and begin to explain the social multiplicity of money.

## The Social Differentiation of Money

### The Theoretical Challenge

Sociologists treat money paradoxically: on the one hand money is considered a central element of modern society, and yet it remains an unanalyzed sociological category. Money is ignored, Collins has suggested, "as if it were not sociological enough" (1979:190).[1] Significantly, the *International Encyclopedia of the Social Sciences* devotes over thirty pages to money but not one to its social characteristics. There are essays on the economic effect of money, on quantity theory, on velocity of circulation, and on monetary reform—but nothing on money as a "réalité sociale," to use Simiand's (1934) apt term. Oddly, while sociologists have long recognized social time and social space, social money has eluded them. Sorokin's *Sociocultural Causality, Space, Time* (1943), for instance, devotes separate chapters to the qualitative heterogeneity of time and space, but only a few speculative lines to the possible multiple symbolism of money.

To be sure, in classic interpretations of the modern world, money occupies a pivotal place. But what kind of place? The classic thinkers had little difficulty recognizing a series of economic effects of monetization: the facilitation of transactions at a distance, extensive division of labor, inequality, and domination. But they also asserted pervasive effects on the quality of social life. As the "most abstract and 'impersonal' element

[1] There are exceptions. See, for example, Turner (1986), Ganssmann (1988), Smelt (1980), Baker (1987).

that exists in human life" (Weber [1946] 1971:331), it was assumed that money spearheaded the process of rationalization. For Simmel and Marx, money revolutionized more than economic exchange: it fundamentally transformed the basis of all social relations by corrupting personal bonds into calculative instrumental ties. As Simmel observed, "The complete heartlessness of money is reflected in our social culture, which is itself determined by money" ([1900] 1978:346). For Simmel, however, in contrast to Marx, money was not only a depersonalizer but also a liberating force. By breaking the personal bondage of traditional arrangements, money allowed each individual the freedom of selecting the terms and partners of economic exchange.

Presumably the revolutionary power of money came from its complete indifference to values. Money was perceived as the prototype of an instrumental, calculating approach; it was, in Simmel's words, "the purest reification of means" ([1900] 1978:211). Unlike any other known product, money was the absolute negation of quality. With money, only quantity mattered: it transformed the world into an "arithmetic problem" (Simmel [1908] 1950:412).

The utilitarian model has had a remarkable grip over theorizing about money. Contemporary sociology still clings to the view of money as an absolutely fungible, qualitatively neutral, infinitely divisible, entirely homogeneous medium of market exchange. For example, in his recent *Foundations of Social Theory,* Coleman builds an extremely sophisticated analysis of social exchange, yet continues to treat money as the ultimate impersonal common denominator (Coleman 1990:119–131). So does Giddens, in *The Consequences of Modernity.* As a "symbolic token," money, in Giddens's analysis, serves as a key example of the "disembedding mechanisms associated with modernity," by which he means the " 'lifting out' of social relations from local contexts of interaction and their restructuring across indefinite spans of time-space" (Giddens 1990:22, 25, 21). Habermas goes as far as to argue that money is the medium by which the economic system "colonizes" the lifeworld; irrepressibly and systematically undermining "domains of action dependent upon social integration" (Habermas 1989:327)[2]. Sociologists thus accept with a notable lack of skepticism the notion that once money invades the realm of personal relations it will inevitably bend those relations in the direction of instrumental rationality.

I propose an alternative differentiated model of money as continually shaped and reshaped by different networks of social relations and varying

---

[2] For a different critique of Habermas, as well as Parsons' and Luhmann's treatment of money, in particular for ignoring power and inequality, see Ganssmann (1988).

systems of meanings. Money is neither culturally neutral nor socially anonymous. It may well "corrupt" values and social ties into numbers, but values and social relations reciprocally transform money by investing it with meaning and social patterns. Despite its transferability, people make every effort to embed money in particular times, places, and social relations. Thus, there is no single, uniform, generalized money, but multiple monies: people earmark different currencies for many or perhaps all types of social interactions, much as they create distinctive languages for different social contexts. And people will in fact respond with anger, shock, or ridicule to the "misuse" of monies for the wrong set of social relations, such as offering a $1,000 bill to pay for a newspaper. Money used for rational instrumental exchanges is not free from social constraints but is another type of socially created currency, subject to particular networks of social relations and its own set of values and norms.

Here we enter delicate terminological terrain. Some analysts will prefer to call an object "money" only when a state issues it and assigns it value. Even there, we have to recognize that in the United States alone all sorts of governments have issued different bills, coins, and any number of other tender. Consider for instance the 5,000 or more state bank notes—not including additional thousands of counterfeit issues—circulating in the nineteenth century. Merchants and bankers had to rely on bank-note directories to keep track of the unwieldy varieties of monies, as the value (as well as the size and style) of bank notes differed from bank to bank and in different states. In fact, apparently it was common for bank customers to specify "in what sort of money deposits were to be withdrawn and with what sort promissory notes were to be repaid" (Hammond 1967:702–703).[3]

Even after the National Banking Act of 1863 created a uniform national currency, the stock of American money remained highly diversified. The new national bank notes circulated alongside other Civil War currency inventions, including U.S. notes ("greenbacks"), interest-bearing legal tender notes, government demand notes, postage and fractional currency as well as gold and silver certificates, and the more traditional gold coins and subsidiary silver (see Friedman and Schwartz 1971:20–29). These multiple official monies were in many cases earmarked for specified purposes. Greenbacks, for instance, were receivable in most payments, but not for duties on imports nor for interest on bonds and notes. Gold on the other hand, although designated largely for foreign trans-

---

[3] The heterogeneity of state notes went beyond their varying economic values; banks also frequently personalized notes with elaborate designs of individuals and scenes meaningful for their locality. For an excellent collection of bank-note illustrations, see *Important Early American Bank Notes, 1810–1874* (1990).

actions, was also reserved for certain domestic payments such as custom duties.[4] Limited regional variation persisted as the West Coast remained mostly on a specie basis. Yet on the whole, after the Civil War, the American state moved toward a more uniform legal tender.[5]

Creating currencies, however, has not been entirely state business. At times, stores, businesses, and other organizations have privately issued tokens, paper notes, or coins. In fact, until an 1862 Congressional prohibition (and even after), Americans responded to the periodic scarcity of small change by the resourceful production of substitute currency. There is even an instance of "church money": 4-pence notes issued in 1792 by a church in Schenectady, New York (Nussbaum 1964:42). Most notably, merchants' copper cents—the "hard-time tokens" of the 1830s—successfully served as both commercial advertising and small change. Other tokens bearing patriotic emblems or political slogans animated economic exchange with timely debates, often satirizing President Jackson's policies. Again in the Civil War, when subsidiary silver became more valuable as metal than coin, privately issued "shin plasters" (paper money in small denominations) along with thousands of tradesmen's and political tokens were used as substitute currency in everyday transactions. And until 1864, a sizeable stock of privately issued gold coins remained in circulation (see Low [1900] 1955; Falkner 1901; Barnard 1917).

Outside the realm of governments, organizations, or business, moreover, people constantly do two further things: they convert selected objects into the equivalent of currencies, as in the case of cigarettes, postage stamps, subway tokens, or baseball cards; and they adapt government-issued currencies so vigorously that it seems reasonable to call these variations monies as well. That is how I will use the term. These objects have no common physical characteristics; they qualify as distinct monies because of the uses and meanings people assign to them, because of the distinctions they represent in everyday social life. I will argue that the earmarking of social monies is a phenomenon as powerful as the official creation of legal tender.

Ironically, when it comes to money, folk sociology seems to be wiser than academic sociology. In their everyday existence, people understand that money is not really fungible: that despite the anonymity of dollar bills, not all dollars are equal. We routinely assign different meanings

[4] For other cases of restricted receivability, see Breckinridge 1903:124–126; and Kemp 1956:59–93.

[5] Bensel (1990) sees the nationalization of currency as further evidence of the general centralization of state activities during and after the Civil War. Southern currency, however, remained in a state of "unbelievable chaos" (Nussbaum 1964:123), as all sorts of paper currencies were being issued not only by the Confederacy, but also by its states and municipalities as well as by state banks.

and separate uses to particular monies. Sometimes the earmarking is quite concrete: for instance, Rainwater, Coleman, and Handel's study of American working-class housewives (1959:154–167) describes the women's careful "tin can accounting": monies for separate expenses were kept apart, in tin cans or labeled envelopes: one for the mortgage, another for utilities, one for entertainment money, and so on. The wives in Bakke's landmark study of unemployed workers in the 1930s ([1940] 1969:142–143) used china pitchers to segregate different types of income earmarked for particular expenses: the rent of an extra room, for instance, might serve to pay off the mortgage, while a child's earnings were designated to purchase school clothes.

### Earmarking

How does this process of social earmarking work? Answering this question is the second task of my project. After all, the physical homogeneity of modern currency is indisputable. How, then, do people distinguish between monies that can so easily remain indistinct? Anthropologists provide some intriguing insights into the differentiation of monies, but only with regards to primitive money. For instance, ethnographic studies show that in certain primitive communities, money attains special qualities and distinct values independent of quantity. How much money is less important than *which* money. Multiple currencies, or "special-purpose" money, to use Karl Polanyi's term (1957:264–266), have sometimes coexisted in one and the same village, each currency having a specified, restricted use (for purchasing only certain goods or services), special modes of allocation and forms of exchange, and, sometimes, designated users (see, e.g. Bohannan 1959). For instance, in Rossel Island, a small traditional community in the southwestern Pacific, separate lower-value coins were reserved exclusively for women. And in Yap, one of the Caroline Islands in the western Pacific, mussel shells strung on strings served as women's money, while men monopolized the more desirable large stones (Baric 1964:422–423; Sumner [1906] 1940:140).

Special monies are often morally or ritually ranked: certain kinds of money may be good for obtaining food but not for purchasing a wife; other monies are appropriate only for funeral gifts or marriage gifts or as blood money; still other monies serve exclusively for paying damages for adultery or insults, for burial with the dead, or for magical rites. In this context, the "wrong" quality or lesser quality money, even in large quantities, is useless or degraded.

These special monies, which Douglas (1967) has perceptively identified as a sort of primitive coupon system, control exchange by rationing and restricting the use and allocation of currency. In the process, money sometimes performs economic functions by serving as a medium of exchange, but it also functions as a social and sacred "marker" used to acquire or amend status or to celebrate ritual events. The point is that primitive money is transformable, from fungible to nonfungible, from profane to sacred.

But what about modern money? Influenced by economic models, most anthropologists established a sharp dichotomy between primitive, restricted, "special-purpose" money and modern "all-purpose" money, which, as a single currency unburdened by ritual or social controls, can function effectively as universal medium of exchange. Only recently have anthropologists begun to cast off the fallacy of a culturally neutral currency. An important collection of essays edited by Parry and Bloch (1989) demonstrates the heterogeneity of money, showing how the multiple symbolic meanings of modern money are shaped by the cultural matrix. But because their cases are restricted to societies outside the centers of capitalism, they cannot fully challenge established assumptions.

A sociological model of money must show how, how much, and why, even in the heartland of capitalism, different networks of social relations and meaning systems mark modern money, introducing controls, restrictions, and distinctions that are as influential as the rationing of primitive money. Multiple monies in the modern world may not be as visibly identifiable as the shells, coins, brass rods, or stones of primitive communities, but their invisible boundaries work just as well. How else, for instance, do we distinguish a bribe from a tribute or a donation, a wage from an honorarium, and an allowance from a salary? How do we identify ransom, bonuses, tips, damages, or premiums? True, there are quantitative differences between these various payments. But surely the special vocabulary conveys much more than diverse amounts. Detached from its qualitative differences, the world of money becomes undecipherable.

One might argue that the earmarking of money is an individual phenomenon. Indeed, in psychology, new studies now reject the notion that money is psychologically general, maintaining that instead money involves "multiple symbolizations" (Lea, Tarpy, and Webley 1987:335). An exciting literature on "mental accounting" challenges economists' assumption of fungibility by showing the ways individuals distinguish between kinds of money. For instance, they treat windfall income very differently from a bonus or an inheritance, even when the sums involved are identical (Thaler 1990; Kahneman and Tversky 1982).

Modern money, however, is marked by more than individual random preferences. As Mauss observed, money is "essentially a social fact" (1914:14). The earmarking of money is thus a social process: money is attached to varying sets of social relations, rather than individuals. There are a number of different techniques for this social production of multiple monies: restricting the uses of money, regulating modes of allocation, modifying its presentation, attaching special meanings to particular amounts, designating proper users, earmarking appropriate sources. To be sure, this phenomenon is not restricted to the uses of state-issued money, but applies as well to other objects, from tokens and commercial paper to art objects, even including kitchen recipes or jokes—anything, in fact, that is socially exchangeable. At issue here, however, is the attempt to show that precisely where interpreters of modernity see the utmost depersonalization of life, in the circulation of state currency, people continually introduce distinctions, doubts, and directives that defy all instrumental calculation.

My current research focuses on fundamental transformations of this earmarking of money in the United States between the 1870s and 1930s. I have selected four general social settings to explore and explain patterns of variation in the conditions and techniques of differentiating monies: the domestic economy, gifts exchanged by relatives and friends, institutional money, and moral money. Let us briefly consider each of these monies.

## Creating Currencies: Four Cases

### First Case: Domestic Money

How do intimate relations of kin define money? What sort of money circulates within the family? How is it allocated, and how is it used? How do changing social and power relationships between husbands and wives and between parents and children affect the meaning of domestic monies? Consider, for instance, married women's money at the turn of the twentieth century. This money, whether given by the husband or earned in the household or in the labor market, was earmarked as a different form of currency from an ordinary dollar. It was obtained in special ways, used for designated purposes, and even had a special vocabulary, "allowance," "pin money," "egg money," "butter money," "spending money," "pocket money," "gift," or "dole," but seldom "wage," "salary," "paycheck," or "profit."

Studying money in the family is entering largely uncharted territory. Curiously, although money is the major source of husband–wife disagreements and often a sore point between parents and children, we know less about family money matters than about family violence or even marital sex. Not only are families reluctant to disclose their private financial lives to strangers, but husbands, wives, and children often lie, deceive, or simply conceal information from each other as well. Perhaps more fundamentally still, the model of what Amartya Sen (1983) calls the "glued-together" family has meant that questions about how money is divided between family members are seldom even asked. Once money enters the family, it is assumed to be somehow equitably distributed among family members, serving to maximize their collective welfare. How much money each person gets, how he or she obtains it, from whom and for what, are rarely considered.

The period between 1870 and 1930 provides some unusual glimpses into this traditionally secret world of family money. As the consumer society was being established, Americans wrote about and studied money matters in an unprecedented manner. Household-budget studies richly documented how the working class and lower-middle class spent their money. And in anonymous, "confessional" articles published in popular magazines, middle-class Americans disclosed their own domestic budgets, transforming the battle over the purse strings into a public issue.

How was a wife's money earmarked and set apart from other domestic monies? First, by its method of allocation. In the hierarchically structured family, husbands gave wives part of their income. Upper- and middle-class wives received an irregular dole, or more rarely, a regular allowance from their husbands for housekeeping expenses, including household goods and clothing. Working-class wives, on the other hand, were given their husbands' paychecks and were expected to administer and distribute the family money. The amount of money wives received was not determined by the efficiency or even the quantity of their domestic contributions but by prevalent beliefs of what was a proper amount. Therefore, a larger paycheck for the husband need not translate into a raise in the housekeeping allowance. On the basis of gender economics, it might in fact simply increase a husband's personal money.

Legally, domestic money was a husband's property. Even if a woman managed to save some money from her housekeeping expenses, the law ultimately considered that money to be her husband's property. For instance, in 1914, when Charles Montgomery sued his wife, Emma, for the $618.12 she had saved from the household expenses during their twenty-five years of marriage, Justice Blackman of the Supreme Court, Brooklyn, ruled for the husband, arguing that "no matter how careful and prudent has been the wife, if the money . . . belonged to the husband it is still his property" (*New York Times*, December 16:22). Thus a wife's channels to additional cash were limited to a variety of persuasion techniques: asking, cajoling, downright begging, or even practicing sexual blackmail.

If these techniques failed, there was also a repertoire of underground financial strategies, ranging from home pocket-picking to padding bills.

Some methods were quite risky. In 1905 Joseph Schultz was taken to the police court of Buffalo by Mrs. Schultz. It seems that Mr. Schultz, determined to stop his wife's nocturnal thefts of the change left in his trousers, set a small rattrap in the trouser pocket. About 2:00 A.M. the trap was sprung, and the next morning the husband was taken to court. *Bench and Bar,* a New York legal journal, reported with some satisfaction that the judge turned down the wife's complaint and upheld the right of husbands to maintain rattraps for the protection of their small change (3 *Bench and Bar* 6).

Changes in gender relations influenced the method of allocation of married women's money. As women's consumer role expanded at the beginning of the twentieth century, the traditional "dole," or asking method, became not only inefficient but also inappropriate in increasingly egalitarian marriages. The allowance—a more definite and regular housekeeping income—was praised as a more equitable method of allocation, but then in turn condemned by home-efficiency experts of the 1920s and 1930s as an unsatisfactory payment for modern wives. The joint account emerged as the new cultural ideal.

A wife's money was further earmarked by its uses. Wives' money meant housekeeping money, a necessary allotment restricted to family expenses and excluding personal spending money. Pocket money was a budgetary expectation for husbands and children, but not for wives. Gender marked the uses of women's money even when their income was earned. Women's wages were still earmarked as separate and treated differently. Among farm families, for instance, women's egg money and butter money were distinguished from husbands' wheat money or corn money, and used for different purposes. In the 1920s and 1930s, as more married women entered the labor force, their earnings, regardless of the sums involved, were treated as pin money and categorized as supplementary income, used for the family's extra expenses, or earmarked by more affluent couples as discretionary "fun" money. A wife's pin money, regardless of its quantity, remained a more frivolous, less serious earning than her husband's wages.

The case of domestic money explores some of the limits of a purely rationalized model of money: the meanings, allocation, and uses of married women's money were shaped not only by considerations of economic efficiency but also by a complex mixture of ideas about family life, by changing gender relations, and by social class.

### Second Case: Gifts of Money

The social relations of kin and friendship also patterned money into a sentimental gift. Today, according to one recent estimate, $45 billion are spent by Americans on money gifts annually, including cash, cheques, and gift certificates (*Volumetric Study of the Gift-Giving Market,* American Express 1986). Typically, however, money has been seen as corrupting the gift economy by introducing improper and overly visible market elements into a sentimental exchange. Yet gift money emerged in the United States in the early twentieth century as a qualitatively distinct personalized kind of money. Americans were remarkably resourceful in "inventing" gift money: for instance, in the late nineteenth century, they had transformed thousands of ordinary coins into "love tokens" by engraving sentimental messages that made the coins a popular romantic gift for lovers as well as a present for family celebrations, such as birthdays, weddings, or anniversaries (Campbell 1972; McClure 1976).

In the first two decades of the twentieth century, money entered the booming gift economy transformed into gift money in a number of ways. In 1910 American Express, for example, first began advertising money orders as an "acceptable Christmas gift" (American Express archive materials). And in the 1920s, greeting-card companies marketed specially designed cards to send holiday or birthday money to friends and relatives (Chase 1926:152–155; Hallmark archive collection). Even etiquette manuals gradually introduced advice on the how-to's of money gifts for weddings, anniversaries, and christenings.

Gift money was not only a middle-class or upper-class privilege. For instance, immigrants' remittances to relatives who stayed behind were sent not only for practical purposes, such as buying a steamship ticket or paying off a debt, but often as money gifts for birthdays, Christmas, Easter, or other festive occasions (Thomas and Znaniecki [1918–1920] 1958; Breckinridge 1921:86). More generally still, immigrant remittances consitute a separate moral economy.

How was money earmarked as a personal gift? First, by designating its proper users: in middle- and upper-class circles, for instance, gifts of money were exchanged only between near relatives or closest friends, while in the working class money seems to have circulated more broadly and with less restraints, especially at weddings or christenings (Kingsland 1910:7; Breckinridge 1921:101–103). Gift money among strangers became a very different sort of currency. It had its own name: "tip" not "gift." At the turn of the century, as tipping became increasingly popular, it provoked much moral and social controversy. There were even nationwide efforts by state legislatures to abolish tipping by turning it into a punishable misdemeanor.

For its critics, the tip was not a gift but "tainted" money; a form of extortion parading as a gift. For what did a gift of money mean between employer and employee? It paid for the personal extra, "the waiter's smile or immunity from the terrible look" (W. Scott 1916:96). Such "sentimental considerations," declared the author of *The Itching Palm* (W. Scott 1916:28), a 1916 study of tipping, distorted market relations by introducing particularism into the impersonal world of economic exchange. Thus, the alchemy of money gifts worked only between intimates or even distant friends; money exchanged by strangers was a different sort of currency.

Money can also be earmarked as a gift by physical transformation: adorning plain cash by enclosing it in special containers. Women's magazines in the early 1900s described the many time-consuming and elaborate strategies for converting ordinary money into gift money. These included gold coins hidden in cookies or concealed by Christmas seals; dollar bills decorating a belt buckle, or encased within a picture frame (see, "New Ways to Give Christmas Money" 1912:70). Or else a money gift was created by using special kinds of money, such as gold coins or new dollar bills, sufficiently distinct to serve as gift items. Gift certificates, invented in 1905, were another mechanism used to transform money into a gift. Materially different from cash and personalized with the recipient's name, certificates were formally set apart from ordinary cash.

Gift money was further earmarked by its uses, designated for particular expenses. Etiquette manuals, for instance, sometimes instructed brides and grooms to acknowledge cash gifts by specifying what the couple bought with their money (see Post [1922] 1937:400). Earmarking was also accomplished by physically segregating gift money in special places. For instance, Christmas money was often saved in home tin banks or, after 1910, in the enormously successful Christmas club accounts promoted by savings banks for separate "Christmas money" deposits.

Thus, as it entered the personal sphere of gift exchange among friends and kin, money did not circulate as a measure of utility but as a sentimental currency, expressing care and affection. Certainly it takes work to make money into a gift, more work, say, than turning a book or flowers into a gift. Yet still people earmark money as a gift by how they obtain it, how and when they present it, how they display it, and how they spend it.

### Third Case: Institutional Money

In contrast to the social "domestication" of family money and the personalization of gift money, the earmarking of money is sometimes bureaucratically prescribed and officially imposed. This raises a separate set of questions for my project. What happens when the state deliberately sets out to break the homogeneity of money by creating visible distinctions between kinds of money? One could certainly raise this question concerning Treasury bonds, commemorative postage stamps, tax exemptions, or even the creation of token economies in total institutions, such as the "convict currency" issued to prisoners. My current research, however, focuses on the persistent conflict between cash and in-kind relief in American social welfare policy, showing the resistance by state agencies as well as private charities to grant unrestricted money support to the poor.

Agencies worked hard to distinguish charitable donations from a wage payment by closely supervising the uses of relief. For most of the nineteenth century and the early 1900s, they did so by directly regulating the household economy of the poor, allocating clothing, fuel, and food to the needy, but seldom cash. Or else agencies dispensed grocery orders that not only specified which goods recipients could purchase but where to buy them. After 1920, however, cash relief emerged as a more dignified form of relief, endorsed by many welfare experts as a way to increase the discretionary power of the poor. A dollar, after all, carries no visible stigma of differentness nor apparent market constraints. Or so the practitioners reasoned (Colcord 1923; 1936).

Despite the rhetoric, the alleged freedom of monetary payments was an illusion. Cash relief was still treated as a very different kind of money than a wage. In fact, the supervision of relief probably intensified as charity organizations teamed with home economists searching for better strategies to assure what they defined as "wise" spending of benefits. Welfare workers undertook the reform of family budgets with the zeal formerly spent in upgrading family morality. Armed with budget books and account ledgers, social workers visited the homes of the poor, showing them what to buy, where to buy, and sometimes even escorting housewives in instructional shopping excursions (Gibbs 1916; Dunn 1922).

To further support official notions of proper spending, charity organizations sponsored a large number of thrift institutions, ranging from stamps savings to fuel clubs and vacation savings clubs, all designed to earmark dependents' money into "proper" expenses (Brown 1899; Brubaker 1906). How successful were they? My preliminary evidence suggests a sort of contest between official and private earmarks as people found strategies to subvert bureaucratic restrictions on the uses of their money, often spending in ways that outraged middle-class observers, paying, for instance, for burial insurance with money allocated for food purchase.

### Fourth Case: Moral Money

This final section of my project explores "moral money": under which conditions does money acquire sacred, religious, or moral value, and when does it become "tainted" money, defined as collectively or individually demeaning? I focus primarily on two cases: "death" money as a special category of ritual payment; and income from prostitution as a case of morally tainted money. My earlier work on insurance and compensation for wrongful death suggests that earmarking money for death payments involves moral work as elaborate as, although distinct from, domestic monies, money gifts, and official money. As for the money involved in sexual exchange, it raises a number of questions about how gender, sexuality, and morality create a separate economy.

A superficial reading of this evidence could lead one to suppose that money was indeed pervading every nook and cranny of social life just as classical social theorists predicted it would. Instead, everywhere we look we find people actively reshaping and creating monies. These historical case studies of multiple monies are indicators of a complex social economy that remains hidden in the dominant economic paradigm of a single, quality-less, and rationalizing market money. My cases are not anomalies or exceptions to value-free market money, but typical examples of money's heterogeneity in modern society.

## Agendas and Strategies

Some general comments on research strategy: first, why choose these four areas? Why not examine, for instance, the social construction of market money and take on economists in their own turf? After all, such analysts as Baker (1987) have done just that. Quite deliberately, however, I chose areas where, according to the traditional dichotomy between the market and personal relations, rationalization should have succeeded best: commodifying core personal and social relations and rationalizing sentiment: family, friendship, charity, sexual relations, death. I show that it is very hard work to suppress the active creative power of supposedly vulnerable social relations.

Second, why focus on the period between the 1870s and 1930s? It looks as if practices on money were changing at that time in the United States on a wide range of behaviors: that is, new forms of earmarking money emerge in a number of different settings, even, for instance, in prisons and orphan asylums. At least public discussions of these issues became much more active in this period. I have not yet formulated a general explanation of these transformations. But surely the postbellum expansion of the economy and the increase in real per capita income, as well as an increasingly consumer-oriented culture and economy, gave Americans the means and incentives for differentiating their monies. Making more money and spending it required not only skillful bookkeeping: they also raised a new set of confusing and often controversial noneconomic quandaries. What did it mean to spend money well? How, for instance, should a family's extra income be used? How much should be saved, how much given to charity, how much spent for leisure? Or, in the public sphere, should relief be paid in cash or in-kind? What should cash benefits pay for?

The relation between the state and the personalization of money is particularly intriguing. Paradoxically, forms of earmarking seem to have multiplied just as official money became *more* uniform and generalized. During the nineteenth century, the state worked hard to eliminate distinctions among currencies. Prompted by the financial crisis of the Civil War, Congress in 1862 authorized the Treasury to print millions of "greenbacks," a new paper currency without gold backing, which circulated nationally as legal tender. And in 1863 and 1864 the National Bank Act allowed newly chartered national banks to create a uniform national currency. A few years later, the multiple state bank notes were taxed out of existence (Friedman and Schwartz 1971:15–25).

Standardization of money, however, was not a smooth, consensual process. In fact, defining American currency became one of the most explosive political and social issues of the late nineteenth century. Significantly, despite a dramatic postbellum increase in people's use of deposits rather than cash, the debates centered on currencies (James 1978:22–27). Were greenbacks "real" money, or did only "hard" metallic money serve as authentic currency? Should gold, as monometallists argued, be the only true standard? Or, could silver, as "free-silver" proponents maintained, serve as equally sound money? Were national bank notes legitimate? Or, as Greenbackers insisted, was only government-issued money acceptable? (On these debates, see Nugent 1968). These were not merely word games nor strictly technical distinctions; the "money question" became a fiercely contested public debate, polarizing social groups and shaping the political process of late nineteenth-century American society. Indeed, one historian notes that only in the United States did "the argument about the form and function of money [become] public" (Nugent 1968:167).

By the turn of the century the controversy had waned, after free-silver proponents lost the 1896 election and the 1900 Gold Standard Act established the gold dollar as the national monetary standard. In short, within some four decades, the American state had achieved a significant degree of monetary standardization—although not until 1933 did Congress formally declare all U.S. coins and currencies as equal legal tender (Nussbaum 1964:181).[6]

That is precisely the irony: while the state and the law worked to obtain a single national currency, people continually disrupted monetary uniformity, actively creating all sorts of monetary distinctions. Outside the world of printing and minting, however, people spent less energy on the adoption of different objects as currencies than on the creation of distinctions among the uses and meanings of existing currencies—that is, on earmarking. Why this proliferation of earmarks? Is there some link between official standardization and personal differentiation of monies? These are some of the many questions raised by a historical model of multiple monies.

Developing a sociological model of money forms part of a broader challenge to neoclassical economic theory. It offers an alternative approach not only to the study of money but to all other aspects of economic life, including the market. In the sociological model, economic processes of exchange and consumption are defined as one special category of social relations, much like friendship, neighboring, or patron-client ties. Thus, economic phenomena such as money, although partly autonomous, are interdependent with historically variable systems of meanings and structures of social relations.

While we can welcome the effort to challenge the explanations economists conventionally offer for well-established phenomena, my research program consists of identifying nuance and variation where others—sociologists and economists alike—have seen flatness and uniformity.

I thank Bernard Barber, Charles Tilly, Pierre Bourdieu, and Loïc Wacquant for their invaluable comments on this paper. Critical suggestions were also made by members of the Russell Sage Seminar in Economic Sociology. I am grateful to Richard Swedberg for his encouragement of this enterprise. I have adapted portions of this argument from three other papers: "Beyond the Polemics on the Market: Establishing a Theoretical and Empirical Agenda," *Sociological Forum* 3 (Fall 1988):614–634; "The Social Meaning of Money: 'Special Monies'," *American Journal of Sociology* 95 (November 1989):342–377; and "Money," *Encyclopedia of Sociology* (vol. 3, pp. 1304–

[6] An expert in monetary legal history points to the decrease in litigation over specific money as another measure of growing monetary uniformity (Nussbaum 1939:59–60). Indeed, Bensel (1990:162 n. 141) explains how, "By making the greenback a 'legal tender' for public and private debts, the Union in effect made the acceptance of paper currency mandatory in all contracts and transactions in which money changed hands if those obligations were to be enforceable in court." There were, however, exceptions. As late as 1864, California and Nevada still upheld "specie contracts," allowing for payment of a specific kind of currency (Breckinridge 1903:126, 158–160).

1310), edited by Edgard F. Borgatta and Marie L. Borgatta (Macmillan, 1992). An extended version will appear in my book *The Social Meaning of Money* (Basic Books, in preparation).

# References

BAKER, WAYNE E. 1987. "What is Money? A Social Structural Interpretation." In Mark S. Mizruchi and Michael Schwartz eds., *Intercorporate Relations.* Cambridge, MA: Cambridge University Press, pp. 109–144.

BAKKE, E. WIGHT. [1940] 1969. *The Unemployed Worker.* Hamden, CT: Archon Books.

BARIC, LORRAINE. 1964. "Some Aspects of Credit, Saving and Investment in a Non-Monetary Economy (Rossel Island)." In Raymond Firth and B. S. Yamey eds., *Capital, Saving and Credit in Peasant Societies.* Chicago: Aldine.

BARNARD, B. W. 1917. "The Use of Private Tokens for Money in the United States." *Quarterly Journal of Economics* 31:600–634.

BENSEL, RICHARD F. 1990. *Yankee Leviathan.* Cambridge, MA: Cambridge University Press.

BOHANNAN, PAUL. 1959. "The Impact of Money on an African Subsistence Economy." *Journal of Economic History* 19:491–503.

BRECKINRIDGE, SOPHONISBA P. 1903. *Legal Tender.* Chicago: University of Chicago Press.

———. 1921. *New Homes for Old.* New York: Harper & Brothers.

BROWN, MARY WILLCOX. 1899. *The Development of Thrift.* New York: Macmillan.

BRUBAKER, HOWARD. 1906. "The Penny Provident Fund." *University Settlement Studies* 2:62–65.

CAMPBELL, LOUISE M. 1972. "Love Tokens." *The MANA Journal* 16:4–17.

CHASE, ERNEST DUDLEY. 1926. *The Romance of Greeting Cards.* Cambridge, MA: Cambridge University Press.

CHRISTIE'S CATALOG. 1990. *Important Early American Bank Notes, 1810–1874.* New York: Christie's Publications.

COLCORD, JOANNA C. 1923. "Relief." *The Family* 4(March):13–17.

———. 1936. *Cash Relief.* New York: Russell Sage Foundation.

COLEMAN, JAMES. 1990. *Foundations of Social Theory.* Cambridge, MA: Harvard University Press.

COLLINS, RANDALL. 1979. Review of *The Bankers,* by Martin Mayer. *American Journal of Sociology* 85:190–194.

DOUGLAS, MARY. 1967. "Primitive Rationing." In Raymond Firth ed., *Themes in Economic Anthropology.* London: Tavistock, pp. 119–145.

DUNN, AMY D. 1922. "The Supervision of the Spending of Money in Social Case Work." M.A. thesis. Ohio State University.

FALKNER, ROLAND P. 1901. "The Private Issue of Token Coins." *Political Science Quarterly* 16(June):303–327.

FRIEDMAN, MILTON, and ANNA J. SCHWARTZ. 1971. *A Monetary History of the United States, 1867–1960*. Princeton, NJ: Princeton University Press.

GALBRAITH, JOHN KENNETH. 1975. *Money*. Boston: Houghton Mifflin.

GANSSMANN, HEINER. 1988. "Money—a Symbolically Generalized Medium of Communication? On the Concept of Money in Recent Sociology." *Economy and Society* 17(August):285–316.

GIBBS, WINIFRED S. 1916. "The Development of Home Economics in Social Work." *The Journal of Home Economics* (February):68–74.

GIDDENS, ANTHONY. 1990. *The Consequences of Modernity*. Stanford, CA: Stanford University Press.

HABERMAS, JURGEN. 1989. *The Theory of Communicative Action*. Volume 2. Boston: Beacon Press.

HAMMOND, BRAY. [1957] 1967. *Banks and Politics in America*. Princeton, NJ: Princeton University Press.

JAMES, JOHN A. 1978. *Money and Capital Markets in Postbellum America*. Princeton, NJ: Princeton University Press.

KAHNEMAN, DANIEL, and AMOS TVERSKY. 1982. "The Psychology of Preferences." *Scientific American* 246:160–173.

KEMP, ARTHUR. 1956. *The Legal Qualities of Money*. New York: Pageant Press.

KINGSLAND, MRS. BURTON. 1910. *The Book of Good Manners*. New York: Doubleday.

Lea, Stephen E. G., Roger Tarpy, and PAUL WEBLEY. 1987. *The Individual in the Economy*. New York: Cambridge University Press.

LOW, LYMAN HAYNES. [1900] 1955. *Hard Times Tokens*. San Jose, CA: Globe Printing Co.

MAUSS, M. MARCEL. 1914. "Les origines de la notion de monnaie." *Institut Français d'Anthropologie. Compte rendu des séances* 2:14–19.

MAZLISH, BRUCE. 1989. *A New Science*. New York: Oxford University Press.

McCLURE, DUDLEY L. 1976. "Love Token Collecting Offers Romantic Glimpse of History." *Numismatic News Weekly* (February 14):14, 20, 22.

"New Ways to Give Christmas Money." 1912. *Ladies' Home Journal* 29(December):70.

NUGENT, WALTER T. K. 1968. *Money and American Society, 1865–1880*. New York: Free Press.

NUSSBAUM, ARTHUR. 1939. *Money in the Law*. Chicago: Foundation Press.

———. 1964. *A History of the Dollar*. New York: Columbia University Press.

PARRY, J., and M. BLOCH, eds. 1989. *Money and the Morality of Exchange*. Cambridge, NY: Cambridge University Press.

PARSONS, TALCOTT, and NEIL J. SMELSER. 1956. *Economy and Society*. New York: Free Press.

POLANYI, KARL. 1957. "The Economy as an Instituted Process." In Karl Polanyi et al. eds., *Trade and Market in the Early Empires*. Glencoe, IL: Free Press, pp. 243–270.

POST, EMILY. [1922] 1937. *Etiquette*. New York: Funk & Wagnalls.

RAINWATER, LEE, RICHARD P. COLEMAN, and GERALD HANDEL. 1959. *Workingman's Wife*. New York: Oceana Publications.

SCOTT, AUSTIN W. 1913. "The Right To Follow Money Wrongfully Mingled With Other Money." 27 *Harvard Law Review* 125.

SCOTT, WILLIAM R. 1916. *The Itching Palm*. Philadelphia: Penn Publishing Co.

SEN, AMARTYA. 1983. "Economics and the Family." *Asian Development Review* I:14–26.

SIMIAND, FRANÇOIS. 1934. "La Monnaie, Réalité Sociale." *Annales Sociologiques,* ser. D:1–86.

SIMMEL, GEORG. [1900] 1978. *The Philosophy of Money*. Tom Bottomore and David Frisby, trans. London: Routledge & Kegan Paul.

———. [1908] 1950. *The Sociology of Georg Simmel,* Kurt H. Wolf, ed. Glencoe, IL: Free Press.

SMELT, SIMON. 1980. "Money's Place in Society." *British Journal of Sociology* 31:205–223.

SOROKIN, PITIRIM A. 1943. *Sociocultural Causality, Space, Time*. Durham, NC: Duke University Press.

SUMNER, WILLIAM GRAHAM. [1906] 1940. *Folkways*. New York: Mentor.

SWEDBERG, RICHARD. 1987. "Economic Sociology: Past and Present." *Current Sociology* 35:1–221.

THALER, RICHARD H. 1990. "Anomalies: Saving, Fungibility, and Mental Accounts." *Journal of Economic Perspectives* 4:193–205.

THOMAS, W. I., and FLORIAN ZNANIECKI. [1918–1920] 1958. *The Polish Peasant in Europe and America*. New York: Dover.

TURNER, BRYAN S. 1986. "Simmel, Rationalisation and the Sociology of Money." *The Sociological Review* 34:93–114.

*Volumetric Study of the Gift-Giving Market*. 1986. New York: American Express.

WEBER, MAX. [1946] 1971. "Religious Rejections of the World and Their Directions." In H. H. Gerth and C. Wright Mills eds., *From Max Weber: Essays in Sociology*. New York: Oxford University Press, pp. 323–359.

WHITE, HARRISON C. 1988. "Varieties of Markets." In Barry Wellman and S. D. Berkowitz eds., *Social Structure: A Network Approach*. Cambridge, MA: Harvard University Press.

ZELIZER, VIVIANA. 1979. *Morals and Markets: The Development of Life Insurance in the United States*. New York: Columbia University Press.

———. 1987. *Pricing the Priceless Child: The Changing Social Value of Children*. New York: Basic Books.

# 9

# Thomas Edison and the Social Construction of the Early Electricity Industry in America

PATRICK McGUIRE, MARK GRANOVETTER, and MICHAEL SCHWARTZ

## The Social Construction of Industry

In 1880 Thomas Edison had only recently perfected the incandescent light, and virtually no homes or factories were yet served by electricity generated either on-site or in separate central stations. Lighting was overwhelmingly dominated by natural gas. By 1890, on-site generation of electric power had been promoted but already overtaken by the central stations of an investor-owned electric utility industry. This fledgling industry consisted of scores of independent local firms using different technologies and organizational structures, hobbled by local government, dependent on local investors and equipment manufacturers, and engaged in destructive competition. By 1929, the industry was dominated by a few large holding companies using standardized methods of generation and organizational structure, and protected by government agencies (Bonbright and Means 1969; Raushenbush and Laidler 1928; Ripley 1927; Federal Trade Commission 1935; McGuire 1986:526–529).

We use this sequence of events to demonstrate what we call the *social construction of industry* in a case that is central to the American industrial infrastructure. Due to a series of struggles between the dominant private investor-owned utilities (IOU's) and publicly owned firms (see Rudolph and Ridley 1986; King 1959; Hubbard 1961; Metcalf and Reinemer 1967; Raushenbush and Laidler 1928; McGuire 1989), there were frequent federal inquiries which created a vast body of primary documents, and inspired extensive secondary analyses which facilitate our investigation (Bureau of Corporations 1912; U.S. Department of Agriculture 1916; Federal Trade Commission 1927, 1934, 1935).

The idea that industries, like other economic institutions, are "socially constructed" follows from Granovetter's work on embeddedness (1985; 1990). His argument presents an alternative to the New Institutional Economics, which contends that a variety of social institutions and arrangements can be understood as the efficient solutions to economic problems (Granovetter 1985:488, 505). Such ahistoric and decontextual analyses assume that social actors (individuals and corporations) are minimally affected by dynamics exterior to the market, and that they therefore pursue economic self-interest without a social environment to mediate their interaction (483–486, 490). Such analyses specifically discount the impact on economic trajectories of such nonmarket phenomena as trade associations and director interlocks as well as social networks such as country clubs, fraternities, and family-based revolving credit associations (496). Granovetter contended that these and other social relationships may be pivotal to economic activity.

In a specific application of this argument, McGuire (1986) argued that industries should not be defined exclusively (or even primarily) on the basis of their commonly produced commodities—the principal classification criterion used by the federal government's Census of Manufactures. He emphasized the need to analyze socioeconomic and institutional links among self-designated competitors, arguing that an industry only becomes a social reality when firms are similarly structured, occupational categories are standardized, and extra-institutional structures are created to manage competition and articulate common goals.

We stress the role of human agency and social structure in determining which groups of firms become associated into an industry, and in defining the scope and structure of the resulting collectivity. Standard discussions of industrial organization conspicuously neglect human agency since they assume that industrial structure is an inevitable and maximally efficient consequence of existing technology and market structure. These functionalist arguments are inadequate both because they fail to demonstrate that the outcome is maximally efficient and because they do not explore the process by which it is produced, though at times there is an implicit or explicit appeal to natural selection (Friedman 1953).

At the opposite extreme from this functionalism, in which the activity of particular individuals is irrelevant because outcomes are more-or-less automatically shaped to efficiently meet the needs of the economic system,[1] is the argument that certain industries, especially those thought to

---

[1] For electric utilities, such an argument appears in Lilley 1965; MacLaren 1943; Hammond 1941; and Bright 1972.

be dominated by one or two crucial technological developments, take the form they do on account of the activity of a few "great men or women."[2] We will argue that human agency is vastly underestimated in the former argument, but overestimated in the latter. Our own argument sees individual and collective action as critical, but only within sharply defined historical and structural constraints.

Thomas Hughes's 1979 article and award-winning 1983 book *Networks of Power* err in both directions. On the one hand, Hughes presents an elaborate and challenging argument that the organization and financing of the industry were ultimately the consequence of innovations developed to address a series of technical problems; on the other hand, he sees these inventions as the masterwork of a group of brilliant inventors, engineers, and businessmen (1983:5–17).

We admire Hughes's painstaking research, and respect the relevance of the causal forces he identifies. And we strongly endorse some of his key findings, for example, that "the [Chicago Edison] system and the way it was created became models for other urban utilities . . . both the leading edge and the representative case of the waves of development that followed" (1983:204). But we argue that his "systems imperative" thesis—that the industry developed as it did as the result of brilliant men finding solutions to economic and technical problems that circumstances presented to them—derives from an analytic framework that conceals a range of possible alternative outcomes (McGuire 1986:104–106; DuBuff 1984; Perrow 1988). We believe that the resulting structure was not the only technologically practical one,[3] nor was it the most efficient in terms of market economics.[4] It arose because a set of powerful actors gained access to certain techniques and applied them in a highly visible and profitable way. Those techniques resulted from the specific and shared personal understandings, social connections, organizational conditions, and historical opportunities available to these actors. This success, in turn, triggered important pressures for uniformity across regions, even when

[2] This notion was captured most succinctly by William James in *From Great Men and Their Environment*: "Originally all things were flashes of genius in an individual head" (quoted in Martin 1922:46). It was most fully elaborated in Sidney Hook's classic book, *The Hero in History* (1943). Some studies of electric utilities that emphasize a "great men" theme are Conot 1979; McDonald 1962; Hammond 1941; Prout 1972; Ramsey 1937; Lindgren 1979; Bush 1973; Miller 1957; and T. Martin 1953.

[3] This is shown in detail for the period 1888–1891 by David (1987) and David and Bunn (1988).

[4] A critique of this tendency in Hughes's work can be found in McGuire (1990). That article specifically emphasizes the different economic logics of different investor groups seeking efficient outcomes, and of conflicting definitions of market efficiency between inventor/entrepreneurs and financiers/investors in the related electric equipment industry.

such uniformity excluded viable and possibly more efficient existing or potential alternative technologies and organizational forms.

In effect, we argue that which industry form eventually dominated was affected but not finally determined by the relative efficiency of different forms. We mean to identify the forces that moved the industry in certain directions, and the advantages that those directions achieved simply by virtue of having been established; these advantages then changed the nature of the contest between industrial forms in such a way as eventually to lock in a form that might not have been abstractly optimal. The new form then itself modified the environment in ways compatible with its needs. Later observers, who then look only at a snapshot of technology and organization, may note the fit between industry and environment and find confirmation for their argument that the industry has arisen in its present form in order to meet the needs posed by that environment. Only a dynamic, historical account can break through the misconceptions that result from confining analysis to comparative statics.

Our argument has a family resemblance to that made by economists Paul David (1986) and Brian Arthur (1989) on the "lock-in" of inefficient technologies (such as the QWERTY keyboard on which this argument is typed—more slowly than it would be on one of better and well-known design), but generalizes the argument from the case of technology to that of institutional and organizational form.

Virtually all analyses, ranging from the early industry publicists and politically motivated federal investigators to more recent scholarly treatises by Hughes and other academics, emphasize the centrality first of Thomas Edison and, later, of Samuel Insull in the development of the electric utility industry. We generally accept these assertions, and therefore focus our analytic attention on their roles.

But in so doing, we challenge the prevailing sense of their individual omniscience and self-conscious historical missions.[5] We argue instead that their social networks were vital in providing the resources and opportunities that facilitated success. Insull's success in Chicago (from 1892 on) established his capacity to disseminate his methods to other electrical utilities, enabling him to coordinate the actions of the newly emerging industry. While acknowledging that Insull was a central actor, we argue that his importance derived from his role as a bridge among previously segregated networks of individuals and organizations. Though he can be credited with perceiving and effectively activating the structural potential

---

[5] See, for example, for Insull, his own memoirs and collected speeches (Insull 1915, 1924); Forrest McDonald's biography (1962); and Hughes (1979, 1983) and Ramsey (1937).

in his network location, Insull was actually no more innovative than many other utility executives. His centrality therefore resulted less from his persona, or from any uniqueness in Chicago Edison's technical infrastructure, than from a more general and enduring phenomenon: the creation of economic formations from congealed networks of personal relationships.

The present chapter is a very preliminary report of one part of our project. In our view, a theory of the social construction of industry ought to account for the social structure of an industry, in which we include: 1) the internal structure of organizations comprising the industry; 2) the structuring of relations between firms and their upstream and downstream trading partners; 3) relations among the firms within the industry (including formal and informal relations, cross-stockholding and interlocking directorates, trade associations, and vertical relations such as those expressed in holding companies); and 4) relations between the industry and government at all levels.

Our completed project will attempt to cover all these bases from the beginning of the industry in about 1880 to its stable form, around 1910. In the following material, we end in 1892, before Samuel Insull moved to Chicago Edison, from which he would revolutionize the industry. Much of the social structuring of electrical utilities was still to be determined at this point, including most of the interfirm relations in the industry and the links to government. But the important issue of whether electricity would be produced on-site in homes and businesses or in central stations had been generally resolved. The issue of whether equipment manufacturers would be nearly indistinguishable from the providers of the service (as was the long-time outcome for telephones) had already been joined, and the ground had been laid for the separation that would become more clear in Insull's Chicago.

## The Birth of the Electric Utility Industry: Bankers, Inventors, and Manufacturers in Conflict, 1880–1894

*Edison, Morgan, and the Conflict over Central Station Development*

Drexel, Morgan and Company, and several affiliated financiers including William Vanderbilt—the largest owner of natural gas stocks in America (Friedel and Israel 1986:22; Wheeler 1973:145) had created the Edison Electric Light Company (hereafter EELC) in 1878 to "support Edison's experiments [on incandescent lighting] at Menlo Park and control the resulting patents" (Friedel and Israel 1986:14; Conot 1979:122–130). Edison encountered several problems and delays through the winter, spring, summer, and fall of 1879 and was forced to relinquish control of the firm to an executive committee controlled by Morgan associates (Hoyt 1966:170). To continue the developmental work on the incandescent bulb system, Edison was forced to sell some of his EELC and other stocks, and some assets and patents. Among the new investors was Henry Villard: President of Northern Pacific Railroad, and a man affiliated with German investment houses (Passer 1953:85–86; Conot 1979:143; Buss 1978:190). Villard also became a member of the EELC executive committee.

The friction between Edison and bankers such as J. P. Morgan continued after Edison finally produced a viable incandescent bulb, on account of their differing conceptions of the basic trajectory of the electrical generation business. Edison's vision of the industry was that it would consist of utility companies that could compete with natural gas by building central generating stations and selling electricity to individual residences and business establishments. EELC investors were loathe to invest in such an enterprise, and so Edison saw that he would have to manufacture generating equipment in his own firms, and secure a monopoly over the production of such equipment, to complement his monopoly power based on patents (Conot 1979:220–221; McGuire 1990).

The major American investors in electrical development sought a decentralized system in which residential and individual users would generate their *own* electricity, using small devices bought from manufacturers and installed (like furnaces) into their buildings. J. P. Morgan and his supporters had invested heavily in the invention of such small devices. They sought to assign their patent rights to manufacturers and collect licensing fees. Their ultimate ambition was an industry composed of scores of manufacturers, each producing its own line of electricity production and distribution equipment based on the Edison patents, for untold numbers of homes and factories. The sales of these tens of thousands of systems would constitute a very large market, with a constant cash flow and huge total revenues, generating substantial royalty payments to EELC and huge dividends for its shareholders.

The creation of the Edison Company for Isolated Lighting as a subsidiary of EELC occurred in response to the early demands for electric service from businesses and a few affluent individuals. In 1882, there were 153 isolated systems sold by Edison Isolated alone; the number increased to 702 by 1886 (Passer 1953:117). Among the initial customers were investors J. P. Morgan, Henry Villard, and William Vanderbilt, as well as such prominent Chicago industrialists as Marshall Field, Rand McNally, and Cyrus McCormick (Bright 1972:72, 75; Passer 1953; 85, 117; Freeman 1952:10; Allen 1950:80).

The crucial fact is that the main point of contention between Morgan and Edison was not the technology as such, but rather the structure of markets and economic returns that would result. In fact, at this stage of technological development, the distinction between isolated systems and central stations was smaller than it might seem in retrospect, since isolated systems were often in commercial establishments that had many lamps, and the early central stations were quite small, most serving only a couple of hundred customers.[6] Using the direct-current technology of the 1880s, which was constrained to a relatively low voltage, long-distance transmission was impractical.[7] Early central stations, such as Edison's first at Pearl Street, New York, could generate electricity only within a radius of half a mile, and thus were limited to densely packed urban centers. What was crucial was that Edison sought to sell electricity in a way that required massive investor capital and little economic outlay from the consumer. Morgan wanted to see equipment sold to consumers with minimal outlay from EELC investors, as would happen if licenses were sold to producers who risked their own capital and paid royalties to EELC rather than such risks being borne by EELC investor's funds.

Edison's attraction to large systems may have been in part aesthetic, an aspect of his own personal style. Thus Hughes, using Isaiah Berlin's distinction between the hedgehog and the fox, refers to "Edison the hedgehog" who relates everything to a single vision (Hughes 1983:18). (Foxes pursue many, often unrelated ends.) But Hughes also notes that when an inventor "created only a component, he remained dependent on others to invent or supply other components. The inventor of components could not have the control over innovation that Edison wanted" (1983:21). He may thus have seen that in the isolated station/equipment

---

[6] For example, by 1885, isolated systems averaged 254 lamps per installation and theater installations of Edison Isolated systems averaged 702 lamps per installation. As late as 1888 the (smaller) Edison central stations (65 percent of total Edison stations, 25 percent of all installed lamps) averaged only 750 lamps (Passer 1953:117, 121). A "lamp," the term always used in the literature on this early period, simply means a single socket and bulb, as we now know it. An electric chandelier, then, might consist of a dozen or more "lamps."

[7] For technical reasons, it is far easier to boost and to reduce ("step down") the voltage of alternating current than direct current. Because of inevitable loss of voltage over transmission lines, the electric power sent at low voltage over long distances would be too weak to serve any useful purpose. This is not to say that direct current cannot be transmitted at high voltage, only that the technical problems to be solved were more complex and little investment capital was available to finance such an effort once alternating current had become dominant. Ironically, during the 1980s, firms began building high-voltage power lines with DC current. As we enter the era of superconductivity in the 1990s, DC current may become far more important. See David and Bunn (1988) for a discussion of related technical and historical issues.

manufacturing model, his profits would depend on patent rights and royalty payments; the patent law was sufficiently ambiguous that he may have feared the outrageous costs associated with possible patent disputes, as well as investor moves to replace his patents with those of other inventors.[8] Revenues from central-station generation of electricity, by contrast, were a direct return to the owners of such stations and thus gave the owners a more powerful position in relation to investors and financiers.

We can only speculate as to why Edison had so strong a preference for the central-station model. But it is clear that, even before he developed the incandescent bulb, he had this model in mind. He used as the analogue for his planned central stations the "image of the central gashouse and its distributing system, of gas mains running to smaller branch pipes and leading into many dwelling places" (Josephson 1959:179), and read extensively about the system of distribution for natural gas. In developing his incandescent bulb, Edison turned away from the low-resistance, high-current lights that others had experimented with because his calculations showed that central stations would have to use fantastic amounts of copper wire in order to connect up any substantial area lighted in this way. Instead, he turned to the high-resistance, low-current model that he eventually made to succeed. He also developed new kinds of generators (then called "dynamos") that could drive such a system. From the "very outset of his work, Edison was guided by his overarching concept of a *whole electric distribution system* of which all the parts must be fitted into place. In contrast with other inventors who searched only for some magical incandescing substance, he worked out all the supporting structure of his system: its power supply, conductors and circuit, and then came back to determine what kind of light would be demanded by it" (Josephson 1959:211).

Morgan and other American and British financiers had a number of structural reasons to oppose centralized power. They had been willing to make long-term commitments of capital to railroads, but not commercial

---

[8] Initially, Edison tried to avoid litigation on patents. In one case where he was prevailed upon to enter litigation, the English Edison Company sued Joseph Swan, another inventor of an incandescent bulb. This suit was settled in 1883 by a merger of the two firms into the Edison and Swan United Electric Company. Edison took personal affront at both the failure to validate his patent and the dual billing of the inventors (Hughes 1983:62; Carosso 1987:271). The situation of dual billing was not only demeaning, but also put the investors in a position to play off the inventors against one another. We have no direct evidence that a similar situation would have occurred in this case, but it is plausible that Edison would fear such an outcome or the leverage that would result even from the possibility—especially since he had done this to Bell's telephone patents, with the backing of financiers (see footnote 11).

ventures. On the other hand, German investors "had from the outset directed most of their capital into long-term industrial and commercial enterprises" (Buss 1978:173).[9] Thus, not surprisingly, the only investor who openly supported Edison's expansionist efforts was the one with connections to German investors—(German-born) Henry Villard.[10] By 1880 it was clear that Edison's scheme would require huge sums of capital to create, nurture, and consolidate central-station systems.

The American bankers sought a positive balance sheet in the short run and a rapid return on their investment, and they feared having to rely on long maturities in their investments. The long and expensive wait for central stations to be perfected and installed—and then for lines to be laid and connected to users—would not only delay returns on their existing investment, but also require huge new capital outlays that would themselves have long-delayed returns. Furthermore, such delayed returns presented the risk that the technology might become obsolete; the long construction period would postpone the introduction of the Edison electrical system, possibly allowing other inventors time to innovate and develop compatible or even improved devices. This could have robbed the Edison system of its "first mover" advantage.[11]

Investors also doubted whether the potential returns from a couple of

[9] To understand the difference in relationships between industry and banks in the United States and Germany requires a consideration of the differing patterns of industrial development. American industry developed more slowly and gradually, with banks playing an important role, but not one in which they directly dominated industry. The inability to dominate directly appears related to the reluctance to commit funds for the long term. By contrast, German industry was developed over a relatively short period of time, and banks played a relatively more dominant role than in the United States. Clapham observes of the period from 1870 to 1914 that bank credits to industrial concerns, "at first short, became longer and longer until they amounted almost to partnerships. Industrialists sat on the directorates of banks and—much more important—bankers tended to control the policy of industry" (1936:393). On the dominating position of German banks in this period see also Gerschenkron 1952 and 1966.

[10] A desire to avoid long-term commitment of capital had previously been shown by several of the EELC investors, who had withdrawn from the telephone industry precisely due to their recognition of the amount of capital needed to make that industry develop. They sold their securities and equipment to the Bell Company—a firm that faced similar funding problems due to investor attitudes (McMahon 1984:15; Irwin 1986:261–263).

[11] A similar delay had impeded the development of Alexander Graham Bell's telephone. Ironically, Edison and his investors were aware of the possible loss of "first mover" advantages, because Edison had invented devices that undermined Bell's advantage. Several of the EELC backers had supported Edison's efforts to modify and improve on Bell's device, and had backed the establishment of a competing and improved technical system that Edison created at the Newark labs before he moved onto Menlo Park and the electric light developments (McMahon 1984:15–24; Conot 1979:81–96, 168–170).

centralized stations could be as high as those for thousands of isolated systems. Not only could isolated stations be sold almost immediately, but their installation would create an immediate market for a range of electrical devices, thus allowing investors to show a positive balance sheet in the short run.

William Vanderbilt in particular had a strong vested interest in keeping the electric incandescent light limited to the affluent. He was the largest owner of natural gas stock in America and (as Edison noted) he only bought the EELC stock as a hedge (Friedel and Israel 1986:21– 22).[12] He had invested millions of dollars in gas equipment, mains, lines, and other fixed capital. Edison's scheme basically called for him to fund a system that would replace and render obsolescent before its time the fixed capital he had already invested in to serve the same purpose. For all these reasons, when Edison proposed that a large central station be built at Pearl Street in New York City in 1880, Morgan and the other investors were hesitant. In addition to the objections we have already cataloged, they did not trust Edison. They felt that he had misled and perhaps deceived them during the late 1870s about the pace of development of incandescent lighting in his laboratories, and that he constantly struggled with them over its direction (Friedel and Israel 1986:13–40). Edison then threatened to resign from the firm, in essence threatening to destroy further development and the value of existing investments. "To avoid dooming the firm," as they described the prospect of EELC without Edison, the Morgan-dominated Executive Committee agreed in mid-December 1880 to authorize $1 million for development at Pearl Street (Friedel and Israel 1986:190); but once he had bullied them into creating a central-station system in New York City, most remaining goodwill between the two sides evaporated. In a seeming concession to stockholders (and in a move that further weakened Edison's stock-based control of EELC), EELC issued and sold an additional $130,000 worth of stock. They used this money to repay the outstanding loans from stockholders and to purchase Edison's patents for the electric railroad for $50,000.

In late 1880, the Edison Electric Illuminating Company of New York (EEIC-NY)—forerunner of the present Consolidated Edison[13]—was es-

---

[12]On the original EELC board, though Vanderbilt had invested heavily in the company, there were only surrogates for the family since, given their gas-company interests, they "did not want to be openly associated with the enterprise" (Conot 1979:129). Vanderbilt himself had a checkered history with electric lighting. Having installed an isolated plant in his Fifth Avenue mansion in the early 1880s, he had to have it removed when Mrs. Vanderbilt became hysterical after a short-circuit and fire made her aware that she had a steam engine and boiler in the cellar, driving the generator (Josephson 1959:261).

[13]Consolidated Edison, known locally as Con Edison, is the utility company currently serving the New York City metropolitan area.

tablished. As a licensee of the parent firm, EELC, it was to be the operating company (we now say "utility") that would build a central generating station at Pearl Street in New York. This station, which would supply direct current electricity throughout a one-square-mile area, was built in the financial district. It was located there not only because the high density of commercial establishments would provide a ready market for the electricity, but also because it would "catch the attention of financiers and the investing public, persons who were needed to fund Edison stations elsewhere" (Hughes 1983:42).

In exchange for its license, EEIC-NY gave $250,000 in securities and $100,000 in cash payment to its parent, EELC. The remaining $750,000 of authorized capitalization had to be raised by sales of EEIC-NY securities. Such sales, which would provide the money for the $100,000 payment and for physical plant construction, needed to occur before construction could begin.[14] The $750,000 in authorized capital for EEIC-NY was offered to EELC stockholders in proportion to their existing ratio of EELC shares (Passer 1953:87–90). Thus, Edison and his associates needed to come up with at least $100,000 to return to EELC and, as majority owners, had to raise most of the remaining $650,000 which was authorized for, and would eventually be needed to complete the project.

At this point, Edison needed cash to purchase EEIC-NY stock in proportion to his EELC shares and to assure the $100,000 payment to EELC (Passer 1953:90). As Friedel and Israel note, most of the investors had decided not to put "more money into the electric light . . . [until they had realized] some returns on the patents for which they had already supported Edison for more than two years" (1986:194).

This also forced Edison and his intimate associates Charles Batchelor, Francis Upton, Edward Johnson, and Sigmund Bergmann (some of whom were investors in EELC) to create a series of industrial firms to produce (under EELC license) devices for Pearl Street and (more generally) other central and isolated systems. It was at this juncture that Johnson, who had just returned from Britain, pressured Edison to hire a twenty-one-year-old Englishman, Samuel Insull, as his private secretary. When Insull arrived in America, on February 28, 1881, he spent the entire day and night meeting with Johnson and Edison (Insull 1915:xxvi). He offered counsel as to which of Edison's European telephone and telegraph patents and which of his European securities could be sold, for what prices, and to whom. By 4:00 A.M. Insull had become "Edison's financial fac-

---

[14]We have been unable to find records that state clearly whether all $750,000 in securities was actually sold, and when exactly the bulk of sales took place in relation to the actual construction.

totum," and at dawn Johnson sailed for Europe to sell the patents and securities (McDonald 1962:22). Subsequently Edison used the cash from these sales, along with his personal wealth and credit, and funds invested by his intimate associates, to finance the series of manufacturing companies that could make, sell, and buy his electric devices and inventions and also to help fund the creation of EEIC-NY and the Pearl Street Station (McDonald 1962:26–27).

### Edison's Empire: His Network of Associates and Firms

Edison had never been the solitary inventor working in his late night laboratory. Francis Jehl, who had worked there, described the Menlo Park operations thus: "Edison is really a collective noun and means the work of many men" (quoted in Lindgren 1979:17). From sometime in the early 1870s, when his lab was in Newark, through the legendary Menlo Park period (1876–1881), when so many important technological breakthroughs took place, Edison employed about 200 inventors and technicians. After the move to New York, when the laboratory on Goerck Street guided the success of the Pearl Street station, at least 200 (and perhaps as many as 500) additional employees passed through the Edison laboratories. These individuals, most of them inventors and tinkerers, became the heart of electrical manufacturing and generation in the United States. Many were promoted internally, so that most of the executives of the various Edison manufacturing companies (including Edward Johnson, who brought Insull to the United States) rose from the laboratory.

Edison had several intimate associates. Before 1877, he worked in a lab in Newark, New Jersey with Sigmund Bergmann, Charles Batchelor, and John Kruesi, among others, and relied on Grosvenor Lowrey for his economic and legal information, and as a link to Wall Street. Bergmann left and formed a licensed company to produce Edison products. Edward Johnson formed and operated another licensed company and also represented Edison in Europe from 1878 to 1880. In 1880, he and Bergmann merged their firms and took Edison as a third partner in Messrs. Bergmann and Company, a Manhattan firm that produced fixtures, meters, sockets, and other small devices (Passer 1953:94; Friedel and Israel 1986:201).

During the Menlo Park period (1876–1881), Edison and his associates were joined by Francis Upton. When Upton and Batchelor actually solved the filament problem in 1879, Edison gave them 5 percent and 10 percent of the future income of the electric light patent respectively, and some EELC stock (Conot 1979:149). Selling some stock and drawing on other financial resources, Upton, Batchelor, Johnson, and Edison formed Edison Electric Lamp Company, which was run first by Batchelor and, after 1881, by Upton (Friedel and Israel 1986:194–195; Passer 1953:93). Batchelor then helped set up Edison Electric Tube Company, run by Kruesi, and Edison Machine Works, run by Charles Dean, Kruesi's former assistant at Menlo Park (Passer 1953:95–97; Friedel and Israel 1986:195). However, after 1883 Batchelor took over management of the Machine Works. The latter two firms were owned directly by Edison and his trusted associates. Thus, as Edwards notes, "[d]uring the early 1880's, Thomas Edison personally directed the operations of his factories . . . [he relied on] personal and loyal associates" as factory managers (1979:25).[15]

While in Newark and Menlo Park, Edison had relied on Grosvenor Lowrey for business and legal matters, and as his principal liaison to Wall Street (Josephson 1959:179–185, 223). After Lowrey, who was intimately tied to Morgan and had his office in Morgan's building, became increasingly identified with the investors and argued against Edison's desires in the struggle over the direction of the firm and technology, Edison sought business advice from other quarters. Johnson and Insull provided a sounding board, partially replacing Lowrey.[16] And Insull, as Edison's personal secretary, was the conduit through which all Edison correspondence passed to and from financiers, businessmen, and the Edison-associate plant managers.

These various firms, needed to construct and equip Pearl Street (and to produce devices for sale to other electrical firms in the future), were established by Thomas Edison and his associates and received exclusive licenses from EELC. Only the Edison Company for Isolated Lighting—carrying forward the Morgan-supported isolated lighting scheme—became a formal subsidiary of EELC (Passer 1953:93–99; Friedel and Israel 1986:198–201). Edison accepted the formation of Edison Isolated only after "tremendous pressure" (Hammond 1941:63).

Edison had forced reluctant investors to support the Pearl Street station and had created an industrial infrastructure to support the project. However, the EELC contract with EEIC-NY indicates that investor sup-

---

[15] The Edison Machine Works was in a plant on Goerck Street, on New York's Lower East Side; the Edison Electric Tube Company was set up on Washington Street in New York in February 1881 to organize the installation of the underground distribution system for the Pearl Street Station (Friedel and Israel 1986:195). These four companies—Lamp, Tube, Machine Works, and the Messrs. Bergmann and Company—were the core of the Edison manufacturing operation for the next decade, and were key elements in the later establishment of Edison General Electric (EGE) in 1889 and General Electric in 1892.

[16] In 1882, Johnson became a member of the EELC board and a vice-president of EELC (Jones 1940:51).

port was highly conditional. The contract for Pearl Street assured exclusive licensing rights for the remainder of New York City *only if* Pearl Street was built for less than $250,000, and if in each year after 1881, Edison would build, equip, and occupy four new plants per year (Passer 1953:119).[17] Due to delays in creating the manufacturing firms, getting supplies, and unforeseen difficulties in manufacturing and construction, Pearl Street cost about $600,000. It supplied electricity free in 1882 (beginning with its first generation of electricity on September 4), and lost $12,000 in the first half of 1883. It turned a profit in the third quarter of 1883 and paid its first dividend in 1885 (Hughes 1983:45; Jones 1940:211).[18]

These dismal results certainly contributed to the tone of the report of the annual meeting of EELC in 1882, in which the Morgan-dominated executive committee expressed their lack of enthusiasm for additional central-station projects. They noted that

> the policy of our Company . . . has always been . . . that of merely paying the expenses of experiments and of taking out and holding patents and not of investing capital in the actual business of lighting. [Passer 1953:98]

Edison's conflict with the committee over central stations was only one, though perhaps the most important, of a series of incidents in which he and they were in active conflict. For example, Edison fought against an attempted trust formation early in 1883 that would have consolidated the six largest electrical firms into the Gramme Electric Company. This merger had been proposed by a group of New York bankers affiliated with U.S. Electric and supported by Morgan-associated EELC executives (Woodbury 1949:108; Flint 1923:293–295; Passer 1953:51–52). Edison also opposed the 1883 merger of his electric railroad patents with those of Steven Field. When he failed at his attempt to block that merger, he responded by halting his work on this important area of electric power application (Conot 1979:207; Passer 1953:220–221).

Next the Edison and Morgan factions clashed over royalties. Between 1882 and 1884, the number of light bulbs sold jumped from 210,000

[17] Dales notes that thirty-six DC stations were planned for Manhattan alone (1957:15). Martin (1922:87) says that thirty-six were planned for the area south of 59th Street, so that the grand total for Manhattan would have been considerably more.

[18] Other early central station projects, such as Appleton Wisconsin and London's Holborn Viaduct, also lost money. The former paid royalties to EELC eventually, but the latter collapsed (McDonald 1957:37; Hughes 1983:62). By 1888, however, the profitability corner had been turned, with only two central station firms out of the roughly 200 Edison-dependent ones losing money (Conot 1979:227).

to 370,000. Revenue per bulb rose from 2.8 to 14.3 cents, a total of over $43,000 profit in the last year. Edison Lamp's contract called for royalty payments for all profit over 3 cents per bulb (Passer 1953:95). But Edison Lamp immediately reinvested all revenue, so that it technically showed no profit, and therefore paid no royalties to EELC. The Morgan associates claimed that this was fraud, and they also accused the manufacturing firms of overcharging the Isolated firm and its cash-paying customers for devices and bulbs. Such practices by Edison would have had the effect of retarding sales of isolated stations. And, when such sales did exist, Edison and associates would have been price-gouging clients of their financier-sponsored sister firm.

Because of this history of conflicts, Edison could not find investors for another central station in New York City; Boston investors, most of whom had close ties either to New York investors at odds with Edison, or to competing companies, shunned an Edison plan for one there (Conot 1979:208). Edison responded to EELC's lack of interest in central stations by announcing

> I have come to the conclusion that my system of lighting, having been perfected, should be promoted and I should take hold and push the system better than anyone else. [Passer 1953:98]

Thus, in the spring of 1883, Edison formed the Thomas A. Edison Construction Department to sell and build central stations, and put Insull in charge of it. During the next eighteen months, he and Insull sold a score of central stations to small towns such as Brockton and Fall River in Massachusetts, Piqua and Tiffin in Ohio, Sunbury and Harrisburg in Pennsylvania, and Newburgh in New York (Passer 1953:99; McDonald 1962:30). Edison secured for the companies operating these stations a license from EELC that entitled them to an exclusive territorial franchise regarding the use and sale of all electrical products whose patent was owned by EELC.[19] What was most significant about these sales was that Edison accepted securities of these firms in lieu of cash payment for equipment and for the EELC license. This further angered EELC investors, who received, instead of cash, securities for which there was no market, and upon which there would not be dividends in the foreseeable future given the absence of any substantial cash flow. This practice also worsened Edison's own economic position by requiring that he cover the

[19] But the value of such a license was diluted by the fact that Edison Isolated continued, during this period, to sell products within these territories to industrial firms and large residential customers, thus competing directly with the new central stations, in violation of contractual provisions.

immediate costs of manufacturing equipment for these stations—a further drain on his limited capital supply. However, it did keep his workforce occupied, and it built a case for there being a central-station business if only investors would support it. Moreover, the indebtedness of the local utilities to the Edison Company—particularly the equity aspect of this indebtedness—created a long-term partnership between them that ultimately established both coordination and control across the market.

Successful operation of these new central stations was by no means trivial, however, especially in this early stage of development. It required considerable technical as well as business expertise, and local firms were difficult to monitor. Corrupt or incompetent local executives could easily fritter away a large investment before their failures were visible at Edison headquarters in New York. Edison, through Insull, addressed this problem when possible by dealing with individuals who were or had been part of the Edison industrial team. Thus Charles Edgar, who had risen through the laboratory ranks to a major position in the organization, was sent to Boston by Edison in 1887 to oversee the installation of the Boston generators and became the chief executive of Boston Edison (Toner 1951:10). John Lieb, who would later become president of New York Edison, was sent to Milan, Italy in 1882 as chief engineer of Italian Edison (Martin 1922:28); and Frank Sprague, H. M. Byllesby, and S. Z. Mitchell, each engineers at the Goerck Street facility, left New York to install and operate Edison central-station plants in Brockton, Massachusetts; Hamilton, Ontario; and Seattle, Washington respectively during this era (Passer 1962:219–220; Tate 1938:148; Dierdorf 1971:2–67).[20]

In July 1884, the Morgan-dominated EELC executive committee proposed merging EELC with the Edison manufacturing firms to stop the diversion of funds and end the acceptance of local securities. Edison rejected their proposal, and EELC threatened not to renew his five-year personal invention contract. They also demanded the elimination of the exclusive production licenses with Edison Lamp and Edison Works. Edison countered by demanding, as a precondition to signing another five-year invention contract, that exclusive production contracts be given to the other two manufacturing firms in which he was a partner: Messrs. Bergmann and Company, and Edison Tube (Conot 1979:220–221).

---

[20] It is difficult, however, to get a clear picture for most of the new central stations of those who were running them, since when the new stations later merged into larger firms, the earlier records were generally lost. It is possible that detailed study of local newspapers during this period would further indicate the extent to which other former Edison associates were important in the early central stations.

Due to their sale of securities and the issuance of additional securities by EELC, Edison and his associates no longer held a majority of the stock in EELC. Morgan knew this because his firm had brokered many of their sales (Carosso 1987:271). Yet Edison directly challenged Morgan and, using his prestige among various minority stockholders and their fear of the threatened loss of the charismatic inventor and his knowledgeable associates, soon had gathered proxies for 3,000 of the 3,500 votes needed to control the firm. Faced with Edison's resistance and recognizing that his own investments in this rapidly growing field might be jeopardized, Morgan acquiesced to Edison's demands (McDonald 1962:25–32).

At the 1884 annual meeting of the EELC, a Board and executive committee more amenable to Edison's wishes and ideas were elected. Eight of the thirteen EELC directors were replaced, including several Morgan and all Vanderbilt associates, and Edward H. Johnson became the top executive (McDonald 1962:32). Yet Morgan continued to have representation on the Board, and twice in the following two years the exit of a Morgan associate was followed by his replacement with another (Passer 1953:101). This highly unusual "broken tie" replacement indicates that Morgan continued to exert influence on the Board (cf. Palmer 1983; Useem 1985:43–46).

Edison-influenced directors then invested EELC funds in central-station projects in Boston and New York (Insull 1915:349; Passer 1953:102). These funds were augmented by Edison's own sales of stocks and patents. Morgan was not about to acquiesce quietly to this move, and he called in existing loans and issued new ones at high interest, thus creating a cash-flow crisis for Edison. Rumors of financial impropriety began circulating, discouraging other investors from assisting him. Edison's problems were compounded when other firms infringed on his patents and produced low-cost compatible bulbs and devices. By the mid-1880s, Edison's firms were in deep financial crisis: they reneged on loan payments, the Menlo Park headquarters complex was sold at a Sheriff's auction, and the firm's efforts to extend its network of central-station facilities was severely hampered.

Morgan and other financiers continued to withhold capital for new or expanded manufacturing production, but this was somewhat mitigated by access to European investment capital. When in 1886 a group of Boston investors, some affiliated with EELC's rival firm Thomson-Houston, and others with the British banking firm of Baring Brothers, joined EELC in a syndicate to create Boston Edison and build a central-station facility, even Morgan was pressured into purchasing a minority share of the stock (McGuire 1986:81–86; Insull 1915:174–175, 399; Passer 1953:85, 239; McMahon 1985:11; Toner 1951:7–10; Carosso 1979:17–19).

In May, 1886, Edison settled a strike at the Goerck Street plant, and promptly moved the entire operation to Schenectady, New York, a rural town with lower wages and skilled but unemployed workers (McDonald 1962:37). During 1887 to 1889, Insull became the chief executive of the newly located Edison Machine Works, his first experience in command of a substantial workforce. In November, 1886, increasingly desperate financially, Edison sold 1,000 shares of his EELC stock to Morgan and associates for a pittance.[21] Now in full control of EELC but not the manufacturing firms, Morgan still prevented cash flow to the latter, hoping to force their consolidation with EELC (Carlson 1984:337; Carosso 1987:271).

### Henry Villard, German Capital, and the Origins of General Electric

In the late 1880s, Edison's group again regained control of the electrical industry, relying more significantly than they had in the early 1880s on capital from the German Empire. To understand these events we must recap the intertwined stories of financier Henry Villard and the vagaries of German banking and electricity. Villard, who appeared in our story earlier as a supporter of Edison's drive to build central stations, was of German origin, coming to the United States in 1853 where he became a journalist. His marriage to the daughter of abolitionist W. L. Garrison opened for him the doors to the Boston elite of business and finance, which complemented his already strong German business contacts. After several trips back and forth to Europe, in which he mobilized German and British capital for various purposes, he led syndicates to buy out the Oregon Steamship Line and later, the Northern Pacific Railroad (1878), of which by 1881 he had gotten complete control. But by 1884 Villard was severely over-extended and revenues from these investments were less than expected. J. P. Morgan used his position as a major investor to force re-organization of Northern Pacific and to force Villard to leave the United States in an effort to reconstruct his personal fortune and mend his strained relations with his financial contacts in Europe (Buss 1978). Not insignificantly, this activity was concurrent with the proxy context between Morgan and Edison, and Villard was an Edison supporter.

The major Edison affiliate in Germany was German Edison,[22] which

---

[21] That is, at $6.00 per share, whereas it had once sold for $5,000 per share.

[22] Deutsche Edison Gesellschaft für angewandte Electrizität (German Edison Company for Applied Electricity), founded in 1883 (see Hughes 1983:67).

in 1887 was reorganized as German General Electric (AEG).[23] The company was founded in 1883 by Emil Rathenau, an engineer who built it into the major force in the German electrical industry by creating what would now be called a holding company. Rathenau was a major figure in German business, and because he had used vast amounts of borrowed money to build AEG, he was well connected to sources of capital. The other major force in German electricity was the equipment manufacturer Siemens and Halske, founded and run by electrical inventor Werner von Siemens, whose cousin, Georg von Siemens, principal director of the powerful Deutsche Bank, had once worked for the firm (Hughes 1983:180). Villard returned to the United States as an agent of the Deutsche Bank to purchase railroad and electric utility stocks. Within a year he was back on the EELC board and involved in the development of Edison systems in several cities (Buss 1978:177–199).

In 1889, when Villard put together a syndicate of German banks and manufacturing firms, he was able to include AEG and Siemens and Halske. This syndicate recruited a group of other financiers to purchase Edison Electric (EELC), the Edison manufacturing companies, and several other companies, and consolidate them into a new entity called Edison General Electric. This scheme was to be the first installment of his grand plan to "form an international cartel to control the electric business the world over" (McDonald 1962:39–40; see also Carosso 1987:272). This action was such a dramatic and definitive breach of the capital boycott that Morgan himself took a minority position in the refinancing, having first, however, altered the terms in a way highly favorable to his own interests (McDonald 1962:40).

Morgan's participation was partially defensive: the consolidation moved the light-bulb patents and manufacturing into the same corporate shell as the new dominant central generation business. If Morgan wished to preserve his access to and influence over the lighting industry, he had to invest in the larger enterprise.

The new firm was placed on a sound financial footing. Villard became president and Insull second vice-president and Board member. Villard put Insull in full charge of manufacturing and sales, whereupon he "reorganized and integrated the manufacturing operations, rendering them vastly more efficient" (McDonald 1962:41). In the next two years, Villard and Insull exploited EGE's financial security to establish a solid foundation for the central-station system that Edison had begun to create many years earlier. Because of their ability to extend credit to fledgling

---

[23] Allgemeine Elektrizitäts-Gesellschaft (General Electric Company); to avoid confusion, we append the adjective *German*, or simply refer to the company as *AEG*.

local suppliers, they were immediately successful. This success stimulated further efforts on the part of EGE's two chief competitors, Westinghouse and Thomson-Houston, in the central-station business. By 1891 the three firms were furiously competing to extend credit and sell equipment to electrical utilities across America.

But in 1891, Edison General Electric entered another era of financial uncertainty, in part because Villard's vast financial manipulations were foundering, and he was forced to sell off much of his stake in EGE to Morgan interests.[24] In 1893, what had begun as a move by EGE to take over one of its two leading competitors, Thomson-Houston, became, at Morgan's instigation, a reverse takeover of EGE by Thomson-Houston (McDonald 1962:45–51; Conot 1979:301–302). This merger, which brought the new company—renamed General Electric—access to Thomson-Houston's alternating-current technology, also gave Morgan complete control. He immediately replaced Villard as president with Thomson-Houston president Charles Coffin. Of the Edison men, only Insull was offered a major executive position in the new General Electric, as second vice-president. He accepted the position on the understanding that it was temporary, and he would resign as soon as the merger was fully accomplished (McDonald 1962:52). Edison, disgusted by the removal of his name from the new enterprise, sold out his remaining interest in the company and abandoned his interest in the electrical industry (Josephson 1959:365).

By the early 1890s, therefore, the die was permanently cast: central-station generating was entrenched as the method by which electrical power

---

[24]The period from 1890 to 1893 was one of increasingly volatile financial markets. The Sherman Silver Purchase Act of 1890, authorizing the government to purchase a large quantity of silver to increase the amount of silver coinage in circulation—in part an effort by President Benjamin Harrison to satisfy the demand of farmers for easier money—had the effect of draining the government's gold reserves, since the notes used to buy the silver could be and usually were redeemed in gold. This in turn made investors jittery and was one cause of the Panic of 1893. One aspect of this uncertainty was that the European creditors on whom Villard counted for support started selling their bonds and stocks, and leading German financiers called in their loans to EGE (Buss 1978:217).

The German banks were also under stress on account of their participation in failed investments in Argentina (Lauck 1907:59, 70). Villard, given his marriage into a prominent Boston family, could conceivably have called on the same Boston financiers that helped finance Boston Edison in 1885, overcoming the Morgan group's opposition to financing of central stations. But the main Morgan rival, Kidder-Peabody, was so closely involved with Baring Brothers in London (who were severely affected by the failed Argentine investments) that they and their other Boston allies were not in a financial position to assist Villard. And Morgan, at this point, was able to call on Vanderbilt connections to buy up the securities dumped by the Europeans at distress-sale prices. Note that Vanderbilt was, at this point, still one of the largest owners of natural-gas securities in the United States.

would be supplied in American cities. This victory was not, however, completely apparent until the end of the decade. Indeed, after the formation of General Electric, Morgan made one final attempt to re-emphasize isolated power at the expense of central-station development by raising the prices of equipment sold to those stations, reducing the prices of isolated plants, and energetically resuming their promotion (McDonald 1962:60; McMahon 1985:17). This effort was abandoned within a few years as economic turmoil led to a series of central-station bankruptcies from 1894 to 1896 (McDonald 1957:56, 1962:71). Since few of these firms had prospered long enough to repay the debts they had incurred to EGE and Thomson-Houston, their crises became a huge burden on General Electric, which now held a vast portfolio of nearly worthless stocks and bonds in central-station utility companies. General Electric, asset rich and cash poor, looked to its owners for financial relief, and Drexel, Morgan and Company supplied $4 million in capital by purchasing notes and stock in these local utilities that GE put on the market at a fraction of their original prices (Passer 1953:328; McDonald 1962:60).

This ironic twist of fate removed the last structural barrier to central station development. The crisis of 1893 left Morgan with a huge stake in such development: in one stroke he had become the largest single owner of central-station securities in the United States. This stake could be made lucrative only if distressed local firms were nurtured and protected. Confronted with the weight of this financial burden, and with rival Westinghouse cutting the costs of its own central-station equipment, Morgan backed away from his commitment to isolated generation and in late 1894 and 1895 GE reduced the price of central station equipment (Dewing 1914:175; Bright 1972:96–98).

## Alternative Outcomes and the Significance of the Early Period for Later Development

The practical and analytic significance of the triumph of central-station generation has been lost in the jumble of more visible events during this period. Superficially, the result was a major victory for finance capital during the first period of financial hegemony in American business history. Certainly it is worth noting that Morgan and his allies eventually wrested control of Edison General Electric from Insull and Edison, and fitted it into the Drexel, Morgan empire. This demonstrated the deep and recurring dependency of manufacturing and operating companies on investment capital, and the capacity of financiers to convert this dependence into both strategic and operational control (cf. Mintz and Schwartz 1985).

But even internationally influential actors like J. P. Morgan are constrained by the congealed actions of other people and organizations. The twelve years of (relative) autonomy—during which Edison, Insull, and Villard first developed central-station technology and then created a network of utilities based on it—produced a set of structural circumstances that even Morgan found irreversible.

The structural constraints that Morgan found irreversible were partly technical, partly organizational, and partly interorganizational. They included:

1. A widespread system of local utilities built around central-station technology. This precluded the realization of Morgan's vision of immediate profits from isolated generation.

2. A highly centralized electrical manufacturing sector, in which a handful of firms developed and marketed the full range of products, from huge generators to light bulbs. This precluded Morgan's preferred outcome—a multitude of small, specialized, licensed producers with little individual market power, who could therefore easily be manipulated by financiers while paying substantial licensing fees.

3. A well-developed interdependence between the electrical equipment manufacturing sector and local utilities, based on credit arrangements that made General Electric and Westinghouse into key actors in the creation of local utility affiliates, and that resulted in influence over and dependence upon them. This prevented the realization of Morgan's intention that financiers would dominate the process of creating and extending local electrical power.

We contend, on the one hand, that none of these outcomes (even central generation) were technically inevitable and, on the other hand, that they are not the single-handed production of geniuses.

Can we demonstrate that the *dominance* of central electrical stations over the generation of power by isolated plants, or over alternative systems such as those based on gas, was not technically inevitable, as the efficiency arguments of Hughes (1979; 1983) and others imply? We find no compelling evidence for such inevitability.

Though speculative history is always perilous, we should recall that it was precisely gas lighting, both indoors and outdoors, that was the norm until challenges from arc and incandescent lighting began around 1880. Indeed, gas light remained the principal source of illumination for most Americans until after World War I. Though the principal market for gas shifted from lighting to heating after 1880 (much more slowly in Europe than in the United States), even today, with hardly any support from capital over the past century, the few gas-powered appliances available, such as clothes-dryers, air conditioners, and ovens, are generally considered more efficient than their electrically powered counterparts. Though problems of safety and noxious fumes were a drawback to gas lighting in the 1880s, these have been subsequently largely overcome in existing gas appliances. Although current suppliers of heating oil often raise the specter of gas explosions, questions have also been raised about the possible health effects of high-voltage electric power lines.[25]

Bright chronicles improvements in gas lighting in the 1890s that "materially increased its advantage over electric lighting. For a number of years the potential superiority of the incandescent electric lamp remained in doubt, and even its survival was sometimes questioned." He goes on to observe that it was not until the "successful introduction of metallic filaments early in the twentieth century that the incandescent lamp pushed permanently ahead of gas lighting and arc lighting" (1972 [1949]:127, 130). We conclude that a full study remains to be done on what the potential was for advances in gas-powered lighting and appliances, had such developments been favored by investors and supported by a well-placed network of inventors and technicians.

Even easier to imagine is an electrical-supply industry in which isolated stations played a significant—perhaps even dominant—role. Here, the fundamental fact is that Edison overcame enormous technical and financial obstacles to erect the first central stations. His heroic efforts first to finance and then build the Pearl Street station in New York, constantly improvising solutions to the most difficult problems, and working himself in the trenches (literally) with his men, have been chronicled many times (Hughes 1983; Josephson 1959; Conot 1979; Friedel and Israel 1986). What requires emphasis here is that success was by no means guaranteed. A similarly ambitious effort on the part of a talented inventor and engineer (S. Z. Ferranti) in London to construct a central station, using equipment not previously tested, was a miserable and extremely costly failure in the late 1880s (Hughes 1983:236–247), setting back large central stations in Britain for a decade or more. And even after Pearl Street went on line, it did not turn a profit for almost three years, despite being in one of the most concentrated urban areas in the world, with a mix of business and residential customers that Edison had care-

[25] In marketing isolated electrical plants, the EELC similarly played on fears of the flammability of gas in such fire-prone places as textile mills, newspapers, and sugar refineries. It "regularly put stories of fires caused by gas systems in its Bulletins" (Friedel and Israel 1986:200).

fully chosen to be optimal. An early London station sponsored by Edison's colleagues and backers, Holborn Viaduct, inaugurated in 1882, never made a profit and was abandoned in 1886 (Hughes 1983:45, 54–62). Thus, by the mid-1880s, the profitability of DC-powered central stations was by no means demonstrated, nor were such stations obviously technically superior to isolated installations.

Although J. P. Morgan and his powerful financial allies preferred the option of isolated stations, there was no other engineer or inventor with Edison's genius and drive to whom they could turn to help develop them; and if they had found one, they would have had to jettison the enormous investments they had made in the Edison Electric Light Company. It was thus left to Edison and his colleagues, who disdained isolated stations, to develop and improve them.

Was the Morgan vision of an industry dominated by isolated systems feasible? The ownership attributes of these systems were similar to those that eventually prevailed in household heating—in which fuel is delivered to homes and businesses that then generate heat on-site,[26] or to some extent in water supply and sewage systems, where both decentralized wells or cesspools and centralized lines have survived. Nor was Morgan's notion of selling isolated systems new: it had been used by such electric arc light producers as Brush Electric and Weston Electric since 1878 and by the American Electric Company and United States Electric Company from 1880 (Passer 1953:14–17, 25–26; Woodbury 1949:98; Carlson 1984:301). Arc lights were used for large indoor areas and street lighting.[27] U.S. Electric (another incandescent firm supported by New York financiers) created and sold some isolated incandescent systems, but their development efforts were hobbled by the patent advantages of Edison (Buley 1967:234; Flint 1923:287–290; Friedel and Israel 1986:193–194). Thus this commodity-sales approach advocated by Morgan was in some ways the norm in the emerging industry at that time. Moreover,

[26] Ironically, this decentralized option came to be called "central heating," because it involved one central power source within a house, as opposed to "space heating" room by room. This illustrates the wide range of technical possibilities for heating, as well as the relativity of terms such as "central." A heating system comparable to modern centrally generated electricity would produce heat in large central plants and deliver it to homes and businesses through pipes. Some modest-sized versions of such a system are in use with steam pipes to heat complexes of buildings such as colleges and military bases, apartment buildings in large cities such as Manhattan, and the entire downtown areas of some European cities.

[27] Arc lamps used glowing carbon rods in front of a reflecting surface, sometimes covered, or focusing light through a lens. It had neither a bulb structure nor a vacuum around the carbon. Further, the carbon rods needed continued adjustment (as the carbon burned) to maintain a circuit and the production of light.

the idea of isolated generation returned to fashion in the 1980s, when industrial firms found they could use waste heat and other cheap sources (including the sun and wind) to produce electricity at below-market rates (see Ridgeway and Connor 1975; Stobaugh and Yergin 1979:158–160; Pollack 1987).[28]

But Edison never seriously turned his efforts to making isolated generation a success. In the early 1880s, though Edison "was receiving thousands of inquiries for lighting installations, he resisted putting up 'isolated, plants for companies and individuals, because he considered such business 'demoralizing'. He was intent on concentrating on municipal systems to rival the gas companies" (Conot 1979:187).[29] In all of 1881, Edison sold only eight isolated plants (Passer 1953:117). Nevertheless, by late 1881, such plants were the main possible source of funding for Edison, and so he capitulated and allowed the formation of the Edison Company for Isolated Lighting. By 1888, 1,291 Edison isolated plants were in operation, with a total of 343,654 lamps. At this point, 185 Edison central stations were in place, lighting 385,840 lamps, thus barely dominant over isolated plants (Passer 1953:119, 121), despite Edison's opposition to the latter. Isolated plants sold to a few affluent households, but mainly to businesses, where they were extremely economical to run. This was especially so if the "hotel, apartment house, theater, and so forth had its own steam boiler for heating purposes," since then this same boiler could drive the generator for the plant (Passer 1953:113).

Thus, it is possible to imagine isolated systems being constantly improved technically and adapted in such a way as to be linked to the growing number of installations of central heating in homes, as was already the case for businesses. But all the energy of Edison and his colleagues was bent to the promotion and improvement of central stations. Once alternating current was developed in the late 1880s, central-generation costs began a dramatic decline, due to the advent of high-voltage transmission with step-down transformers, and central stations achieved an economic superiority over isolated generation that is only now being challenged. If, however, dramatic improvements in isolated systems had occupied Edison in the early 1880s, both the motivation for and the impact of AC development would have been greatly attenuated. Indeed, isolated systems actually convey many of the same advantages that led to

[28] Thus, a recent commentator on these trends, noting Morgan's preference for isolated generation, asks: "Was J. P. Morgan the first believer in the soft path? Is Amory Lovins really a secret admirer of the Rockefellers?" (Weiss 1989:7–8).

[29] Presumably Conot uses "municipal" to mean on a scale larger than one or a few buildings. None of Edison's stations involved municipal ownership: all were private, investor-owned utilities.

the adoption of AC power: less use of copper wire, less real estate occupied for stations, and fewer problems in serving sparsely populated areas. With a large installed base of isolated systems in place, as might have occurred by the late 1880s with suitable improvements, the appeal of central generation for customers would have diminished, and the system with first-mover advantage, isolated generation, might well have remained dominant as has the QWERTY typewriter keyboard (David 1986).

Isolated systems might also have played a far more important role even without Edison's imprimatur, had he failed in his efforts to promote central stations. Such failure might easily have occurred for technical reasons: the Pearl Street station was plagued by cost overruns and technical difficulties that nearly prevented it from operating (Passer 1953:119), much as has occurred for many nuclear power plants of the late twentieth century, and did occur for the Holborn Viaduct station in London and its later, ill-fated successor, the Deptford station of Ferranti. Such a technical failure would have given isolated systems a new boost and discouraged further central-station development in France, Italy, Germany, and England, all of which were heavily dependent on Edison technology.

Failure of Edison central stations might also have been brought about by the capital boycott of this effort by the Morgan forces. When Edison regained control of EELC in the proxy fight of 1884, he did so with the crucial support of Henry Villard and Villard's brother-in-law, both members of the EELC board. Several months later, these two resigned from the board after Villard suffered financial disaster with the collapse of his railroad empire. Had these resignations come six months earlier, it is by no means certain that Edison would have prevailed. And later, in 1889, it is difficult to imagine a successful breach of the Morgan boycott without access to European capital markets that was facilitated by such go-betweens as Villard (who had made a financial comeback within a few years) and Insull. Thus, we can also see the central-station effort as having been rescued by the international mobility of capital, especially German capital, which was possible only because the German Empire was a rapidly expanding financial and industrial power in search of promising international investments, and because Edison happened to be allied to Villard, who was intimately tied to German bankers. Thus, central stations owe their predominance at least as much to international financial and political circumstances as to any inherent technical superiority.

Had isolated stations become a significant force in electrical generation, the electrical utility industry as we know it would be far different. Isolated generation in business firms would have deprived utilities of most of the load they now provide and would likely have resulted in far smaller central stations. Edison realized as much, since he inserted a clause in the contracts of Pearl Street and other central stations that prohibited any other entity from using Edison equipment in the central-station franchisee's territory: this constituted a prohibition on the sale of Edison isolated systems within Edison central-station territories, a clear indication of where Edison's own sympathies lay (Bryant 1926:150–151). Indeed, as late as 1913, Samuel Insull was still calling for the elimination of isolated plants operating in the Chicago area. He was still trying to convince factories that, due to economies of scale, load diversity, and special rates for large customers, Commonwealth Edison could provide them with power less expensively than they could produce it for themselves (Insull 1915:419–420, 439). Insull's success in this effort was one part of his building of giant utility companies.

Even if central stations had eventually prevailed, the process could have been significantly different in other ways that would have produced permanent differences in technology and industry structure. The domination of electrical equipment manufacturing by a few large firms was typical of widespread business consolidation in the late nineteenth and early twentieth centuries. Certainly this was a period in which virtually all major sectors of American industry came to be dominated by a handful of companies which had acquired or destroyed their competition.[30]

Although such domination may have been inevitable, we argue that the product boundaries were eminently flexible. By 1896, it was established that the same companies would produce (or license others to produce) virtually all electrical equipment, from generators to light bulbs. This coexistence had (and has) no technical inevitability. It was a straightforward consequence of Edison's early vision. Westinghouse and Thomson-Houston only began producing central generators because of the immense competitive pressure from EELC, and later from Edison General Electric under Insull's leadership. If central generation had ultimately been successfully established under the auspices of some other company that did not produce light bulbs and had less access to capital, then Westinghouse and Thomson-Houston would have had less motivation to enter that sector.

In the absence of what became Edison General Electric, central-station generators might have been produced by a separate industry that had little or no stake in light bulbs or appliances. It might well have been, therefore, that two (or more) electrical manufacturing industries would have arisen, as separate oligopolies. Such a structure would have functioned much differently vis-à-vis consumers, local utilities, the financial

---

[30] Every standard history documents this process. See, for example, Chandler 1969; 1977; Edwards 1975; Nelson 1959.

community, and the government. Here again, therefore, we are struck by the permanent structural consequences of the vision and resourcefulness of Edison and his associates.

Finally, the financial and equity ties between manufacturers and utilities were by no means inevitable, but were rather a direct consequence of the capital scarcity created by Morgan's opposition to central-station generation. Under the circumstances, Edison had little alternative but to fund local utilities. Insull later converted this into a strength and ultimately forced Westinghouse and Thomson-Houston to follow suit. But this arrangement was not inevitable; nor is there much evidence to suggest that it introduced efficiency into the creation or operation of the electrical industry. Moreover, street railways, subways, and bus systems, not to mention systems for the distribution of water or heating and cooling, have all been developed without such intimacy between the manufacturer and the local affiliate. We see no evidence that this different relationship reflected some underlying imperative, related to either technology or efficiency. Indeed, once Samuel Insull became president of a utility company (Chicago Edison, beginning in 1892), he had as a major objective to break this dependence on manufacturing companies. This will be a major focus of our forthcoming (1994) book: *The Social Construction of Industry: Human Agency in the Development, Diffusion, and Institutionalization of the Electric Utility Industry.*

# References

ALLEN, FREDERICK L. 1950. *The Great Pierpont Morgan.* London: Victor Gollancy Ltd.

ARTHUR, W. BRIAN. 1989. "Competing Technologies and Lock-In by Historical Events." *Economic Journal* 99 (394) (March):116–131.

BONBRIGHT, JAMES, and GARDINER MEANS. [1932] 1969. *The Holding Company.* New York: Augustus Kelley Publishing.

BRIGHT, ARTHUR, JR. [1949] 1972. *The Electric-Lamp Industry.* New York: Macmillan.

BRYANT, GEORGE S. 1926. *Edison, the Man and his Work.* Garden City, NY: Garden City Publishing Company.

BULEY, R. CARLISLE. 1967. *The Equitable Life Assurance Society of the United States 1859–1964,* Volume 1. New York: Appleton-Century-Croft.

BUREAU OF CORPORATIONS. 1912. *Report of the Commissioner of Corporations on Water Power Development in the United States.* Washington D.C.: Government Printing Office.

BUSH, GEORGE. 1973. *The Future Builders: The Story of Michigan's Consumer's Power Company.* New York: McGraw-Hill.

BUSS, DIETRICH. 1978. *Henry Villard: A Study of Transatlantic Investments and Interests 1870–1895*. New York: Arno Press.

CALDWELL, GEORGE. 1907. "Value of Bond Department to a Bond or Trust Company." *Annals* 30:230–232.

CARLSON, W. BERNARD. 1984. "Invention, Science, and Business: The Professional Career of Elihu Thomson 1870–1900." Unpublished Ph. D. Dissertation, Department of the History and Sociology of Science, University of Pennsylvania.

CAROSSO, VINCENT. 1979. *More Than a Century of Investment Banking: The Kidder, Peabody Story*. New York: McGraw-Hill.

———. 1987. *The Morgans: Private International Bankers 1854–1913*. Cambridge, MA: Harvard University Press.

CHANDLER, ALFRED. 1969. "The Structure of American Industry in the Twentieth Century." *Business History Review* 43:255–298.

———. 1977. *The Visible Hand: The Managerial Revolution in American Business*. Cambridge, MA: Harvard University Press.

CLAPHAM, JOHN H. 1936. *Economic History of France and Germany*. Fourth Edition. London: Cambridge University Press.

COLEMAN, CHARLES M. 1952. *P.G. & E. of California 1852–1952*. New York: McGraw-Hill.

CONOT, ROBERT. 1979. *A Streak of Luck*. New York: Seaview Books.

CONOVER, MILTON. 1923. *The Federal Power Commission: Its History, Activities and Organization*. Baltimore: Johns Hopkins Press.

DALES, JOHN. 1957. *Hydro Electricity and Industrial Development: Quebec 1898–1942*. Cambridge, MA: Harvard University Press.

DAVID, PAUL A. 1986. "Understanding the Economics of QWERTY: The Necessity of History." In William N. Parker ed., *Economic History and the Modern Economist*. London: Basil Blackwell, pp. 30–49.

———. 1987. *Hero and the Herd in Technological History: Reflections on Thomas Edison and the Battle of the Systems*. Stanford, CA: Center for Economic Policy Research, LEFR Pub. #100.

DAVID, PAUL A., and JULIE ANN BUNN. 1988. *The Economies of Gateway Technologies and Natural Evolution: Lessons from Electric Supply History*. Stanford, CA: Center for Economic Policy Research.

DAWSON, ALBERT F. 1938. *Columbia System: A History*. New York: J. J. Little and Ives Co.

DEWING, ARTHUR. 1914. *Corporate Promotions and Re-Organizations*. Cambridge, MA: Harvard University Press.

DIERDORF, JOHN. 1971. *How Edison's Lamp Helped Light the West: The Story of Pacific Power and Light Company*. Portland: Pacific Power and Light Company.

DOMHOFF, G. WILLIAM. 1970. *The Higher Circles: The Governing Class in America*. New York: Vintage Press.

DORAU, HERBERT. 1930. *The Changing Character and the Extent of Municipal Overlap in the Electric Light and Power Industry.* Chicago: Institute for Research in Land Economies and Public Utilities.

DU BUFF, RICHARD. 1984. "Networks of Power: A Review." *Business History Review* 58:283–284.

EDGAR, CHARLES L. 1926. *The Boston Edison's Place in the Electrical Industry.* Boston: Metropolitan Electrical League of Boston.

EDWARDS, RICHARD. 1975. "Stages in Corporate Stability and Corporate Growth." *Journal of Economic History* 35:426–457.

———. 1979. *Contested Terrain: The Transformation of the Workplace in the Twentieth Century.* New York: Basic Books.

FEDERAL TRADE COMMISSION. 1927. *Control of Power Companies: Electric Power Industry.* FTC Re.-Senate Resolution 329, 68th Congress. Washington, D.C.: Government Printing Office.

———. 1934. *Efforts by Associations and Agencies of Electric and Gas Utilities to Influence Public Opinion: Investigations of Utility Companies.* FTC Summary Report to Senate Resolution 83, 1st session, 70th Congress. Washington, D.C.: Government Printing Office.

———. 1935. *Investigations of Utility Companies—Laws and Regulations,* Part 73A, 1st session, 70th Congress, Volume 12. Washington, D.C.: Government Printing Office.

FLINT, CHARLES R. 1923. *Memories of an Active Life: Man, and Ships, and Sealing Wax.* New York: G.P. Putnam and Sons.

FREEMAN, CHARLES Y. 1952. *The Miracle of Electric Light and Power.* New York: Newcomen Society.

FRIEDEL, ROBERT, and PAUL ISRAEL. 1986. *Edison's Electric Light: Biography of an Invention.* New Brunswick, NJ: Rutgers University Press.

FRIEDMAN, MILTON. 1953. *Essays in Positive Economics.* Chicago: University of Chicago Press.

GERSCHENKRON, ALEXANDER. 1952. "Economic Backwardness in Historical Perspective." In Bert Hoselitz ed., *The Progress of Underdeveloped Countries.* Chicago: University of Chicago Press, pp. 3–30.

———. 1966. "The Modernization of Entrepreneurship." In Myron Weiner ed., *Modernization: The Dynamics of Growth.* New York: Basic Books, pp. 246–257.

GRANOVETTER, MARK. 1985. "Economic Action and Social Structure: The Problem of Embeddedness." *American Journal of Sociology* 91(3):481–510.

———. 1990. "The Old and the New Economic Sociology: A History and an Agenda." In Roger Friedman and A. F. Robertson eds., *Beyond the Marketplace: Rethinking Economy and Society.* New York: Aldine de Gruyter, pp. 89–112.

GROSSER, HUGO. 1906. "The Movement for Municipal Ownership in Chicago." *Annals* 27:72–90.

HAMMOND, JOHN. 1941. *Men and Volts: The Story of General Electric.* Philadelphia: Lippincott.

HELLMAN, RICHARD. 1972. *Government Competition in the Electric Utility Industry.* New York: Praeger Press.

HOOK, SIDNEY. 1943. *The Hero in History.* Boston: Beacon Press.

HOYT, EDWIN. 1966. *The House of Morgan.* New York: Dodd, Mead, and Company.

HUBBARD, PRESTON. 1961. *Origins of the TVA: Muscle Shoals 1920–32.* Nashville: Vanderbilt University Press.

HUGHES, THOMAS. 1979. "The Electrification of America 1870–1930." *Technology and Culture* 20(1):124–161.

———. 1983. *Networks of Power: Electrification in Western Society 1880–1930.* Baltimore: Johns Hopkins University Press.

INSULL, SAMUEL. 1915. *Central Station Electric Service,* William Kelly, ed. Chicago: Privately Printed.

———.1924. *Public Utilities and Modern Life: Selected Speeches 1914–1923.* William Kelly, ed. Chicago: Privately Printed.

IRWIN, MANLEY. 1986. "The Telecommunications Industry." In Walter Adams ed., *The Structure of American Industry.* New York: Macmillan, pp. 260–283.

JEHL, FRANCIS. 1938. *Menlo Park Reminiscences.* Volume 2. Dearborn, MI: The Edison Institute.

JENSEN, GORDON M. 1956. *The National Civic Federation—American Business in the Age of Social Change and Reform, 1900–1910.* Unpublished Ph.D. Dissertation, Department of Philosophy, Princeton University.

JONES, PAYSON. 1940. *A Power History of the Consolidated Edison System.* New York: Consolidated Edison of New York.

JOSEPHSON, MATTHEW. 1959. *Edison: A Biography.* New York: McGraw-Hill.

KING, JUDSON. 1959. *The Conservation Fight.* Washington, D.C.: Public Affairs Press.

KRAMER, ALBERT. 1905. "Securities of Public Service Corporations as Investments." *Annals* 25:101–116.

LAUCK, W. JETT. 1907. *Causes of the Panic of 1893.* Boston: Houghton-Mifflin.

LILLEY, SAMUEL. 1965. *Men, Machines and History.* New York: International Publishing.

LINDGREN, NILS. 1979. "Seizing the Moment." *EPRI Journal* 4: Special Issue.

MARTIN, COMMERFORD. 1922. *Forty Years of Edison Service 1882–1922.* New York: New York Edison Press.

MARTIN, THOMAS. 1953. *The Story of Electricity in Alabama.* Birmingham: Alabama Power Company.

MC CRAW, THOMAS. 1971. *TVA and the Power Fight, 1930–1939.* Philadelphia: Lippincott.

McDONALD, FORREST. 1957. *Let There Be Light: The Electric Utility Industry in Wisconsin, 1881–1955*. Madison, WI: American History Research Center.

————. 1962. *Insull*. Chicago: University of Chicago Press.

McGUIRE, PATRICK. 1986. *The Control of Power: the Political Economy of Electric Utility Development in the United States 1870–1930*. Unpublished Ph.D. Dissertation, Department of Sociology, SUNY–Stony Brook.

————. 1989. "Instrumental Class Power and the Origin of Class-Based State Regulation in the U.S. Electric Utility Industry." *Critical Sociology* 16:2–3;181–203.

————.1990. "Money and Power: Variance in Support by Financiers and the Electrical Manufacturing Industry 1878–1896." *Social Science Quarterly* 71(3):510–530.

McGUIRE, PATRICK, MARK GRANOVETTER, and MICHAEL SCHWARTZ. Forthcoming. *The Social Construction of Industry: Human Agency in the Development, Diffusion, and Institutionalization of the Electric Utility Industry*. New York: Cambridge University Press.

MacLAREN, MALCOLM. 1943. *The Rise of the Electrical Industry During the Nineteenth Century*. New Jersey: Princeton University Press.

McMAHON, A. MICHAEL. 1984. *The Making of a Profession: A Century of Electrical Engineering in America*. New York: IEEE Press.

————. 1985. *Reflections: A Centennial Essay on the Association of Edison Illuminating Companies*. New York: Association of Edison Illuminating Companies.

METCALF, LEE, and VICTOR REINEMER. 1967. *Overcharge*. New York: David McKay and Company.

MILLER, RAYMOND. 1957. *Kilowatts at Work: A History of the Detroit Edison Company*. Detroit, MI: Wayne State University Press.

MILLS, C. WRIGHT. 1956. *The Power Elite*. New York: Oxford University Press.

MINTZ, BETH, AND Michael Schwartz. 1981. "Interlocking Directorates and Interest Group Formation." *American Sociology Review* 46 (December):851–869.

————. 1985. *The Power Structure of American Business*. Chicago: University of Chicago Press.

MITCHELL, SIDNEY A. 1960. *S.Z. Mitchell and the Electric Industry*. New York: Ferrar, Strauss and Cudahy.

MIZRUCHI, MARK. 1982. *The American Corporate Network: 1904–1974*. Beverly Hills, CA: Sage Press.

NATIONAL CIVIC FEDERATION. 1907. *Municipal and Private Operations of Public Utilities*, (2 Volumes). New York: National Civic Federation.

NATIONAL ELECTRIC LIGHT ASSOCIATION. Various years. *National Electric Light Association: Proceedings of Annual Meetings*. New York: National Electric Light Association.

NELSON, RALPH. 1959. *Merger Movements in American Industry—1895–1956*. National Bureau of Economic Research. Princeton, NJ: Princeton University Press.

PALMER, DONALD. 1983. "Broken Ties: Interlocking Directorates, the Inter-Organizational Paradigm and Intercorporate Coordination." *Administrative Science Quarterly* 28(1):40–55.

PASSER, HAROLD. 1952. "Development of Large Scale Organizations: Electrical Manufacturing Around 1900." *Journal of Economic History* 12(4):370–395.

———. 1953. *The Electrical Manufacturers, 1875–1900: A Study of Competition, Entrepreneurship, Technical Change, and Economic Growth.* Cambridge, MA: Harvard University Press.

———. 1962. "Frank Julian Sprague: Father of Electric Traction, 1857–1934." In William Miller ed., *Men in Business: Essays on the Historical Role of the Entrepreneur.* New York: Harper Torch Books, pp. 212–237.

PERROW, CHARLES. 1988. "The Power of Capitalist Networks: A Critique of Hughes." Unpublished Paper, Conference on the Development of Large Technical Systems. Cologne, Germany: Max Planck Institute.

POLLACK, ANDREW. 1987. "Non-Utility Electricity Rising." *The New York Times* August 12: D1.

PROUT, HENRY. [1921] 1972. *The Life of George Westinghouse.* New York: Arno Press.

RAMSAY, MARION L. 1937. *Pyramids of Power: The Story of Roosevelt, Insull and the Utility Wars.* Indianapolis: Bobbs-Merrill Publishing.

RAUSHENBUSH, STEPHEN, and HARRY LAIDLER. 1928. *Power Control.* New York: New Republic, Inc.

RIDGEWAY, JAMES, and BETTINA CONNER. 1975. *New Energy: Understanding the Crisis and a Guide to an Alternative Energy System.* Boston: Beacon Press.

RIPLEY, WILLIAM. 1927. *From Main Street and Wall Street.* Boston: Little, Brown.

ROSE, MARK. 1985. "Cities of Light and Heat: Urbanization of Electric and Gas Systems 1880–1930." *Urban Resources* 3:47–53.

RUDOLPH, RICHARD, and SCOTT RIDLEY. 1986. *Power Struggle: The Hundred-Year War Over Electricity.* New York: Harper and Row.

SPITZER, LYMAN. 1907. "Industry Bonds as an Investment." *Annals* 30:374–383.

STOBAUGH, ROBERT, and DANIEL YERGIN, eds. 1979. *Energy Future: Report of the Energy Project at the Harvard Business School.* New York: Random House.

TATE, ALFRED. 1938. *Edison's Open Door: The Story of Thomas A. Edison—A Great Individualist.* New York: E. P. Dutton.

THOMPSON, CARL. 1925. *Public Ownership.* New York: Thomas Crowell and Company.

TONER, JAMES. 1951. *The Boston Edison Story 1886–1951: 65 Years of Service.* New York: Newcomen Society.

U.S. DEPARTMENT OF AGRICULTURE. 1916. *Electric Power Development in the U.S.* 64th Congress, 1st session, Document #316, Senate, V-8, 9, 10. Washington, D.C.: Government Printing Office.

USEEM, MICHAEL. 1985. *The Inner Circle.* Cambridge: Cambridge University Press.

VARIOUS AUTHORS. 1906. "The Relation of the American Municipalities to the Gas and Electric Light Service." *Annals* 27:200–233.

WAINWRIGHT, NICHOLAS. 1961. *History of the Philadelphia Electric Company 1881– 1961.* Philadelphia: Philadelphia Electric Company.

WEAVER, GLEN. 1969. *The Hartford Electric Light Company.* Hartford, CT: Hartford Electric.

WEINSTEIN, JAMES. 1967. *The Liberal Ideal and the Corporate State.* Boston: Beacon Press.

WEISS, LAWRENCE. 1989. "Giant Power Redux." *Wheeling and Transmission Monthly* 1(7):7–8.

WHEELER, GEORGE. 1973. *Pierpont Morgan and Friends.* Englewood Cliffs, NJ: Prentice-Hall.

WOODBURY, DAVID O. 1949. *A Measure for Greatness—A Short Biography of Edward Weston.* New York: McGraw-Hill.

WOODRUFF, CLINTON. 1906. "Municipal Progress: 1904–5." *Annals* 27:191–199.

WRIGHT, WADE O. 1957. *History of the Georgia Power Company 1885–1956.* Atlanta, GA: Georgia Power Company.

# IV

# THE PERFORMANCE OF FIRMS
# AND THEIR ENVIRONMENTS

# 10

# Organizational Design and the Performance Paradox

## MARSHALL W. MEYER
## with KENNETH C. O'SHAUGHNESSY

This chapter attempts to explain why the measurement and explanation of organizational performance have proved so intractable. It is, however, somewhat broader in scope than the title implies. The core argument is that the properties of performance measures desirable for purposes of organizational control are comparability and variability. This argument, in turn, bears on some very fundamental issues in organizational theory. Among these issues are Williamson's M-form hypothesis, which is reinterpreted here; the tendency of organizations to cluster into distinct fields and then to mimic one anothers' structures and practices as noted by institutional organizational theorists; and some limits of the finance conception of the firm of which much has been written recently.

The chapter is organized into several sections. The first frames the problem by outlining a paradox of performance—while performance measures and measurement activity have proliferated over time, performance measures tend to be very weakly correlated with one another—and by reviewing conventional explanations for this paradox. The second section begins to construct a theory of the performance paradox by focusing narrowly on the properties of performance measures that contribute to efficient capital allocation and decentralization in divisionalized firms. The third section extends the analysis of performance measures in divisionalized firms to other organizational settings, including what I label pseudo-divisionalized organizations (e.g., franchisees and members of trade associations) as well as institutionalized organizations (e.g., schools, government bureaus, etc.). The fourth section attempts a partial test of the theory of the performance paradox, which is successful but limited by the nature of the data at hand. The final section outlines some implications of the theory of the performance paradox for research on organizations and strategic management.

## The Performance Paradox Described

Organizational theory has all but foundered on the problem of performance. The difficulty is not that we cannot theorize about the causes of performance. Indeed, we do so all the time, although mainly implicitly. It is rather that we do not know what performance is. The elusive nature of organizational performance is illustrated in a recent comment in *Public Utilities Fortnightly*. John F. Childs, a Kidder Peabody vice-president, in a response to a 1989 report of the National Association of Regulatory Utility Commissioners (NARUC), questioned whether utility performance is adequately measured by return to shareholders. The NARUC report had found that " '. . . the ultimate and most meaningful indicator of corporate profitability is total return to common stockholders' " and concluded, based on total return to stockholders, that utility earnings were more than adequate. But Mr. Childs demurred: ". . . a company can be performing very poorly and continue to perform very poorly but if there is an improvement, even though still unsatisfactory, the market price may increase and produce a high return to investors . . . Stock market performance . . . is not a proper measure of company performance . . ." (Childs 1990:50–52). Whether or not the NARUC and Mr. Childs would have held their respective opinions had earnings been higher and market performance of utility shares lower is immaterial. The point is that commonly used performance measures can and often do diverge, sometimes dramatically so. This is the nemesis of measuring organizational performance.

The issue raised by Mr. Childs's comment is in fact more complicated than first meets the eye. In general, *organizational* performance measures tend to be weakly correlated with one another save for common factors (such as a returns measure in the numerator). This has been known for years. The literature on organizational effectiveness, which dates from the late 1960s and 1970s, treats performance as multidimensional. For example, Molnar and Rogers (1976) argue that the goal and systems approaches to effectiveness tap different dimensions of performance. Campbell (1977) lists some thirty criteria of organizational effectiveness, which while "not orthogonal" do not readily cluster: "In the best of all possible worlds, it would be nice to have a hierarchical map of how the criteria fit together . . . Almost by definition, such a map will be impossible to construct . . ." (p. 40). Campbell then goes on to note that interrater agreement on performance measures can be quite low, negative correlations among performance measures abound, and that "it is probably unproductive to follow the multivariate approach in the development of effectiveness measures" (p. 45). Overall, the effectiveness literature concludes that no single measure of organizational performance is adequate and that, for this reason, the concept of organizational performance (Yuchtman and Seashore, 1967) if not organizational effectiveness itself (Hannan and Freeman, 1977) may be suspect.

Recent studies in the organizational strategy literature reinforce the generalization that performance measures tend to be disparate in several respects. To begin, accounting and financial performance indicators tend not to correspond closely. Keats and Hitt (1988:583) report correlations of three accounting measures, return on equity (ROE), return on investment (ROI), and return on assets (ROA) with two financial measures (return to shareholders, one measure adjusted for risk, the other not) to range from $-.14$ to $-.23$, none statistically significant, in a set of 110 manufacturing firms. Using the CRISP and COMPUSTAT data files describing 241 firms in the 1963–1982 interval, Jacobson (1987) found a correlation of .14 between ROI and total stock returns. Murray (1989) similarly finds accounting and financial measures of performance to be essentially uncorrelated in a sample of eighty-four *Fortune 500* food and oil companies: a factor analysis of two stock-market-based and three earnings-based measures yields two orthogonal dimensions, one labeled short-term performance (earnings), the other labeled long-term performance (dominated by the market-based measures). Gomez-Mejia, Tosi, and Hinkin (1987) generated similar results from a factor analysis of performance measures in seventy-one large manufacturers: accounting measures of sales and profits are essentially independent of financial measures such as market value, return on equity, and change in share prices. There are many other studies reproducing this result (e.g., Dubofsky and Varadarajan 1987), and for this reason the weak relationship of accounting to market-based measures of performance need not be belabored. Additionally, although firm reputations for financial performance tend to correlate with accounting measures of profitability, reputational measures tapping other dimensions of performance tend not to. Chakravarthy (1986) finds corporate reputations for excellence, judged by both *Fortune* and Peters and Waterman (1982), to be uncorrelated with returns measures (specifically return on sales, capital, and book equity) among fourteen firms in the mainframe computer industry. McGuire, Sundgren, and Schneeweis (1988) find a significant positive correlation of corporate reputation for social responsibility (as judged by a 1983 *Fortune* poll covering 131 firms) with ROA—which Fombrun and Shanley (1990:237) find to be artifactual—but all other correlations of social responsibility with returns and market-based performance measures are nonsignificant among the firms studied. Fombrun and Shanley (1990) did find positive correlations between a composite measure of corporate reputation taken from a 1985 *Fortune* survey and several accounting measures of economic performance, but the composite measure included items tapping opinions about firms' financial soundness, use of corporate assets, and long-term investment value. These empirical results, or non-results, reflect fundamental dissension as to the meaning and measurement of performance. So deep is this dissent that a recent issue of the *Strategic Management Journal* published three studies utilizing wholly different performance measures. Wooldrige and Floyd (1990) used subjective measures obtained from questionnaires administered to CEOs; Fiegenbaum and Thomas (1990) used market share and the ratio of performing to total policies to assess performance in the insurance industry; and Zajac (1990) used average return on assets.

Even though organizational performance measures tend to be weakly correlated with one another, performance measures have increased in number and sophistication over time, and staffs charged with monitoring performance have burgeoned correspondingly. In the nineteenth century, performance measures consisted mainly of industry-specific cost and output measures (e.g., the cost of moving railway freight, expressed as cents per ton mile). Cost measures were supplemented with accounting-based return measures (e.g., return on investment) in the 1920s, and with purely financial measures of performance reflecting dividends and gains in share prices (e.g., return on equity) in the 1960s and 1970s. (See Chandler 1977 for a description of the development of cost accounting during the nineteenth century and ROI accounting early in this century.) New professions, accounting and financial analysis especially, have grown rapidly as demands for more refined performance measures have burgeoned. Indeed, not only has second-order performance assessment by external auditors and financial analysts become endemic, but third-order performance assessment—evaluation of investment decisions made by fund managers—has become a minor growth industry.

The performance paradox, then, is the simultaneous proliferation and noncorrelation of performance measures. Several explanations for this paradox readily come to mind. One explanation is self-serving managerial behavior, which is suggested in the emerging accounting literature on the quality of earnings forecasts (see Moses 1990). The argument is straightforward: managers routinely exercise discretion with respect to performance measures, smoothing year-to-year results or trading one outcome for another (for example, quality for return on sales) depending on which outcome is being attended to. Since constraints and hence performance trade-offs are expected to be more severe for low performing than for high performing organizations, one might expect to find very low, sometimes even negative, correlations among performance measures for low performers and somewhat higher correlations among firms considered high performers, resulting, overall, in correlations hovering about zero. This was the expectation when this research began but, as will be shown, it was not confirmed. Moreover, self-serving managerial behavior cannot account for the observed tendency for the range of performance measures to increase over time. Quite the opposite, such behavior would give rise to selective performance measurement biased toward those measures most favorable to an organization.

Macro-organizational theory also has little difficulty accommodating the performance paradox, although it operates from very different premises. The macro-organizational theory explanation runs along the following lines: performance measures reflect the interests of powerful external interests and constituencies, which themselves have proliferated over time. Examples are unions, big government, market analysts, and predatory stockholders, which are all comparatively recent developments. The interests of these groups differ—for example, predatory shareholders are interested in immediate return on equity; managers in long-term growth and careers; unions in jobs and wages; and the government in compliance with an array of employment, environmental, and nondiscrimination statutes. Therefore weak to degenerate correlations among some performance indicators are to be expected. This explanation for simultaneous proliferation and noncorrelation of performance measures, while elegant, leaves organizations themselves hamstrung, for it portrays firms as largely externally governed, managers as having little discretion over what dimensions of performance are measured and not knowing what performance is in any case, and internal control systems as progressively weakened due to cross-pressures arising externally. It denies the possibility that performance measurement can actually improve performance, as managers believe to be the case, by portraying firms implicitly as "permanent failures" (Meyer and Zucker 1989). Perhaps unintentionally, macro-organizational theory fuels the agency theory argument that high performance can be induced in firms only through radical simplification of environments, for example, by tying managers' compensation very closely to gains for shareholders (see Jensen and Meckling 1976). And, most importantly, organizational theory ignores the fact that the performance measures used in the research cited above—accounting, financial, and reputational measures—are mainly of interest to owners and managers and are of little relevance to other constituencies.

## The Case of the Divisionalized Firm

What alternative exists to the self-serving managerial behavior and organizational theory explanations for the paradoxical facts of performance, whereby performance measures proliferate over time yet tend not to correlate with one another? Let me suggest, to begin, that an alternative explanation should operate at an intermediate level, relying neither on individual maximization (as in self-serving managerial behavior) nor on uncontrollable forces in the environment (as in macro-organizational theory). This intermediate level of explanation, I propose, involves mainly organizational design and control considerations. The organizational design component is this: organizations are designed to achieve comparability of performance measures. The control component is somewhat different: once comparability is achieved, variability across performance measures is sought so that comparisons yield meaningful information. The comparability argument is familiar, as it is central to the theory of the divisionalized firm—divisionalization is intended to yield performance measures comparable across subunits. The variability argument is not familiar, or at least not readily so, but I believe it to be implicit in some recent work linking change to organizational control (Eccles and White 1988). The notion that organizations seek performance measures having comparability and variability seems counterintuitive in the extreme, for it suggests that long-term gains in performance depend on maintaining divergences across performance outcomes rather than on seeking convergences among them. Somewhat differently, it suggests that organizations exhibiting low correspondences among performance indicators are more likely to achieve high levels of performance overall.

The organizational design and control explanation of the performance paradox begins with a detailed analysis of performance assessment in divisionalized or M-form firms whose subunits are largely autonomous, largely because M-forms are believed to be advantaged with respect of comparability of performance measures. The argument has two parts. To begin, I argue that the strategic superiority Williamson (1975) attributes to the M-form, particularly the fundamental attribute of efficient capital allocation, depends crucially on both comparability and variability of performance measures *across* divisional units, not comparability alone. Second, I argue that operational advantages associated with decentralized operations that Chandler (1977) and others attribute to the M-form depend crucially on both comparability and variability of performance measures *within* divisional units.

### Efficient Allocation of Capital

Divisionalization may seem an unlikely place to begin understanding why performance measures tend to be disparate yet to proliferate over time, but two reasons suggest that it is a promising place to begin. First, divisionalization is alleged to benefit performance. This will be assumed for present purposes. Second, the alleged key benefits of divisionalization—transactional efficiencies arising from separation of strategic decisions from operating ones and assignment of capital flows to their most efficient uses—hinges on variation in performance outcomes across divisions. This will be demonstrated presently.

Oliver Williamson's M-form hypothesis argues that divisionalized firms will be advantaged overall compared to their functionally organized counterparts: "The organization and operation of the large enterprise along the lines of the M-form favors goal pursuit and least-cost behavior more nearly associated with the neoclassical profit maximization hypothesis than does the U-form organizational alternative" (1975:150). The M-form hypothesis, it turns out, is very much contingent on the existence of an appropriate control apparatus, presumably one that monitors divisional performance (measures of which are not indicated) so that the general office can make strategic choices, such as allocating capital and recruiting executive talent, without otherwise meddling in divisional matters. In comparison with the M-form, the H-form (holding company) organization, which looks structurally like the M-form, is one where "the requisite control apparatus has not been provided." The corrupted M-form also looks structurally like the M-form, save that "general management has become extensively involved in operating affairs" (1975:152, 153). The M-form hypothesis, thus, might be restated as follows: divisionalization (usually) gives rise to a control apparatus for monitoring divisional performance and making strategic choices, which, in turn, yields profit maximization. The nature of the control apparatus, importantly, is not specified in detail, although it is stipulated that it must be powerful but not too intrusive. If it is too weak, the H-form results; if it is too intrusive, the uncorrupted M-form gives way to the corrupted M-form where subunits lose control over operations.

What kind of control apparatus does Williamson have in mind? Specifics are lacking, although clearly Williamson believes that the controls consist mainly of accounting measures of performance (such as return on sales or return on investment) made available to the general office. The

**Figure 10.1a   Unitary Organization**

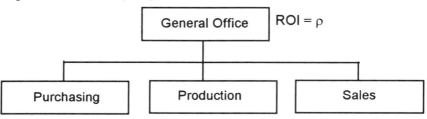

**Figure 10.1b   M-Form Organization**

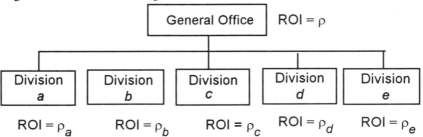

question I wish to raise is whether M-form organization *necessarily* yields significantly more information to the general office than the U-form, organized along functional lines. An affirmative answer to this question is normally assumed. Divisionalization reorganizes firms into self-contained profit centers whose performance is comparable with one another. Comparability of performance measures, in turn, allows the general office to allocate resources, formulate and execute strategic plans, and reward managers according to performance. But it is not at all clear that comparability is sufficient to promote effective control of operating divisions.

Consider a firm operating in several markets simultaneously, say markets for products $a$, $b$, $c$, and so on, and having a unitary structure. This firm is sketched in Figure 10.1a. It has a general office and three major functional units: purchasing, production, and sales. The same firm, reconfigured along divisional lines, is sketched in Figure 10.1b. The divisional design is perfectly conventional, or apparently so: a general office and five divisions operate as profit centers. Consider now the nature of the accounting measures in this firm, both before and after divisionalization. Let us assume, for the purpose of argument, only a single accounting measure, say return on investment (ROI), which can be calculated only at the level of the firm in the unitary structure but can be also monitored for the five operating divisions under divisionalization.[1]

Let us assign an arbitrary value, say $\rho$, to ROI for the entire firm, both immediately before and immediately after divisionalization (nothing save for organizational form changes overnight). Let us also denote divisional ROI in Figure 10.1b by $\rho_a$, $\rho_b$, $\rho_c$, and so on. Consider now the following conditions:

$$\rho = \rho_a = \rho_b = \rho_c = .\ .\ ., \tag{1}$$

and

$$\rho \neq \rho_a \neq \rho_b \neq \rho_c \neq .\ .\ .\ . \tag{2}$$

The issue here is whether the general office can best exercise control and therefore maximize $\rho$ under the first condition, where $\rho_i$'s are equal, or under the second condition, where they are not. Under the first condition, where the $\rho$'s are invariant across divisions, divisionalization yields little information with which the general office might exercise control, even though performance measures are comparable. For this reason, few gains in overall firm performance are likely to arise from divisionalization under the first condition. Gains in information, and hence in control and performance, are more likely under the second condition, where variation in divisional performance exists. This occurs for several reasons. Given interdivisional variation, the general office can focus attention on areas of high performance so that those areas serve as exemplars for less stellar units and expose areas of low performance, which can either be corrected or divested. Interdivisional variation can also generate information-laden "wheeling and dealing" of the sort described by Eccles (1985), which is useful in allocating capital flow toward high-performing units and away from low performers. This is consistent with Williamson's argument: *"the assignment of cash flows to high yield uses is the most fundamental attribute of the M-form enterprise . . ."* (1975:148). But it renders the argument contingent on variation across divisions, in the absence of which high-yield uses for capital cannot be readily identified.

The control apparatus crucial to the M-form hypothesis, thus, turns out to have two components: 1) one or more performance measures comparable across the more or less self-contained divisions of an organization, and 2) variation across subunits in one or more of these mea-

---

[1] The actual computation of ROI is unimportant. Indeed, it is unimportant whether the accounting measure is ROI or any other measure allowing comparisons of divisional performance.

sures. The first, needless to say, is contingent on divisionalization. And the second is contingent on the first, since no indicator of performance measurable solely at the firm level can exhibit variation. Without variation across divisions in performance outcomes, then, few positive benefits of reorganization along the lines of the M-form are likely to accrue.[2] In this sense, interdivisional variation in performance facilitates performance gains. A testable hypothesis, therefore, is as follows: *gains associated with divisionalization will be greatest in organizations exhibiting the greatest variation in performance across divisions.*

### Decentralization

Decentralization, like assignment of cash flows to high-yield uses, is believed to be to the advantage of M-form organizations because it removes operating decisions from the general office and allows coordination of marketing, production, and sales activities at the divisional level. Decentralization is thus hypothesized to economize on coordination costs specifically and bounded rationality generally. Indeed, Chandler (1966) as well as Stinchcombe (1990) argue that decentralization, or what Stinchcombe calls centralization of decision-making authority at the divisional level, is the principal advantage of the divisionalized firm. Compared to the unitary or functional organizational design, advantages with respect to coordination costs do accrue to divisionalized firms. But compared to the holding company or, even more extremely, compared to autonomous firms, the M-form appears to offer few savings in coordination costs. Consistent with Williamson, then, absent efficiencies in capital allocation M-form firms might be encouraged to devolve into H-forms and even weaker forms of association.

However, a strong case for the M-form exists even where no efficiencies in capital allocation obtain. The argument is as follows: to the extent that the M-form generates performance measures (plural) that are comparable across and variable within divisions, it promotes effective decentralization—that is, effective control on the part of division managers—and hence gains in performance as hypothesized by both Chandler and Stinchcombe. Consider, first, settings where divisions are more or less sovereign, perhaps units of a holding company, perhaps independent business units capitalized by a larger firm but otherwise autonomous, perhaps units about to be divested by the larger firm. To the extent that

---

[2] Williamson might disagree by arguing that without these conditions the M-form gives way to the H-form. But this is a matter of semantics. Moreover, the issue of variance is not addressed in Williamson's work.

**Figure 10.2a**    **M-Form Organization Performance Measure $=P_1$**

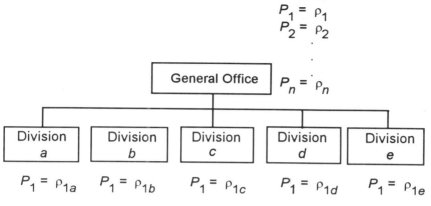

**Figure 10.2b**    **M-Form Organization Performance Measures $=P_1, \ldots, P_n$**

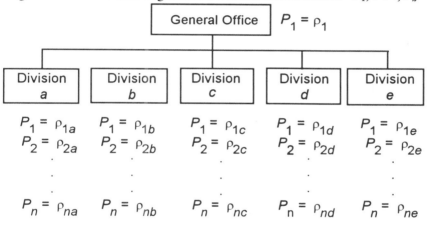

divisional units have sovereignty, comparability of performance measures is not enforced. Total decentralization exists, but so does total anomie: division managers have no basis on which to assess, much less to improve, their performance. In this sense, sovereignty undermines effective decentralization. (See, however, the discussion of pseudo-divisionalization below.)

Consider next settings where divisions are supervised by an active general office, which attends to a single performance measure. This is illustrated in Figure 10.2a, identical to Figure 10.1b save for notation: ROI has been replaced by $P_1$, which denotes the sole performance measure of concern, and a subscript (1) has been added to the $\rho$'s such that each division is described by a measure taking values $\rho_{1a}, \ldots, \rho_{1e}$. Consistent with the earlier discussion, decisions concerning cash flows are centralized at the level of the general office; other decisions are left to division heads who have relatively little information, save for the single performance yardstick provided by the general office, with which to make choices.

Consider finally settings where multiple performance measures are available at both the general office and division levels. This is illustrated in Figure 10.2b, which generalizes Figure 10.2a to a range of $P_i$'s, where $i$ runs from 1 to $n$. Each division in Figure 10.2b, then, is described by several performance measures, $\rho_{ia} \neq \rho_{ib} \neq \ldots \neq$ where $i = 1, \ldots, n$. These performance measures, importantly, are not identical, as they measure different things (e.g., ROI, growth, etc.). Even so, all are comparable across divisions because their measurement is standardized by the general office. What is important is that the existence of multiple but comparable measures describing each division renders these measures comparable within each division. Comparability is achieved because divisions can be (and usually are) ranked relative to one another on each of the $n$ performance criteria. In principle, then, M-forms measuring multiple dimensions of performance generate considerable information that aids division managers in assessing and improving performance on a decentralized basis.

In fact, the amount of information available to division heads in M-forms like that of Figure 10.2b depends very much on variability across the $n$ performance measures within divisions. Recall from the earlier discussion that invariance of performance measures across divisions yields little information with which the general office might exercise control. Invariance across performance measures within divisions is similarly un-informative and unhelpful to division managers. Somewhat differently but parallelling the earlier discussion, should $\rho_{ia} = \rho_{ib} = \ldots$ and so on within each division $i$, $\rho_{ij}$'s expressed as ranks, then any one measure yields the same information as any or all of the others, reducing the firm described in Figure 10.2b effectively to that in Figure 10.2a. Should, however, $\rho_{ia} \neq \rho_{ib} \neq \ldots$ and so on within each division $i$, $\rho_{ij}$'s expressed as ranks, then these performance measures allow division managers to identify areas of relatively high and relatively low performance, the former to be preserved, the latter to be corrected.[3] Exposing areas of relatively high and low performance within divisions may also generate data beyond those contained in the performance measures themselves, for it

[3] This argument is consistent with basic motivational theory. Variability across performance outcomes yields very specific, as opposed to global, suggestions for improvement, which contributes positively to motivation. And they permit proximate (within-division) comparisons rather than distant (across-division) comparisons, which also contributes positively to motivation.

is conducive to internal conflict and an upward flow of information to division managers. A second testable hypothesis, therefore, is the following: *gains associated with divisionalization will be greatest in organizations exhibiting the greatest variation across performance measures within divisions.*

Two potential concerns about this analysis of decentralization should be addressed. One is whether the availability of multiple performance measures for divisions allows the M-form firm to be readily recentralized rather than decentralized, given that the general office possesses the same data as division managers and hence is capable of second guessing division managers. This risk is surely present. Should recentralization occur, however, the M-form is compromised substantially. Indeed, as already noted, Williamson describes this situation as the corrupted M-form, which occurs due to the general office's extensive involvement in divisional matters.

A second potential concern is whether subdivisionalization and variation across subdivisions on a single performance measure offer the same positive benefits as multiple performance measures exhibiting variation within divisions. In some sense this possibility begs the question: if subdivisions are appropriate, why have divisional structures in the first place? Whether units are called divisions or subdivisions, however, is unimportant. What is important is that performance assessment places upper bounds on divisionalization. The critical features of performance measures, it will be remembered, are comparability and variability across units. The first is the precondition for the second, firms benefit to the extent that both are present, and comparability suffers as units become more numerous and hence more specialized. Few industries can be organized like Good Humor trucks, where each operator is a profit center. That there is an upper limit to divisionalization is evident in the experience of some large U.S. firms that have consolidated operating divisions in recent years. General Motors, which maintained five automotive divisions through the early 1980s, now has two. And General Electric, which once had 110 semiautonomous product divisions is now configured as eighteen business units.

### Divisionalization: A Summary

The case of the divisionalized firm is of interest, as it has been shown that the M-form's advantages with respect to both efficient capital allocation and decentralized decision making depend on both comparability and variability of performance measures. This result is not entirely new. Divisionalization has always been understood as a means of generating comparable performance data for operating units. Not previously understood, however, is that the benefits of comparability hinge on variability of performance outcomes *across* units (for capital allocation) as well as variability across performance outcomes *within* units (for decentralization). Inconsistent outcomes across comparable performance measures, then, provide advantage to the M-form as compared to unitary or functional organizational structures. The question this raises is whether the benefits of comparability and variability of performance measures are unique to divisionalized firms or hold more generally for other organizational forms.

## Generalizing the M-Form

Here I develop several generalizations of the M-form by arguing that some of its desirable properties can be reproduced in organizational designs that are wholly different or apparently so. I introduce first the notion of pseudo-divisionalization, which describes the tendency of otherwise autonomous organizations to affiliate so as to realize the advantages of comparability and variability of performance measures without actually merging. I then interpret institutionalization as an organizational design one step removed from pseudo-divisionalization. Rather than relying on formal affiliation, institutionalization operates through informal (if powerful) social definitions of organizations as comparable, so that variability in performance and other outcomes can be identified and used for purposes of control. Finally I ask whether variety or variability alone in performance outcomes is sufficient to sustain organizations whose units are not comparable.

### Construction of Pseudo-Divisions

I have argued above that divisionalization benefits organizations to the extent that it yields performance measures having two properties: comparability across divisional units and variability across, and therefore within, these units. I now want to raise the question of whether at least part of this argument can be extended to organizations configured as other than divisionalized firms. I believe it can be, as there exist organizational designs other than the M-form that help render performance outcomes comparable across otherwise autonomous units. Some possible ways of arraying organizations as pseudo-divisions include the following.

FRANCHISES.   Franchising allows an organizational form to replicate itself rapidly through the action of individual entrepreneurs, who purchase the right to use a firm's name in return for meeting certain performance standards. Replication occurs in several dimensions: product, production process (or organizational design), and performance assessment. Franchising renders performance measures strictly comparable, and certain minimum standards or benchmarks are carefully monitored by the franchisor and must be met as a condition of keeping the franchise. As a result, franchisees can readily compare their performance with one another on a variety of measures.

TRADE ASSOCIATIONS. Trade associations (or associations of nonprofit organizations) have a number of functions, among them compilation of performance data allowing individual members to gauge themselves against industry norms. To illustrate: the National Retail Merchants Association provides its membership with statistics on sales volume, gross markups, markdowns, inventory turnover, and the like for a number of merchandise lines for stores of different sizes and types. Since trade associations normally recruit their membership from a single industry, comparability of the performance measures they disseminate is assured.

The discussion of pseudo-divisions could be extended substantially, but the general point, I believe, is clear. There exist a variety of organizational designs and devices other than divisionalization that render performance comparable on a variety of dimensions. Sometimes comparability is built into organizational forms from the outset, as in franchising. But sometimes comparability is an emergent property, as in trade associations. Whichever is the case, once comparability is established, variability across performance measures follows since pseudo-divisions generate a lot of information for one another. The following hypothesis is thus suggested: *performance gains will be greatest in organizations that are arrayed as pseudo-divisions through organizational designs such as franchising, trade association membership, and the like.*

### Institutionalization

The theory of institutionalization emerged in the 1970s as an alternative to rational theories explaining organizations in terms of their efficiency properties. While there are several versions of institutional organizational theory (Scott 1987), the core proposition of institutionalization is that organizations are social actors, responsive to, yet at the same time sources of, beliefs about their social value. Institutional processes, largely invisible, are said to have tangible consequences, including the tendency of organizations to array themselves into identifiable fields within which pressures toward isomorphism or imitation operate (DiMaggio and Powell

1983), and also including the tendency of resources to flow to organizations fitting social expectations of how they ought reasonably to be structured.

Some organizations are more institutionalized than others. Organizations are institutionalized to the extent that expectations of how they ought reasonably to be organized are widespread and reciprocated (Meyer and Rowan 1977). These reciprocated expectations, I wish to point out, establish comparability among organizations. Sometimes institutionalized beliefs categorize organizations in order to make their activities understandable and their performance measures comparable. To use the most common example, there must be widespread understanding of not only what a school is but also of grade-level and subject-matter distinctions before the activities of schools can be made sense of and measures of student and school performance made usable. Institutional categorization also occurs in the sorting of baseball teams into major and minor leagues, college football teams into the Ivy League, Big Ten, and so on, and prize fighters into lightweight, middleweight, and heavyweight groups. As with schools, comparison of teams' or of pugilists' performance is rendered impossible or meaningless without categorization of this sort.

In addition to categorizing organizations, institutionalized beliefs also define performance measures along which organizations are compared. Accounting measures, for example, are mainly outcomes of institutional pressures. Bodies of accounting doctrine, such as generally accepted principles, are established through consensual processes involving accountants, their clients, and regulatory bodies rather than through market competition. And specific accounting standards, once legitimated, tend to diffuse swiftly whether or not they are advantageous for individual organizations. For example, fund accounting was adopted rapidly by local governments in the United States following publication of an influential text on municipal finance (Meyer et al. 1985). The flow-through method of accounting for investment tax credits was adopted nearly universally among *Fortune 200* firms following the reversal of the Accounting Principles Board's long-standing policy against the flow-through method, even by firms for which this change was disadvantageous (Mezias 1990).

Many more examples could be used to illustrate the general principle that institutional processes help define sets of organizations as comparable as well as the standards used to make comparisons. Institutionalization, then, like divisionalization and pseudo-divisionalization, can be understood as an organizational design alternative, especially in settings where the divisional model or variations of it are not readily available (as sometimes occurs in the public and nonprofit sectors). A hypothesis that might be tested, therefore, is as follows: *other things being equal, performance gains will be greatest in organizations where structures and standards are institutionalized.* An implication of this hypothesis should not be missed, namely that institutionalization, rather than a cover for nonperformance, contributes positively to performance by rendering organizations and their performance measures more comparable.

## Locating Variance in Performance

No single or simple test could adequately evaluate the many implications of the performance paradox, let alone the specific hypotheses laid out above. But it is possible to explore the notion that variance across performance indicators is distributed differentially among organizations. The approach taken here departs substantially from other work on performance. We are not attempting to explain performance causally (see, for example, Zajac 1990), although the results below carry implications for causal explanation for performance. Nor are we attempting to remove noise or variance from performance measures (as does Jacobson 1990). Quite the opposite: we are trying to locate noise or variance in performance measures, starting from the hunch that more successful organizations will exhibit greater variance across performance measures than less successful ones.

### The PIMS Data Base

The data are taken from the PIMS (Profit Impact of Market Strategy) data base assembled by the Strategic Planning Institute. The PIMS data files describe strategic business units within firms (normally divisions of M-form enterprises), not entire firms, in North America and Europe. I have chosen to use the SPI4 data file, which describes a cross-section of some 2,700 business units. SPI4 measures are expressed as either four-year averages (to smooth temporal fluctuations) or as change measures (percentage change over four years). All measures used here describe business units in the most recent years for which data are available. PIMS data have a number of well-known limitations. The business units covered are not representative of firms, much less organizations, generally, as retail and service businesses are greatly underrepresented. Measurement error in some items is alleged (Jacobson and Aaker 1987:35–36). And the data are disguised (for example, expressed as ratios), making it virtually impossible to identify individual business units, much less the larger firms of which they are parts. These limitations notwithstanding, the SPI4 data file yields a large number of performance measures (we use nine) for a large sample of organizational units.

Nine performance measures are utilized in the present analysis. Three returns-based measures are return on investment (ROI), return on sales (ROS), and internal rate of return (IRR). Three quality measures are productivity (PROD), measured as change in value added per employee; product quality (QUAL), which taps change in quality relative to a firm's top three competitors; and image (IMAG), which is also measured as change in comparison with the three largest competitors. Finally, I include three measures describing growth: growth in sales (SALES), growth in market share (SHARE), and growth in assets (ASSET). The last is critical. Business units are classified as having high asset growth, flat assets, or declining assets, and variance across the other eight performance measures is compared within these groups. High asset growth units are those having annual rates of assets growth exceeding 11.5 percent (the top quintile of the distribution); declining units are losing assets at an annual rate of greater than 7.5 percent (the bottom quintile); and flat asset units are those between these figures.

The choice of asset growth as a criterion measure is somewhat arbitrary, but it is no more arbitrary than choosing a returns-based measure, and it is justified on several grounds. Affirmatively, growth in an organization's assets—not simply in its sales—is one of the few performance indicators for which there is strong theoretical justification in the literature.[4] In particular, theories of economic evolution equate success with doing more of the same (Winter 1990), that is, increasing plant and production. Also affirmatively, most constituencies surrounding a firm favor asset growth. To be sure, some groups, especially managers (McEachern 1975) and bureaucrats (Niskanen 1971), have especially strong preferences for growth outcomes, but few constituencies oppose asset growth actively. Measures taken to increase productivity and returns may, by contrast, provoke severe opposition (as at General Motors' Lordstown, Ohio plant in the early 1970s). Negatively, returns measures are deliberately excluded as criterion measures because they are highly correlated with one another, much more so than growth measures. To classify business units, for example, according to ROI would severely restrict the variance of ROS and IRR measures within high, medium, and low ROI groups. This would effectively restrict our analysis to variance across quality and growth measures.

---

[4]Agency theory *asserts* the primacy of shareholder returns, but this is assumed rather than derived from other first premises.

**Table 10.1  Correlations among Performance Measures**

| | High Asset Growth Business Units Only (N = 548) | | | | | | |
|---|---|---|---|---|---|---|---|
| | ROS | IRR | PROD | QUAL | IMAG | SALES | SHARE |
| ROI | .811 | .517 | .124 | −.137 | −.057 | .056 | −.124 |
| ROS | — | .409 | .197 | −.149 | −.035 | −.019 | −.094 |
| IRR | — | — | .033 | .057 | .110 | .415 | .148 |
| PROD | — | — | — | .032 | −.024 | −.050 | −.022 |
| QUAL | — | — | — | — | .413 | .171 | .171 |
| IMAG | — | — | — | — | — | .194 | .222 |
| SALES | — | — | — | — | — | — | .498 |
| | Constant Asset Business Units Only (N = 1648) | | | | | | |
| ROI | .845 | .328 | .290 | −.075 | −.092 | .059 | −.031 |
| ROS | — | .306 | .269 | −.087 | −.086 | .058 | −.034 |
| IRR | — | — | .010 | .088 | .049 | .431 | .233 |
| PROD | — | — | — | .045 | −.092 | −.038 | −.074 |
| QUAL | — | — | — | — | .348 | .171 | .225 |
| IMAG | — | — | — | — | — | .136 | .176 |
| SALES | — | — | — | — | — | — | .529 |
| | Declining Asset Business Units Only (N = 550) | | | | | | |
| ROI | .872 | .283 | .293 | −.013 | .016 | .201 | .141 |
| ROS | — | .292 | .287 | .015 | .022 | .241 | .165 |
| IRR | — | — | .044 | .132 | .131 | .425 | .238 |
| PROD | — | — | — | .096 | −.116 | .239 | .046 |
| QUAL | — | — | — | — | .349 | .174 | .185 |
| IMAG | — | — | — | — | — | .230 | .230 |
| SALES | — | — | — | — | — | — | .485 |

## Variability across Performance Measures

The research question, then, is whether variability across performance measures is distributed equally or unequally among the business units in the SPI4 data base. We begin by comparing zero-order correlations among the three returns measures, three quality measures, and two of three growth measures (asset growth is excluded). Table 10.1 displays these correlations for high asset growth, flat asset, and declining asset business units. Casual inspection of Table 10.1 reveals several patterns. To begin, the returns measures ROI, ROS, and IRR, are highly correlated. Indeed, the correlation of ROI and ROS exceeds .8 in all three groups of business units. Two of the three quality measures, QUAL and IMAG, are moderately correlated, as are the two remaining growth measures, SALES and SHARE, again, for all three groups of business units. Secondly, correlations generally increase as one moves from high asset growth to flat asset to declining asset business units. There are ten negative coefficients (of twenty-five) among high asset growth units, nine negative coefficients in the flat asset group, and only two negative correlations among declining asset units. Moreover, while thirteen of the twenty-five correlations increase monotonically as one moves from high asset growth to flat asset to declining asset business units, only three decline monotonically. These correlations suggest somewhat greater variance across performance measures in high asset growth compared to flat and declining asset units, but they do not indicate whether the observed differences are significant, and, if so, where significant differences are located in the correlation matrices.

In order to determine the significance of these differences, an unusual statistical procedure was devised, as follows: each of the business units in the SPI4 data base was ranked (from 1 to 2,746) on each of the eight performance measures used in Table 10.1. Variances of ranks on individual performance measures were then computed for each business unit, and these variances were, in turn, ranked (again, from 1 to 2,746). Rankings of variances were then compared using Wilcoxon two-sample ranksum tests. The Wilcoxon tests yield significance levels of differences in variances across performance measures between high asset growth business units and the remaining business units in the SPI4 data base. (Differences between high asset growth and declining asset business units, needless to say, are even more pronounced than those reported here; differences between declining asset business units and others are comparable to the results below.) The use of rank-order tests removes effects of outliers, which abound in the SPI4 data, frees us from distributional assumptions, and yields tests of statistical significance that are extremely conservative.

Table 10.2 displays the basic results of the Wilcoxon tests comparing variance across performance measures for high asset growth business units with the same variance measures computed flat and declining asset units. The results are displayed first for returns measures, quality measures, and growth measures separately; then for returns and quality measures together, returns and growth measures together, and quality and growth measures together; and, finally, for returns, quality, and growth measures combined. The expectation, again, is that high asset growth business units will exhibit significantly greater variance across performance measures than flat or declining asset units. This variance effect is expected to be en-

**Table 10.2   High Asset Growth Business Units versus Others: Wilcoxon Tests of Differences in Variance across Performance Measures (N = 2746)***

|  | Comparison** | Z-score | Prob. < |
|---|:---:|:---:|:---:|
| Returns measures (ROS, ROI, IRR) *only* | − | −2.18 | .03 |
| Quality measures (productivity, product quality, image) *only* | + | 2.50 | .01 |
| Growth measures (sales growth, market share growth) *only* | 0 | −1.40 | n.s. |
| Returns and quality measures | + | 4.39 | .0001 |
| Returns and growth measures | + | 5.87 | .0001 |
| Quality and growth measures | + | 6.41 | .0001 |
| Returns, growth, and quality measures | + | 7.71 | .0001 |

* See text for explanation of variance measures.

** Comparisons are between high asset growth business units and others; "+" indicates higher variance in high asset growth units.

demic: no single performance measure or set of similar measures is expected to account for the overall pattern of higher than expected variance across performance measures in high asset growth units.

Let us consider, first, the results for returns, quality, and growth measures combined, which appear in the bottom row of Table 10.2. The Wilcoxon test reveals that variation across all eight performance measures is much greater in high asset growth business units than in units experiencing flat or declining assets. The difference is significant well below the .0001 level. This outcome, importantly, is not due to differences between any one of the three types of performance measures and the other two. When returns and quality measures are considered together (and growth measures excluded), variance across these items remains significantly greater in high asset growth business units than in flat or declining asset units. When returns and growth measures are considered together (and quality excluded), the result is exactly the same. And when quality and growth measures are taken together (and returns excluded), this outcome again obtains. Nor are overall differences between high asset growth and flat or declining units attributable to variance across the individual returns, quality, and growth measures. Indeed, when returns, quality, and growth measures of performance are considered separately, the results are quite mixed. Variance across the three returns measures (which, as already noted, are highly correlated) is actually *lower* among high asset growth business units than among the others. Variance across the three quality measures, by contrast, is somewhat higher among growing units compared to units with flat or declining assets. And variance across the two growth measures is not significantly different for high asset growth compared to flat and declining asset business units.

Together, the results displayed in Table 10.2 are consistent with the expectation that variance across performance measures is disproportionately concentrated in units experiencing substantial growth in assets. This outcome, moreover, is not due to the behavior of any one of the eight individual performance measures used in the analysis. Nor is it due to untoward variation in any one of the three dimensions of performance tapped by individual measures used—again, returns, quality, and growth. Quite the opposite: disproportionately high variance across performance measures in high asset growth business units is due to differences *between* returns and quality, returns and growth, and quality and growth measures.

### Controlling for Heterogeneity

Many explanations could be offered for the patterns of variation across performance measures indicated in Tables 10.1 and 10.2. One is that growth is somehow more lumpy than decline, and that this lumpiness causes performance measures to diverge sharply in high asset growth firms. While this explanation cannot be dismissed out of hand, it seems very unlikely given that decline processes are often highly conflictual. Another potential explanation is that rapidly growing business units face more diverse demands than units whose assets are flat or declining. Again, this seems unlikely for reasons cited in the discussion of organizational theory above—environmental constraints are most intrusive in mature firms. A further explanation is that growing business units are somehow exempt from the normal rules of the performance game such that substandard outcomes on one or two dimensions is overlooked, at least temporarily. All of these explanations imply that the effects observed in Table 10.1 are due to one or another unobserved variable—lumpiness, environmental constraints, or relief from normal performance constraints—rather than the tendency of organizations to seek performance measures having both comparability and variability.

The SPI4 data does not permit me to control for all potential sources of heterogeneity, but some can be controlled. Of particular concern is the possibility that high asset growth business units are more heterogeneous in function, and therefore in actual performance criteria, than flat or declining asset business units, yielding high variance across actual performance outcomes. The possibility of undetected heterogeneity was investigated in two ways. To begin, business units were classified by industry, consumer goods versus industrial goods, and differences in variances across performance were calculated as before. (Service and retail industries are so underrepresented in the SPI4 data base that they could not be analyzed separately.) The results for business units producing consumer goods are displayed in the three left-hand columns of Table 10.3, while the results for business units manufacturing industrial goods appear in the three right-hand columns of the table. For the most part, Table 10.3 reproduces what was found in Table 10.2: variance *within* returns, quality, and growth measures is not significantly higher in high asset growth business units compared to flat and declining asset units, but variance *between* returns, quality, and growth measures is significantly higher for business units whose assets are growing rapidly. These effects hold among producers of both consumer and industrial products. It should be noted, however, that Z-scores are somewhat higher and significance levels correspondingly lower for consumer goods business units. Business units were also classified by whether their principal products are at the growth or mature stages of the product life cycle. (The SPI4 data base also includes codes for the initial and declining stages of the product life cycle, but so few units fall into these categories that they cannot be analyzed.)

In Table 10.4, the three left-hand columns display results for business units at the growth stage of the product life cycle, which comprise about one-fifth of the SPI4 sample, while the three right-hand columns describe mature units. As shown in this table, the earlier results are not reproduced for business units at the growth stage, since the expected differences in variance across performance measures between high asset growth and other business units are not statistically significant.[5] Stated differently, business units in growing markets whose assets are flat or declining exhibit as much variation across performance measures as rapidly expanding business units in growing markets. The earlier results do hold, however, for the great majority of business units in mature markets. The right-hand columns of Table 10.4, which describe these mature business units, reproduce the earlier finding that significantly greater variance between returns, quality, and growth measures appears in high asset growth compared to flat or declining asset business units.

---

[5] In fact, the one significant difference, which holds for returns measures of performance only, is not in the expected direction.

Table 10.3  High Asset Growth Business Units versus Others: Wilcoxon Tests of Differences in Variance across Performance Measures by Industry Type

| | Consumer Products Only (N=766)* | | | Industrial Products Only (N=1426)* | | |
|---|---|---|---|---|---|---|
| | Comparison** | Z-score | Prob. < | Comparison | Z-score | Prob. < |
| Returns measures (ROS, ROI, IRR) *only* | 0 | -.94 | n.s. | - | -2.56 | .01 |
| Quality measures (productivity, product quality, image) *only* | + | 2.54 | .01 | 0 | 0.96 | n.s. |
| Growth measures (sales growth, market share growth) *only* | (-) | -1.94 | .052 | 0 | -.14 | n.s. |
| Returns and quality measures | + | 3.94 | .0001 | + | 2.37 | .02 |
| Returns and growth measures | + | 4.24 | .0001 | + | 2.70 | .007 |
| Quality and growth measures | + | 5.04 | .0001 | + | 3.55 | .0004 |
| Returns, growth, and quality measures | + | 6.14 | .0001 | + | 4.25 | .0001 |

*See text for explanation of variance measures

**Comparisons are between high asset growth business units and others; "+" indicates higher variance in high asset growth units.

**Table 10.4  High Asset Growth Business Units versus Others: Wilcoxon Tests of Differences in Variance across Performance Measures by Stage of Product Life Cycle**

| | Growth Stage Only (N = 556)* | | | Mature Stage Only (N = 2010)* | | |
|---|---|---|---|---|---|---|
| | Comparison** | Z-score | Prob. < | Comparison** | Z-score | Prob. < |
| Returns measures (ROS, ROI, IRR) *only* | − | −2.15 | .03 | 0 | −1.40 | n.s. |
| Quality measures (productivity, product quality, image) *only* | 0 | .43 | n.s. | (+) | 1.76 | .08 |
| Growth measures (sales growth, market share growth) *only* | 0 | .07 | n.s. | − | −2.18 | .03 |
| Returns and quality measures | 0 | 1.21 | n.s. | + | 2.46 | .014 |
| Returns and growth measures | 0 | .95 | n.s. | + | 4.12 | .0001 |
| Quality and growth measures | 0 | .85 | n.s. | + | 4.89 | .0001 |
| Returns, growth, and quality measures | 0 | 1.22 | n.s. | + | 5.41 | .0001 |

*See text for explanation of variance measures

**Comparisons are between high asset growth business units and others; "+" indicates higher variance in high asset growth units.

*Summary of Results*

A brief summary of empirical results is in order. To begin, correlations among performance measures improve, overall, rather than deteriorate as one moves from high asset growth to flat asset to declining asset business units represented in the SPI4 data base. Variance across performance measures within business units was therefore found to be highest in the high asset growth units. This variance effect holds whenever dissimilar performance measures are considered. It holds for business units in industries producing both consumer and industrial goods. And while the variance effect is attenuated for business units in the growth stage of the life cycle, possibly because there are so few flat or declining asset units in these industries, it does hold for mature business units. Overall, then, the evidence supports the empirical generalization that high asset growth business units exhibit greater variance across performance measures than units experiencing flat or declining assets.

# Conclusion: the Performance Paradox Revisited

At the outset, I noted that performance measures tend to be weakly or not at all correlated with one another, but that these measures have nonetheless proliferated over time. The simultaneous proliferation and noncorrelation of performance measures I labeled the performance paradox, and the remainder of this chapter has sought to explain this paradox. Self-interested managerial behavior and organizational theory explanations of the performance paradox were reviewed but determined to be inadequate on several grounds, among them the observed tendency for correlations among performance measures to deteriorate among rapidly growing business units. An alternative explanation of the performance paradox was then proposed. The explanation combines organizational design with organizational control considerations. With respect to design, it was argued that organizational units are arrayed so as to maximize comparability of performance measures across units. Divisionalization is the normal method for achieving comparability, but it is not always feasible. Alternatives to divisionalization involve the construction of pseudo-divisions through means such as franchises and trade associations, and institutionalization of both organizational forms and performance measures themselves. With respect to organizational control, it was argued that once comparability of measures is achieved, variability of performance outcomes both within and between organizational units is sought. Variability is sought because it exposes areas of both low and high performance, allowing correction of the former and emulation of the latter, and because, more generally, it induces requisite variety in organizations. Variability is achieved by using multiple performance measures that are not strongly correlated with one another.

The theory of the performance paradox, thus, carries several implications for received ideas about motivation, agency, compensation, and public/private differences.

IMPLICATIONS FOR MOTIVATION AND AGENCY.   Motivation theory asserts that job performance is maximized when goals are specific rather than general or vague. But the use of multiple and weakly correlated performance measures favored by managers, if the theory developed above is correct, may undermine the kind of goal specificity sought by subordinates. Agency theory parallels motivation theory in this respect, for it assumes that principals can readily specify the performance outcomes desired of their agents. The performance paradox suggests that simple agency arrangements may prove difficult, as outcomes sought by principals are likely to be somewhat inconsistent with one another or to prove inconsistent over time.

IMPLICATIONS FOR EXECUTIVE COMPENSATION.   It is all but a matter of faith that executive compensation should be linked to corporate performance, even though this principle readily yields the conclusion that U.S. executives are underpaid (see, for example, Jensen and Murphy 1990a; 1990b). The pay for performance commandment, however, assumes that performance is readily gauged by one or two straightforward metrics, for example, returns to shareholders. The performance paradox is utterly at odds with any simple performance-based pay scheme because of the elusiveness of performance itself, all the more so in successful firms. If anything, the performance paradox suggests an approach to compensation sensitive to the range of performance measures used and the balance of gains and losses across them.

IMPLICATIONS FOR PUBLIC/PRIVATE DIFFERENCES.   The public/private distinction has been widely debated and accepted by many economists, but rejected by most organizational theorists. Privatization remains a rallying point for those who believe the public sector to be inherently incapable of efficient conduct due to its multiple constraints. The performance paradox, however, suggests that firms may deliberately seek the kinds of inconsistent feedback that is said to plague public management. If this is so, then the public/private distinction is blurred somewhat, and the possibility of developing performance measures comparable across public and private organizations is opened.

The above notwithstanding, some cautions are in order. The theory of the performance paradox developed here requires testing at a number of levels. Fine-grained data on the processing of performance data are needed to verify that variability across measures is actually sought. Data at the firm level are needed alongside business-unit level data to assess whether variability across business units in performance outcomes is to the advantage of the larger firm, as well as to control for the possibility of spillover effects whereby prosperous firms augment the assets of all divisions regardless of their performance. Longitudinal data are needed to follow the process through which gains in performance follow variability across individual performance measures—presumably, gains occur in discontinuous, steplike increments—as well as the creation of new performance measures themselves. The organizational design and control explanation for the performance paradox here must also be tested against competing explanations. Most important, however, performance must be built explicitly, rather than implicitly (as has been the case until now), into our thinking about organizations. If nothing else, the arguments and data developed above suggest that this can and should be done in a way that is sensitive to the multiple and conflicting constraints faced by organizations in the real world.

Support from the Reginald H. Jones Center for Management Policy, Strategy, and Organization is gratefully acknowledged. This chapter is part of a larger work on organizational performance that ventures much beyond issues of organizational design, portions of which have been presented to the General Motors strategy seminar at the Kellogg School, Northwestern University, the economic sociology seminar of the Russell Sage Foundation, the 1991 Stanford organizations conference at Asilomar, the Management Department colloquium at the Wharton School, University of Pennsylvania, and the 1991 meetings of the American Sociological Association. The participants in these seminars and meetings have provided much valuable input. I am especially indebted to Weijian Shan, Harbir Singh, Andrew van de Ven, Harrison White, and Lynne Zucker for their extensive comments. Gerald Salancik, however, bears ultimate responsibility for this paper. He challenged me to bring some fresh thinking to the classic problem of organizational coordination and control. I hope I have met the challenge.

# References

CAMPBELL, JOHN P. 1977. "On the Nature of Organizational Effectiveness." In Paul S. Goodman, Johannes M. Pennings, and Associates, *New Perspectives on Organizational Effectiveness*. San Francisco: Jossey-Bass, Ch. 2.

CHAKRAVARTHY, BALAJI S. 1986. "Measuring Strategic Performance." *Strategic Management Journal* 7:437–458.

CHANDLER, ALFRED. 1966. *Strategy and Structure*. Cambridge, MA: MIT Press.

―――. 1977. *The Visible Hand*. Cambridge, MA: Harvard University Press.

CHILDS, JOHN F. 1990. "A Review of Electric and Telephone Stockholder Returns from 1972 to 1988." *Public Utilities Fortnightly* (February 15): 50–52.

DiMAGGIO, PAUL J., and WALTER W. POWELL. 1983. "The Iron Cage Revisited: Institutional Isomorphism and Collective Rationality in Organizational Fields." *American Sociological Review* 48:147–160.

DUBOFSKY, PAULETTE, and P. "RAJAN" VARADARAJAN. 1987. "Diversification and Measures of Performance: Additional Empirical Evidence." *Academy of Management Journal* 30:597–608.

ECCLES, ROBERT G. 1985. *The Transfer Pricing Problem: A Theory for Practice*. Lexington, MA: Lexington Books.

ECCLES, ROBERT G., and HARRISON C. WHITE. 1988. "Price and Authority in Inter-profit Center Transactions." *American Journal of Sociology* 94 (supplement):S17–S51.

FIEGENBAUM, AVI, and HOWARD THOMAS. 1990. "Strategic Groups and Performance: The U.S. Insurance Industry, 1970–84." *Strategic Management Journal* 11:197–215.

FOMBRUN, CHARLES, and MARK SHANLEY. 1990. "What's In a Name? Reputation Building and Corporate Strategy." *Academy of Management Journal* 33:233–258.

GOMEZ-MEJIA, LUIS R., HENRY TOSI, and TIMOTHY HINKIN. 1987. "Managerial Control, Performance, and *Executive Compensation*." *Academy of Management Journal* 30:51–70.

HANNAN, MICHAEL T., and JOHN FREEMAN. 1977. "Obstacles to Comparative Studies." In Paul S. Goodman, Johannes M. Pennings, and Associates, *New Perspectives on Organizational Effectiveness*. San Francisco: Jossey-Bass, Ch. 6.

JACOBSON, ROBERT. 1987. "On the Validity of ROI as a Measure of Business Performance." *American Economic Review* 77:470–478.

―――. 1990 "Unobservable Effects and Business Performance." *Marketing Science* 9:74–95.

JACOBSON ROBERT, and DAVID A. AAKER. 1987. "The Strategic Role of Product Quality." *Journal of Marketing* 51:31–44.

JENSEN, MICHAEL E., and WILLIAM MECKLING. 1976. "Theory of the Firm: Managerial Behavior, Agency Costs, and Ownership Structure." *Journal of Financial Economics* 3:305–360.

JENSEN, MICHAEL C., and KEVIN J. MURPHY. 1990a. "CEO Incentives—It's Not How Much You Pay, But How." *Harvard Business Review* 68:138–149.

―――. 1990b. "Performance Pay and Top Management Incentives." *Journal of Political Economy* 98:225–264.

KEATS, BARBARA W., and MICHAEL A. HITT. 1988. "A Causal Model of Linkages among Environmental Dimensions, Macro Organizational Characteristics, and Performance." *Academy of Management Journal* 31:570–598.

MCEACHERN, WILLIAM A. 1975. *Managerial Control and Performance.* Lexington, MA: Lexington Books.

MCGUIRE, JEAN B., ALISON SUNDGREN, and THOMAS SCHNEEWEIS. 1988. "Corporate Social Responsibility and Firm Performance." *Academy of Management Journal* 31:854–872.

MEYER, JOHN W., and BRIAN ROWAN. 1977. "Institutionalized Organizations: Formal Structure as Myth and Ceremony." *American Journal of Sociology* 83:340–363.

MEYER, MARSHALL W., WILLIAM STEVENSON, and STEPHEN WEBSTER. 1985. *Limits to Bureaucratic Growth.* Berlin and New York: de Gruyter.

MEYER, MARSHALL W., and LYNNE G. ZUCKER. 1989. *Permanently Failing Organizations.* Newbury Park, CA: Sage Publications.

MEZIAS, STEPHEN J. 1990. "An Institutional Model of Organizational Practice: Financial Reporting at the Fortune 200." *Administrative Science Quarterly* 35:451–457.

MOLNAR, J. J., and D. L. ROGERS. 1976. "Organizational Effectiveness: An Empirical Comparison of the Goal and System Resource Approaches." *Sociological Quarterly* 17:401–413.

MOSES, O. DOUGLAS. 1990. "On Analysts Earning Forecasts for Failing Firms." *Journal of Business Finance and Accounting* 17:101–118.

MURRAY, ALAN I. 1989. "Top Management Heterogeneity and Firm Performance." *Strategic Management Journal* 10:125–141.

NISKANEN, WILLIAM A., JR. 1971. *Bureaucracy and Representative Government.* Chicago: Aldine.

PETERS, THOMAS J., and ROBERT H. WATERMAN, JR. 1982. *In Search of Excellence: Lessons from America's Best-Run Companies.* New York: Harper & Row.

SCOTT, W. RICHARD. 1987. "The Adolescence of Institutional Theory." *Administrative Science Quarterly* 32:493–511.

STINCHCOMBE, ARTHUR L. 1990. *Information and Organizations.* Berkeley: University of California Press.

WILLIAMSON, OLIVER. 1975. *Markets and Hierarchies.* New York: Free Press.

WINTER, SIDNEY G. 1990. "Survival, Selection, and Inheritance in Evolutionary Theories of Organization." In Jitendra V. Singh ed., *Organizational Ecology: New Directions.* Newbury Park, CA: Sage Publications, pp. 269–297.

WOOLDRIGE, BILL, and STEVEN W. FLOYD. 1990. "The Strategy Process, Middle Management Involvement, and Organizational Performance." *Strategic Management Journal* 11:231–241.

YUCHTMAN, EPHRAIM, and STANLEY E. SEASHORE. 1967. "A System Resource Approach to Organizational Effectiveness." *American Sociological Review* 32:891–903.

ZAJAC, EDWARD J. 1990. "CEO Selection, Succession, Compensation, and Firm Performance: A Theoretical Integration and Empirical Analysis." *Strategic Management Journal* 11:217–230.

# 11

# Corporate Financing: Social and Economic Determinants

## LINDA BREWSTER STEARNS
## and MARK S. MIZRUCHI

From 1930 to 1980, managerialism was the dominant model of corporate control in advanced capitalist societies. Managerialists argued that large corporations had become powerful, independent institutions controlled by inside managers, who were free from the constraints of stockholders and financial institutions (Berle and Means, 1932; Berle, 1954; Dahrendorf, 1959; Bell, 1961; Baran and Sweezy, 1966; Galbraith, 1967; Herman, 1981). This model had important implications for organizational theory. The claim that large corporations are independent of external influence encouraged researchers to focus on characteristics of the individual firm and to downplay its environment. Although interest in the business environment has increased among organizational theorists in the past two decades, managerialists remain influential.

In recent years three perspectives have challenged the managerialist model. First, finance-capital theorists have criticized the empirical adequacy of the model (Fitch and Oppenheimer 1970a–c; Zeitlin 1974). Interlocking directorates studies, for example, have consistently shown banks and insurance companies to be among the most central firms in regional and national corporate networks (Mizruchi 1982; Mintz and Schwartz 1985). Second, organizational theorists within the resource-dependence school have emphasized the limitations of managerial autonomy (Zald 1970; Pfeffer and Salancik 1978). Resource-dependence models view corporations as neither self-contained nor self-sufficient, but rather as organizations that must rely on their environment to supply necessary resources. Third, two new economic theories of the firm, transaction-cost theory (Williamson 1988) and agency theory (Jensen and Meckling 1976), suggest that the governance costs connected with external financing circumscribe managerial autonomy. In an effort to monitor debtor firms, financial institutions may restrict managerial prerogatives by attaching covenants to lending agreements or positioning themselves on the boards of directors of these firms.

Managerialists and their critics agree that the autonomy of corporate management is in large part determined by corporations' dependence on external financing.[1] They disagree, however, over the extent to which this dependence actually exists. Managerialists argue that since large corporations are able to finance their investments with retained earnings, financial control is no longer prevalent (Bell 1961; Baran and Sweezy 1966; Galbraith 1967; Sweezy 1971; Herman 1981). According to these theorists, large corporations, if they borrow, do so only because they find it more economical than using their own funds. Transaction-cost and agency theorists, however, argue that any use of external funds involves governance costs (Williamson 1988; Jensen and Meckling 1976). Finance-capital and some resource-dependence theorists argue that corporations' dependence on external financing has increased in recent years (Stearns 1990).

In this chapter, we examine the extent to which corporations' use of external funds is discretionary. In addition, we investigate the extent to which corporate borrowing is socially embedded. We ask two questions: 1) do corporations borrow money primarily because they need it? and 2) are corporations' borrowing decisions determined by market forces alone or are they affected by the firm's embeddedness in a structure of social relations with financial institutions? These questions are examined using a time-series model, which enables us to identify the effects of the general economic environment as well as firm-specific variables on the borrowing patterns of twenty-two large corporations over a twenty-eight-year period.

## Corporate Autonomy and Financial Control

Writings on financial control date back to the early twentieth century, when financiers such as J. P. Morgan wielded enormous power within the American business community (Hilferding 1910; U.S. House of Representatives 1913; Brandeis 1914; Lenin 1917). Investment bankers

---

[1]This view assumes that stock ownership is no longer a primary basis for financial control. Although some researchers have challenged this view (Kotz 1978), most agree that considerable stock dispersal has taken place since the early part of the century. See Mizruchi 1982:Ch. 1.

played an important role in corporate formations and mergers because of their central position in the issuance and sale of new securities (Navin and Sears 1955; Carosso 1970; Mizruchi 1982; Roy 1983). As the major providers of capital in a period of intense competition and increasing concentration, investment banks appropriated a major share of the promoters' profits for themselves, appointed their own representatives to sit on corporations' boards, and exerted influence over corporate policy (Sweezy 1942; Chandler 1977).

After 1920, the relation between investment banks and corporations changed (Berle and Means 1932; Sweezy 1942). According to Sweezy (1942), the specter of cutthroat competition ceased in most industrial sectors as large industrial monopolies came to dominate the market. Fewer combinations occurred; in some industries, they ceased altogether. Investment banks' power decreased correspondingly as the issuing of new securities, the basis of their power, became less important. Between the 1920s and the 1970s, financial control theories virtually disappeared from economic and business writings (for exception see Rochester 1936, and Perlo 1957). Managerialism became the dominant theory of corporate control.

According to managerialists, because corporations could successfully and regularly produce enough internal funds they no longer had to depend on external capital sources (Berle 1954; Dahrendorf 1959; Bell 1961; Baran and Sweezy 1966; Galbraith 1967). Oligopolistic market structures ensured adequate profits, and the state, as a major consumer, intervened to prevent crisis situations (Baran and Sweezy 1966; Galbraith 1967). As a result, firms could finance their own investments and thereby escape dependence upon financial institutions. Galbraith succinctly captures the managerialists' argument:

> . . . the corporation accords a much more specific protection . . . . That is by providing . . . a source of capital, derived from its own earnings, that is wholly under its own control. No banker can attach conditions as to how retained earnings are to be used. . . . It is hard to over-estimate the importance of such a source of capital. Few other developments can have more fundamentally altered the character of capitalism [1967:92–93].

Nevertheless, two studies (Lintner 1959; Stearns 1990) showed that the managerialists had underestimated corporations' use of external capital sources. Lintner (1959) found that from 1900 through 1953, non-financial corporations consistently met between 40 and 45 percent of their total current financial needs with external funds. In addition, although large manufacturing firms relied primarily on internal funds in the 1920s, they increasingly drew on external funding over the next thirty years, a finding directly contrary to the managerialist argument. Stearns (1990) showed that the proportion of total funds obtained from external sources fluctuated after World War II. While corporations obtained approximately one-third of their total funds from external sources between 1946 and 1965, they obtained almost half of their total funds from these sources between 1965 and 1980. Stearns suggested that this pattern may indicate a parallel fluctuation in bank influence on nonfinancial firms.

Proponents of managerialism often counter such evidence by maintaining that although corporations do borrow, their borrowing is discretionary:

> The corporation may still, as a matter of policy, borrow from or through financial institutions, but it is not normally forced to do so and hence is able to avoid the kind of subjection to financial control which was so common in the world of Big Business fifty years ago [Baran and Sweezy 1966:15–16].

Instead, they argue, corporations borrow to take advantage of favorable interest rates, tax benefits (Modigliani and Miller 1963) and investment opportunities (Herman 1981).

Based on the preceding discussion, it is evident that the extent to which corporations are dependent on external funding is a crucial empirical issue for the managerialist thesis. But, to date, no research has established whether corporations' borrowing is need based. Most studies of corporate financing have been carried out by specialists in finance whose primary goal has been to discover corporations' optimal capital structure (the best mix of debt, equity, cash, etc.), rather than to investigate corporate dependence on external financing. Scholars within this field have not reached a consensus on how borrowing decisions are made or even whether such decisions affect firms' performance (Myers 1984; Barton and Gordon 1987).

### Determinants of External Financing

In order to test whether corporations need the funds they obtain externally, we examine the extent to which borrowing is discretionary. Specifically, we look at the effect of three variables—the cost of borrowing, the availability of internal funds, and the stage in the business cycle—on the amount borrowed. We also examine the effects of type of control and three alternatives to external financing.

COST OF BORROWING. One way to determine whether borrowing is discretionary is to examine the degree of elasticity surrounding the demand for capital. *Elasticity* refers to changes in the demand for a commodity (in this case, capital) relative to changes in the commodity's price (in this case, interest rates). In situations of low demand elasticity, an increase in interest rates has little effect on borrowing; corporations borrow regardless of price. In situations of high demand elasticity, borrowing is sensitive to changes in interest rates; corporations borrow when interest rates are low but not when interest rates are high. As a result, low demand elasticity indicates that corporate borrowing is nondiscretionary (i.e., corporations stay in the market regardless of interest rates because they need the funds), while high demand elasticity indicates that corporate borrowing is discretionary (i.e., corporations leave the market when interest rates become too high). Therefore, if managerialists are correct and corporations do not need the funds they borrow, the amounts borrowed will be negatively related to interest rates.

AVAILABILITY OF INTERNAL FUNDS. Managerialists and economists often argue that corporations borrow because investing borrowed funds is more cost-efficient than investing internal funds. This is because borrowed money is a tax-deductible expense (Modigliani and Miller 1963). If external financing is discretionary, that is, not need based, we would expect to find no systematic relation between the amount of internal funds and the amount of capital borrowed. In contrast, if external financing is nondiscretionary, done primarily because corporations do not have adequate internal funds of their own to cover their expenses or investments, we should observe a negative relation between the amount of internal funds and the amount borrowed.

PHASE OF THE BUSINESS CYCLE. We can also examine whether borrowing is discretionary by examining the phase of the business cycle in which corporations do most of their borrowing. Corporations borrow during the expansion phase of the business cycle to replenish depleted inventories, finance peak selling cycles, and invest in new capital expenditures (such as plant enlargement or modernization and new equipment). In these situations, borrowing is both discretionary (to promote corporate growth) and nondiscretionary (to enable corporations to compete). In contrast, when corporations borrow during the recession phase, it is often to meet payoff schedules on their short-term debt or to provide the working capital necessary to remain afloat (Stearns 1990). In such situations, borrowing is nondiscretionary (to ensure corporate survival). Therefore, a finding that corporations make greater use of external financing during recessions would suggest that managerialists are incorrect in assuming that corporations do not need the funds they borrow.

TYPE OF CONTROL.   To our knowledge, no one has tested whether management-controlled and family-controlled firms differ in the amounts they borrow. Managerialists argue that widespread stock dispersion decreases stockholders' power to press for high dividend payouts. Lower stock dividends result in increased retained earnings, thus lowering the need for external financing. According to agency theory, however, management-controlled firms may be more prone to borrow. Since managers do not own the firms they control, agency theorists view them as less risk averse than owners. As a result, they may be more willing to place the firm in financial jeopardy. Therefore, we make no prediction regarding the relation between type of control and the amount of external financing.

ALTERNATIVE FORMS OF FINANCING.   Finally, we control for corporations' attempts to decrease their dependence on external financing. First, it is well established that organizations often seek to decrease environmental uncertainty through vertical integration (Chandler 1962; Thompson 1967; Williamson 1975). Since securing external financing is a major source of uncertainty, corporations may acquire their own financial institution in order to decrease their dependence on external sources.[2] Second, corporations interested in acquiring another firm may avoid raising funds in external markets by choosing instead to tender their own stock as payment. And third, by selling stock directly to their employees, corporations may rely less on external markets for this type of funds.

### Data and Variables

Our data consist of information about twenty-two major U.S. industrial corporations between 1956 and 1983. These consist of firms whose primary production was in eleven two-digit Standard Industrial Classification manufacturing industries. For each of the eleven industries, one of the largest and one of the smallest firms whose primary activities took place in that industry were selected for study. Because firms had to be in the *Fortune* 500 at both the beginning and end of the period encompassed by our study, in some industries, such as electronic equipment,

---

[2] By financial institutions we mean firms that sell financial services (e.g., Hartford Insurance acquired by IT&T). We are not referring to subsidiaries such as GMAC, whose role is to help consumers finance the purchase of General Motors products.

**Table 11.1    Corporations in the Sample**

Name (as of 1983)

American Motors
Beatrice
Colgate-Palmolive
Crown Central Petroleum
Dayco
DuPont
Exxon
General Motors
General Tire
Grumman
Interlake Iron
International Business Machines
International Telephone & Telegraph
Johnson & Johnson
Koppers
NCR
Procter & Gamble
Sterling Drug
United States Steel
United Technologies
Westinghouse
Wrigley (William)

both firms were among the largest in the *Fortune* 500. A list of the twenty-two companies is presented in Table 11.1.

We sampled on the basis of primary industry in order to observe a wide range of manufacturing firms. Thus, these firms do not constitute a random sample. In fact, the data could be viewed as a population of major manufacturing firms over a twenty-eight-year period. In this case, the use of statistical significance tests might be viewed as unnecessary. We have included significance tests in the analyses presented below for two reasons: first, as a heuristic device for interpreting the strength of relations among variables; second, because our aim is to make generalizations about "the causal processes that generated [the] data" (Blalock 1979:242). Whether or not the tests are employed does not affect our substantive conclusions. Although the limitations of our sample make it difficult to generalize our findings to all corporations, we believe, based on our previous work with this data set, that our findings would apply at a more general level (Stearns and Mizruchi 1986; Mizruchi and Stearns 1988).

For each company-year, we collected general financial data such as sales and assets, net income, short- and long-term debt, use of the stock and bond markets, mergers and acquisitions, and any restrictive covenants attached to loans. We also collected information on the firm's top management and board of directors, including the number of inside and outside directors and representatives of financial institutions, as well as the type of financial institution.

In addition, we coded data on general economic conditions such as the prime rate of interest among the largest New York banks, cost of AAA bonds, the aggregate demand for capital of all nonfinancial corporations in the economy (in the U.S. capital market), whether the Federal Reserve was following a "tight" or "easy" monetary policy, and whether the economy was in an expansion or contraction phase of the business cycle. Our primary data sources were *Moody's* for director and financial data, *Standard and Poor's Directory of Executives* for information about the principal affiliations of outside directors, and the *Federal Reserve Board Bulletins* and *Federal Reserve Flow of Funds Accounts* for data on economic conditions.

The operationalization of the dependent and independent variables are presented in Appendix 11.A.

### Estimation Procedure

Our design is a pooled cross-sectional time series commonly found in econometric analyses. In these models, the unit of analysis is the "company-year." With twenty-two firms and twenty-eight time points, our data set contains 616 observations. Because the same companies are observed at several points in time, however, the observations are not statistically independent. Thus our "true" number of observations is somewhere between 22 and 616. There are three potential sources of bias in analyses of this type: serial and contemporaneous correlation of the residuals and heteroskedasticity. This suggests the need for a generalized least squares (GLS) approach (Hannan and Young 1977; Maddala 1977. For recent applications see Friedland and Sanders 1985; and Pampel and Williamson 1985). There are several GLS estimation procedures. The approach best suited to our data is a modified GLS estimation technique discussed by Parks (1967). This model assumes the existence of a first-order autoregressive process, indicating that the correlations of the within-company error terms are likely to be highest in one-year intervals and

Table 11.2   Determinants of Total External Financing (MGLS Estimates)

| Independent Variables | B | SE |
|---|---|---|
| Available Internal Funds | −.326*** | .020 |
| NY Prime Interest Rate | .0004** | .0001 |
| Expansion Phase of Cycle | .010*** | .002 |
| Control (Management vs. Family) | .035*** | .009 |
| Own Financial Company | .014 | .010 |
| Employee Stock-Ownership Plan | −.010 | .010 |
| Acquisition through Stock | .087*** | .008 |
| Constant | .350*** | .015 |
|  | d.f. | 608 |

*p < .05
**p < .01
***p < .001; all probabilities are two-tailed

smaller as the time between the observations increases. This assumption is particularly useful when relatively long time periods are examined. The Parks model also corrects for heteroskedasticity and contemporaneous correlation of the residuals. The SAS routine used to compute our equations provided two additional estimation procedures. We tried these as a check on the robustness of our results. The results produced a few minor differences but none large enough to alter our substantive conclusions.

## Results

The regression equation for the determinants of corporate external financing are presented in Table 11.2. The results provide no support for the position that large corporations employ external financing in a primarily discretionary manner. First, contrary to the managerialist argument, management-controlled firms use external financing to a greater extent than do family-controlled firms. Second, two of the three measures of financial dependence indicate that external financing is primarily nondiscretionary: The use of external funds is negatively related to reserves of internal funds. In other words, as a firm's retained earnings decline, its use of external financing increases. Moreover, the use of external financing is positively related to interest rates. That is, an increase in use of external financing is not a simple response to favorable interest rates.[3] In short, our results suggest that, contrary to what managerialists would predict, need determines the use of external financing.

Corporations increase their use of external financing during expansionary periods. This finding neither supports nor contradicts the managerialist thesis, since such borrowing may be either discretionary or nondiscretionary.

Of the alternatives to external financing, the use of the corporation's stock for acquisitions has a significant positive effect on the amount of external financing. Thus, it appears that this means of raising funds complements, rather than replaces, the use of external capital markets. The effects of owning a financial institution and having an employee stock ownership plan are not significant.

In summary, the results show that managerialists are incorrect in their assertion that nonfinancial corporations are no longer dependent on external financing. The managerialist argument hinges to a great extent on the view that corporations' borrowing is discretionary. Our findings suggest that borrowing is not discretionary. This indicates that nonfinancial corporations are more dependent on financial institutions than managerialists have claimed.

We turn now to the second major issue of the chapter: the extent to which corporate borrowing is socially embedded.

## The Social Embeddedness of Corporate Borrowing

Sociological and organizational theorists argue that business transactions are influenced by the network of social and interorganizational relations in which firms are embedded (Granovetter 1985. See also Abolafia and Kilduff 1988; White 1981; Burt 1983; Baker 1984; 1990; Leifer and White 1987). Despite the failure of economic models to predict a firm's borrowing behavior (Myers 1977; 1984), financial economists have not examined whether interfirm relations influence financing patterns.

Corporations seeking financial information or ready access to capital are likely to invite a representative from a financial institution onto their boards of directors (Dooley 1969; Allen 1974; Pfeffer 1972; Pfeffer and Salancik 1978; Pennings 1980; Useem 1984). In addition, financial institutions trying to protect their investments often demand representation on borrowing firms' boards (Kotz 1978; Fama and Jensen 1983; Richardson 1987; Mizruchi and Stearns 1988).

---

[3] What our findings reflect, we believe, is the strong relation between demand and interest rates. The higher and the more nondiscretionary corporations' demand for external funding, the more interest rates are driven up. See Mizruchi and Stearns (1991) for further examination of this issue.

An interlock between two firms often reflects an already established business relation (Palmer, Friedland, and Singh 1986; Stearns and Mizruchi 1986). This relation may consist of positive past experiences that would encourage further transactions (Granovetter 1985) or an unequal distribution of power that could mandate them (Stearns and Mizruchi 1986).

Once a social relation is established, the corporation's freedom to shop among financial institutions for a cheaper source of capital is constrained. The social and political "price" of not borrowing from the board member's financial institution may figure into the corporation's "cost" analysis (Baker 1990). It may be "cheaper" to borrow from the director's institution than to alienate a powerful member of the financial community.

On the other hand, some financial institutions refrain from doing business with the firms on whose boards they sit to avoid charges of conflict of interest (Hirsch 1982; Baker 1990). In these cases, financial representatives still provide advice as well as contacts that can facilitate access to external funds. Advice on the type of financing to secure may vary, based on the type of financial representation on the firm's board. Therefore, regardless of whether the firm transacts business with the financial institutions on its board, the presence of these directors may affect the firm's borrowing behavior.

Using an expanded version of the time-series model discussed above, we examine whether a corporation's social ties with the financial community affect the amount and type of external financing it obtains. If borrowing decisions reflect financial control or resource dependence, we would expect to find a positive association between the types of financial representation on corporations' boards and the amount and type of funds firms borrow. If borrowing decisions are driven only by market behavior, no such association should exist.

Before presenting our results, it is necessary to discuss the types of financing available to corporations and the division of labor among financial institutions, that is, which institutions handle which type of external financing. This section provides background information for understanding the specific hypotheses. In addition, we argue that corporations cannot obtain external financing without placing themselves under some form of external constraint.

### External Financing and Constraint

Corporate external financing can take several forms, including short- and long-term debt, both public and private, and equity.

*Short-term debt* is defined as debt originally scheduled for repayment within one year. Firms generally secure short-term debt to finance peak selling or manufacturing cycles, to finance shipment of goods and storage of commodities, and to cover cash needs until long-term money is available. The three major types of credit supplied are: 1) loans from commercial banks, 2) commercial paper, and 3) trade credit among firms. Trade credit provides goods, not cash. Bank loans and commercial paper provide the cash necessary for a firm to expand more rapidly than is possible through trade credit.

Bank loans establish an ongoing relation between the corporation and the commercial bank. After the terms of the loan are set between the banker and the corporation's CFO (chief financial officer), a "lending partnership" exists until the loan is repaid. Commercial paper, by contrast, does not result in a partnership arrangement. After the CFO and his or her commercial paper trader (usually an investment banker) set the terms of the deal, the commercial paper is sold in a broad, impersonal market.

While interest rates in the commercial paper market are usually the lowest available to business borrowers, this form of borrowing has several drawbacks. Only financially strong firms borrowing at least $10 million have access to the commercial paper market, and the amount of funds available to them is limited to the excess liquidity that corporations (who are the main suppliers of these funds) have at the time. Perhaps most importantly, corporations in temporary financial difficulty increase their chances of bankruptcy because the impersonal nature of commercial paper makes it more difficult to re-negotiate (commercial banks, on the other hand, are generally available to help their good customers weather temporary storms).[4] For these reasons, corporations have preferred bank loans; between 1946 and 1980, approximately three-fourths of corporations' short-term debt (excluding trade debt) was financed through commercial banks (Stearns 1990).

In general, financial institutions can constrain their debtors' corporate strategies by controlling the latter's access to capital (Mintz and Schwartz 1985; Glasberg 1989). Corporations' access to short-term funds is limited by their line of credit, which is an informal agreement by a bank to

---

[4]This point was emphasized dramatically in the aftermath of the Penn Central bankruptcy. Penn Central had a large amount of commercial paper that went into default and embarrassed corporate treasurers who had been holding the paper. Immediately after the bankruptcy, the commercial paper market dried up, and some companies that had relied heavily on this market found themselves under severe liquidity pressure as their commercial paper matured and could not be refunded. Chrysler, for example, had to seek bank loans of over $500 million because it could not sell commercial paper. Without adequate bank lines, Chrysler might well have been forced into bankruptcy itself, even though at that time (1970) it was basically sound (Weston and Brigham 1981).

lend up to a stated maximum amount to a firm. Without a line of credit to guarantee a ready supply of short-term funds, corporations must slow down their rate of growth or cut back their operations. In addition, banks can exert direct control over financially unstable corporations that depend on them to issue or renew short-term loans by attaching covenants (such as dollar limits on dividends, management salaries, and capital expenditures) to loan agreements.

*Long-term debt* has a maturity of more than one year. Corporations borrow long-term debt to refinance short-term debt, to expand production facilities, and to finance acquisition of another firm's assets. Long-term debt is financed privately with financial institutions in the form of private-placement bonds, term loans, and commercial mortgages; or sold publicly in the form of common stock, preferred stock, and corporate bonds. Like short-term funds, long-term debt offers different advantages and disadvantages to corporations in terms of cost, availability, and the potential for control.

Common stocks are securities that represent ownership in a corporation. The advantages to corporations are that: 1) the securities do not entail fixed charges; and 2) they carry no fixed maturity date. The disadvantages are that: 1) the sale of common stock extends voting rights and hence opportunities to exert control to additional stock owners; 2) the costs of underwriting and distributing common stock are usually higher than those for underwriting and distributing bonds; and 3) common stock dividends cannot be deducted as an expense on corporations' federal income tax.

Preferred stocks also represent ownership interests in a corporation. These securities offer the same advantages and disadvantages of common stock, except that they do not extend voting rights. However, they come with provisions that restrict management's discretion over paying dividends on common stock and borrowing additional long-term funds.

Most long-term funds are obtained in the form of corporate bonds rather than in the stock market. Between 1945 and 1980, corporations raised $67 billion in stock as compared to borrowing $360 billion in bonds (Stearns 1990). The advantages of raising long-term funds via bonds are that: 1) the cost of debt is limited, that is, bondholders do not participate in profits; 2) the cost is typically lower than that of stock; 3) debt does not extend voting rights; and 4) the interest payment on debt is tax deductible. The disadvantages are that: 1) the debt is a fixed charge, which the company must meet even if its earnings fluctuate; 2) the debt usually has a fixed maturity date; and 3) in a long-term contractual relationship, restrictive covenants are likely to be stringent.

Finally, long-term bonds can be sold publicly in the capital market or placed privately with a financial institution. Private issues have some definite advantages over public ones. The firm is spared the time, trouble, and expense of having to register the issue with regulatory authorities and comply with their requirements. In addition, if the firm encounters difficulties later on, it can discuss the problem directly with the lender and make modifications in the debt agreement. Because a public bond issue has many holders, renegotiating the debt is much more difficult. The disadvantage of privately placed debt is that the lender is more likely than the purchaser of a public issue to monitor and influence corporate strategy.

In summary, while corporations' alternatives for obtaining external funds differ in price and availability, none are without costs—there are no "free lunches"—in terms of managerial autonomy. Corporations cannot avoid the constraints accompanying the ongoing relation with a commercial bank or insurance company without incurring other constraints or possible losses of control. By choosing to sell commercial paper or public bonds, corporations increase the difficulty of re-negotiating the debt, risking bankruptcy if they cannot meet their payments. In addition, by dealing in public capital markets, corporations limit their flexibility in developing strategies; lines of credit make cash readily available, while public issues take months to organize. By selling stock, corporations avoid the temporary constraints that accompany private loans; however, they permanently dilute future profits as well as increase their chances of unfriendly takeovers. Thus, control disadvantages accompany all sources of external funding.

### Division of Labor Among Financial Institutions

Although the 1980s brought some deregulation of the financial industry and the rise of the financial supermarket, there was a clear division of labor among financial institutions for most of the period under study (1955 through 1983). Corresponding to the different types of external financing were different types of financial institutions that specialized in providing a particular type of fund. Three types of financial institutions—commercial banks, life insurance companies, and investment banks—handle the vast majority of corporations' financial business. We briefly discuss each financial institution's sources of funds, lending restrictions, and market concentration to provide background information on the organizations from which corporations obtain their funds.

COMMERCIAL BANKS.   Commercial banks accept demand deposits subject to check withdrawals and make short-term loans to business enterprises. Most commercial banks also accept savings deposits and make consumer loans. As with all financial institutions, the types of investments commercial banks make are determined by their sources of funds and by government regulations. Because of the high turnover and demand nature of deposits, commercial banks specialize in short-term loans that can be quickly converted into liquid assets. Commercial banks also extend term loans of one to five years for such business needs as expansion, plant modernization, working capital, and mergers and acquisitions. The biggest users of these loans are medium- and small-sized firms, since they usually cannot issue bonds to raise long-term funds.

Commercial banks' trust departments administer the majority of private pension funds.[5] These funds supply long-term funds to corporations through stock and bond purchases. Between 1965 and 1980, private trusteed pension funds spent approximately $36 billion on corporate bonds and $95 billion on corporate stocks (Stearns 1983). As a result, private trusteed pension funds' share of outstanding stocks equaled 12 percent and their share of outstanding bonds equaled 13 percent.

Commercial banks vary in their power and clientele. The most powerful are money market banks, comprising about twenty giant banks located in financial centers such as New York, Chicago, San Francisco, and Los Angeles. The power of these banks is reflected in their disproportionate influence on the cost of loans, their partial control over the money supply, their correspondent relations with thousands of other banks, and their access to huge pools of unregulated international funds. Their clientele consist of the largest corporations (*Fortune* 500 and multinational firms). At the next level, there are about 100 regional banks in major cities across the country that finance large local corporations. These regional banks grew rapidly during the 1970s and began to compete with money market banks. The remaining 14,000 local banks primarily serve

[5] Pension funds can be divided into two categories: public and private. Public plans cover state, local, and federal government companies, while private plans cover companies, unions, and nonprofit organizations. Private plans can be insured or uninsured (trusteed) plans. Insured plans are administered by insurance companies, and uninsured plans are generally administered by bank trust departments (although sometimes they are handled internally by the corporations themselves or by outside investment counselors). Public funds are usually internally administered. The investment policies of pension plans differ considerably. Federal pension funds do not make capital available to corporations, since law requires that these funds be invested in treasury securities. Insured pension plans were comingled with the other assets of the life insurance companies during most of the period under study. In 1978, state and local pension funds totalled $153 million. Fifty-three percent of this amount was invested in corporate bonds and 22 percent in corporate stock. In 1978, private pension funds totalled $199 million. Fifty-four percent was invested in corporate stock and 24 percent in corporate bonds (Stearns 1983).

small businesses and consumers. In 1977, all 14,642 commercial banks had $207.3 billion in short-term and term loans outstanding. The ten top New York City commercial banks (or 0.0007 percent of all banks) held over $36.2 billion (or 17 percent) of these loans (Corporate Data Exchange 1980). In the same year, the twenty top trust departments controlled 46 percent of all trust (including pension) funds.

LIFE INSURANCE COMPANIES. The primary source of external funds for life insurance companies is premiums (regular periodic payments made by policyholders). A secondary source is pension plans administered by life insurance companies. The stable, long-term nature of these funds, together with state laws designed to protect policyholders, encourages life insurance companies to invest large amounts in long-term assets such as bonds and mortgages.

Life insurance companies are the leading buyers in the private placement market, where an entire corporate bond issue is sold directly to a few institutional buyers. In fact, since the 1930s, life insurance companies have been the single largest source of corporate long-term funds. Between 1946 and 1980, they held approximately 40 percent of all corporate bonds (public and privately placed) and commercial mortgages outstanding (Stearns 1983).

The life insurance industry is highly concentrated. Of the approximately 1,750 companies in the United States, the fifty largest owned 76 percent of the total industry assets of $390 billion in 1977 (Corporate Data Exchange 1980).

INVESTMENT BANKS. Investment banks, unlike commercial banks and insurance companies, are not depositories of capital. Deposits were prohibited by the Glass-Steagall Act of 1933. Investment banks, however, serve three very important functions within the business community and the capital market. First, they underwrite new corporate stock and bond issues. The usual practice is for one or more investment bankers to buy a new issue of stocks or bonds outright from a corporation. The group forms a syndicate to sell the securities to individuals and institutions. Between the time they pay the firm for the issue and sell the stocks or bonds, investment bankers bear all of the risk of market price fluctuations. Second, investment banks act as agents for the private placement of bonds, advising a company of the financial structure of the issue, locating prospective investors, and negotiating the interest rate and restrictive covenants. Private placements, however, produce less income for investment banks than do underwriting stocks and bonds. Third, investment bankers arrange corporate mergers and acquisitions. During the 1980s, this activity generated enormous revenues for the industry.

Investment banking is the most highly concentrated business in the financial sector. The top twenty banks manage or participate in virtually all large issues and many smaller ones. In 1977, five investment banks acted as lead managers in 64 percent of the $37 billion in new public financing (Corporate Data Exchange 1980).

## Hypotheses

Since each form of borrowing is provided by a different kind of financial institution, we expect that the type of financial institution represented on a firm's board of directors will affect the type of financing the firm secures. The following paragraphs describe the associations we expect to observe.

SHORT-TERM BORROWING.    Money-market commercial banks are the primary suppliers of short-term loans for the largest corporations (all corporations in our sample are *Fortune* 500 firms). Therefore, we expect the presence of a money-market banker on the board to increase the amount of short-term borrowing.[6] Regional commercial banks are also lenders of short-term funds, but they lack the capital necessary to make large short-term loans. As a result, we make no prediction regarding the relation between having a regional banker on the board and amount of short-term loans borrowed. Since investment banks and life insurance companies specialize in long-term lending, we expect to observe a negative relation between the amount of short-term funds firms borrow and the presence of a representative of one of these institutions on their board.

LONG-TERM PRIVATE FINANCING.    Life insurance companies are the primary suppliers of long-term private financing. We, therefore, expect the presence of a life insurance executive on the board to increase the amount of long-term private borrowing. Although investment bankers are occasionally involved in negotiating private placement loans, this form

[6] Short-term loans can be in the form of bank loans or commercial paper. While commercial banks provide bank loans, commercial paper is sold on the public market. Our hypothesis is based on the fact that separate data for bank loans and commercial paper were unavailable, and bank loans accounted for over 75 percent of short-term financing prior to 1980 (Stearns 1990). It should be noted, however, that the proportion of bank loans to commercial loans varies over time for large corporations (their use of commercial paper increased after 1980, for example). Consequently, changes in these proportions would alter this hypothesis.

of long-term financing is less lucrative for investment banks than is the underwriting long-term public bonds. As a result, we make no prediction regarding the relation between the presence of an investment banker on the board and the amount of long-term private funds borrowed. Since money-market banks specialize in short-term lending, we expect to find a negative relation between the presence of a money-market banker and private long-term financing. The effect of the presence of a regional banker on the board on long-term private financing is more complex. On the one hand, since regional banks specialize in short-term funds, we expect a negative relation to exist. On the other hand, regional banks compete with money-market banks for the banking business of large corporations. Since regional banks cannot provide the large sums of short-term debt that money-market banks can, they might encourage firms to borrow more long-term funds in order to keep the firms' short-term fund requirements within regional banks' lending limits. As a result, we make no prediction regarding the relation between the presence of a regional banker on the board and the amount of long-term private financing.

LONG-TERM PUBLIC BONDS. Long-term public bonds are underwritten by an investment bank or a syndicate of investment banks. Money-market and regional commercial banks are also involved in the issuance of public bonds. These banks are commissioned to process interest payments and to act as the issue's trustee (the firm that represents the bond-holders in dealing with the corporation) until the bond is retired. We, therefore, expect the presence of an investment banker, a money-market banker, or a regional banker on the board to increase the amount of long-term public bonds. Since insurance companies benefit more directly from private than public bonds, we expect to observe a negative relation between the presence of an insurance executive on the board and the amount of public bonds.

ALTERNATIVE TYPES OF EXTERNAL FINANCING. We control for alternative types of external financing (stock issues, short-term, long-term private, and long-term public funds) for the three types of borrowed funds. Corporations generally do not finance large sums of short-term debt in the same year they secure long-term funds (Stearns 1990), probably because short-term amounts are consolidated into the long-term debt. We, therefore, expect short-term financing to be negatively related to both forms of long-term borrowing. In addition, we expect long-term private and long-term public financing to be negatively related, since they are functional substitutes for one another. Finally, because corporations must not devalue their offerings by flooding the market, we expect to observe

**Table 11.3   Statement of Hypotheses**

| Independent Variables | Hypothesized Effect on Amount Borrowed | | |
|---|---|---|---|
| | Short-term | Long-private | Long-public |
| Social Determinants (Board Composition) | | | |
| Investment Banker | − | | + |
| Money Market Banker | + | − | + |
| Regional Banker | | | + |
| Insurance Executive | − | + | − |
| External Financing Alternatives | | | |
| Short-Term Borrowing | | − | − |
| Long-Term Private Loans | − | | − |
| Long-Term Public Bonds | − | − | |
| Stock Issue | − | + | − |

a negative relation between the amount of public issues (stock issued and long-term public bonds) offered in a given year.

The above hypotheses are summarized in Table 11.3. The operationalization of the dependent and independent variables is presented in Appendix 11.B.

*Results*

The MGLS regression equations for the three types of corporate financing are presented in Table 11.4. In each case, the amount of funds borrowed was positively associated with the presence of a financial representative from the institution that was the primary supplier of those funds. The presence of a money-market banker on the board increases a corporation's use of short-term debt, the presence of an insurance executive increases long-term private debt, and the presence of an investment banker increases long-term public funds borrowed.

The presence of a money-market banker is negatively related to long-term private debt, and the presence of a life insurance executive on the board negatively affects the amount of long-term public debt. Finally, having a money-market and regional banker on the board are both positively associated with long-term public debt. All of these findings are consistent with our hypotheses.

Contrary to expectation, however, the presence of a life insurance executive on the board is positively related to short-term borrowing. Per-

**Table 11.4  Determinants of Specific Types of External Financing (MGLS Estimates)**

| Independent Variables | Short-Term Borrowing | | Long-Term Private Loans | | Long-Term Public Loans | |
|---|---|---|---|---|---|---|
| | B | SE | B | SE | B | SE |
| Social Embeddedness | | | | | | |
| Investment Banker | .0005 | .001 | −.003 *** | .0006 | .0004 *** | .0001 |
| Money Market Banker | .026 *** | .003 | −.006 *** | .001 | .009 *** | .0004 |
| Regional Banker | −.0001 | .003 | .0005 | .001 | .002 *** | .0002 |
| Insurance Executive | .032 *** | .004 | .009 *** | .001 | −.001 ** | .0004 |
| Control (Mgt. vs. Family) | .023 *** | .005 | −.0009 | .001 | −.001 *** | .0003 |
| Economic | | | | | | |
| Available Internal Funds | −.113 *** | .010 | −.067 *** | .004 | −.007 *** | .0007 |
| Interest Rate | .0006 *** | .0001 | .0005 *** | .0001 | .0006 *** | .0001 |
| Phase of Business Cycle | .006 *** | .002 | .0005 | .0004 | .0003 | .0003 |
| Internal Alternatives | | | | | | |
| Own Financial Company | −.014 ** | .005 | −.008 *** | .001 | −.007 *** | .0004 |
| Employee Stock Plan | −.0005 | .006 | −.001 | .002 | −.005 *** | .0006 |
| Acquisition Through Stock | −.016 | .038 | .538 *** | .025 | .112 *** | .027 |
| External Alternatives | | | | | | |
| Short-Term Borrowing | — | — | −.028 *** | .006 | −.021 *** | .001 |
| Long-Term Private Loans | −.144 *** | .012 | — | — | −.040 *** | .002 |
| Long-Term Public Bonds | −.199 *** | .019 | −.116 *** | .024 | — | — |
| Stock Issue | .008 | .004 | .028 *** | .006 | .015 *** | .001 |
| Constant | .253 *** | .008 | .025 *** | .004 | −.015 *** | .002 |
| | d.f. | 601 | d.f. | 601 | d.f. | 601 |

*p<.05
**p<.01

haps corporations with high amounts of short-term borrowing place life insurance executives on their board to gain access to private long-term funds should liquidity (having to pay off short-term debt) become a problem and bankruptcy become a threat.[7]

The finding (reported in Table 11.2) that external financing is nondiscretionary remains robust when the three types of borrowing are examined separately. All three types increase as corporations' internal funds decrease and interest rates increase. Long-term private and long-term public borrowing are unrelated to the stage of the business cycle. Short-term borrowing, however, occurs more often during the expansionary phase of the business cycle. As discussed above, borrowing at such times may be either discretionary or nondiscretionary.

The effect of type of control (management versus family) differs for the three kinds of borrowing. Management-controlled firms borrow significantly more short-term funds than do family-controlled firms; family-controlled firms borrow significantly more long-term public bonds than do management-controlled firms; and type of control has no effect on long-term private borrowing.

The effect of the presence of an employee stock-ownership plan and of using the corporation's stock for acquiring firms also differs by type of borrowing. The existence of an employee stock-ownership plan is unrelated to the amount of short-term and long-term private loans, but it is negatively related to the amount of long-term public bonds. Furthermore, using stock to acquire another firm is not related to short-term borrowing, but it is positively related to both kinds of long-term borrowing.

Although owning a financial institution did not have a significant effect on the total amount of external funding (Table 11.2), it had a negative effect on the three types of borrowing once financial board representation was controlled.[8] This suggests that the extent to which corporations use the capital resources of their own financial institution is in part determined by whether a financial representative sits on their board of directors.

---

[7] Such intercorporate ties would represent Laumann and Marsden's third principle of organizational bonding—redundancy. According to them, linkages between organizations are maintained "as a form of social insurance against the failure of a particular source of resource supply and as potential alternative by which dependence on a given source of supply can be limited" (1982:333).

[8] The consolidated model included the amount of stock (preferred and common) issued in total external financing. To test whether this variable accounts for the difference, we recomputed the equation in Table 11.2, deleting stocks issued. The results were virtually identical; the effect of owning a financial institution was positive but not statistically significant.

Finally, as predicted, short-term borrowing is negatively related to both types of long-term funds, while long-term private and long-term public funds are negatively related to one another. The issuance of stock is positively related to long-term private financing (as predicted) and to long-term public financing (contrary to prediction). Thus, it appears that corporations needing long-term funds issue stock and borrow from financial institutions simultaneously.

## Conclusion

In the managerialist model, large corporations are viewed as financially self-sufficient systems because they can meet their capital requirements with internally generated funds. According to this view, to the extent that corporations do use the capital market, this use is not out of necessity but because external funds offer cost and tax advantages. Yet we found that corporations were more likely to borrow when their own internal funds were low. Furthermore, borrowing increased when interest rates were high (indicating that the aggregate demand for capital is high). These findings suggest that corporations borrow precisely during those times in which their dependence on financial institutions is greatest.

We find that some corporations decrease their reliance on external financing by acquiring a financial institution. Do corporations choose to acquire a financial institution rather than obtain funds in external capital markets because, as transaction-cost economists argue, hierarchies are more efficient (Williamson 1975; 1981)? Or do corporations acquire a financial institution, as resource-dependence theorists argue, as a way of decreasing their dependence and limiting their vulnerability to external control (Pfeffer and Salancik 1978; Perrow 1981; Burt 1983)? Both explanations are plausible, and they are not necessarily mutually exclusive. Further research is necessary, however, in order to identify the conditions under which corporations acquire financial institutions.

Classical and neoclassical economists view the market as the chief determinant of corporate behavior, generally ignoring the importance of social relations. Our findings indicate that although firms do respond to market forces (short-term borrowing increased during the expansionary phase of the business cycle, for example), the character of social relations between corporations and financial institutions is an equally strong predictor of the amount and type of funds borrowed. The types of financial institutions represented on firms' boards of directors were associated with each of the three types of corporate borrowing. Our data do not enable us to ascertain whether the board-represented financial institution is supplying the financing. Both Palmer, Friedland, and Singh (1986) and Stearns and Mizruchi (1986), however, found a correlation between ties to financial directors and economic transactions.[9]

We also cannot ascertain the causal ordering between interlocking and type of borrowing. In an earlier study (Mizruchi and Stearns 1988), we showed that financial directors are added to corporations' boards during periods of declining solvency and profitability as well as during periods of expansion and increasing aggregate demand for capital. These results suggest that interlocks are used for both cooptation and monitoring purposes. That is, during periods of expansion and increased demand for capital, firms may voluntarily appoint financial directors to ease their access to capital. When corporations face declining solvency and profitability, however, financial representatives may join their boards to monitor corporate strategies in order to protect their investments.

Interlocks and borrowing may also be nonrecursive. In some cases, a firm embarking on a particular financial strategy may appoint a specific financial representative to its board; in other cases, a firm's financing strategy may reflect the influence of a financial representative already on its board. In support of the latter interpretation, it is worth noting that the average tenure of financial representatives in our data is thirteen years. This indicates that in most cases, the presence of financial board members preceded the firm's borrowing behavior.

We have focused on two issues to examine the extent to which corporations are autonomous relative to financial institutions. First, we investigated whether corporations are dependent on financial institutions for external sources of capital. Our findings suggest that they are. Second, we examined whether corporations' borrowing decisions are embedded in their social relations with financial institutions. Our findings indicate that this too is the case. Rather than being independent, autonomous entities, the large corporations in our sample were involved in a network of intercorporate relations with financial institutions. Such involvement does not necessarily mean that financial institutions have the power over corporations that they did at the turn of the twentieth century. Given the importance of the largest corporations to our economy (Heilbroner 1966), however, it does suggest that sociologists should in-

---

[9] In a study of investment banking, Baker (1990) found considerable variation in the extent to which firms did business with the investment banks represented on their boards. A preliminary analysis with data on commercial bank loans in the 1930s (Go 1987; Mizruchi, Dordick, and Han 1990) indicates similar variation in the extent to which firms do business with the commercial banks on their boards. A corresponding study based on relations with insurance companies remains to be done.

quire into the behavioral consequences of the relations between financial
and nonfinancial firms.

# Appendix 11.A

We have operationalized the variables in Table 11.2 as follows:

### Dependent Variable

*Total external financing*. The total amount of money borrowed (short-
term and long-term funds) plus the amount raised through stock (preferred and common) sales (see Appendix 11.B). We controlled for
corporate size by dividing total external financing by total assets. The
dependent variable and all independent variables affected by inflation
(interest rates, availability of internal funds, acquisition through stock,
and stock issues) were deflated to constant dollars (1967 = 100).

### Independent Variables

*Available internal funds*. We used retained earnings, which is the amount
of internal funds left after a corporation has paid its debts and stock
dividends for the year. We controlled for corporate size by dividing
retained earnings by total assets.

*Interest rate*. We used the New York Prime Rate.

*Expansion*. A dummy variable coded 0 for contraction and 1 for expansion.

*Control*. A dummy variable coded 0 for family-controlled firms and 1
for management-controlled firms (see Stearns and Mizruchi 1986 for
further details).

*Own financial company*. A dummy variable coded 0 for no and 1 for
yes.

*Employee stock-ownership plan*. A dummy variable coded 0 for no and 1
for yes.

*Acquisition through stock*. The value of the corporation's stock given to
finance the acquisition of another firm. The value was calculated on
the number of shares times the average stock price for the year.

# Appendix 11.B

We have operationalized the variables in Table 11.4 as follows:

## Dependent Variables

*Short-term borrowing.* We used current liabilities (debt due in one year) to represent corporations' short-term borrowing. Current liabilities was used (rather than bank notes) because it provided the only consistent data for short-term debt between firms and within firms across time. Because current liabilities includes bank notes, commercial paper, bond and tax anticipation notes, warrants, and trade debt, it provides a more conservative estimate of the hypothesized effects. We controlled for corporate size by dividing the amount of current liabilities by total assets.

*Long-term private borrowing.* To calculate the amount of long-term privately borrowed funds for a given year, say 1956, we subtracted the amount of long-term debt outstanding in 1955 and any new public bond issue in 1956 from the amount of long-term debt outstanding in 1956. We controlled for corporate size by dividing the amount of long-term private borrowing by total assets.

*Long-term public bond financing.* Public bonds are listed separately in *Moody's*. Information includes the date of issue, date of maturity, amount, bond rating, purpose of borrowing, restrictive covenants, underwriters, trustees, interest commissioners, and so on. We controlled for corporate size by dividing the amount of long-term public bond financing by total assets.

## Independent Variables

*Board composition.* Dummy variables were created for all four types of financial institutions (investment banks, money-market banks, regional banks, and life insurance companies). A financial institution was coded as represented on a corporation's board (0 = no and 1 = yes) if one of its officers was a member present in either the preceding year or the year the borrowing took place.

*Interest rate.* We used the New York Prime Rate for the interest rate on short-term borrowing and the AAA bond rate for the interest rate on long-term private and public borrowing.

*Stock issue.* The value of preferred and common stock issued. The preferred stock value was calculated as the number of shares times the callable dollar amount. The common stock value was equal to the amount listed in *Moody's* as underwritten by the investment bank. We controlled for corporate size by dividing total amount of stock issued by total assets.

We would like to thank Wayne Baker, Ivar Berg, David Jacobs, and K. Jill Kiecolt for their comments on a previous draft. We are especially grateful to Paul DiMaggio for his detailed suggestions. Stearns was supported by the Russell Sage Foundation and Howard Foundation. Mizruchi was supported by a National Science Foundation Presidential Young Investigator Award (SES-8858669). Please direct correspondence to Linda Brewster Stearns, Department of Sociology, University of California, Riverside, California 92521.

# References

ABOLAFIA, MITCHEL Y., and MARTIN KILDUFF. 1988. "Enacting Market Crisis: The Social Construction of a Speculative Bubble." *Administrative Science Quarterly* 33:177–193.

ALLEN, MICHAEL P. 1974. "The Structure of Interorganizational Elite Cooptation: Interlocking Corporate Directorates." *American Sociological Review* 39:393–406.

BAKER, WAYNE E. 1984. "The Social Structure of a National Securities Market." *American Journal of Sociology* 89:775–811.

———. 1990. "Market Networks and Corporate Behavior." *American Journal of Sociology* 96:589–625.

BARAN, PAUL A., and PAUL M. SWEEZY. 1966. *Monopoly Capital*. New York: Monthly Review Press.

BARTON, SIDNEY L., and PAUL J. GORDON. 1987. "Corporate Strategy: Useful Perspective for the Study of Capital Structure?" *Academy of Management Review* 12:67–75.

BELL, DANIEL. 1961. *The End of Ideology*. New York: Collier.

BERLE, ADOLPH A. 1954. *The 20th Century Capitalist Revolution*. New York: Harcourt, Brace and World.

BERLE, ADOLPH A., and GARDINER C. MEANS. [1932] 1968. *The Modern Corporation and Private Property*. New York: Harcourt, Brace and World.

BLALOCK, HUBERT M., JR. 1979. *Social Statistics*. Second Edition. New York: McGraw-Hill.

BRANDEIS, LOUIS D. 1914. *Other People's Money*. New York: Frederick A. Stokes Company.

BURT, RONALD S. 1983. *Corporate Profits and Cooptation: Networks of Market Constraints and Directorate Ties in the American Economy*. New York: Academic Press.

CAROSSO, VINCENT. 1970. *Investment Banking in America*. Cambridge, MA: Harvard University Press.

CHANDLER, ALFRED D., JR. 1962. *Strategy and Structure*. Cambridge, MA: MIT Press.

———. 1977. *The Visible Hand*. Cambridge, MA: Harvard University Press.

CORPORATE DATA EXCHANGE. 1980. *Banking & Finance: The Hidden Cost*. New York: Corporate Data Exchange, Inc.

DAHRENDORF, RALF. 1959. *Class and Class Conflict in Industrial Society.* Stanford: Stanford University Press.

DOOLEY, PETER C. 1969. "The Interlocking Directorate." *American Economic Review* 59:314–323.

FAMA, EUGENE, and MICHAEL JENSEN. 1983. "Separation of Ownership and Control." *Journal of Law and Economics* 26:301–325.

FITCH, ROBERT, and MARY OPPENHEIMER. 1970a–c. "Who Rules the Corporations?" *Socialist Revolution* 4:73–108; 5:61–114; 6:33–94.

FRIEDLAND, ROGER, and JIMY SANDERS. 1985. "The Public Economy and Economic Growth in Western Market Economies." *American Sociological Review* 50:782–799.

GALBRAITH, JOHN KENNETH. 1967. *The New Industrial State.* New York: New American Library.

GLASBERG, DAVITA SILFEN. 1989. *The Power of Collective Purse Strings.* Berkeley: University of California Press.

GO, TIAN KANG. 1987. "Concentration of Term Loans in the United States, 1938–41." *Research Papers,* No. 8. Tokyo: The Institute of Business Research.

GRANOVETTER, MARK. 1985. "Economic Action and Social Structure: The Problem of Embeddedness." *American Journal of Sociology* 91:481–510.

HANNAN, MICHAEL T., and ALICE A. YOUNG. 1977. "Estimation in Panel Models: Results on Pooling Cross-Sections and Time-Series." In David R. Heise ed., *Sociological Methodology.* San Francisco: Jossey-Bass, pp. 52–83.

HEILBRONER, ROBERT. 1966. *The Limits of American Capitalism.* New York: Harper and Row.

HERMAN, EDWARD S. 1981. *Corporate Control, Corporate Power.* New York: Cambridge University Press.

HILFERDING, RUDOLF. [1910] 1981. *Finance Capital.* London: Routledge and Kegan Paul.

HIRSCH, PAUL. 1982. "Network Data Versus Personal Accounts: The Normative Culture of Interlocking Directorates." Paper presented at Annual Meeting of American Sociological Association, San Francisco.

JENSEN, MICHAEL C., and WILLIAM H. MECKLING. 1976. "Theory of the Firm: Managerial Behavior, Agency Costs and Ownership Structure." *Journal of Finance* 3:305–360.

KOTZ, DAVID M. 1978. *Bank Control of Large Corporations in the United States.* Berkeley: University of California Press.

LAUMANN, EDWARD O., and PETER V. MARSDEN. 1982. "Microstructural Analysis in Interorganizational Systems." *Social Networks* 4:329–348.

LEIFER, ERIC M., and HARRISON C. WHITE. 1987. "A Structural Approach to Markets." In Mark S. Mizruchi and Michael Schwartz eds., *Intercorporate Relations: The Structural Analysis of Business.* New York: Cambridge University Press, pp. 85–108.

LENIN, V. I. (1917) 1977. *Imperialism: The Highest State of Capitalism.* New York: International Publishers.

LINTNER, JOHN. 1959. "The Financing of Corporations." In Edward S. Mason ed., *The Corporation in Modern Society.* Cambridge, MA: Harvard University Press, pp. 166–201.

MADDALA, G. S. 1977. *Econometrics.* New York: McGraw-Hill.

MINTZ, BETH, and MICHAEL SCHWARTZ. 1985. *The Power Structure of American Business.* Chicago: University of Chicago Press.

MIZRUCHI, MARK S. 1982. *The American Corporate Network, 1904–1974.* Beverly Hills: Sage Publications.

MIZRUCHI, MARK S., and LINDA BREWSTER STEARNS. 1988. "A Longitudinal Study of the Formation of Interlocking Directorates." *Administrative Science Quarterly* 33:194–210.

———. 1991. "Governance Costs, Network Ties, and Institutional Processes: Why Do Corporations Borrow?" Paper presented at Annual Meeting of American Sociological Association, Cincinnati, OH.

MIZRUCHI, MARK S. and GWEN DORDICK, and SHIN-KAP HAN. 1990. "Do Corporations Do Business with the Bankers on Their Boards?: Direct and Functional Resource Representation." Paper presented at Annual Meeting of American Sociological Association, Washington, D.C.

MODIGLIANI, FRANCO, and MERTON H. MILLER. 1963. "Taxes and the Cost of Capital: A Correction." *American Economic Review* 53:433–443.

MYERS, STUART C. 1977. "Determinants of Corporate Borrowing." *Journal of Financial Economics* 5:147–175.

———. 1984. "The Capital Structure Puzzle." *Journal of Finance* 39:575–591.

NAVIN, THOMAS R., and MARIAN V. SEARS. 1955. "The Rise of a Market for Industrial Securities, 1877–1902." *Business History Review* 29:105–138.

PALMER, DONALD, ROGER FRIEDLAND, and JITENDRA V. SINGH. 1986. "The Ties that Bind: Determinants of Stability in a Corporate Interlock Network." *American Sociological Review* 51:781–796.

PAMPEL, FRED C., and JOHN B. WILLIAMSON. 1985. "Age Structure, Politics, and Cross-National Patterns of Public Pension Expenditures." *American Sociological Review* 50:782–799.

PARKS, RICHARD W. 1967. "Efficient Estimation of a System of Regression Equations when Disturbances are Both Serially and Contemporaneously Correlated." *Journal of the American Statistical Association* 62:500–509.

PENNINGS, JOHANNES M. 1980. *Interlocking Directorates.* San Francisco: Jossey-Bass.

PERLO, VICTOR. 1957. *The Empire of High Finance.* New York: International Publishers.

PERROW, CHARLES. 1981. "Markets, Hierarchies, and Hegemony." In Andrew Van de Ven and William Joyce eds., *Perspectives on Organization Design and Behavior.* New York: Wiley, pp. 371–386.

PFEFFER, JEFFREY. 1972. "Size and Composition of Corporate Boards of Directors: The Organization and Its Environment." *Administrative Science Quarterly* 17:218–228.

PFEFFER, JEFFREY, and GERALD R. SALANCIK. 1978. *The External Control of Organizations: A Resource Dependence Perspective.* New York: Harper & Row.

RICHARDSON, R. JACK. 1987. "Directorship Interlocks and Corporate Profitability." *Administrative Science Quarterly* 32:367–386.

ROCHESTER, ANNA. 1936. *Rulers of America: A Study of Finance Capital.* New York: International Publishers.

ROY, WILLIAM G. 1983. "The Unfolding of the Interlocking Directorate Structure of the United States." *American Sociological Review* 48:248–257.

STEARNS, LINDA BREWSTER. 1983. "Corporate Dependency and the Structure of the Capital Market, 1946–1980." Ph.D. dissertation, State University of New York at Stony Brook.

———. 1990. "Capital Market Effects on External Control of Corporations." In Sharon Zukin and Paul DiMaggio eds., *Structures of Capital: The Social Organization of the Economy.* New York: Cambridge University Press, pp. 175–201.

STEARNS, LINDA BREWSTER, and MARK S. MIZRUCHI. 1986. "Broken-Tie Reconstitution and the Functions of Interorganizational Interlocks: A Reexamination." *Administrative Science Quarterly* 31:522–538.

SWEEZY, PAUL M. 1942. *The Theory of Capitalist Development.* New York: Monthly Review Press.

———. 1971. "The Resurgence of Financial Control: Fact or Fancy?" *Monthly Review* (November):1–33.

THOMPSON, JAMES D. 1967. *Organizations in Action.* New York: McGraw-Hill.

U.S. HOUSE OF REPRESENTATIVES (COMMITTEE ON BANKING AND CURRENCY). 1913. *Investigation of Concentration of Control of Money and Credit.* Washington, D.C.: U.S. Government Printing Office.

USEEM, MICHAEL. 1984. *The Inner Circle.* New York: Oxford University Press.

WESTON, J. FRED, and EUGENE F. BRIGHAM. 1981. *Managerial Finance.* Hinsdale, IL: Dryden Press.

WHITE, HARRISON C. 1981. "Where Do Markets Come From?" *American Journal of Sociology* 87:517–547.

WILLIAMSON, OLIVER E. 1975. *Markets and Hierarchies.* New York: Free Press.

———. 1981. "The Economics of Organization: The Transaction Cost Approach." *American Journal of Sociology* 87:548–577.

———. 1988. "Corporate Finance and Corporate Governance." *The Journal of Finance* 18:567–591.

ZALD, MAYER N. 1970. "Political Economy: A Framework for Comparative Analysis." In Mayer N. Zald ed., *Power in Organizations.* Nashville: Vanderbilt University Press.

ZEITLIN, MAURICE. 1974. "Corporate Ownership and Control: The Large Corporation and the Capitalist Class." *American Journal of Sociology* 79:1073–1119.

# 12

# Shareholder Power and the Struggle for Corporate Control

## MICHAEL USEEM

## Managerial Prerogatives and Corporate Performance

Much of the corporate restructuring during the 1980s and early 1990s can be traced to a more open contest for control of large business firms. The intensified struggle derived from a weakening of the long-standing dominance of professional managers over the fate of many major corporations. In decades past, there had been a gradual but seemingly inexorable shift of control of large corporations from founding owners and shareholders to nonowning professional managers. This was the "managerial revolution" identified by Adolph Berle and Gardiner Means in their 1932 landmark study of corporate organization and governance. A company's board of directors was, in principle, the instrument for shareholder sovereignty over management, but in practice the board had often evolved instead into an instrument of management. Unable to change an unresponsive board, unhappy shareholders were left with the sole alternative of exiting. The "Wall Street Rule" of disinvesting, rather than challenging management, became a norm of necessity.

Later analysis confirmed that ownership control of the corporation by the 1970s had been replaced with managerial control in a substantial proportion of the largest firms in the United States. One of the major studies reported that 82 percent of the country's 200 largest nonfinancial corporations had come under management control by 1974, up from 40 percent in 1929. Of the 40 largest companies in 1900, just 22 percent were management controlled (Berle and Means 1967; Herman 1981). While outside financial institutions and family groups continued to exercise considerable influence on some companies, inside professional management acquired active control of many other publicly traded corporations (Fligstein 1990; Herman 1981; Kotz 1978; Larner 1970; Mintz and Schwartz 1985).

As the managerial revolution took hold, senior managers had lost virtually all of what little ownership stake they had once had in large firms. Chief executives of the nation's 120 largest companies and their families held an average 0.30 percent of the companies' shares in 1938; by 1974 this had declined to a scant 0.047 percent (Jensen and Murphy 1990). Yet despite the decline of personal ownership, many had wrested control on the premise that they would be more effective at serving ownership interests than the owners themselves. The premise had been persuasive. The enormous scale of the new organizational forms and the task of operating them in highly complex environments placed a premium on sophisticated leadership. As Alfred Chandler characterized it in *The Visible Hand*, the founding family and favored financier had relinquished all but residual control over company decisions. "They could say no," observed Chandler, "but unless they themselves were trained managers with long experience in the same industry and even the same company, they had neither the information nor the experience to propose positive alternative courses of action" (1977:491). Decision making came to be viewed as a learned rather than intuitive or inherited skill.

The solution to one set of organizational problems, however, ushered in a new set of dilemmas. While professional non-owning managers might come to be the technocratic masters of problem solving, it proved inherently difficult for the owners to ensure that the managers did so in a way that best served shareholder interests. Once professional managements were installed as the owners' agents, the door was opened for career, power, and other motives to intrude into decision making. So too was the decision-making door opened to the concerns of local communities, company employees, nonprofit organizations, and other corporate stakeholders as they prodded their companies to be more "socially responsible." Despite the institution of a host of organizational mechanisms to link managerial and ownership interests better, such as the widespread use of performance-based executive compensation schemes, the door could never be fully closed (Eisenhardt 1989; Fama 1980; Fama and Jensen 1983; Jensen and Meckling 1976).

When large corporations entered a prolonged period of profit decline during the 1970s, blame was at first placed on neither this "agency" problem nor other possible shortcomings of professional management.

Rather, business executives tended to single out the growing role of the federal government in costly areas of social regulation, above all environmental protection, occupational health and safety, and equal employment opportunity. Instead of suggesting internal restructuring or new business strategies to overcome the long-term problem of declining performance, many company leaders chose to target reduction of government intervention in the marketplace. Large corporations aggressively sought a roll-back through Washington lobbying, political donations, and employee mobilization (Himmelstein 1990; Silk and Vogel 1976; Useem 1984; Vogel 1989).

Yet despite the reduction in state interference and the improved political climate following inauguration of the Reagan Administration in 1981, performance and competitiveness for many firms were still not restored to full health. Then, in a fateful turn, the search for causes veered inward on management itself. Poor business performance came finally to be blamed by some on entrenched managers who, it seemed, had become unresponsive to shareholder concerns. Senior managers did not generally share this view, but it gained currency among many takeover specialists, major shareholders, and academic critics. The assessment of Michael Jensen, a leading advocate of change in top management of publicly traded corporations, illustrates the critique that became widespread during the late 1980s: the autonomy of professional management from ownership oversight, he concluded, had caused "widespread waste and inefficiency of the public corporation and its inability to adapt to changing economic circumstances" (1989:65). Peter Drucker echoed the appraisal: "What made takeovers and buyouts inevitable . . . was the mediocre performance of enlightened-despot management, the management without clear definitions of performance and results and with no clear accountability to somebody" (1991:109).

While professional managers and their policies came to be viewed by many outsiders as the problem, the solutions proposed for improving performance depended on the proponent. Incumbent managements naturally preferred to remain so and to stimulate earnings through internal reform, such as workforce downsizing. Corporate "raiders," by contrast, placed little stock in the ability of incumbent management ever to reform itself. "We're supporting managements who produce nothing," complained Carl Icahn, one of the most active practitioners of hostile corporate acquisitions, in justifying his actions: "Not only are we paying those drones to produce nothing, but we're paying them to muck up the works" (Icahn 1988). Still other outsiders proposed to install management teams that also possessed a major ownership stake through leveraged buyouts, thereby recombining ownership and control of the corporation in the same individuals.

Corporate downsizing, acquisitions, and buyouts were thus among the varied responses in a more active market for control of the corporation that emerged during the 1980s. Incumbent managements, outside raiders, and investment groups vied for the opportunity to restructure the corporation. Lining up behind those with the most promising strategy were a new set of moneyed actors, the institutional investors. Slowly, almost imperceptibly, they had gained ground as vast numbers of company shares became concentrated in their hands. At first it was a largely passive ground, with institutions routinely supporting incumbent management against challengers from the outside. During the 1980s, however, the institutions moved onto more active ground, still siding with management in most cases but increasingly pressing for changes and, failing that, joining the challengers. The result was a rediscovery of "shareholder rights." This chapter focuses on the forces outside the organization that fostered that new found shareholder power.

## The Rise of Institutional Shareholding

The accumulating resources and prospective power of institutional investors had been little noticed during the early 1980s. Then, with scant warning, they loomed large on many company radar screens. Leading the attack were those institutions first to shed the Wall Street Rule. Exit was no longer necessary since they had now accumulated the power to be heard by management. Equally important, exit was no longer feasible. Few untapped opportunities remained, and almost the only buyers large enough to acquire an institution's holdings were other institutions.

Institutional investors include pension funds (company and state and local government funds), mutual funds, investment trusts, insurance companies, nonpension funds managed by banks, and foundation and nonprofit endowment funds. Pension funds, both private and public, were responsible for more than two-fifths of the total institutional holdings of $5,249 billion in 1988 (Table 12.1). The ten largest private and public pension funds in 1990 alone managed more than $500 billion in assets (*Institutional Investor* 1991). The single largest fund, the California Public Employees' Retirement System, commonly abbreviated as Calpers, presided over more than $55 billion. It was increasing its holdings in 1990 by some $20 million per day, and, indicative of pension funds' inability or unwillingness to churn their funds, Calpers held its average investment for eight years.

**Table 12.1    Holdings of Institutional Investors, 1981 and 1988**

| Institutional Investor | 1981 | 1988 | Annual Growth 1981–1988 |
| --- | --- | --- | --- |
| | (billions of dollars) | | (Percent) |
| Pension Funds | 891.2 | 2,266.8 | 14.3 |
| Private trusteed | 486.7 | 1,139.9 | 12.9 |
| Private insured | 180.3 | 516.8 | 16.2 |
| State/local gov't | 224.2 | 610.1 | 15.3 |
| Investment Companies | 248.3 | 816.5 | 18.5 |
| Open end/mutual funds | 241.4 | 777.8 | 18.2 |
| Closed end/invest trusts | 6.9 | 38.7 | 27.9 |
| Insurance Companies | 559.0 | 1,258.8 | 12.3 |
| Life insurance | 347.0 | 781.8 | 12.3 |
| Property/casualty | 212.0 | 476.9 | 12.3 |
| Bank Trusts (Nonpension) | 334.9 | 774.6 | 12.7 |
| Foundations and Endowments | 56.0 | 133.0 | 13.2 |
| Total | 2,089.4 | 5,249.7 | 14.0 |

Source: Brancato and Gaughan 1990.

Shareholding by institutional investors had steadily increased during the post-war period. Estimates of the specific levels of institutional shareholding vary somewhat with the particular definitions and data sources employed, but the trends all point in the same upward direction (Brancato and Gaughan 1988; Securities Industry Association 1990). Estimates also indicate that the 1980s were marked by a far more rapid concentration of institutional ownership than during earlier decades. From 1970 to 1980, the proportion of stock in the hands of institutional investors rose, according to one time series, from 31 to 33 percent, but during the next six years it jumped another 10 points. The proportion, according to a second time series, rose during the 1970s from 21 to 29 percent, but during the next decade it added 16 points (Figures 12.1a and 12.1b).

Institutional investors also became a more potent force on the stock exchanges during the 1980s. This could be seen, for instance, in the rise of large-block trading, defined by the New York Stock Exchange (NYSE) as trades of 10,000 or more shares. In 1965, only 3 percent of the shares traded on NYSE were exchanged in blocks of 10,000 or more. In 1980, the proportion had reached 29 percent. By the middle part of the decade, it soared to some 50 percent (New York Stock Exchange, 1991).

During the late 1980s, many companies found that a majority of their shares were in the hands of the institutions. By decade's end, for in-

**Figure 12.1a   Holdings of Equities Distribution of Stock Value, 1965–1990**

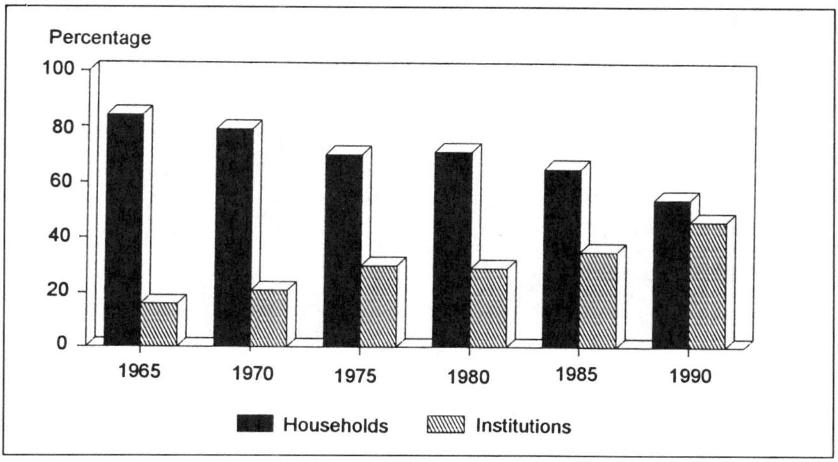

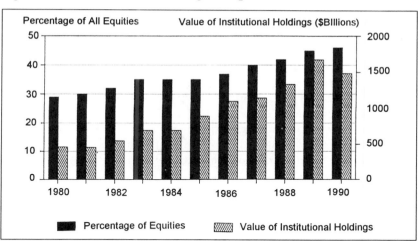

Source: Securities Industry Association (1990); 1990 data for end of third quarter.

**Figure 12.1b   Institutional Holdings of Equities, 1980–1990**

Source: Securities Industry Association (1990); 1990 data for end of third quarter.

stance, institutional investors held 52 percent of General Electric, 59 percent of Johnson and Johnson, 71 percent of Digital Equipment, 83 percent of Intel, and 84 percent of Dayton Hudson (Standard and Poor's *Stock Reports* 1991). Of the 1,000 largest publicly traded firms in 1990, the average institutional shareholding stood at 50 percent, up from 43 percent five years earlier (*Business Week* 1991 and earlier years). A small set of the largest institutional investors was responsible for a large portion of the holdings. One study, for example, examined the holdings of a random sample of 25 companies in 1990 from the Standard and Poor's 500, the 500 largest companies ranked by market capitalization. Most companies among the largest 500 had at least several hundred institutional investors, but the 20 largest investors accounted on average for more than a third (34.1 percent) of the outstanding shares (Lowenstein 1991).

## The Mobilization of Shareholder Power

The increased rates of turnover in corporate ownership, buyouts of public companies, and concentration of institutional ownership placed more power to shape company enterprise in the hands of owners, less in the hands of top managers. Some firms experienced abrupt restructuring, as fresh ownership groups radically redesigned their new possessions. All power here had gone to the takeover engineers. Other firms experienced nothing at all, as incumbent managements continued to enjoy full control of their boards and shareholders. The umbrella of Berle and Means' managerial revolution was not leaking, and it appeared to them that it never would be. These were the extremes, however, and most major firms found themselves somewhere in between. Still free from ownership control, they could no longer afford to ignore it.

Firms experienced several kinds of pressures to be more responsive to shareholder interests and demands. The distinctive forms reflected well-known alternatives for the exercise of power (Etzioni 1968). Some firms came under direct ownership control; others became more responsive as they developed mutually dependent relations with major investors; and still others were the target of concerted shareholder actions.

### *Direct Control through Organizational Fusion*

Direct control was achieved as companies and units previously insulated from ownership pressures were placed under the oversight of owners and managers-cum-owners. Led by leveraged buyouts, this wholesale transformation in corporate control drew attention out of proportion to the actual number of firms affected. Buyouts reached but a tiny fraction of publicly traded firms during the 1980s (Useem 1990). Their special salience lay in the completeness with which ownership control was re-imposed, an appealing model to advocates of reform. For one proponent, they even heralded the "eclipse of the public corporation" (Jensen 1989).

The leveraged buyout of RJR Nabisco by Kohlberg Kravis Roberts was illustrative. R. J. Reynolds Industries, the larger of the two entities that had merged to form RJR Nabisco in 1985, had been solidly controlled by professional management in the 1970s, the period of the most recent assessment of control among major manufacturers (Herman 1981:318). In purchasing all stock in 1989 for nearly $25 billion, KKR completely transformed the control structure. As a firm of little more than a dozen professionals, KKR could not hope to exercise day-to-day control over this and its more than a dozen other companies whose aggregate value was near $60 billion (Kohlberg Kravis Roberts 1989). Nor did the past owners aspire to do so. But the new owners did exercise tight financial control, which the previous owners could not, even if they had so aspired. There "is no mistaking who calls the shots," observed two journalists who examined KKR's operating strategy (Burrough and Helyar 1990:166). KKR principals reviewed all budgets and retained full power over all executive appointments (Burrough and Helyar 1990; Bartlett 1991a).

When a buyout fell short of its targets, as in the case of KKR's second purchase, an oil-field services firm, intervention was swift. Incumbent management was ousted, new management swiftly installed (Burrough and Heylar 1990:139–140). When buyouts did not fall short, the leash was long, its only tug toward strategic thinking. Duracell, the maker of alkaline batteries, was one of Kohlberg-Kravis's later successes (1988). Its chief executive, who with other managers owned some 13 percent of the company (the rest held by KKR), had free reign to make money for both sets of owners. "When I talk with Henry Kravis at lunch," he said, "we don't spend time talking about cost reductions. We talk about how we're increasing the strategic value of the company" (Kidder 1990:8–9).

Unlike the organizations described in Meyer and Zucker's (1989) account of permanent under-performance, there would be no room for failing organizations here (though the performance record of KKR firms and other companies that had been taken private is a matter of dispute—see Long and Ravenscraft 1991). Thousands of independent shareholders in the past had looked to their elected board to police management, a policing function that the managerial revolution had effectively thwarted. Now, the owners themselves were both on the board and in the management. The resulting organizational fusion ensured that all primary agents remained closely wedded to ownership principles.

## Mutual Dependency through Shareholding

Organizational theorists have long argued that resource dependency is a critical lever of power: the greater the reliance of organization $A$ on resources of organization $B$, the greater the power of $B$ over $A$ (Aldrich and Pfeffer 1976; Pfeffer and Salancik 1978; Aldrich 1979; Burt 1983). When shareholding was widely dispersed, there were so many $B$s that $A$ was dependent on none in particular. Companies enjoyed, in the framing of Mintzberg, an environment characterized by a "dispersed and detached ownership" (1983:32–37). With shareholding far more concentrated, however, they now faced instead a "concentrated and involved ownership," with a corresponding loss of autonomy. The fewer $B$s could rightfully demand far more of $A$'s attention. Other kinds of outside organizations, such as suppliers, political institutions, and employees, vied for attention as well, and their resources too had concentrated in some cases. Yet other theorists remind us that their case was inherently weaker since their resources were less essential (Jacobs 1974). Equity sources came first; other providers followed.

Investor profiles of two companies featured in the broader study from which this chapter is drawn illustrate the degree of this concentration. One company was a manufacturer of special machinery with annual revenues in the range of $2 to 5 billion; the other was a retail services firm with annual sales in the range of $5 to 10 billion. Nearly two-thirds of the special machinery firm's shares were held by some 200 institutional investors, and the top ten held more than a fifth. The three largest investors owned 4.0, 2.4, and 2.2 percent of the company. A little more than half of the retail service firm's shares were held by 475 institutions. The top ten investors possessed about 15 percent, and the three largest held 2.1, 2.0, and 2.0 percent.

Though companies saw increasingly concentrated institutional holdings, large investors rarely placed more than 1 or 2 percent of their own equity holdings in a given company. The relative positions of several investors in a pharmaceutical company also featured in the broader study (with sales in the $2 to 5 billion range) illustrate the variation. While the New York State Retirement Fund held 1.0 percent of the firm's shares in 1990, the fund had invested less than 0.5 percent of its total equity. A reverse skew could be seen in the case of the Chubb Corporation (an insurance company), which held only 0.1 percent of the pharmaceutical's stock. That amount, however, constituted 2.4 percent of all Chubb investments. More typical of the largest shareholders was the investment by Citibank's trust department: it held 0.8 percent of the company's stock, which constituted 0.9 percent of the bank's equity holdings.

Investor profiles from a range of firms generally indicate that neither specific companies nor particular institutions were vitally dependent upon one another. The relative stake of each side in the other rarely exceeded several percentage points of total value. Most companies were beholden to no single shareholder, and most institutional investors were reliant on no one firm. The steady aggregation of holdings among the institutional investors during the 1980s had made each side more important to the other. But the symbiotic dependency was still built on networks involving many players. No institution could expect to exercise major influence, at least by virtue of its holdings alone.

### *Promoting Shareholder Interests through Concerted Action*

Until the 1980s, few conventions in the financial work had seemed as bedrock as the Wall Street Rule. The concentration of shareholding changed that. Dissident voices emerged from the high end of institutional investing, particularly large public pension funds. They pressed companies for reform in a variety of areas, ranging from governance structures to executive succession, lines of business, and managerial compensation. Illustrative of the actions are those of Calpers, one of the half dozen most active. Displeased with the financial performance of the General Motors Corporation in 1990, and mindful of GM's planned replacement of the chief executive, the top officer of Calpers, Dale Hanson, wrote each of GM's directors. He asked about their standards for managerial performance, and about the "kinds . . . of policies and structure . . . you contemplate for an on-going relationship with your shareholders" (Hanson in Sommer 1991:39). The directors' response was largely noncommittal but the company invited Hanson for an informal visit to headquarters. Subsequently he wrote the chief executives of other companies, complaining of their financial performance and notifying them that a proxy resolution was being submitted for shareholder vote. In a letter to J. Peter Grace, chief executive of W. R. Grace & Co., Hanson stated that the company was "one of our poorest performing holdings" of the 1,300 companies in Calpers' portfolio (it held 644,300 shares in W. R. Grace). An accompanying analysis noted that despite the poor performance, Mr. Grace's "compensation had risen significantly" and in 1989 was "82% over market, after taking into account the Company's size, performance and other factors." The shareholder resolution would amend the firm's bylaws to create a board compensation committee comprised of "independent directors" with access to outside advisers (Hanson 1990). Rather than face an embarrassing proxy defeat, the company voluntarily accepted Calpers' proposal and the measure was dropped before going to shareholder vote.

As is common in political mobilization in general and corporate political action in particular, the largest players optimized their interests by pursuing both individual and collective strategies. The smaller players of necessity sought strength through numbers. Finding common cause in the mid-1980s, both large and small institutional investors coalesced in several collective initiatives. Even individual shareholders discovered that there could be strength in numbers. The formation of collective action organizations for the advancement of shareholder interests was less surprising than their historic absence.

The primary vehicle for collective voice among the pension funds was the *Council of Institutional Investors*. Created in 1985 as an association of large public and private pension funds, the Council included more than 60 members by 1990 whose combined assets exceeded $300 billion. The Council had formed on the premise that "the enormity of pension fund holdings limits their ability to sell stock and move money into other companies," and thus "pension funds' interests are truly inseparable from those of the country's economy" (Council of Institutional Investors 1990). The association's services concentrated on timely circulation of information among its members, promoting public policies serving pension interests, and fostering reform in corporate governance to increase responsiveness to shareholders. Indicative of the implicit political alliances created to advance their joint interests, several of the largest buyout and takeover groups such as Kohlberg Kravis Roberts and Fortsmann Little annually provided $7,500 as sustaining members of the Council.

The small shareholder found collective voice in the *United Shareholders Association* (USA). Founded in 1986 by one of the most prominent hostile takeover specialists, T. Boone Pickens, USA claimed more than 64,000 members in 1991. The barriers to entry were small: the $50 annual membership fee brought full association services. USA offered an annual rating of the 1,000 largest publicly traded companies on their "responsiveness to shareholders," combining measures of financial performance, governance policies (under the rubric of shareholder rights) and executive compensation. Among its leading tactics was the submission of shareholder proposals for governance changes at 50 companies per year rated as among the worst performers (its "Target 50" program).

A range of other players, some nonprofit, others for profit, furnished additional services and political clout for groups of shareholders. The *Analysis Group* (formed in 1981) compiled detailed financial information on company performance and policies for institutional investors, and its data were actively used by those waging campaigns to pass shareholder resolutions or unseat incumbent management (as during a campaign by Harold Simmons and NL Industries to replace the Lockheed board of directors in 1989–1991). *Institutional Shareholder Services* (established in 1985) provided money managers, public pension funds, bank trusts and other clients with an array of information on proxy and corporate governance questions (e.g., it issued a "Proxy Alert" in January, 1991, recommending that its clients holding NCR shares vote for a special shareholders meeting requested by AT&T in its battle to acquire NCR). *Institutional Shareholder Partners* (founded in 1990) offered consulting services to clients concerned with enhancing shareholder power (its principal, Robert A. G. Monks, unsuccessfully sought election as a shareholder dissident to the board of Sears, Roebuck in 1991). *Investor Responsibility Research Center* (established in 1972), the largest of the information services, offered extensive data on a broad range of corporate governance and shareholder issues.

The legal environment, however, inhibited collective mobilization. Rules of the Securities and Exchange Commission created significant barriers to joint action. Holders of more than 5 percent of a company's stock who have joined together for the purpose of voting their securities are required to follow several onerous procedures. If just the top three institutional shareholders of the special machinery or retail service companies were to have joined forces in 1990, their aggregate holdings of 8.6 and 6.1 percent, respectively, would have required such steps. They would have to have filed a document (Schedule 13d) with the SEC reporting substantial information about their group and the purpose of their shareholding. Even if not formally constituted as a group, if the three institutional investors had simply communicated with one another about the two companies, such action could be construed as the formation of a group that would fall under the special reporting provisions. The institutional investors would then have been required to give advance notification to the Justice Department and Federal Trade Commission (under the Hart-Scott-Rodino Act) if they and the target met certain size standards and if the purchase was for any purpose other than passive financial investment (e.g., seeking to influence or control management). Most major institutional investors and the target firms would meet the size requirement. And the FTC had chosen to regard the solicitation of proxies or other means of acquiring shareholder support as nonpassive investment—and thus grounds for prior reporting (Sommer 1991).

Despite such constraints, both the associations and individual institutional investors increased their pressure on companies during the late 1980s. While avoiding formal and even informal alliance, in de facto fashion the institutions often acted in concert. With access to the same information and sharing similar concerns, they took parallel actions whose aggregate impact was virtually the same as if they were formally coordinated.

One avenue for doing so was through placement of investments in takeover and buyout funds of Kohlberg Kravis Roberts and like organizations (Bartlett 1991b). Buyout fund managers were typically free to draw on the cash as they found undervalued opportunities. Companies attracting their interest knew that the bulk of such funds had been supplied by major institutional investors. The buyout fund device circumvented any legal constraints on collective action since the owners were not technically acting in concert.

A second avenue was opened by proxy contests and stock solicitations initiated during hostile takeover bids. This could be seen in an effort by AT&T in 1991 to acquire NCR. After NCR had turned down a tender offer by AT&T, AT&T sought the votes of shareholders to call a special meeting of the shareholders to replace four members of the board who were up for re-election, a group that included the chief executive. Some 64 percent of NCR's stock in mid-1990 was in the hands of institutions, and AT&T's bid necessarily required strong support from them if it were to be successful. NCR vigorously resisted: "Do you really want to entrust your NCR investment to AT&T's handpicked nominees?" it asked in full-page advertising directed to the investment community. "Don't hand over your investment in NCR for less than its full value. . . . Act in your own best interest. Keep NCR's board intact" (NCR 1991). Both NCR and AT&T also sought the support of the institutions by direct contact with their managers. Though the institutions' response could not be formally orchestrated, for most the answer was much the same: the AT&T offer was too attractive to forego. This brought NCR to the negotiating table, and it finally agreed to an acquisition by AT&T, though at a considerably higher price than had first been offered (Smith 1991; Davis 1991).

Still, legal constraints prevented more overt forms of collective action. And with the waning of buyout funds and hostile takeovers at the end of the 1980s, major shareholders sought new vehicles for exercising their voice. After experimental fits and starts, one of the preferred vehicles became the shareholder proposal.

## Shareholder Proposals

Shareholder proposals are resolutions on company proxy statements inviting shareholders to vote for reform of company governance structures.

**Figure 12.2  Shareholder Proposals Voted on Corporate Governance, 1985–1990**

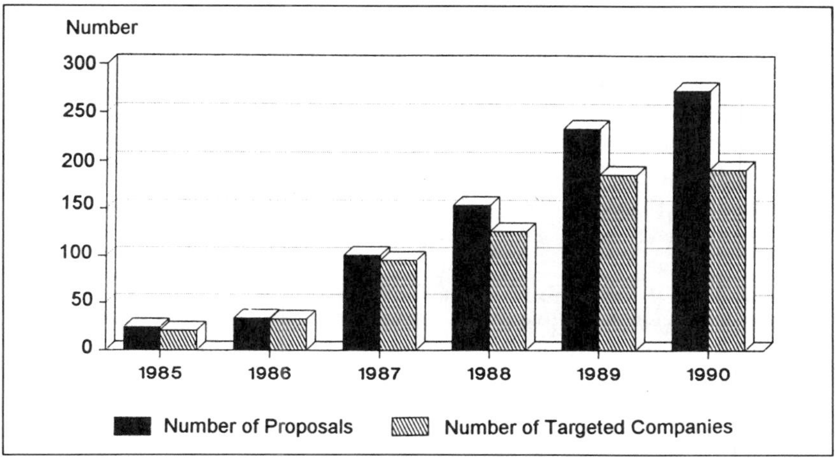

Source: Investor Responsibility Research Center (1990)

The reforms are intended to favor shareholder interests, and they are almost universally opposed by management. During the late 1980s and early 1990s, such proposals attracted increasing shareholder support, a trend indicative of intensifying investor resolution and power.

The five leading areas of shareholder governance proposals near the turn of the decade were 1) rescinding a poison pill, a financial device intended to make an unfriendly takeover prohibitive; 2) instituting confidential voting, a provision that insulates shareholders from company pressure to vote with management; 3) repealing staggered board terms for directors, a policy that prevents wholesale replacement of the board by a hostile suitor; 4) implementing cumulative voting, a procedure that permits shareholders to cast all of their proxy votes for a single director candidate, thereby heightening the chance of electing dissident directors; and 5) requiring minimum stock ownership for directors, a provision that presumably more closely links their interests with those of shareholders. Other areas of shareholder governance proposals included creation of shareholder advisory committees, opting out of anti-takeover laws in Delaware and other states, fuller disclosure of executive compensation, and elimination of golden parachutes (Krasnow 1989; Black 1990). Drawing on a number of data summaries compiled by the Investor Responsibility Research Center, Figure 12.2 shows that the total number of shareholder resolutions and the number of companies targeted rose sharply from 1985 to 1990 (shareholder resolutions are counted in the year in which they are voted).

It should be kept in mind that a relatively small number of institutions and individual shareholders were responsible for the bulk of the institutionally sponsored proposals. Of the 358 proposals pending or voted during the first six months of 1990, for instance, fifteen institutional investors accounted for almost all of the institutional sponsorships. The fifteen leading proposal sponsors were either large public pension funds or union pension funds. Their proposals and those of the United Shareholders Association constituted nearly a third of all shareholder resolutions (Investor Responsibility Research Center 1990a:79–88).

Whatever the origin of the shareholder proposals, some attracted large proportions of the vote. Few of the proposed reforms attracted sufficient favorable votes to pass, but the number that were approved increased at the turn of the decade. During the first half of 1990, for example, at least 16 of the 358 shareholder proposals had passed, higher than the same period in 1989. Moreover, the average vote in nearly all areas of shareholder initiative was higher in 1990 than 1989, as shown in Table 12.2.

Proxy contests increased in number as well, and the challenger's rate of success expanded (Wines 1991). Proxy contests are generally defined to include conflicts in which a challenger or dissident set of shareholders offer their own slate of nominees for the board. Proxy contests are also considered to include situations in which the challenger or dissident shareholders stand in opposition to management on a governance proposal, and both sides actively solicit shareholder votes through the distribution of competing proxy materials.

Though the outcomes of the proxy challenges indicate substantial rates of dissident success, the observed rates could underestimate the potential power of future proxy challenges by shareholders. One study of 100 proxy contests in the 1981 to 1985 period revealed that the practical costs of proxy vote solicitation gave management the advantage (Pound 1988). As a result of the apparent bias, shareholder pressures on company governance and federal regulation to "level the playing field" mounted significantly during the late 1980s and early 1990s. Several large institutional investors and shareholder action groups pressed companies to introduce confidential voting (reducing the ability of management to lobby large investors to alter their vote on shareholder proposals). They also pressed for new proxy regulations by the Securities and Exchange Commission. In late 1989, the California Public Employees' Retirement System petitioned the SEC to undertake extensive revision of the federal proxy rules, and the United Shareholders Association filed a similar pe-

**Table 12.2  Average Level of Voting Support for Shareholder Governance Proposals to Companies, 1989–1990**

| Shareholder Proposal | 1989 % For | (N) | 1990 % For | (N) | Percent Change 1989–1990 |
|---|---|---|---|---|---|
| Rescind poison pill | 39.5 | (18) | 42.7 | (40) | 3.2 |
| Confidential voting | 27.4 | (39) | 33.6 | (50) | 5.2 |
| Repeal classified dirs. | 21.5 | (46) | 25.3 | (38) | 4.2 |
| Cumulative voting | 15.6 | (39) | 20.6 | (45) | 5.0 |
| Minimum stock ownership for directors | 9.0 | (17) | 14.4 | (14) | 5.4 |
| Restore pre-emptive rights | 9.8 | (9) | 11.0 | (7) | 1.2 |

Sources: Krasnow 1989; Investor Responsibility Research Center 1990b, 1990c.

Note: The 1989 figures are for the period from mid-September, 1988, through mid-August, 1989. The 1990 figures are based on proposals voted during the first eight months of 1990. The (N) represents the number of proposals upon which the voting percentage is averaged. Types of shareholder proposals that were brought before fewer than seven companies in 1989 or 1990 are not included. The percentage vote represents the percentage of votes for the shareholder proposal relative to the number of shares voted.

tition in early 1990 (California Public Employees' Retirement System 1989; United Shareholders Association 1990). The proposals were comprehensive in nature (the Calpers petitions included 48 separate points), and both requests included proposals to give challengers better vehicles for communicating with other shareholders, more open access to proxy statements, and better protection from corporate lobbying through confidential voting provisions. Indicative of the political challenge, however, the Business Roundtable and other groups associated with management (e.g., the American Society of Corporate Secretaries, with a membership representing more than 2,000 corporations) rejected many or most of the recommendations. The Business Roundtable, a select association of chief executives of the nation's 200 largest corporations, offered a blunt appraisal: "[A]ll the evidence we have seen confirms that the proxy system is working very well for shareholders. While it is certainly appropriate for the S.E.C. to examine the proxy rules periodically, our preliminary analysis suggests the absence of any compelling case for major change" (Business Roundtable 1990:6). Nonetheless, in 1992 the SEC significantly relaxed its rules restricting investor communication.

# Corporate Defense

Individual companies were not to remain passive during the rising take-over threat and shareholder pressure. A majority of large publicly traded firms instituted governance devices designed to thwart unwanted acquirers. Many of the measures were financial in character but political in purpose. In making hostile acquisitions more difficult, management also implicitly reduced the power of large shareholders. A range of defensive measures were available, some just the mirror reverse of shareholder proposals (Rosenbaum 1990a:vii–xii; Weston et al. 1990:481–529):

*Poison pill.* If a board does not approve a takeover bid and the bidder nonetheless seeks to acquire the firm, a poison pill policy typically gives shareholders rights to purchase stock in the company at a discount price once a hostile buyer accumulates a certain number of shares. Poison pills are also termed "shareholder rights plans."

*Classified directors.* Directors are classified into several groups, usually three, which are up for re-election at different times. Their staggered terms prevent a hostile suitor from placing an unfriendly majority on the board during a single electoral cycle.

*Golden parachutes.* Severance agreements for senior executives provide for generous cash and noncash benefits if they are fired or resign following a change in control of the firm. They are not an anti-takeover device per se, but they may serve to discourage unwanted acquisitions by giving executives sufficient comfort to mount more vigorous resistance to takeover initiatives (Wade et al. 1990 offer indirectly supportive evidence, reporting that chief executives who exercise more influence over their boards of directors are also more likely to institute golden parachutes).

*Fair price requirements.* Bidders sometimes make two-tier offers in which above-market price is offered for some of a company's shares, and then a lower price is offered for the remaining shares after control of the company is secured. A fair price requirement discourages such two-tier bids in hostile takeovers.

*Super-majority vote to approve merger.* Going beyond state law, a super-majority provision requires as much as 75 percent or more of a company's shareholders must approve an unfriendly merger. Since minority blocks of stock may be controlled by managers, directors, and employee stock-option plans, a relatively small minority can defeat an unwanted acquisition.

**Figure 12.3   Percentage of Fortune 500 Manufacturing Firms with Take-over Defenses, 1985–1990**

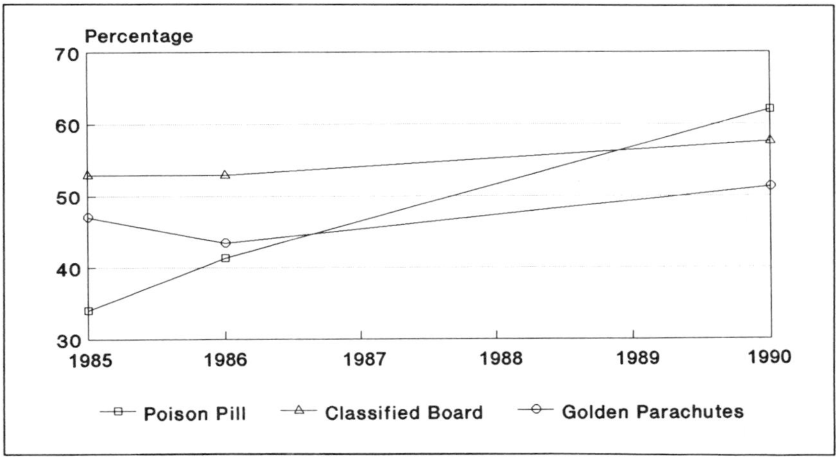

Source: Rosenbaum (1989, 1990b).

*Eliminate cumulative voting.* Under cumulative voting for directors, shareholders can cast votes equal to the number of shares times the number of board positions up for re-election. A dissident shareholder could thus concentrate its votes on a single nominee, heightening the likelihood of electing a director friendly to shareholder interests and hostile to incumbent management.

*Dual capitalization.* Companies sometimes issue two classes of stock, one class having more votes per share than the other. If management purchases a large block of the higher-voting stock, it can dilute the voting power of other shareholders.

*Require boards to consider nonfinancial effects of mergers.* Firm charters require or permit directors to consider the impact of a change in control on groups other than shareholders. These typically include employees, local communities, and buyers and suppliers.

Time series on company adoption of these takeover defenses confirm the heightening of resistance. Comparing three of the most common anti-takeover provisions among *Fortune* magazine's 500 largest manufacturing firms in 1985 and 1986 with 1990, Figure 12.3 reveals net growth in all. Using a more limited time span but larger set of firms, Table 12.3 shows expansion of virtually every major tactics. Among the nation's 1,500

Table 12.3   Percentage of 1,500 Large Corporations with Takeover Defenses, 1989–1990

| Takeover Defense | 1989 (Percent) | 1990 (Percent) | Percent Change 1989–1990 |
|---|---|---|---|
| Classified directors | 54.2 | 57.2 | 3.0 |
| Poison pill | 42.8 | 51.0 | 8.2 |
| Fair price requirement | 31.6 | 31.9 | 0.3 |
| Supermajority vote to approve merger | 16.7 | 16.9 | 0.2 |
| Eliminate cumulative voting | 7.8 | 8.8 | 1.0 |
| Dual capitalization | 7.3 | 7.5 | 0.2 |
| Require boards to consider nonfinancial effects of mergers | 6.0 | 6.5 | 0.5 |
| (No. of companies) | (1440) | (1487) | |

Source: Rosenbaum (1989; 1990b).

largest publicly traded firms, more than half had adopted poison pills and provisions for classified directors. The value of the classified board as a takeover defense was evident in the effort by NCR to resist purchase by AT&T in 1991. After NCR management rejected AT&T's offer, AT&T sought to replace NCR's directors with those more favorable to the offer. Yet because only four of thirteen NCR members were up for re-election at its 1991 annual meeting, AT&T could not secure a majority on the board using the normal proxy process (Smith 1991; Shapiro 1991).

The overall impact of the corporate shift to classified boards can be seen in studies by the Conference Board. Of 851 companies surveyed in 1972, the policies of 81 percent called for one-year terms. By 1989, only 43 percent of 589 surveyed companies retained such provisions, a majority having adopted three-year staggered terms for board members (Bacon 1990).

# The Impact of Owner Challenges on Company Policies

Systematic evidence of the impact of the rising shareholder pressures on company policies and practices confirms that their influence is certainly felt, if not always in predictable or intended ways. Scattered studies permit the construction of a partial mosaic, with some areas still largely unexplored. We consider the areas of impact as they relate to the three major avenues for the exercise of ownership influence.

### Areas of Impact

DIRECT CONTROL. The placement of companies and units previously insulated from ownership pressures under direct ownership control is observed to transform a number of financial and organizational elements of the corporation. A study of large leveraged buyouts between 1979 and 1985, for example, finds that under new ownership, corporate strategy was more centrally controlled while operating decisions became more decentralized (Easterwood et al. 1989).

MUTUALLY DEPENDENT INFLUENCE. The mutual inter-dependence of large corporations and large investors created a nexus in which influence is subtly transmitted. There are few distinctive events to mark the flow, but some outcomes become notable events. Texaco, for example, announced in 1990 that it would bring an independent director onto its board who was suggested by major shareholders rather than management. The action constituted a kind of *quid pro quo* in return for Calpers' earlier decision to support Texaco management in a successful rebuff of an unwanted takeover. Similarly, General Motors announced in 1991 that it would adopt a corporate bylaw that called for a majority of its board to be independent directors, a decision that Calpers, a major GM shareholder, had asked the company to make (White 1991).

The concept of mutual symbiosis achieved widespread acceptance among major companies. A 1990 survey of 130 large companies, all listed on the New York Stock Exchange (the revenues of three-fifths of them exceeded $1 billion), reported that only a single responding firm viewed the current level of shareholder activism as a "serious detrimental challenge to corporate control," and 38 percent saw it as a "positive influence on corporate governance." Similarly, 22 percent of the companies accepted the view that "institutional investors, because of the size of their holdings, [should] have special influence on corporate policy and/or management"; and 58 percent asserted that the importance of "institutional investors to the financial viability" of the company was "vital" (National Investor Relations Institute 1991; Mahoney 1991). The symbiosis, at least judging by such responses, was less developed among smaller firms. Of 70 companies in a parallel survey whose shares were traded over the counter, the comparable figures were, respectively, 10 and 39 percent.

The symbiosis between companies and institutional investors is reported to have measurable impact on certain areas of company policy. In the area of research and development, for instance, one study found a positive correlation between the level of institutional investment and company investment in research and development (R&D). Examining R&D spending relative to total revenue by more than 300 companies in the early 1980s, the analysis showed that firms with higher levels of institutional ownership were also those with higher levels of R&D investments (Jarrell et al. 1985). By contrast, however, a focused look at 22 computer-manufacturing firms from 1976 to 1985 reported a negative relationship between these two factors (Graves 1988). A third study examined the impact of ownership concentration related to all sources, not just institutional holdings, on R&D spending per employee. Focusing on 122 large manufacturing firms in 1980, the investigation revealed that companies with higher concentrations of ownership (among all sources taken together) were also those with higher rates of R&D investment (Hill and Snell 1989).

Mutual dependency is also evident in an observed correlation between the level of institutional shareholding in a firm and its capital structure. One study focused on 40 paired manufacturing firms, where the companies with the largest and smallest level of institutional shareholding in each of 40 industries were compared during the 1983 to 1985 period. The investigation found that firms with high institutional shareholding were also those with low debt-to-equity ratios (the two factors correlated 0.23; Chaganti and Damanpour 1991). The causal ordering of the association was not clear, but the symbiosis between low debt and high shareholding was.

CONCERTED ACTION. Direct action by owners of company shares, either individually or collectively, also had measurable impact. Institutional investors, for example, were more likely to vote for shareholder proposals than individual shareholders. This inference is based on a 1987 study of voting on 30 shareholder proposals to rescind poison pill provisions. Most of the proposals had been sponsored by just three major institutional shareholders (College Retirement Equities Fund, California Public Employees' Retirement System, and California State Teachers' Retirement System). Support for the proposals averaged 28.1 percent. In detailed analysis of the records, the study found that about 10 percent of the votes of individual shareholders had been cast for the proposals, while approximately 30 percent of the institutional shares had been so cast (Georgeson & Company 1987). Re-analysis of these data shows that companies with higher proportions of their shares in institutional hands received larger anti-management votes. The correlation between the percentage of institutional ownership and the percentage of votes for the shareholder proposal relative to the number outstanding shares was 0.20. These results are corroborated by a study of voting on anti-takeover amendments, which revealed that institutional investors and other large blockholders voted more actively on anti-takeover amendments than did small holders (Brickley et al. 1988).

Most shareholder proposals still fail to win a majority, but indirect evidence indicates that even failed challenges sometimes succeeded. Failed tender offers, for example, are often followed by a set of company changes that the bidder had suggested it would have made had the offer been successful. Polaroid Corporation, for example, resisted an unwanted take-over attempt in 1988–1989 by cutting costs, reducing the workforce, reorganizing top management, and promising enhanced earnings. All were actions that the unfriendly acquirer had stated it would take if its tender prevailed (Simon 1988; 1990). Cross-sectional evidence confirming the importance of takeover threats in changing corporate behavior comes from a study of severance packages for top managers in the event of a threatened takeover. Comparing companies that had successfully resisted a hostile takeover attempt with companies that had not been so threatened, the analysts find that the former were significantly more likely to have implemented "golden parachute" policies for their senior managers (Singh and Harianto 1989). Companies thus often make significant policy changes in response to direct ownership pressures even when such challenges are successfully rebuffed.

## Conclusion

After half a century of unchallenged supremacy, senior management at many corporations faced a revolt from one of the least likely of sources, the shareholders. They were, after all, the owners. But their real ownership powers had long been lost in an atomization of holdings that had left them weak and divided. The disenfranchisement seemed so irreversible that the managerial revolution appeared to be one of those fixed and perhaps even eternal qualities of advanced capitalism.

The ownership challenges of the 1980s shattered such conceptions. The surge of corporate mergers and acquisitions was not just another of the shufflings that periodically sweep through American business. The surge carried unique qualities, qualities presaging the owners' revolt. Battles for corporate control ensnarled some of the country's largest enterprises. And a new type of winner appeared, as leveraged owners installed themselves at the center of some companies command and control structure.

The waning of such transactions at the close of the decade signaled more a shift in strategy than any stilling of the revolt. The capacity of shareholders to express their voice only further intensified as atomization gave way to coherence. Stockholding concentrated in fewer hands, and the larger of the hands became adept in tugging at corporate management through new means. Shareholder proposals and proxy fights moved to the cutting-edge, less radical but often more effective strategies. The struggle for direct control through buyouts was displaced by a struggle for indirect influence through reformation of corporate governance and restoration of shareholder rights.

Managerial capitalism and its conception of control no longer prevailed unchallenged. Management's power to define the parameters of debate and decision making remained enormous. But alongside it emerged an institutional capitalism, its conception of rightful control radically different. Shareholders, not professional managers, were to specify and evaluate a company's achievements. The board of directors was to protect outsider interests, not insider perquisites.

As institutional capitalism gained ground and occasionally even the upper hand, a new logic of assessment emerged. The logic called for a distinctive set of organizational principles, for the company was being asked to measure up to different objectives. Major companies, as a consequence, moved to restructure their operations, to mollify if not always satisfy the challengers. The internal organization of the firm was redesigned in the process, better aligning company structure with shareholder objectives.

The chapter is drawn from the author's *Executive Defense: Shareholder Power and Corporate Reorganization* (Harvard University Press, 1993). The support and assistance of the National Planning Association, Edward E. Masters, Phillip Ray, and Peter B. Doeringer are gratefully acknowledged.

# References

ALDRICH, HOWARD. 1979. *Organizations and Environments.* Englewood Cliffs, NJ: Prentice-Hall.

ALDRICH, HOWARD, and JEFFREY PFEFFER. 1976. "Environments of Organizations." *Annual Review of Sociology* 2:79–105.

BACON, JEREMY. 1990. *Membership and Organization of Corporate Boards.* New York: Conference Board.

BARTLETT, SARAH. 1991a. *The Money Machine: How KKR Manufactured Power & Profits.* New York: Warner Books.

————. 1991b. "Big Funds Pressing for Voice in Management of Companies." *The New York Times,* February 23, p. 1.

BERLE, ADOLPH, JR., and GARDINER C. MEANS. 1967. *The Modern Corporation and Private Property.* New York: Harcourt, Brace and World (reprint edition).

BLACK, BERNARD S. 1990. "The Legal and Historical Contingency of Shareholder Passivity." *Michigan Law Review* 89:520–608.

BRANCATO, CAROLYN, and PATRICK A. GAUGHAN, 1988. *The Growth of Institutional Investors in U.S. Capital Markets.* New York: Columbia University Institutional Investor Project.

————. 1990. "The Growth of Institutional Investors, Updated Data: 1981–1988." New York: Columbia University Institutional Investor Project.

BRICKLEY, JAMES A., RONALD C. LEASE, and CLIFFORD W. SMITH, JR. 1988. "Ownership Structure and Voting on Antitakeover Amendments." *Journal of Financial Economics* 20:267–291.

BURROUGH, BRYAN, and JOHN HELYAR, 1990. *Barbarians at the Gate: The Fall of RJR Nabisco.* New York: Harper & Row.

BURT, RONALD S. 1983. *Corporate Profits and Cooptation: Networks of Market Constraints and Directorate Ties in the American Economy.* New York: Academic Press.

BUSINESS ROUNDTABLE. 1990. Letter of December 17, 1990, to U.S. Securities and Exchange Commission. New York: Business Roundtable.

*Business Week.* 1991. "The Business Week Top 1000." Annual Special Issue, *Business Week.*

CALIFORNIA PUBLIC EMPLOYEES' RETIREMENT SYSTEM. 1989. Letter of November 3, 1989, to U.S. Securities and Exchange Commission. Sacramento: California Public Employees' Retirement System.

CHAGANTI, RAJESWARARAO, and FARIBORZ DAMANPOUR. 1991. "Institutional Ownership, Capital Structure, and Firm Performance." *Strategic Management Journal* 12:479–491.

CHANDLER, ALFRED D., JR. 1977. *The Visible Hand: The Managerial Revolution in American Business.* Cambridge, MA: Harvard University Press.

COUNCIL OF INSTITUTIONAL INVESTORS. 1990. "Council of Institutional Investors." Washington, D.C.: Council of Institutional Investors.

DAVIS, L. J. 1991. "When A.T.&T. Plays Hardball." *The New York Times Magazine,* Part 2, June 9:14ff.

DRUCKER, PETER. 1991. "Reckoning with the Pension Fund Revolution." *Harvard Business Review,* March–April:106–109, 111.

EASTERWOOD, JOHN C., ANJU SETH, and RONALD F. SINGER. 1989. "The Impact of LBOs on Strategic Direction." *California Management Review* 32:30–43.

EISENHARDT, KATHLEEN M. 1989. "Agency Theory: An Assessment and Review." *Academy of Management Review* 14:57–74.

ETZIONI, AMITAI. 1968. *The Active Society: A Theory of Societal and Political Processes.* New York: Free Press.

FAMA, EUGENE. 1980. "Agency Problems and Theory of the Firm." *Journal of Political Economy* 88:288–306.

FAMA, EUGENE, and MICHAEL JENSEN. 1983. "Separation of Ownership and Control." *Journal of Law and Economics* 26:301–325.

FLIGSTEIN, NEIL. 1990. *The Transformation of Corporate Control.* Cambridge, MA: Harvard University Press.

GEORGESON & COMPANY. 1987. *Georgeson Reports.* New York: Georgeson & Company.

GRAVES, SAMUEL B. 1988. "Institutional Ownership and Corporate R&D in the Computer Industry." *Academy of Management Journal* 31:417–428.

HANSON, DALE M. 1990. Letter of December 6, 1990, to J. Peter Grace. Sacramento: California Public Employees' Retirement System.

HERMAN, EDWARD S. 1981. *Corporate Control, Corporate Power.* New York: Cambridge University Press.

HILL, CHARLES W. L., and SCOTT A. SNELL. 1989. "Effects of Ownership Structure and Control on Corporate Productivity." *Academy of Management Journal* 32:25–46.

HIMMELSTEIN, JEROME L. 1990. *To the Right: The Transformation of American Conservatism.* Berkeley, CA: University of California Press.

ICAHN, CARL. 1988. "Icahn on Icahn." *Fortune* 29 (February):54–58.

*Institutional Investor.* 1991. "The 1991 Pensions Directory." *Institutional Investor* 25 (January):153–192.

INVESTOR RESPONSIBILITY RESEARCH CENTER. 1990a. *Corporate Governance Bulletin* 7(3) (May/June). Washington, D.C.: Investor Responsibility Research Center.

——. 1990b. *Corporate Governance Bulletin* 7(4) (July/August). Washington, D.C.: Investor Responsibility Research Center.

——. 1990c. *Voting Results 1990.* Washington, D.C.: Investor Responsibility Research Center.

JACOBS, DAVID. 1974. "Dependency and Vulnerability: An Exchange Approach to the Control of Organizations." *Administrative Science Quarterly* 19:45–59.

JARRELL, GREGG A., KEN LEHN, and WAYNE MARR. 1985. "Institutional Ownership, Tender Offers, and Long-Term Investments." Washington, D.C.: Securities and Exchange Commission, Office of Economic Analysis.

JENSEN, MICHAEL C. 1989. "Eclipse of the Public Corporation." *Harvard Business Review* 89(5):61–74.

JENSEN, MICHAEL C., and WILLIAM H. MECKLING. 1976. "Theory of the Firm: Management Behavior, Agency Costs, and Ownership Structure." *Journal of Financial Economics* 3:305–360.

JENSEN, MICHAEL C., and KEVIN J. MURPHY. 1990. "CEO Incentives—It's Not How Much You Pay, But How." *Harvard Business Review* (May–June).

KIDDER, ROBERT. 1990. Quoted in "CEO Roundtable On Corporate Structure and Management Incentives." *Journal of Applied Corporate Finance* 3(Fall):7–35.

KOHLBERG KRAVIS ROBERTS & CO. 1989. "Presentation on Leveraged Buy-Outs." New York: Kohlberg Kravis Roberts.

KOTZ, DAVID M. 1978. *Bank Control of Large Corporations in the United States.* Berkeley, CA: University of California Press.

KRASNOW, LAUREN G. 1989. *Voting by Institutional Investors on Corporate Governance Issues in the 1989 Proxy Season.* Washington, D.C.: Investor Responsibility Research Center.

LARNER, ROBERT J. 1970. *Management Control and the Large Corporation.* New York: Dunellen Publishing Company.

LONG, WILLIAM F., and DAVID J. RAVENSCRAFT. 1991. "The Record of LBO Performance." In Arnold W. Sametz ed., *The Battle for Corporate Control.* New Homewood, IL: Business One Irwin, pp. 517–541.

LOWENSTEIN, LOUIS. 1991. *Sense and Nonsense in Corporate Finance.* Reading, MA: Addison-Wesley.

MAHONEY, WILLIAM F. 1991. "Survey: How Companies View Investor Activism, Interest in Governance." *Investor Relations Update* (January):8–9.

MEYER, MARSHALL W., and LYNNE C. ZUCKER. 1989. *Permanently Failing Organizations.* Newbury Park, CA: Sage Publications.

MINTZ, BETH, and MICHAEL SCHWARTZ. 1985. *The Power Structure of American Business.* Chicago: University of Chicago Press.

MINTZBERG, HENRY. 1983. *Power In and Around Organizations.* Englewood Cliffs, NJ: Prentice-Hall.

NATIONAL INVESTOR RELATIONS INSTITUTE. 1991. "Results of 1990 Corporate Governance Survey." Washington, D.C.: National Investor Relations Institute.

NCR. 1991. "A Question for NCR Shareholders. . . ." *The New York Times,* March 11:D3, advertisement.

NEW YORK STOCK EXCHANGE. 1991. *Yearbook.* New York: New York Stock Exchange.

PFEFFER, JEFFREY, and GERALD SALANCIK. 1978. *The External Control of Organizations: A Resource Dependence Perspective.* New York: Harper & Row.

POUND, JOHN. 1988. "Proxy Contests and Efficiency of Shareholder Oversight." *Journal of Financial Economics* 20:237–265.

ROSENBAUM, VIRGINIA K. 1989. *Corporate Takeover Defenses, 1989.* Washington, D.C.: Investor Responsibility Research Center.

———. 1990a. *Corporate Takeover Defenses, 1990.* Washington, D.C.: Investor Responsibility Research Center.

———. 1990b. "Special Reanalysis of Corporate Takeover Defense Data Base." Washington, D.C.: Investor Responsibility Research Center.

SECURITIES INDUSTRY ASSOCIATION. 1990. *The Securities Industry of the Eighties.* New York: Securities Industry Association.

———. 1991. "Analysis of Statistics Provided by the Federal Reserve Bank." Washington, D.C.: Securities Industry Association.

SHAPIRO, EBEN. 1991. "NCR Establishes an Employee Stock Plan." *The New York Times,* February 22:D1.

SILK, LEONARD, and DAVID VOGEL. 1976. *Ethics and Profits: The Crisis of Confidence in American Business.* New York: Simon & Schuster.

SIMON, JANE. 1988. "Polaroid's Booth Talks Back." *Boston Globe,* October 4:27, 46.

———. 1990. "Same Managers, Same Problems: Polaroid One Year After Shamrock." *Boston Globe,* March 11:33, 38–39.

SINGH, HARBIR, and FARID HARIANTO. 1989. "Management-Board Relationships, Takeover Risk, and the Adoption of Golden Parachutes." *Academy of Management Journal* 32:7–24.

SMITH, RANDALL. 1991. "AT&T's Bid to Buy NCR Is Hampered by the Recent Surge of Computer Stocks." *The Wall Street Journal,* February 20.

SOMMER, A. A., JR. 1991. "Corporate Governance in the Nineties: Managers vs. Institutions." Washington, D.C.: Morgan, Lewis & Bockius.

STANDARD AND POOR'S. 1991. *Stock Reports.* New York: Standard and Poor's Corporation.

UNITED SHAREHOLDERS ASSOCIATION. 1990. Letter of March 20, 1990, to U.S. Securities and Exchange Commission. Washington, D.C.: United Shareholders Association.

USEEM, MICHAEL. 1984. *The Inner Circle: Large Corporations and the Rise of Business Political Activity in the U.S. and U.K.* New York: Oxford University Press.

———. 1990. "Business Restructuring, Management Control, and Corporate Organization." *Theory and Society* 19:681–707.

VOGEL, DAVID. 1989. *Fluctuating Fortunes: The Political Power of Business in America.* New York: Basic Books.

WADE, JAMES, CHARLES A. O'REILLY, III, and IKE CHANDRATAT. 1990. "Golden Parachutes: CEOs and the Exercise of Social Influence." *Administrative Science Quarterly* 35:587–603.

WARTZMAN, RICH. 1991. "A Raider Stalks It, But Leaner Lockheed Has Begun to Take Off." *The Wall Street Journal,* February 14:A1, 6.

WESTON, J. FRED, KWANG S. CHUNG, and SUSAN E. HOAG. 1990. *Mergers, Restructuring, and Corporate Control.* Englewood Cliffs, NJ: Prentice-Hall.

WHITE, JAMES A. 1991. "GM Bows to California Pension Fund By Adopting Bylaw on Board's Makeup." *The Wall Street Journal,* January 31.

WINES, RICHARD A. 1991. *Proxy Contest Study: October 1984 to September 1991.* New York: Georgeson & Company.

# 13

# The Coming of Post-Industrial Society Revisited: Manufacturing and the Prospects for a Service-Based Economy

FRANK P. ROMO
and MICHAEL SCHWARTZ

In the last thirty years, many regions of the United States have experienced considerable changes in the structure of their economies. The rise of international competition, combined with the failure of U.S. industrial leaders to modernize outmoded manufacturing technologies, has wrought decline in this nation's industrial competitiveness and provoked widespread job loss (Bluestone and Harrison 1982; Rains, Berson, and Gracie 1982; Cohen and Zysman 1988; Wallace and Rothschild 1988). These developments have sparked increasing interest in the growing concentration of employment in a set of private business activities defined as the *service sector* of the economy (Shelp 1981; Stanback, Blaue, Noyelle, and Konasek 1981; Noyelle and Stanback 1984; Cohen and Zysman 1987). Indeed, domestic economic policy throughout the Reagan-Bush administrations have treated the service sector as a panacea for North America's decline in manufacturing employment and its mounting economic problems. Aggregate statistics on the U.S. economy have inflamed this optimism: while, between the years of 1979 and 1989, manufacturing lost over 1.4 million jobs, the service-producing industries (not including government) increased by over 17.8 million jobs (see Table 13.1 below).

**335**

In this chapter, we address the prospects of *regional* growth in a service-based economy vis-à-vis a declining manufacturing sector. We adopt Cohen and Zysman's (1987) thesis of the myth of the post-industrial economy based solely on services. We review federal industrial policy about services and manufacturing and, after Cohen and Zysman, argue that it has been, at least from a regional viewpoint, misguided. The logic of our critique rests upon the interpretation of the nature and extent of economic linkages between regional services and manufacturing. We contend that growth in a regional service-sector economy is inexorably intertwined with the health of local manufacturing.

Based on our past research of New York State's manufacturing economy, we propose a developmental model of service establishments in which economic transactions with manufacturing are not only seen as always necessary, but are also, by necessity, bounded and embedded in regional social and cultural aspects of production systems. These systems are characterized by idiosyncratic (i.e., locally relevant) exchanges of information, mutual administrative and production adjustments, personnel transfers, and the existence of a wide range of jointly held assumptions and trusts (see Romo, Korman, Brantley, and Schwartz 1986; 1988; Korman, Romo, Lee, Chan, and Schwartz 1989; Romo and Schwartz 1990; 1991). In the words of Cohen and Zysman (1987:17), we view manufacturing and services as "tightly linked." Thus we contend that decline in a region's manufacturing sector will have a negative impact on growth in the service-producing sector.

We test our model with employment data from New York State's nine major regional labor markets for the periods 1979 through 1989 and 1963 through 1989. We find that manufacturing matters. When compared with employment data in the U.S. as a whole, New York State has lost a much greater proportion of its manufacturing jobs. Thus, although service-sector employment in the state has grown proportionately, this growth is considerably less than that exhibited by the nation during the same period. In addition, we observe that regional losses in manufacturing employment differentially suppress growth in regional service jobs: the most highly deindustrialized sections of the state exhibit the weakest growth in service employment. Our investigation also uncovers a more ominous sign. A large proportion of service growth in the state is comprised of employment in health, educational, and social services, which are heavily subsidized by the government. This trend is particularly pronounced in the most deindustrialized regions. Moreover, our analysis reveals that regional changes in direct government employment respond to offset losses in manufacturing. These findings suggest that a significant share of the muted growth in New York's service sector may be artificial, lasting only as long as tax payers can bear it.

In the conclusion of this chapter, we draw out some of the implications from the New York case for the nation as a whole and for the prospects of the coming of a post-industrial service society.

## Natural Succession: U.S. Economic Policy in the 1980s

Youngstown, Buffalo, Detroit, Cleveland, and Pittsburgh were once major industrial centers of the Northeast, but have now come to epitomize urban decay, recession, and despair. All have suffered the departure of major manufacturing plants, and much has been written about the devastating effects that have followed (see, e.g., Bluestone and Harrison 1982:51–56). By the end of the 1970s and well into the 1980s, scholarly works, television news programs, and articles in, for example, *The New York Times* (September 21, 1981), *BusinessWeek* (May 11, 1980), *The Washington Post* (February 9, 1979), and *The Wall Street Journal* (August 7, 1978), all contained stories about another plant closing down, or about another thousand jobs disappearing from a region, or about the frustration of workers unable to find full-time jobs utilizing their skills and providing enough income to support their families. Despite all of the hyperbole about the emergence of high-tech industries in the North and West, the expansion of boomtowns in the South, and the growth of a post-industrial service economy throughout the United States, some academic researchers, policy makers, and journalists were coming to recognize that something was amiss: the economic system that seemed so capable of sustaining a growing standard of living during the turbulent 1960s had become incapable of providing people with such basic things as home mortgages, stable jobs, or secure pensions (see, e.g., *BusinessWeek* June 30, 1980; Bluestone and Harrison 1982; Harris 1987; Wallace and Rothschild 1988; Root 1988; Moore 1988). Our own research in New York State reveals a similar and no less gloomy picture of the manufacturing economy (see Yago, Korman, Wu, and Schwartz 1984; Romo, Korman, Brantley, and Schwartz 1986; 1988; Romo and Schwartz 1990; 1991). We find that every manufacturing sector in the state has been in decline for at least a quarter of a century. To get an idea of the impact of this decline, consider Figure 13.1, which presents annual employment statistics for New York State's manufacturing sector between 1960 through 1986. It reveals a protracted decline in New York that has been underway from at least the beginning of the 1970s.

**Figure 13.1   Annual Employment Trends in Manufacturing in New York State from 1960 to 1985**

Because so much regional deindustrialization is invisible to all but those who work on the shop floor, or to the managers who actually plan it, there has been a tendency for researchers and other reporters to acknowledge it only when there are plywood shutters over the windows and the "OUT OF BUSINESS" sign is posted, or when the plant is relocated to another community elsewhere in the country or abroad. Moreover, among U.S. academics and policy makers, there is a deeply seated Social Darwinistic assumption that business failures are probably good for the economy: the invisible hand of the free market weeds out the less efficient, or less *fit,* in favor of the fittest. This narrow view of the phenomenon has provoked some to depict any concern over capital flight and regional decline in manufacturing as essentially groundless (see, e.g., Mckenzie 1979; Birch 1979; Lawrence 1983). This view suggests that the recent rash of plant closures is a transitory phenomenon and reflects natural adjustments in the economy or labor force.

Some analysts suggest that perhaps the duration of such decline is due to social policies that protect outmoded, low-productive industries. Indeed, there are those who believe that the pace of disinvestment, especially in the older sunset industries, has not been fast enough. Thurow (1980), for example, contends that labor and capital must be withdrawn from old, low-productive sectors in order to facilitate growth in the newer and high-value-added industries. Thus, Thurow writes that rather than "adopting public policies to speed up the process of disinvestment, we act to slow it down with protection and subsidies for the inefficient" (1980:77). Thurow believes that unless American businesses and the government learn to disinvest more rapidly, the United States will never again be able to compete effectively in the international marketplace.

This idea of the *creative destruction* of industries [1] implicit in Thurow's arguments provides the underpinnings of positions extended by the federal policy,[2] and it is also dominant in debates about deindustrialization in the government, in economics, and in the business press. The prevailing logic envisions a service-based, *post-industrial* economy as the natural successor to a manufacturing-based economy. This is seen as an evolutionary process in which a service and information age is the next stage of political and economic development (for classic statements of this position, see Fisher 1935; Clark 1940; Touraine 1971; Bell 1973; and Gersuny and Rosengren 1973). In *BusinessWeek* (January 27, 1986:22), Gary Becker writes that "strong modern economies do not seem to require a dominant manufacturing sector." The New York Stock Exchange (1984), in a report on trade, manufacturing, and jobs, proclaims that "a strong manufacturing sector is not a requisite for a prosperous economy." Acceptance of the idea of service-sector sovereignty has led investigators to suggest that services are developing into basic industries that lead to a self-supporting export trade (see, e.g., Shelp 1981; Keil and Mack 1986; Gillis 1987; Groshen 1987; Austrian and Zlatoper 1988; Goe 1990).

---

[1] Schumpeter (1942:81–87) wrote that capitalist economies can only evolve to higher levels of prosperity through a "process of creative destruction." Accordingly, a healthy economy requires that its industries be perpetually reincarnated. The old industrial order, like a forest with its cycle of decay and renewal, constantly undergoes transformation to provide the material sustenance for fresh enterprise.

[2] This is especially the case in the Reagan administration, which had a clearly articulated policy about the decline in manufacturing as a positive development in the rise in services (see Cohen and Zysman 1988). Since the Reagan years are particularly relevant to the analysis presented here, we shall concentrate on the federal industrial policy of this period. The Bush administration—largely through its inarticulate and incoherent industrial policy—has extended the impact of the Reagan administration policies. Very recently, however, especially with respect to the United States providing technology to Japan to build the FSX jet fighter, the Bush administration has backtracked somewhat on Reagan's industrial policy, adopting a more protectionistic stance (see *BusinessWeek* August 7, 1989:44).

Indeed, some even believe that the great service transformation has already taken place. An article in *Forbes* suggests that the decline in manufacturing is largely irrelevant because the U.S. has been a service economy, and not an industrial manufacturing society, for the past fifty years. According to this report, "most of the breast-beating about our industrial decline is a kind of masochism—much like the hysteria in 18th-century Britain that building roads fit for stagecoaches would weaken the national fiber and lead to decline in equestrian skills." The article goes on to say, "Instead of following the Pied Piper of 'reindustrialization,' the U.S. should get concentrating on efforts at strengthening services" (*Forbes* April 11, 1983:143, 146).

From this point of view comes the comforting interpretation that current economic difficulties in U.S. manufacturing sectors is not a sign of failure at all. Notwithstanding the nation's budget deficit—a problem often blamed on the international exchange rates and interest rate differentials (both of which are bothersome but temporary and amenable to conventional, albeit tough, treatment), loss in market share and employment in such industries as steel, textiles, autos, consumer electronics, and computer peripherals is treated neither as a surprise nor a bad thing. It is, rather, the price of success. The U.S. economy should be shedding its sunset industries of rustbelt states such as New York, and these industries should be taken over by other nations, while America moves on to dominate the sunrise service sectors of the future. After all, this is part of an ever-evolving international division of labor from which we all will benefit. The general composition of the national product, then, should be a matter of indifference to policy.

The federal government agrees with this perspective. The government's indifference to the composition of national product is clearly expressed in Reagan's industrial policy of removing as many regulations as possible, encouraging freer trade and international capital mobility, and cutting business taxes (Quick 1988). There is in this policy, however, a strong underlying theme peddling post-industrialism. The command that this view has over industrial policy was demonstrated in a report to Congress in the mid-1980s on trade agreements, where the President of the United States set forth the following framework for understanding the troubling trade situation: "The move from an industrial society toward a post-industrial service economy has been one of the greatest changes to affect the development of the world since the Industrial Revolution. The progression of an economy such as America's from agriculture to manufacturing to service is a natural change" (Office of the United States Trade Representative 1984–1985:43; Cohen and Zysman 1987:5). As recently as 1988, President Reagan echoed this position in his last *State of the*

*Union* address to Congress. Far from being indifferent to the composition of the U.S. economy, federal industrial policy has sought to speed up the replacement of manufacturing by service.

According to Cohen and Zysman (1987), the basic idea behind the post-industrial policy is, among other things, founded on erroneous interpretations of the data-generating processes that produce statistical information about the U.S. economy. First, consider the notion that we are undergoing a developmental shift out of manufacturing and into a post-industrial, service-based economy. As Cohen and Zysman argue, this shift is logically legitimated by theoretically constructing a parallel shift out of agriculture and into manufacturing. This is clearly seen in Bell's (1973) description of the historical transition. Bell begins his argument by noting that, although agriculture employed over 20 percent of the workforce in 1929, it now employs less than 4 percent. This shift—from low-productive, low-paying farm jobs to more productive, higher-paying employment in manufacturing—is precisely what economic development is all about. The U.S. economy has sloughed off all those farm jobs and is now better off. The prevailing wisdom maintains that the same developmental movement—i.e., the same *creative destruction*—is currently being repeated in the dislocation of resources and employment out of manufacturing and into service.

For Cohen and Zysman (1987), there is a fundamental problem with the post-industrial logic, namely that its cyclical view of economic history may be misleading. Post-industrial theory assumes that economic history is: 1) comprised of a long process of shifting from one economic sector to another; and 2) that each transition is associated with higher and higher levels of productivity. Implicitly, it accepts the view that older modes of economic activities are largely abandoned in a natural manner and for the better, through some process of economic evolution and progress. This logic is not at all supported by the history of the U.S. economy.

First consider the assumption that manufacturing production has succeeded agricultural production, and the implications of this idea on the current view that service is the new successor to a manufacturing-based economy. As Cohen and Zysman (1987) note, the curtailing, or the offshoring, of U.S. manufacturing production is currently understood by many analysts and policy makers as a development parallel to the historical shift out of agricultural production. Cohen and Zysman contend that the problem with this logic is that the historical shift out of agriculture never occurred. The United States did not abandon agriculture in any way. American agricultural production did not go offshore to another country, nor did it shrivel up and die. On the contrary, it increased by vast amounts, whether this increase is measured by weight or money.

The apparent disinvestment, reported in terms of employment figures, is a mirage: to be sure, farm-labor inputs decreased; but they were replaced by capital (both human and financial) and new technology, while agricultural outputs actually rose (Council of Economic Advisers 1985:339–340).

There appears to be confusion about just what sort of transition has occurred. On the one hand, there is a transition that involves a curtailment of production; on the other hand, there is one that consists of a transfer of labor out of production. Labor productivity in agriculture has been increased by adding capital and technology; it has been automated; it has not been moved offshore or deserted. Nonetheless, policy makers and academic adherents of the post-industrial persuasion advise us to disenfranchise manufacturing even though their agricultural model is largely erroneous.

Another problem with post-industrial theory is its image of economic transactions. The model is founded upon a highly atomized view of economic decision making. It takes the *ceteris paribus* assumptions of the most commonsense neoclassical economic reasoning and treats them as a reality. From this perspective, all economic transactions are the same. They are loose couplings involving the simplest of market relationships: a buyer and a seller with no other interdependence than a traded good. None involves exchanges of services or information; there are no mutual adjustments or tailoring of activities to one another's needs and special problems; and there are certainly no emotions, no loyalties or fidelities necessitated by such transactions, nor do such phenomena affect the way economic transactions are carried out. They are stripped of all components typical to human relationships. Political, cultural, and social differences between transacting parties are of no consequence. Economic transactions, in this view, represent the loosest linkages imaginable. No activity is in any way bound to another. If one industrial activity of such a loosely coupled pair is excised, or offshored, in principle, this should not affect the other (see Lawrence [1984:98–99] for a clearly stated example of this logic). From this point of view, U.S. agriculture production was not necessary to the development and growth of the U.S. farm equipment industry. It makes little difference where food is grown, for whoever produces it will still need farm equipment, and U.S. manufacturers could provide it.

One alternative framework for studying U.S. manufacturing history incorporates the ways in which particular social, organizational, and technological developments in other sectors of the economy acted as initiating conditions, setting a specific course of manufacturing development (see, e.g., Rosenberg 1982). This requires that one pay attention to the linkages between sectors of the economy. For example, the internationally dominant position of the United States as an industrial power has rested, for more than half a century, on two historical innovations: mass production and the giant corporation. As Chandler (1977) shows, one of these innovations, the giant corporation, emerged in two steps. The first step came in the late nineteenth century, about the same time as mass production. Before then, the image of a business as a small-scale entrepreneurial entity was a reasonable portrayal of productive establishments in the U.S. economy. Complex organizational hierarchies, or bureaucracies, were only found in the government, not in private businesses. Complex hierarchies within private-sector companies emerged to solve specific problems with traditional customers. One such problem was the need to provide continuing service after the sale of agricultural machinery. Without such after-sale service, the value of the machinery would be far less. When farmers could no longer repair their farm equipment themselves, the machinery would simply lie in waste. It is conceivable that a service industry, responding to farmers' repair demands, might have sprung up. But in the geographically dispersed U.S. agricultural industry, independent repair businesses were slow to materialize. Consequently, to promote sales, farm equipment manufacturers provided the service through their own organizations. Controlling such activities engendered problems which led to the development of hierarchical organizational structure and large corporations.

These early hierarchical corporations were roughly divided into functional divisions such as sales, production, and service (i.e., a centralized functional or F-form organization). This social-organizational technology contributed to the tremendous economic growth in such companies as duPont, and by early twentieth century, companies like duPont began taking profits and using them to enter new product areas (Chandler 1969; 1977). The F-form organization could manage the production of one or more highly related goods, but it confronted severe structural and coordinative strains if production and market strategy involved a variety of different goods. The problems engendered by product differentiation lead to the next step of development, the multi-divisional or M-form organization (Chandler 1969; 1977). In essence, the M-form corporation is a conglomeration of F-form substructures (each dealing with its own production, sales, and service strategies) with synergism tied together and directed from a corporate headquarters.

In Chandler's rendition of economic history, the F-form paved the way for the development of the M-form organizational innovation, and the M-form innovation further contributed to the world dominance of U.S. industry. The important insight from this story, however, is what it reveals about the role that the U.S. agricultural sector played in the development of the F-form organization. The immense productivity of nineteenth-century U.S. agriculture, organized as it was into small family farms distributed across a broad geographical area, created a far-flung market for manufactured products. But it also engendered service and distributive problems that incubated social-organizational developments that, today, are seen as crucial to the productivity of U.S. manufacturing. What if, in the middle of these developments, agriculture were moved offshore or disappeared? Would U.S. manufacturing businesses have developed these innovative organizational forms, or would such development have been stifled or retarded?

The same sort of crucial linkages found in Chandler's U.S. history of the giant corporation may be in operation today in U.S. manufacturing and service industries. Take, for example, the computer industry. The industry is characterized by tight, long-term linkages—involving information exchanges, joint development and marketing efforts, and a host of other mutual services—between software and hardware manufacturers, which appear to be crucial for further growth and development (see, for example, *Forbes* April 1, 1991; *Fortune* June 17, 1991; *BusinessWeek* October 23, 1989). The United States currently dominates the world in this industry, especially in software production. However, U.S. dominance in software manufacturing largely rests on the huge homogenous market created when the huge U.S. computer maker IBM set hardware standards by opening its personal computer architecture to other manufacturers, and thereby stimulated the abundant availability of inexpensive IBM and IBM-clone computers to the U.S. population. The wide-ranging U.S. market has created unique problems for software manufacturers in providing after-sale support services, which are crucial to making their products valuable to a broad array of customers. Software makers are now responding by developing ingenious user-support divisions that use advanced telecommunication and computer technologies to aid their customers in the use of their products. The feedback that software companies get from their customers via these new service divisions are then applied to new releases of their products, making them useful to a broader range of real-world applications, and thereby strengthening the world dominance of U.S. software industry. These telecommunication service divisions have required special organizational adaptations that perhaps represent the beginnings of the modern-day developmental equivalent of Chandler's F-form and M-form. Moreover, the industry's ability to provide sophisticated software and to make hardware easily available has also spawned development in the U.S. service industries that use these technologies to provide a host of accounting, marketing, engineering, and architectural services to other businesses.

What would happen to this industrial development, and to the ongoing emergence of (quite possibly) innovative industrial organizational forms, if computer manufacturing were suddenly moved offshore or if it declined and disappeared? According to John Armstrong, vice-president for science and technology at IBM, we may soon find out. He believes that U.S. hardware manufacturers are not investing enough to keep up with Japanese manufacturers. Japan's growing skills in hardware are beginning to threaten U.S. software hegemony. Says Armstrong: "You don't ask a juggler which ball is his highest priority. Success is to do all. You can't be a success in computing if you're a whiz at software and can't do hardware" (*Fortune* June 17, 1991:60). The Japanese appear to be moving up the techno-food chain, from dominating the manufacturing of memory and other computer peripherals, to the designing and manufacturing of the computer's central processing unit and its architecture, through software and the services industries that it is now spawning. To be sure, as the Japanese have come to dominate various aspects of computer manufacturing (e.g., monitors, printers, dynamic random access memory chips), the U.S. industry has lost its capability to produce and compete (see, e.g., *BusinessWeek* October 23, 1989; *Fortune* June 17, 1991). What does this portend for the future of U.S. software?

## Employment Figures and Tight Linkages

A central element in our discussion thus far is that economic linkages among industries, and among the establishments within and from different industrial sectors, are comprised of more than simple commodity exchanges. They are embedded in a host of sociological phenomena that in theory can be held constant, but that in practice have important consequences for how business is enacted, for what business produces, for how it produces, and for whether or not it can produce at all. On the proverbial "level playing field," where all parts are interchangeable, where information is cheap and transmitted to everyone instantaneously, and where cultural differences are eliminated and political boundaries are vanquished, tight linkages would be meaningless. Unfortunately, such conditions only exist in theory.

In reality, tight linkages are extremely consequential, and this is especially the case for linkages between services and manufacturing. As Bell points out, in an economy based on services, "the game is between persons. What counts is not raw muscle power, or energy, but information"

(1973:5). Nowhere are cultural, social, and political factors more likely to invade economic transactions than in a game between persons exchanging information. For starters, language is essential for delivering information, be it written or spoken language; and language varies widely, not only across national political boundaries, but also across regions within a country. More specifically, such service activities as market research, business consulting, and accounting and auditing services must adjust to the idiosyncratic activities of the businesses that they serve. An architectural service must incorporate the needs of particular customers with exigencies engendered by the geographical, seismic, social, and architectural history of the city or region in which it operates. Consulting engineers must not only comprehend the general technologies of the machines that they work on, but they must understand the specific needs of particular plants that singularly apply such technologies to the production of special products. These conditions intimately couple service activities with their customers.

Unfortunately, there is not much data on the nature and extent of linkages between industrial activities, and testing the hypothesis of tight linkages is difficult. National input-output tables are one type of data that can address interdependencies among industrial activities. Elsewhere, we have used these data to study the impact of linkages on migration decision in New York State's manufacturing sector (see, e.g., Romo and Schwartz 1990; 1991). At the national level, such tables have been useful in providing a glimpse of the role of manufacturing in the growth of the service economy. For example, a study by the Office of the U.S. Trade Representative found that 25 percent of U.S. GNP is founded on services used as inputs to goods-producing industries. According to the study, this was more than the value added to GNP by manufacturing alone (Office of the U.S. Trade Representative 1983). Input-output studies, however, are performed very infrequently (the most recent study was done in 1977), and the tables only provide national information.

More often, studies of the economy rely on employment statistics. Employment data are very dynamic. Monthly measures broken down by detailed industrial classification, occupation, and other demographic categories are available. Moreover, local state governments often maintain such detailed employment figures for highly detailed geographical areas such as counties and cities. There are significant problems with such statistics, especially in a study of linkages. Take, for example, agriculture employment. Today, the generally accepted figure is about three million, or about 3 percent of the U.S. workforce (see Liesner 1985:55 Table US.9; Council of Economic Advisers 1984:225 Table B–29). But characterizing agricultural employment in this way—only counting farm jobs—

is tantamount to viewing manufacturing employment only in terms of people on the production lines. Are tractor-repair people or veterinarians or ketchup bottlers or orange-juice makers not employed in agriculture? While this question is rhetorical, it begins to show that the three-million figure is blind to the social organizational realities discussed above. Employment figures such as these provide virtually no insight into what would happen if an economy were to abandon agricultural production or manufacturing altogether, or, if it were to be moved offshore rather than automated.

Nonetheless, employment statistics can be made useful for a study of the impact of inter-sectorial linkages on the economic development of economically entangled sectors. To accomplish this, however, the statistics must be viewed through the lens of a theory that magnifies those behavioral tendencies that might be possible only if tight linkages were operating. The presence of such behavioral tendencies would signal the importance of tight linkages in economic development, while their absence would indicate a lack of impact.

Our ideas about the operation of tight linkages in economic development imply a strong regional component. Economic transactions involve more than the exchange of commodities. They also entail exchanges of unique services and information, transacting parties mutually adjust and tailor their activities to one another's needs and special problems, and they develop loyalties that express themselves in the form of long-term relationships. Behemoths like USX, General Motors, or IBM possess the economic wherewithal, the labor capacity, and the organizational capabilities to extend their relationships over large geographical areas. In the words of Barnett and Muller (1974), such firms have "global reach." For example, IBM in Armonk, New York, has established and maintained very close long-term relations with Microsoft in Richmond, Washington, for the last ten years. This has been the tightest of tight linkages involving crucial information exchanges, joint research and development efforts, name sharing,[3] and a host of other mutual services (see *Forbes* April 1, 1991: 108–114). But these are the exceptions. The vast majority of manufacturing and service enterprises do not have the capabilities to establish or maintain such long-distance relationships. Thus, most business transactions are spatially bound to a place. In this view, if inter-sectorial linkages are important, they will be relevant to proximate industrial activities. Moreover, even among giant establishments like IBM and Gen-

[3] In the earlier 1980s, IBM lent its name to Microsoft's first successful operating system, "IBM PC-DOS," which transformed the then tiny company into a major U.S. software manufacturer.

eral Motors, there is a considerable agglomeration of smaller supplier industries in the regions where they locate (see, e.g., Romo and Schwartz 1990; 1991; also see *Fortune* [July 15, 1991:84], which reports the same sort of regional industrial buildup around Honda and Toyota auto plants located in the Midwest).

In terms of employment, regional declines in manufacturing can indicate two things: 1) they can mark a loss in productive capacity; or 2) they can indicate substitution of capital, technology, and indirect labor for direct labor. Under the tight-linkage hypothesis, the former condition will depress regional economic activity and employment in the service sector, while the latter condition will increase regional economic activity and employment in the service sector. But by the logic of post-industrial theory, manufacturing does not matter. From this point of view, service employment is independent of manufacturing. Indeed, the service sector is replacing manufacturing. The post-industrial hypothesis, then, maintains that growth or decline in manufacturing employment will be unrelated to service employment.

## Declining Manufacturing and the Coming of Post-Industrial Society

Recent national employment figures appear to support the post-industrial hypothesis. As reported in the introduction of this chapter, manufacturing lost 1.4 million jobs between 1979 and 1989, while service producing industries gained over 17.8 million. Such aggregate statistics, however, are insensitive to the underlying social structural mechanisms that generate them. The service sector is composed of different sectors that can be related to manufacturing activities in fundamentally different ways. We shall consider three major categories of services: 1) producer services; 2) whole and retail trade; and 3) private-consumptive services. As we demonstrate below, most of the growth in service employment in both the United States and New York State has occurred in these three categories.

A major component of the growth in U.S. service economy has been the so-called producer-service industries (Gershuny and Miles 1983). As the term indicates, producer services are activities that directly provide inputs into establishments in the productive sector of the economy (i.e., manufacturing, construction, mining, and agriculture).[4] Producer ser-

---

[4]Generally, the concept of "producer services" is an attempt to identify the basic distinction between services that are used by households (personal consumption), and those services that are ultimately consumed by business firms and other productive enterprises.

vices can also be indirect providers insofar as the destination of their outputs are other producer services that are directly linked to productive enterprises (Goe 1990). Although definitions of producer-service industries vary across investigations, Greenfield (1966) and Tschetter (1987) indicate that between 1950 and 1960 employment in these industries increased faster than employment in all other nonagricultural sectors; and Noyelle and Stanback (1984) establish that for the period between 1947 to 1977, the share of GNP in the United States attributable to producer services expanded at a greater rate than any other sector of the economy.

Adapting the definition of producer-services industries established by Gellespie and Green (1987; also see Goe 1990),[5] we find that about a third of service-sector growth in the United States during the ten-year period from 1979 to 1989 has been in the producer services.[6] Table 13.1 provides national figures on employment trends by industry for the ten-year period. It shows that between 1979 and 1989, the entire service sector ("All Services") grew by 17.8 million jobs (a 37.6 percent increase), which represented 94.9 percent of all the jobs added to the national economy. As Table 13.1 shows, employment in producer services grew by almost 5.6 million jobs. This is an increase of 61.1 percent, which constitutes 29.8 percent of all new jobs and 31.4 percent of all service-sector jobs added to the national economy during the ten-year period. The other 70 percent increase in service sector employment was dominated by: 1) wholesale and retail trade,[7] which accounted for 29.9 percent of the new jobs added to the economy and 31.5 percent of the

The latter category are producer services (Greenfield 1966). More refined attempts at conceptualizing producer services involve specifying the role of these activities in the social division of labor in production systems (see, e.g., Walker 1985; Gellespie and Green 1987; Goe 1990).

[5] This classification includes as producer-service industries the following standard industrial codes (SIC): banking (SIC 60); credit agencies other than banks (SIC 61); security and commodity brokers and services (SIC 62); insurance carriers (SIC 63); insurance agents, brokers, and services (SIC 64); real estate (SIC 65); business services including advertising, market research, consulting, R & D, and other business-specific services (SIC 73); legal services (SIC 81); and miscellaneous services including engineering and architectural services, accounting, auditing, and bookkeeping (SIC 89).

[6] It should be noted that not all of the outputs of producer services are consumed by business. However, in most of the SIC categories that constitute producer services (see footnote 5), other businesses constitute the overwhelming majority of customers. In a questionnaire study of Ohio services providers, Goe (1990:335) found that in a major metropolitan area such as the Cleveland PMSA almost 68 percent of the output from producer services was consumed by other business establishments.

[7] The trades (SIC 50–59) involve the distribution of durable and nondurable goods, retailing of building materials, general merchandise and as well as food stores, auto dealers, apparel and furniture stores, and eating and drinking establishments.

Table 13.1   Employment Trends by Industry in the U.S. for 1979 and 1989

|  | 1979 | 1989 | Growth |
|---|---|---|---|
| TOTAL (Nonagricultural) | 89,823,000 | 108,581,000 | 18,758,00 |
| Manufacturing | 21,040,000 | 19,612,000 | −1,428,00 |
| All Services | 47,416,000 | 65,220,000 | 17,804,00 |
| Producer Services | 9,147,600 | 14,737,100 | 5,589,50 |
| (60) Banking | 1,498,500 | 1,774,300 | 275,80 |
| (61) Credit agencies other than banks | 554,000 | 907,500 | 353,50 |
| (62) Security, commodity brokers, etc. | 204,200 | 435,200 | 231,00 |
| (63) Insurance carriers | 1,199,800 | 1,468,000 | 268,20 |
| (64) Insurance agents, brokers, etc. | 430,100 | 659,800 | 229,70 |
| (65) Real estate | 954,500 | 1,348,000 | 393,50 |
| (73) Business services | 2,905,900 | 5,788,700 | 2,882,80 |
| (81) Legal services | 459,900 | 896,300 | 436,40 |
| (89) Miscellaneous services | 940,700 | 1,459,300 | 518,60 |
| Private-Consumptive (7, 70–72, 74–80, 82–86) | 12,805,500 | 18,747,700 | 5,942,20 |
| Wholesale & Retail Trade (50–59) | 20,193,000 | 25,809,000 | 5,616,00 |
| Transportation & Utilities (40–49) | 5,136,000 | 5,705,000 | 569,00 |
| Government | 15,947,000 | 17,727,000 | 1,780,00 |

Source: Plunkert (1990: 8–9).

growth in services; and 2) private-consumptive services,[8] which consti-tuted 31.7 percent of the all new jobs and 33.4 percent of the growth in services (see Table 13.1).[9]

Indeed, growth in producer services over the 1980 decade was as great as the growth in retail trade, and fell just short of the growth in private-

[8] Private-consumptive services (SIC 07, 70–72, 75–80, and 82–86) involve, for ex-ample, lodging, personal services, auto and other repair services, as well as entertainment, education, and health services.

[9] It should also be noted that 65 percent of growth in private-consumptive services can be accounted for by health (SIC 80), educational (SIC 82), and social (SIC 83) services. A large proportion of the operating income for such service establishments is subsidized by federal, state, and local governments (e.g., government-sponsored medical insurance, subsidies for students, and direct grants). Thus, much of the growth in private-consumptive services may be funded by the government and may not actually represent independent service sector growth.

| % Growth | % of Total Growth | % of Service Growth | % of Prod. Serv. Growth |
|---|---|---|---|
| 20.88% | | | |
| −6.79% | −7.61% | | |
| 37.55% | 94.91% | | |
| 61.10% | 29.80% | 31.39% | |
| 18.41% | 1.47% | 1.55% | 4.93% |
| 63.81% | 1.88% | 1.99% | 6.32% |
| 113.12% | 1.23% | 1.30% | 4.13% |
| 22.35% | 1.43% | 1.51% | 4.80% |
| 53.41% | 1.22% | 1.29% | 4.11% |
| 41.23% | 2.10% | 2.21% | 7.04% |
| 99.21% | 15.37% | 16.19% | 51.58% |
| 94.89% | 2.33% | 2.45% | 7.81% |
| 55.13% | 2.76% | 2.91% | 9.28% |
| 46.40% | 31.68% | 33.38% | |
| 27.81% | 29.94% | 31.54% | |
| 11.08% | 3.03% | 3.20% | |
| 11.16% | 9.49% | | |

consumptive services. While producer services are tightly coupled with goods-producing activities (either by servicing such establishments directly or by servicing other producer-service establishments that transact directly with manufacturing establishments), the other two categories—which together constitute almost 65 percent in the growth of the service sector—are only loosely linked to manufacturing. In terms of employment, however, they are related in a very important way. Through multiplier effects on the demand side, large incomes from manufacturing and producer-service jobs create demands for items such as stereo components, camcorders, clothes, pizza, cars, auto services, amusement and recreation; and shrinkage in such sources of personal income will reduce the demand for retail trade and private-consumptive services.

The national figures have offered no evidence that changes in manufacturing employment have any impact on the changes in services employment. If anything, those figures continue to support the post-indus-

trial hypothesis. One reason for this is that national statistics obscure
regional variation. As Walker (1985) points out, the very existence of
producer services is attributable to shifts in the social division of labor
characterized by increasing externalization of service activities from prod-
uct-producing firms to business-service firms (also see Noyelle and Stanback 1984; Daniels 1985; Marshall 1985; Wood 1986; Gellespie and
Green 1987; Hutton and Ley 1989). For Walker, the social division of
labor refers to a web of business transactions, information exchanges,
and mutual administrative and production adjustments linking work groups
from various industries together to form regional production systems
(1985:52). Thus, the concept of producer services implies a strong regional component characterized by spatial concentrations of manufacturing establishments and dependent service firms insofar as transactions,
interaction exchanges, and mutual business-monitoring adjustments are
facilitated by face-to-face interactions. The growth in retail trade and the
private-consumptive services are also regionally bound. While regional
retailing services would not be directly affected if products came from
foreign manufacturers—the same sales effort is involved in selling a Ford
as in selling a Honda[10]—the demand for such services, as mentioned
above, is affected by the personal incomes from jobs in local manufacturing and producer-service establishments. The same logic applies to private-consumptive services.

To capture the regional relationship between manufacturing and services, we present data from a multi-year study of the effects of manufacturing declines on New York State's economy (see Romo, Korman,
Brantley, and Schwartz 1986; 1988; Korman, Romo, Lee, Chan, and
Schwartz 1989; Romo and Schwartz 1990; 1991). Figure 13.2 displays
a map of New York State depicting the nine major labor-market regions
under investigation. As previously discussed, losses in regional manufacturing employment can result from either loss of productive capacity (i.e.,
plant closures due to business failures or migrations out of the state), or
it can be brought about by substituting capital, technology, and indirect
labor for direct labor. In New York State, there is strong evidence that
much of the decline in manufacturing jobs has resulted from a decline in
productive capacity (see, e.g., Yago, Korman, Wu, and Schwartz 1984;
Perry 1987). Thus, in the case of New York State, if manufacturing matters, we expect that regional declines in production jobs will have a negative impact on service jobs. If it does not matter, as post-industrial the-

[10]This assumes that foreign products are made available to U.S. dealers in the first
place; a condition—as we reported above—that does not always hold true, especially in the
case of Japanese computer-chip equipment companies, which the U.S. Department of
Commerce has accused of discriminating against U.S. customers.

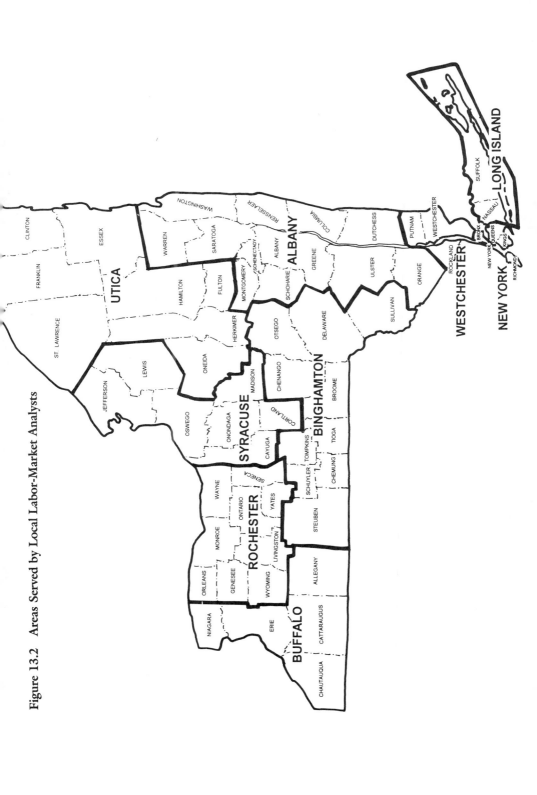

**Figure 13.2    Areas Served by Local Labor-Market Analysts**

**Table 13.2   Employment Trends by Industry in New York State for 1979 and 1989**

|  | 1979 | 1989 | Growth |
|---|---|---|---|
| TOTAL (Nonagricultural) | 7,101,121 | 8,131,550 | 1,030,429 |
| Manufacturing | 1,497,545 | 1,185,862 | −311,683 |
| All Services | 4,069,249 | 5,154,211 | 1,084,962 |
| Producer Services | 1,093,812 | 1,514,806 | 420,994 |
| (60) Banking | 207,085 | 260,604 | 53,519 |
| (61) Credit agencies other than banks | 27,029 | 20,961 | −6,068 |
| (62) Security, commodity brokers, etc. | 79,579 | 154,514 | 74,935 |
| (63) Insurance carriers | 116,364 | 120,402 | 4,038 |
| (64) Insurance agents, brokers, etc. | 47,411 | 63,359 | 15,948 |
| (65) Real estate | 110,819 | 143,027 | 32,208 |
| (73) Business services | 351,978 | 446,839 | 94,861 |
| (81) Legal services | 61,822 | 109,817 | 47,995 |
| (89) Miscellaneous services | 91,725 | 195,283 | 103,558 |
| Private-Consumptive (7, 70–72, 74–80,82–86) | 1,072,127 | 1,499,226 | 427,099 |
| Wholesale & Retail Trade (50–59) | 1,476,443 | 1,724,540 | 248,097 |
| Transportation & Utilities (40–49) | 413,391 | 397,359 | −16,032 |
| Government | 1,267,560 | 1,389,284 | 121,724 |

Source: New York Department of Labor.

ory claims, then growth in the service sector will be independent of employment changes in manufacturing.

Table 13.2 presents the 1979 and 1989 employment figures for New York State's manufacturing, service, and governmental sectors. In this ten-year period, the state added just over a million jobs. This is a 14.5 percent increase, but it is also substantially lower than the 20.9 percent increase observed in the entire nation (see Table 13.1). Like the United States as a whole, New York lost jobs in manufacturing (about 312,000). This 20.8 percent decrease is dramatically greater than the 6.8 percent loss recorded for the entire nation during the same period. Also like the nation, the New York's service employment grew over the period; it actually increased by over a million jobs. While the state's proportional growth in the "All Services" category was not as great as that recorded in the United States as a whole (i.e., 26.7 versus 37.6 percent), it repre-

| % Growth | % of Total Growth | % of Service Growth | % of Prod. Serv. Growth |
| --- | --- | --- | --- |
| 14.51% | | | |
| −20.81% | −30.25% | | |
| 26.66% | 105.29% | | |
| 38.49% | 40.86% | 38.80% | |
| 25.84% | 5.19% | 4.93% | 12.71% |
| −22.45% | −0.59% | −0.56% | −1.44% |
| 94.16% | 7.27% | 6.91% | 17.80% |
| 3.47% | 0.39% | 0.37% | 0.96% |
| 33.64% | 1.55% | 1.47% | 3.79% |
| 29.06% | 3.13% | 2.97% | 7.65% |
| 26.95% | 9.21% | 8.74% | 22.53% |
| 77.63% | 4.66% | 4.42% | 11.40% |
| 112.90% | 10.05% | 9.54% | 24.60% |
| 39.84% | 41.45% | 39.37% | |
| 16.80% | 24.08% | 22.87% | |
| −3.88% | −1.56% | −1.48% | |
| 9.60% | 11.81% | | |

sents about three-quarters of all the new jobs added to the state's economy during the period (after accounting for losses in manufacturing). Finally, the state governmental sector added close to 122,000 jobs, which constitutes a 9.6 percent increase and 11.8 percent of all the new jobs added to the economy.

It appears that, as for the United States as a whole, the service sector has grown in New York State. But the similarity ends here. In the national economy, as Table 13.1 shows, the growth in the producer services (61.1 percent) outpaced growth in both the wholesale and retail trade (27.8 percent) and in private-consumptive services (46.4 percent). However, as proportions of total growth, all three sectors contributed approximately equal shares (about 30 percent each; see Table 13.1). Proportional growth in New York's private-consumptive service lagged behind U.S. growth (39.8 versus 46.4 percent), yet changes in this sector constituted a larger share of overall growth. As a proportion of all new jobs added to the economy, the state's private-consumptive services contributed 41.5 percent, while in the United States as a whole, this sector contributed only 31.7 percent. This is significant because a more detailed examination of New York's employment figures reveals that over 78 percent of the growth in the private-consumptive sector came from health, education, and social services, all of which are heavily subsidized by government expenditures.[11] This implies that tax monies may be responsible for a large share of the growth in the service sector. It also echoes findings from an earlier period in the state's economic history, as reported by Wu and Korman (1987). They discovered that, between 1962 and 1976, declines in manufacturing were associated with increases in government outlays for social services. This represents, in other words, the state's strategy toward the devastating economic effects of deindustrialization.

The wholesale and retail trades in New York also grew at a slower pace, and contributed less total growth, than they did in the United States as a whole. In the ten-year period under investigation, the state's economy added a little over 248,000 wholesale and retail jobs. This marks an increase of 16.8 percent (as compared to the U.S. growth of 27.8 percent), and represents about 24.1 percent of the total employment growth (as compared to the U.S. proportion of the total of 29.9 percent). The trades, dominated as they are by retailing, are sensitive to multiplier effects. New York's weak showing may indicate a reduction in personal income resulting from massive losses in its manufacturing sector. As Cohen and Zysman (1987:21) point out, manufacturing is a wage-setting force in regional economies: when manufacturing declines, so do the wage levels in all the sectors of the economy. It would consequently have a negative impact on personal purchasing power and retailing.

Finally, New York added some 421,000 producer-services jobs to the economy. While its growth almost equaled the proportional growth in the state's private-consumptive services, the 38.5 percent increase registered by the producer services lagged well behind the national growth of 61.1 percent. However, the overall contribution of producer services to the state's total employment growth was considerably higher than that observed for the United States as a whole (40.9 versus 29.8 percent). This may be a bright spot in an otherwise dismal economic picture. As

[11] As reported in Table 13.2, private-consumptive services grew by just over 427,000 jobs between 1979 and 1989. Of this growth, the health services (SIC 80) added 185,000 or 43.3 percent of the new private-consumptive service jobs; education (SIC 82) added 68,600 or 16.0 percent of the new private-consumptive service jobs; and social services (SIC 83) added 80,200 or 18.8 percent of the new private-consumptive service jobs.

mentioned above, the outputs of producer services are likely to be consumed by goods-producing establishments. Perhaps the large contribution made by producer services to the state's overall employment growth indicates that the manufacturing activities remaining in the state are prosperous enough to generate growth in this sector. We will return to this issue in the conclusion of the chapter.

Overall, however, the comparison between the United States as a whole and New York State suggests that the state's substantially larger proportional losses in the manufacturing sector has significantly dampened growth in its service sectors. This finding lends some support to Cohen and Zysman's (1987) "manufacturing matters" hypothesis. Yet the mechanisms that produce this relationship—tight linkages—are, as we have argued above, likely to express themselves mainly in the regional impact of manufacturing on services. This is something that the statewide analysis obscures. Table 13.3 presents data on the growth of manufacturing, government, and services for each of the nine New York State labor markets between 1979 and 1989. In the bottom half of the table, service is further disaggregated into the "Wholesale & Retail" trades, "Producer Services," and "Private-Consumptive" services; the table also shows their proportional growth as a percentage of "All Services." The regions have been sorted by loss in manufacturing to facilitate comparisons (where the regions with the greatest losses come first).

The top half of Table 13.3 reveals that there is a moderate relationship between proportional loss in manufacturing and growth in the combined service sector (i.e., "All Services"): the biggest losers (e.g., New York City, Buffalo) sustain the most muted service growth. There are, however, exceptions. Albany, which bore heavy losses in manufacturing (about a 22.7 percent decline) displayed the greatest proportional growth in the services (44.3 percent). This may in part be attributable to this region's excessive growth in government employment. We will have more to say about this below, but first we consider a much more dramatic pattern revealed in Table 13.3: the relationship between proportional loss in manufacturing and the share of service growth attributable to the private-consumptive services. Service growth in regions that suffer the greatest losses in manufacturing is dominated by growth in the private-consumptive services. For example, of all the service jobs added to New York City's service sector, nearly half (49.6 percent) were in the private-consumptive services. At the other end of the continuum, only 31.3 percent of the service growth on Long Island—which almost managed to hold an even keel in manufacturing jobs during the period—could be attributed to private-consumptive services.

As discussed above, over 78 percent of the state's growth in the pri-

**Table 13.3   Employment Trends by Major Labor-Market Area in New York State for 1979 and 1989**

| Labor Market | Manufacturing | | | |
| --- | --- | --- | --- | --- |
| | 1979 | 1989 | Growth | % Growth |
| New York | 517,634 | 357,407 | −160,227 | −30.95% |
| Buffalo | 145,226 | 100,360 | −44,866 | −30.89% |
| Utica-Rome | 32,333 | 24,437 | −7,896 | −24.42% |
| Albany | 60,361 | 46,680 | −13,681 | −22.67% |
| Westchester | 75,514 | 58,520 | −16,994 | −22.50% |
| Syracuse | 61,304 | 53,466 | −7,838 | −12.79% |
| Rochester | 157,146 | 138,265 | −18,881 | −12.01% |
| Binghamton | 40,667 | 36,310 | −4,357 | −10.71% |
| Long Island | 164,819 | 160,904 | −3,915 | −2.38% |

| Labor Market | Wholesale & Retail | | | |
| --- | --- | --- | --- | --- |
| | 1979 | 1989 | Growth | % of Serv. Growth |
| New York | 607,825 | 613,303 | 5,478 | 1.60% |
| Buffalo | 114,658 | 133,111 | 18,453 | 27.52% |
| Utica-Rome | 21,598 | 27,473 | 5,875 | 40.06% |
| Albany | 68,514 | 89,349 | 20,835 | 29.13% |
| Westchester | 78,329 | 91,039 | 12,710 | 19.50% |
| Syracuse | 57,738 | 73,631 | 15,893 | 32.37% |
| Rochester | 76,767 | 102,472 | 25,705 | 33.81% |
| Binghamton | 20,041 | 25,692 | 5,651 | 41.21% |
| Long Island | 231,321 | 293,396 | 62,075 | 30.05% |

Source: New York State Department of Labor.

vate-consumptive sector is charged to the state-subsidized subsectors of health, education, and social services. The figures in Table 13.3 suggest that service-sector growth in deindustrializing regions is greatly bolstered by tax dollars. To explore this possibility further, we analyze the growth in health, education, and social services during the ten-year period. Table 13.4 presents these figures. It gives the 1979 and 1989 employment figures for the three subsectors as well as their combined growth, their

| Government | | | | All Services | | | |
|---|---|---|---|---|---|---|---|
| 1979 | 1989 | Growth | % Growth | 1979 | 1989 | Growth | % Growth |
| 539,300 | 582,600 | 43,300 | 8.03% | 2,118,783 | 2,461,095 | 342,312 | 16.16% |
| 83,700 | 84,500 | 800 | 0.96% | 251,059 | 318,116 | 67,057 | 26.71% |
| 28,400 | 28,700 | 300 | 1.06% | 49,480 | 64,146 | 14,666 | 29.64% |
| 95,800 | 107,700 | 11,900 | 12.42% | 161,324 | 232,859 | 71,535 | 44.34% |
| 54,900 | 54,000 | −900 | −1.64% | 193,728 | 258,905 | 65,177 | 33.64% |
| 46,900 | 49,700 | 2,800 | 5.97% | 132,191 | 181,286 | 49,095 | 37.14% |
| 58,000 | 62,200 | 4,200 | 7.24% | 176,790 | 252,815 | 76,025 | 43.00% |
| 22,200 | 20,700 | −1,500 | −6.76% | 42,928 | 56,640 | 13,712 | 31.94% |
| 165,200 | 174,900 | 9,700 | 5.87% | 504,099 | 710,678 | 206,579 | 40.98% |

| Producer Services | | | | Private-Consumptive | | | |
|---|---|---|---|---|---|---|---|
| 1979 | 1989 | Growth | % of Serv. Growth | 1979 | 1989 | Growth | % of Serv. Growth |
| 749,784 | 959,343 | 209,559 | 61.22% | 509,863 | 679,721 | 169,858 | 49.62% |
| 45,358 | 65,407 | 20,049 | 29.90% | 67,407 | 96,346 | 28,939 | 43.16% |
| 7,771 | 11,829 | 4,058 | 27.67% | 16,373 | 20,817 | 4,444 | 30.30% |
| 30,532 | 54,188 | 23,656 | 33.07% | 49,406 | 74,870 | 25,464 | 35.60% |
| 38,942 | 64,235 | 25,293 | 38.81% | 59,472 | 84,450 | 24,978 | 38.32% |
| 27,675 | 40,449 | 12,774 | 26.02% | 33,075 | 49,136 | 16,061 | 32.71% |
| 30,731 | 52,261 | 21,530 | 28.32% | 57,143 | 83,147 | 26,004 | 34.20% |
| 7,119 | 10,443 | 3,324 | 24.24% | 11,596 | 16,392 | 4,796 | 34.98% |
| 111,635 | 181,879 | 70,244 | 34.00% | 123,469 | 188,073 | 64,604 | 31.27% |

combined proportional contribution to private-consumptive service growth, and their combined proportional contribution to growth of the entire service sector in each region. As before, regions are sorted by the proportional losses in manufacturing employment registered in Table 13.3.

The most striking trend in Table 13.4 is revealed in the last column ("% of All Service Growth"), which records the proportional contribution of health, education, and social services (HE & S services) to all

**Table 13.4  Employment Trends in Health, Education, & Social Services in New York State for 1979 and 1989**

|  | 1979 | | |
| --- | --- | --- | --- |
| Labor Market | Health | Education | Social | Total |
| New York | 189,053 | 75,659 | 58,213 | 322,925 |
| Buffalo | 30,221 | 6,137 | 6,082 | 42,440 |
| Utica-Rome | 7,245 | 1,278 | 1,910 | 10,433 |
| Albany | 22,408 | 7,375 | 5,099 | 34,882 |
| Westchester | 22,904 | 8,144 | 8,376 | 39,424 |
| Syracuse | 11,390 | 6,508 | 3,043 | 20,941 |
| Rochester | 22,800 | 10,906 | 6,777 | 40,483 |
| Binghamton | 5,907 | 411 | 1,394 | 7,712 |
| Long Island | 52,626 | 15,396 | 7,321 | 75,343 |

Source: New York State Department of Labor.

service growth in each region. Figure 13.3 charts this trend with respect to losses in manufacturing. Also included in the graph is the overall contribution of the entire private-consumptive sector to all services growth (from Table 13.3). Figure 13.3 reveals that, in regions where proportional losses in manufacturing are greatest, service growth is largely driven by HE & S services. At the other extreme, where manufacturing losses are lighter, private-consumptive and HE & S services make up a smaller share of overall service growth. Moreover, HE & S services compose a smaller share of private-consumptive services. In general, Figure 13.3 indicates that the more deindustrialized the region, the more government-backed services activities dominate service-sector employment.

A clear picture of the direct role of manufacturing and government in service-sector employment can be ascertained by extending the historical scope of the investigation. As Figure 13.1 demonstrates, a considerable portion of New York State's losses of manufacturing occurred prior to 1979. Table 13.5 presents data covering the twenty-four year time period between 1965 and 1989. Unfortunately, New York Department of Labor figures for 1963 do not provide the level of detail in standard industrial classifications that they do for later years. For the regional data,

| | 1989 | | | Combined Health, Education, & Social Services | | | |
|---|---|---|---|---|---|---|---|
| Health | Education | Social | Total | Growth | % Growth | % of Priv.-Consump. Growth | % of All Service Growth |
| 248,006 | 99,857 | 117,545 | 465,408 | 142,483 | 57.45% | 83.88% | 41.62% |
| 48,156 | 8,040 | 10,923 | 67,119 | 24,679 | 51.25% | 85.28% | 36.80% |
| 9,940 | 1,779 | 2,966 | 14,685 | 4,252 | 42.78% | 95.68% | 28.99% |
| 31,647 | 10,231 | 11,317 | 53,195 | 18,313 | 57.87% | 71.92% | 25.60% |
| 35,777 | 10,224 | 11,089 | 57,090 | 17,666 | 49.38% | 70.73% | 27.10% |
| 19,194 | 9,705 | 5,353 | 34,252 | 13,311 | 69.35% | 82.88% | 27.11% |
| 35,269 | 15,430 | 10,013 | 60,712 | 20,229 | 57.36% | 77.79% | 26.61% |
| 8,683 | 584 | 2,047 | 11,314 | 3,602 | 41.48% | 75.10% | 26.27% |
| 89,644 | 19,221 | 14,169 | 123,034 | 47,691 | 53.20% | 73.82% | 23.09% |

**Figure 13.3  Growth in the Personal-Consumptive Services as a Percent Growth in All Services by Changes in Manufacturing between 1979 and 1989**

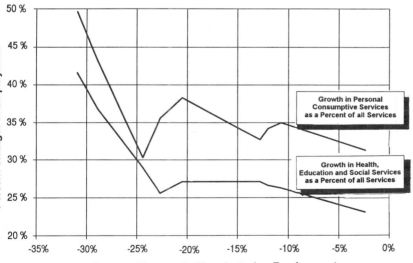

**Table 13.5   Employment Trends by Major Labor-Market Area in New York State for 1963 and 1989**

| Labor Market | Manufacturing | | | |
| | 1963 | 1989 | Growth | % Growth |
|---|---|---|---|---|
| New York | 877,234 | 357,407 | −519,827 | −59.26% |
| Buffalo | 165,057 | 100,360 | −64,697 | −39.20% |
| Utica-Rome | 37,970 | 24,437 | −13,533 | −35.64% |
| Binghamton | 53,571 | 36,310 | −17,261 | −32.22% |
| Albany | 61,811 | 46,680 | −15,131 | −24.48% |
| Syracuse | 64,126 | 53,466 | −10,660 | −16.62% |
| Westchester | 66,180 | 58,520 | −7,660 | −11.57% |
| Long Island | 141,673 | 160,904 | 19,231 | 13.57% |
| Rochester | 108,162 | 138,265 | 30,103 | 27.83% |

| Labor Market | Wholesale & Retail | | | |
| | 1963 | 1989 | Growth | % of Serv. Growth |
|---|---|---|---|---|
| New York | 719,843 | 613,303 | −106,540 | −15.36% |
| Buffalo | 83,365 | 133,111 | 49,746 | 29.98% |
| Utica-Rome | 16,511 | 27,473 | 10,962 | 33.54% |
| Binghamton | 14,124 | 25,692 | 11,568 | 39.42% |
| Albany | 45,847 | 89,349 | 43,502 | 29.22% |
| Syracuse | 38,981 | 73,631 | 34,650 | 31.73% |
| Westchester | 53,282 | 91,039 | 37,757 | 24.69% |
| Long Island | 123,296 | 293,396 | 170,100 | 34.88% |
| Rochester | 48,753 | 102,472 | 53,719 | 33.43% |

Source: New York State Department of Labor.

service-employment figures are highly aggregated into "Wholesale & Retail Trades" (including SIC 50–59), "Financial Services" (including SIC 60–67), and "Other Services" (including SIC 7, 70–86, 89, and 99). Thus we are unable to construct the producer-service and private-consumptive service categories, since these classifications are comprised of an amalgamation of detailed standard industrial codes from both the financial and other service categories (see footnote 5 above).

Consequently, we concentrate on the data in the top half of Table 13.5. This involves 1965 and 1989 employment data for all manufactur-

| | Government | | | | All Services | | |
|---|---|---|---|---|---|---|---|
| 1963 | 1989 | Growth | % Growth | 1963 | 1989 | Growth | % Growth |
| 482,000 | 582,600 | 100,600 | 20.87% | 1,767,566 | 2,461,095 | 693,529 | 39.24% |
| 63,700 | 84,500 | 20,800 | 32.65% | 152,201 | 318,116 | 165,915 | 109.01% |
| 25,000 | 28,700 | 3,700 | 14.80% | 31,467 | 64,146 | 32,679 | 103.85% |
| 15,400 | 20,700 | 5,300 | 34.42% | 27,298 | 56,640 | 29,342 | 107.49% |
| 59,600 | 107,700 | 48,100 | 80.70% | 83,989 | 232,859 | 148,870 | 177.25% |
| 28,600 | 49,700 | 21,100 | 73.78% | 72,086 | 181,286 | 109,200 | 151.49% |
| 35,900 | 54,000 | 18,100 | 50.42% | 105,978 | 258,905 | 152,927 | 144.30% |
| 100,600 | 174,900 | 74,300 | 73.86% | 223,002 | 710,678 | 487,676 | 218.69% |
| 37,700 | 62,200 | 24,500 | 64.99% | 92,124 | 252,815 | 160,691 | 174.43% |

| | Financial Services | | | | Other Services | | |
|---|---|---|---|---|---|---|---|
| 1963 | 1989 | Growth | % of Serv. Growth | 1963 | 1989 | Growth | % of Serv. Growth |
| 382,365 | 891,686 | 509,321 | 73.44% | 446,361 | 679,721 | 233,360 | 33.65% |
| 15,690 | 65,407 | 49,717 | 29.97% | 31,238 | 96,346 | 65,108 | 39.24% |
| 3,892 | 11,829 | 7,937 | 24.29% | 6,413 | 20,817 | 14,404 | 44.08% |
| 3,337 | 10,443 | 7,106 | 24.22% | 4,752 | 16,392 | 11,640 | 39.67% |
| 9,163 | 54,188 | 45,025 | 30.24% | 18,253 | 74,870 | 56,617 | 38.03% |
| 9,004 | 40,449 | 31,445 | 28.80% | 14,170 | 49,136 | 34,966 | 32.02% |
| 11,656 | 64,235 | 52,579 | 34.38% | 27,308 | 84,450 | 57,142 | 37.37% |
| 20,797 | 181,879 | 161,082 | 33.03% | 56,762 | 188,073 | 131,311 | 26.93% |
| 11,679 | 52,261 | 40,582 | 25.25% | 17,254 | 83,147 | 65,893 | 41.01% |

ing industries, government, and all services within each of the nine labor market areas. As in the cases of Tables 13.3 and 13.4, we have sorted the regions into descending order by proportional losses in manufacturing employment to facilitate comparisons among the different sectors. Table 13.5 reveals a clearer relationship between the proportional changes in manufacturing employment over the twenty-four period and proportional changes in service employment, and Figure 13.4 provides a graphical representation of these same data. The graph compares the proportional changes in employment for the manufacturing, governmental, and service sectors by each of the nine regions (which appear on the X-axis of the graph). To further illustrate the relationships between employment changes in these three sectors, we have also calculated a simple OLS regression model in which the percentage of change in service employment (PCSE) in each of the nine regions is regressed on the percentage of change in manufacturing employment (PCME) and the percentage of change in government employment (PCGE).[12] Predicted values from the regression model have been plotted in Figure 13.4 along with the observed values. As the figure indicates, the pattern of predicted values is quite close to the pattern of observed values.

In the estimated regression model, the constant of 99.9 percent indicates the average growth in the service sector across all regions after the effects of changes in manufacturing and service employment are controlled. On average, service employment almost doubled over the twenty-four period. The regression model also indicates that for each positive percentage point of change in manufacturing employment, the proportional growth in service employment increases by 11 percent; and for every positive percentage point of change in government employment, service employment increases by over 9.6 percent. The magnitude of these estimates indicates that regional manufacturing and government activities, as measured by changes in employment, have very strong positive effects on regional service employment.

Figure 13.4 clearly shows how government employment counterbalances losses from manufacturing to sustain high levels of service employment. Consider the Syracuse and Albany labor-market areas. Both main-

---

[12] Estimating this model generated the following coefficients:

$$PCSE = 99.9\% + (11.2\% \times PCME) + (9.6\% \times PCGE) + e.$$

| | s.e. = 0.270 | s.e. = 0.423 | s.e. = 0.390 |
| | t-test = 3.591 | t-test = 2.633 | t-test = 2.475 |

Here, s.e. indicates the standard error of each estimate, the t-test is the ratio of the estimate divided by its standard error; and $e$ is unexplained variation. The t-tests for each estimate are associated with observed probability values that are less than 0.05. Under standard statistical assumptions, the magnitude of the observed probabilities indicate that we can reject the null hypothesis for each individual estimates that it equals zero. This result is further confirmed by the F-test of the regression, which equals 20.87. With 2 degrees of freedom in the numerator and 5 degrees of freedom in the denominator, the F-test is associated with a probability that is less than 0.05. Thus, we can reject the more general null hypothesis that the modeled relationship between the dependent and independent variables is equivalent to zero. Finally, $R^2$ measures the amount of observed variation in the nine observations that is explained by the predicted values. This statistic varies between 0 (i.e., no variance explained by the model) and 1 (i.e., 100 percent of the variance explained by the model). In this case, $R^2$ equals 0.87, which indicates a very good fit between model and data.

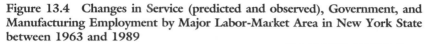

Figure 13.4 Changes in Service (predicted and observed), Government, and Manufacturing Employment by Major Labor-Market Area in New York State between 1963 and 1989

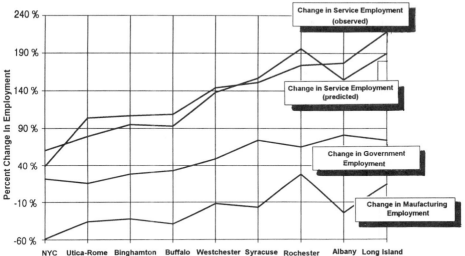

tain high levels of service growth in the face of greater-than-expected declines in manufacturing employment: that is, they maintain relatively high proportional gains in service employment while sustaining relatively large losses in manufacturing employment. Each region, however, also shows comparatively high growth in government employment that offsets losses in manufacturing. These patterns imply that government employment, through the multiplier effects of the salaries it provides, operates to maintain service-sector growth in regions that have experienced high levels of deindustrialization. In other words, we observe patterns in the data that indicate that the government is sponsoring growth in the service with tax dollars (also see Table 13.4 and Figure 13.3 above).

## Conclusion

There is a lingering belief, held by many academics and policy makers, that U.S. manufacturing—the producer side of the economy—will inevitably be replaced by the service side of the economy as a normal transition to the next stage of economic development. This conviction, or the idea of a post-industrial society, is deeply rooted in the neoclassical free market conception of economic transactions. Here highly atomized actors compete with one another for the best deal on a level playing field, where all things traded are interchangeable, and where information is cheap and transmitted to everyone instantaneously. Accordingly, the post-industrial perspective suggests that any particular service activity is interchangeable and can be used by almost anyone, no matter what they do or where they do it. From this point of view, services can develop independently, without the support of other parts of the economy, including manufacturing.

In this chapter we have presented an alternative view of service development. While we agree that the service sector is vital to the economy, it is only a partner—not the successor—of manufacturing. In our model, economic transactions between service and manufacturing establishments are not only crucial to the continued growth of both sectors, they are bound together and embedded in regional production systems. These systems are characterized by locally relevant exchanges of information, mutual administrative and production adjustments, personnel transfers, and the existence of a wide range of jointly held assumptions and trusts. Such systems tightly bind regional service activities and manufacturing activities. Other regional services, such as retail trade and personal-consumptive services, depend upon multiplier effects engendered by the personal incomes from the economic activity of the region's production system. Accordingly, our point of view suggests that the post-industrial service economy can only be a partial economy. Historically, the production of goods has been the principal component of the economic base of many U.S. communities and regions, and the fate of the service sector is, in our opinion, inalienably tied to the soundness of regional manufacturing.

We examined employment data from New York State and observed a strong positive relationship between the magnitude of regional manufacturing activities and the growth of the state's service sector. While service employment grew in the face of declines in manufacturing, it was far less than what the United States as a whole experienced over the time period of our study. In addition, service-sector growth was significantly stifled by the degree of regional deindustrialization. We also observed that a large portion of the state's service-sector growth was in private-consumptive activities such as health, education, and social services, which are all heavily subsidized by tax dollars. This trend was more prevalent in regions that have suffered the greatest losses in manufacturing employment. In general, our findings revealed that government employment operated in a way that offset declines in manufacturing. These observations replicate Wu and Korman's (1987) conclusions that the state attempts to ward off the negative effects of deindustrialization by sponsoring growth in the service sector. But such service-sector growth must be considered largely artificial. By attempting to counterbalance declines in manufacturing, the state government has incurred a tremendous fiscal burden that, without renewed economic growth in the private sectors, ultimately exhausts its resources and results in huge deficits.

There was one bright spot in New York State's employment profile. Producer services displayed an unusually high level of employment growth. The outputs of producer services are likely to be consumed by goods-producing industries. This may indicate some strength among those manufacturing establishments that are still operating in the state. Moreover, Goe (1990) has demonstrated that producer services can generate their own exports, making them a potential source of surplus revenues for a regional economy. There is, however, a caveat. In a questionnaire study of producer-service establishments in four of Ohio's regions, Goe presents evidence that strongly suggests that a region's loss in manufacturing jobs, coupled with the magnitude of its manufacturing employment, are highly related to the degree to which outputs from its producer services are consumed by businesses rather than by local households (1990:335, Tables 1 and 4). For example, in the Cleveland PMSA, the 1974 manufacturing work force was 287,000. Between 1974 and 1986, the region experienced a 28.6 percent decline in the manufacturing employment. In 1986, about 68 percent of its producer-services output went to other business and productive enterprises. At the other end of the continuum, the Youngstown/Warren MSA lost almost 52 percent of its 92,000 manufacturing jobs over the same period. In 1986, about 29 percent of its producer services output went to other business and productive enterprises. This finding suggests that, in heavily deindustrialized regions and/or in regions with a small manufacturing economy, producer services come to resemble private-consumptive services, relying on local households as key consumers. Thus, the strong growth in New York State's producer service, especially in its most deindustrialized regions, may not indicate anything positive about the remaining manufacturing base, nor indicate anything about the potential for exporting services.

This study has focused on regions rather than on the United States as a whole, but it offers solid evidence that the United States can no longer afford to ignore its manufacturing sector. Long-term economic decline in New York State can be generalized to the nation as a whole. Once upon a time, when a region in the United States lost its capacity to manufacture a product, it usually meant that some other U.S. region could do it better or cheaper or both. For example, the turn-of-the-century decline of textiles in the Northeast was accompanied by increased activity in the Southeast (Heckman 1984). While New England lost, the U.S. economy as a whole gained, since textiles were still thriving in southeastern states such as North Carolina. If New Englanders lost their jobs, they could move to some other place in the United States where work was easier to find. The growth in California's population surged as the Midwestern dustbowlers in the 1930s sought work in the promised land. In that distant time and from a national perspective, such glib concepts as "creative destructions" almost made sense.

Today, the game has radically changed. U.S. markets no longer belong to U.S. producers, and we have a global economy where political boundaries, ethnic and cultural differences, and a host of other sociological phenomena heavily influence the way business is conducted. In the past, the U.S. government could level some of the more obvious humps on the playing field where economic actors encountered one another through such legal anti-trust devices as the Sherman and Clayton Acts. Nowadays, the political realities of international competition handcuff such efforts. A region's loss in market share and employment in such industries as steel, textiles, autos, consumer electronics, or computer peripherals—all of which have drastically declined in the United States as a whole—more than likely means that another nation has come to control production. The result is not only a loss in the nation's capacity to provide people with employment, but it also involves a loss in the nation's ability to manufacture these products. And if the experience of New York State is any indication of this process, losses in productive capacity asphyxiate the growth in the service economy, ultimately leading to its demise.

The moral of our story is simply this: the United States is not likely to witness the coming of a post-industrial service society without a flourishing manufacturing sector. To ensure this coming, the United States must reorient its priorities and use government policy to reestablish a competitive manufacturing sector. But this will require an industrial policy that is sensitive to the ways that U.S. economic activities are linked to one another, something that is completely absent from the current stock of ideas that dominate today's policy makers.

We wish to thank Jennifer Parker for her help in preparing the statistical analysis presented in this paper and Ann Rotchford for her comments and assistance during the preparation of this and other drafts of the manuscript. Research for this paper was supported by NSF Grant Soc. 8609718 and the Russell Sage Foundation.

# References

AUSTRIAN, Z., and T. J. ZLATOPER. 1988. "The Role of Export Services." *REI Review* (Autumn): 24–29.

BACON, R., and W. ELTIS. 1976. *Britain's Economic Problem: Too Few Producers.* London: Macmillan.

BARNETT, R. J., and R. E. MULLER. 1974. *Global Reach: Power in Multinational Corporations.* New York: Simon and Schuster.

BELL, D. 1973. *The Coming of Post-Industrial Society: A Venture in Social Forecasting.* New York: Basic Books.

BERGMAN, E. M., and H. A. GOLDSTEIN. 1983. "Dynamics of Structural Change in Metropolitan Economies." *American Planning Association Journal* (Summer):263–279.

BEYERS, W. B. 1989. *The Producer Services and Economic Development in the United States: The Last Decade.* Washington, D.C.: Economic Development Administration, Technical Assistance and Research Division, U.S. Department of Commerce.

BIRCH, D. L. 1979. *The Job Generation Process.* Cambridge, MA: MIT Program on Neighborhood and Regional Change.

BLUESTONE, B., and B. HARRISON. 1982. *The Deindustrialization of America: Plant Closings, Community Abandonment, and the Dismantling of Basic Industry.* New York: Basic Books.

BROWNING, H., and J. SINGELMANN. 1978. "The Transformation of the US Labor Force: the Interaction of Industry and Occupation." *Politics and Society* 8:481–509.

*BusinessWeek.* June 30, 1980. "The Reindustrializing of America." Pp. 56–146.

———. January 27, 1986. "The Prophets of Doom have a Dismal Record." P. 22.

———. August 7, 1989. "Rethinking Japan: the New Harder Line toward Tokyo." Pp. 44–52.

———. October 23, 1989. "Computers: Japan Comes on Strong." Pp. 104–112.

CHANDLER, A. D. 1969. *Strategy and Structure: Chapters in the History of the American Industrial Enterprise.* Cambridge, MA: MIT Press.

———. 1977. *The Visible Hand: the Managerial Revolution in American Business.* Cambridge, MA: Harvard University Press.

CLARK, C. 1940. *The Conditions of Economic Progress and Security.* London: Macmillan.

COHEN, S. S., and J. ZYSMAN. 1987. *Manufacturing Matters: the Myth of the Post-Industrial Society.* New York: Basic Books.

———. 1988. "Manufacturing Innovation and American Industrial Competitiveness." *Science* 239:1110–1115.

COUNCIL OF ECONOMIC ADVISERS. 1985. *Economic Report of the President.* Washington, D.C.: Government Printing Office (February).

DANIELS, P. W. 1983. "Business Service Offices in British Provincial Cities: Location and Control." *Environmental Planning* 15:101–120.

———. 1985. *Service Industries: A Geographic Apprisal.* London: Methuen.

FELLOWS, J. 1988. "America's Changing Economic Landscape." In F. Hearn ed., *The Transformation of Industrial Organization: Management, Labor and Society in the United States.* Belmont, CA: Wadsworth, pp. 312–333.

FISHER, A. 1935. *The Clash of Progress and Security.* London: Macmillan.

*Forbes.* April 11, 1983. "You Mean We've Been Speaking Prose All These Years?" Pp. 143–149.

———. April 1, 1991. "Can Anyone Stop Bill Gates?" Pp. 108–114.

*Fortune.* June 17, 1991. "Who's Winning the Computer Race?" Pp. 58–70.

———. July 15, 1991. "Why Japan Keeps on Winning." Pp. 76–85.

GELLESPIE, A. E., and A. E. GREEN. 1987. "The Changing Geography of Producer Services Employment in Britain." *Regional Studies* 21:397–411.

GERSHUNY, J., and I. MILES. 1983. *The New Service Economy: the Transformation of Employment in Industrial Society.* London: Frances Pinter.

GERSUNY, W., and W. R. ROSENGREN. 1973. *The Service Society.* Cambridge, MA: MIT Press.

GILLIS, W. R. 1987. "Can Service-Producing Industries Provide a Catalyst for Regional Economic Growth?" *Economic Development Quarterly* 1:249–256.

GOE, W. R. 1990. "Producer Services, Trade, and the Social Division of Labor." *Regional Studies* 24:327–342.

GRANOVETTER, M. 1985. "Economic Action and Social Structure: the Problem of Embeddedness." *American Journal of Sociology* 91:481–510.

GREENFIELD, H. I. 1966. *Manpower and Growth in the Producer Services.* New York: Columbia University Press.

GROSHEN, E. G. 1987. "Can Services be a Source of Export-led Growth? Evidence from the Fourth District." *Economic Review Federal Reserve Bank of Cleveland* 3:2–15.

HARRIS, C. S. 1987. "Magnitude of Job Loss." In P. D. Staudohar and H. E. Brown eds., *Deindustrialization and Plant Closure.* Lexington, MA: Lexington Books, pp. 89–100.

HECKMAN, J. S. 1984. "The Product Life Cycle and New England Textiles." *Quarterly Journal of Economics* 74:697–717.

HUTTON, T., and D. LEY. 1989. "Location, Linkage and Labour: the Downtown Complex of Corporate Activities in a Medium Size City, Vancouver, British Columbia." *Economic Geographer* 63:126–141.

KEIL, S. R., and R. S. MACK. 1986. "Identifying Export Potential in the Service Sector." *Growth and Change* (April):2–10.

KORMAN, H., F. P. ROMO, J. LEE, D. CHAN, and M. SCHWARTZ. 1989. "Comparative Costs as the Engine of Industrial Migration: Another Pseudo Fact." Paper presented at the American Sociological Association Meetings, San Francisco (August).

LAWRENCE, R. Z. 1983. "The Myth of Deindustrialization." *Challenge* (November & December):12–21.

———. 1984. *Can America Compete?* Washington, D.C.: Brookings Institution.

LIESNER, T. 1985. *Economic Statistics 1900–1983: United Kingdom, United States of America, France, Germany, Italy, Japan.* London: The Economist Publications Ltd.

MARSHALL, J. N. 1982. "Linkages Between Manufacturing Industry and Business Services." *Environmental Planning* 14:523–540.

———. 1983. "Business-Service Activities in British Provincial Conurbations." *Environmental Planning* 15:1343–1359.

———. 1985. "Business Services, the Regions and Regional Policy." *Regional Studies* 19:353–364.

———. 1989. "Corporate Reorganization and the Geography of Services: Evidence from the Motor Vehicle Aftermarket in the West Midlands Region of the U.K." *Regional Studies* 28:139–150.

MCKENZIE, R. B. 1979. *Restrictions on Business Mobility.* Washington, D.C.: American Enterprise Institute.

MOORE, T. S. 1988. "Deindustrialization and the Dynamics of Local Employment Change." In M. Wallace and J. Rothschild, eds., *Research in Politics and Society: Deindustrialization and the Restructuring of American Industries.* Greenwich, CT: JAI Press, pp. 109–126.

NEW YORK STOCK EXCHANGE. 1984. *U.S. Competitiveness: Perception and Reality.* New York: New York Stock Exchange (August):32.

NORTHCLIFFE, G. B. 1975. "A Theory of Manufacturing Places." In L. Collins and D. F. Walker, eds., *Locational Dynamics of Manufacturing Activities.* New York: John Wiley and Sons, pp. 19–25.

NOYELLE, T. J., and T. M. STANBACK. 1984. *The Economic Transformation of American Cities.* Totowa, NJ: Rowman and Allenheld.

OCHEL, W., and M. WAGNER. 1987. *Service Economies in Europe: Opportunities for Growth.* Boulder, CO: Westvies.

OFFICE OF THE U.S. TRADE REPRESENTATIVE. 1983. *Annual Report of the President of the United States on the Trade Agreements Program.* Washington, D.C.: Government Printing Office.

———. 1984–1985. *Annual Report of the President of the United States on the Trade Agreements Program.* Washington, D.C.: Government Printing Office.

PERRY, D. C. 1987. "The Politics of Dependency in Deindustrializing America: The Case of Buffalo, New York." In M. P. Smith and J. R. Feagin, eds., *The Capital City.* New York: Basil Blackwell, pp. 113–137.

PLUNKET, L. M. 1990. "Job Growth and Industry Shifts in the 1980's." *Monthly Labor Review* 9:3–17.

QUICK, P. D. 1988. "Businesses: Reagan's Industrial Policy." In F. Hearn, ed., *The Transformation of Industrial Organization: Management, Labor and Society in the United States.* Belmont, CA: Wadsworth, pp. 342–355.

RAINS, J. C., L. BERSON, and D. GRACIE. 1982. *Community and Capital in Conflict: Plant Closings and Job Loss.* Philadelphia, PA: Temple University Press.

ROMO, F. P., H. KORMAN, P. BRANTLEY, and M. SCHWARTZ. 1986. "The Causes of Industrial Decline: An Analytical Model." Paper presented at the American Sociological Association, New York (August).

———. 1988. "The Rise and Fall of Regional Political Economies: a Theory of the Core." In M. Wallace and J. Rothschild, eds., *Research in Politics and Society 3: Deindustrialization and the Economic Restructuring of American Business.* Greenwich, CT: JAI Press, pp. 37–64.

ROMO, F. P., and M. SCHWARTZ. 1990. "Escape from New York." *Challenge* (January & February):18–25.

———. 1991. "The Structural Embeddedness of Business Decisions: a Sociological Assessment of Migration Behavior of Manufacturing Plants from New York between 1960 and 1995." *Russell Sage Foundation Working Papers* 16 (February).

ROOT, K. 1988. "Job Loss: Whose Fault, What Remedies?" In M. Wallace and J. Rothschild, eds., *Research in Politics and Society: Deindustrialization and the Restructuring of American Industries.* Greenwich, CT: JAI Press, pp. 65–84.

ROSENBERG, N. 1982. *Inside the Black Box: Technology and Economics.* New York: Cambridge University Press.

SCHUMPETER, J. 1942. *Capitalism, Socialism and Democracy.* New York: Harper & Row.

SHELP, R. K. 1981. *Beyond Industrialization: Ascendancy of the Global Service Economy.* New York: Praeger.

STANBACK, T. M. 1979. *Understanding the Service Economy.* Baltimore, MD: The Johns Hopkins University Press.

STANBACK, T. M., P. J. BLAUE, T. J. NOYELLE, and R. A. KONASEK. 1981. *Services: The New Economy.* Totowa, NJ: Allanheld Osmun.

THUROW, L. 1980. *The Zero-Sum Society.* New York: Basic Books.

TOURAINE, A. 1971. *The Post-Industrial Society.* New York: Random House.

TSCHETTER, J. 1987. "Producer Service Industries: Why Are They Growing So Fast?" *Monthly Labor Review* (December): 31–39.

USDA, ECONOMIC RESEARCH SERVICE. 1984. *Economic Indicators of the Farm Sector: Farm Sector Review 1983,* Report #ECIFS3–2. Washington, D.C.: USDA (August).

U.S. DEPARTMENT OF LABOR. 1988. "Employees in Nonagricultural Payrolls by Major Industries, 1936 to Date." *Employment and Earnings* 35:43.

WALKER, R. A. 1985. "Is There a Service Economy? The Changing Capitalist Division of Labor." *Science and Society* 49:42–83.

WALLACE, M., and J. ROTHSCHILD. 1988. "Plant Closings, Capital Flight and Worker Dislocation: the Long Shadow of Deindustrialization." In M. Wallace and J. Rothschild, eds., *Research in Politics and Society 3: Deindustrialization and the Economic Restructuring of American Industries.* Greenwich, CT: JAI Press, pp. 1–35.

WOOD, P. A. 1986. "The Anatomy of Job Loss and Job Gain: Some Speculations on the Role of the 'Producer Service' Sector." *Regional Studies* 20:37–46.

WU, S. Y., and H. KORMAN. 1987. "Socio Economic Impacts of Disinvestment on Communities in New York State." *The American Journal of Economics and Sociology* 46:261–271.

YAGO, G., H. KORMAN, S. Y. WU, and M. SCHWARTZ. 1984. "Investment and Disinvestment in New York State, 1960–1980." *Annals, AAPSS* 475:28–38.

# V

# SMALL FIRMS IN NETWORKS

# 14

# Small Firm Networks

## CHARLES PERROW

It is clear that the last fifteen years have seen dramatic changes in the form taken by economic organizations in North America, Europe, and Japan, generally favoring decentralized structures and loose alliances. In this chapter I briefly characterize this development, review three explanations for it, and argue that none of them have provided fully satisfactory accounts for the changes. One of the new forms to emerge, *nondependent subcontracting,* is discussed next. The most interesting form, *networks of small firms,* is the focus for the rest of the chapter. It is the least significant form in terms of economic output—on a worldwide basis the output of small firm networks is probably trivial—but I will argue that, although it is small and fairly new, it is a diverse and possibly durable economic phenomenon that deserves attention, and that conventional economic theories and leftist theories in particular have failed to grasp its importance. Small firm networks (SFNs) are significant in three respects that I consider: their potential for what I call the *production of trust,* a generally neglected and always unspecified factor of production; their welfare implications, such as effects on the distribution of wealth and power in society (which should be the final referent in all we do, I believe); and the fact that SFNs reverse a 150-year-old trend toward the absorption of society by large organizations. Before discussing the third significance of SFNs, I review the fundamental question of whether it is size or networks that is important, and conclude that one must have both small size and networking to realize the advantages of SFNs.

**Figure 14.1  Integrated Firm Model**

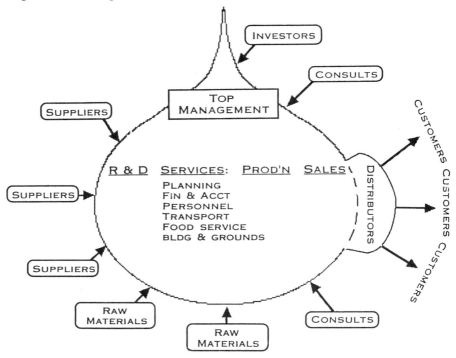

# The Integrated Firm, the M-Form, and Devolution

Figure 14.1 pictures the integrated firm (IF). This type of firm buys out as many of its competitors as it can and also integrates backward and forward to control as much of the "throughput," as Chandler (1977) calls it, from raw materials to final consumer as it can. It absorbs the sources of uncertainty in its environment, and in the process reduces the number of autonomous organizations in its environment. I have listed a few of its business and financial service functions to remind us that these also might have been performed by independent organizations before the integration took place. The IF deals with consultants and suppliers, of course, but in order to control transaction costs and throughput coordination it prefers to produce something itself rather than to buy it, according to theory. (The onion shape in Figure 14.1 indicates the post-1945 swelling of middle levels and the relative decline of the hourly workforce).

**Figure 14.2**

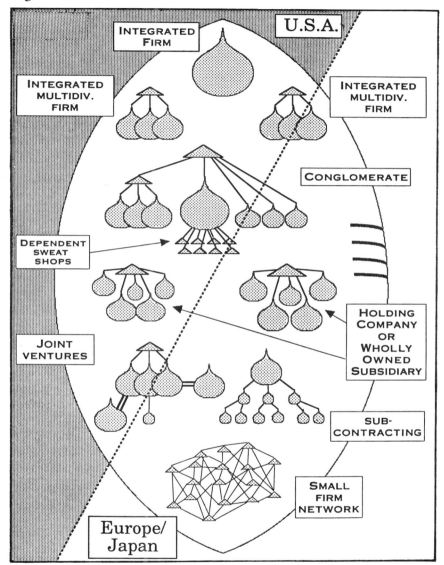

Figure 14.2 pictures some of the other forms of economic organizations we need to consider. It is shaped like an American football rather
than a continuum, because in between the two extremes—the integrated
firm and the SFN—there exist a variety of possibilities. Uniting a few

integrated firms in different products or in related industries produces the multidivisional firm, and uniting a multidivisional with some integrated firms—possibly including some with highly dependent subcontractors or sweat shops—produces the conglomerate. If the state owns conglomerates, we have command economies; if they are in private hands, we have advanced capitalism.

That is roughly an account of the economic history of the United States from, say, 1850 to 1970 or so. Most of the firms of the industrial United States are still at the integrated production end of the football; the large and powerful ones have become multidivisional (and multinational, of course) or conglomerate firms. But, supposedly in response to competition from abroad, U.S. firms have been devolving, downsizing, delayering, breaking up, spinning off, and combining in joint ventures. The forms in the figure that indicate joint ventures and the holding company or the wholly owned subsidiary only feebly represent the variety of forms involved in this change (see Powell 1990 and Sabel 1992 for a better indication of these). These forms have been much in evidence in Europe and Japan at least since the 1960s, but my impression is that they are less evident in the United States.

More radical forms are illustrated by the subcontracting and the small firm network diagrams in Figure 14.2. Both of these will be discussed in detail shortly, but for the present suffice it to say that the subcontracting model involves a greater degree of devolution, with perhaps 70 percent of the components produced by independent firms, which are generally under 100 employees in size. The small firm network is even more radical, with nothing but small firms of five to ten to twenty persons who produce a large variety of goods and services—almost everything except extractive goods and basic industrial output.

## Why the Change toward Decentralized Structure?

Three arguments provide reasons for the emergence of SFNs and nondependent subcontracting.

### Argument I: Flexible Production

Proponents of this theory are optimistic about the efficiencies of deconcentration, and cite such things as:

- a flexible response to changing and fragmented markets, because small suppliers have more direct information and have it more quickly than the specialized units of a large bureaucracy;

- small units have more widely skilled personnel who can be redeployed more quickly;
- information technology reduces transaction delays and costs when firm A searches for the best supplier among firms B, C, and D, thus offsetting the advantage large firms have from centralized purchasing or in-house suppliers;
- technological changes that make the production of small runs and changes in products more feasible;
- in the small firm effort is more directly related to reward, and there are more chances of ownership status;
- nonspecialized tasks in smaller organizations reduce the separation between conception and execution.

Note that while I have emphasized the role of size in this list, there is nothing to prevent a large bureaucracy from restructuring itself to realize most of the gains on the list. The grand outlines of this school are best represented by Charles Sabel, Michael Piore, and Jonathan Zeitlin (see, e.g., Piore and Sabel 1984, Sabel 1989, Sabel and Zeitlin 1985).

### *Argument 2: Capitalist Failure*

Less sanguine are the critics of capitalism, who cite the externalization of social costs to smaller units. In particular, they cite harder work, longer hours, less pay, no union protection, and the absorption of risk by the small firm (see, e.g., Murray 1983; 1987; Hyman 1988; Smith 1989; Pollert 1988; Sakai 1990; Wood 1988; and—for an ambivalent effort to come to terms with flexible specialization by the Left—Thompson 1989.) Ironically, for capitalism's critics, as bad as big organizations are, big organizations are better than small ones if capitalism reigns. Big organizations have better labor practices, internal labor markets, more social services, and there is even evidence from the United States that large, bureaucratic firms promote more cognitive complexity among employees than do small firms.[1] Though I have not seen it discussed, I would anticipate a "self-exploitation" argument here as well: the fetish of consump-

---

[1] Kohn and Schooler's 1983 work (Ch. 2) shows that men who work in bureaucratic organizations—blue-collar as well as white-collar—are more likely than those in nonbureaucratic organizations to display cognitive complexity and flexibility, open-mindedness, personal responsibility, and self-direction, and to value change. They emphasize the protection that large, permanent bureaucratic organizations provide, rather than the attributes of size per se, but it is still a warning about the dynamics of small organizations in the United States.

tion drives the people in small firms to work long hours in order to accumulate and spend. An additional anticapitalist explanation, independent of the above claims about exploitation, asserts that the deconcentration in the United States can be explained by the collapse of U.S. industrial hegemony. Rather than buying up cheap industrial property to further integrate vertically and horizontally, the giants are getting rid of their own property and speculate with the proceeds. Here the U.S. response is different from that of other countries. Having acquired hegemony through market control and monopsony, when faced with superior quality and more efficient production from other countries, the U.S. firms can only sell off units and trade with the proceeds. But there is a worldwide decline of profits and intensification of competition, according to this branch of the "capitalism's failure" argument, and this affects the Japanese and European firms that have emphasized flexibility and quality. These firms are externalizing social costs through contracting out, thus contributing to the changes in organizational forms.

### Argument 3: Organizational Failure

Along with the first argument—flexible production—this theory emphasizes flexibility and speed, but it is less concerned with broad upskilling, independency, and, still to be discussed, fostering cooperation through networks. Instead, this type of explanation looks more to organizational efficiency concerns that are often associated with management schools, even with "agency theory" (see Perrow 1986a or 1986b for a critique of agency theory). Here, in the organizational failure argument, big firms have gotten too big; internal vested interests create a small-numbers bargaining position with which top management cannot cope: these vested interests create inflexibilities and inefficiencies when markets are fragmenting and technologies changing.[2]

There are two variants of interest in this approach, a structural and an entrepreneurial one. As an example of the first, Swedish organizational theorist Bengt Stymne (1989: 16–17) argues that management is whipped at both ends of the labor market by a "rigid wage structure," which prevents rewarding the specialized people much in demand ("management experts, software experts, engineers, etc."), so they leave to form

---

[2] There is a rueful acknowledgement of these organizational failures in Williamson's work, both the 1975 and the 1985 volumes, but it hardly encumbers his transaction cost analysis. Similarly, Chandler jolts one out the somnolence of ever-increasing production figures in the very last pages of his very long 1977 volume, *The Visible Hand,* with a plaintive query about the costs of giganticism. Neither acknowledgments deflect their authors' relentless efficiency arguments.

their own companies. At the other end, the rigid wage structure overpays unskilled workers for such jobs as cleaning, transport, and copying, so outside firms offer cleaning people at lower prices. The second variant emphasizes the stifling of initiative for true entrepreneurs in large firms. Instead these break free and start their own companies. (That these entrepreneurs hope to make their own firms large and thus stifling never receives comment.)

## Inadequacies of the Explanations

All three of these arguments or explanations—flexible production, capitalist failure, and organizational failure—have their merits. But I am still puzzled by the deconcentration of U.S. firms that is said to be going on, because I should think they would have the wit to capture the profit stream of suppliers and distributors, and enlarge that stream because of the increased market control that would come from vertical integration. And they certainly could continue their historical role of buying out the best of the entrepreneurs after a niche is discovered and made profitable.

The big firm does not need to spin off or sell off parts of itself and become smaller to be efficient as so many claim; each time it does so, it loses some of the profit stream. Most of the advantages of flexible specialization can be achieved by the judicious restructuring of the big firm— by flattening the overall hierarchy through the creation of many extra subunits, each with considerable autonomy. This way the firm keeps the ultimate prize, namely the contribution to overall profit that the effort of each unit brings. But if the firm downsizes by creating a subsidiary, it must give up part of the profits to the head, who takes the risks. It is the same with a joint venture. If the head of the unit is salaried, then the firm takes the profits. But if downsizing means loss of profit opportunities, why has it happened?

It was only yesterday that we were told by economists that the success of the multidivisional form, and of large firms in general, was due to their ability to innovate and provide for a bewildering variety of styles and models. Diversification was an appropriate hedge as well as a source of innovative ideas. Economies of scale appeared to have no upper bounds, since the bigger the firm, the more power it would have in the capital market, and the more cross-subsidization it could do to help a struggling line. Technological changes also made flexible and decentralized, short product runs available to the rich big firms, permitting "flexible mass production." With all of these advantages, plus their market power and their political power, the big corporation's need to restructure should be minimal.

One factor surely seems to have changed substantially that might account for the new competition: the new technologies allow multipurpose machines and equipment, and rapid data processing. These undoubtedly facilitate decentralized production. But they also make it just as possible to have highly flexible *centralized* production with attendant economies of scale in terms of research and development, personnel allocation, and so on. The technological tide should raise the level of both big and small firms; the big firms should be able to benefit sufficiently to not need to spin off, sell off, contract out, and engage in joint ventures. However, these technological changes may still favor small firms in the sense that they put them closer to technological parity with the big firms. Both benefit, in other words, but the small firm benefits more.

In any case, integrated production is a way to capture returns while allowing for market and firm growth. It is effective for owners if 1) markets are controlled sufficiently also to control the rate of product and technological change (it is not necessary to suppress it); 2) if the market is stable for other reasons, such as oligopoly, near saturation, technological stability, or government regulation; or, though this is less frequent, 3) if small firms are unable to evade governmental laws and regulations and thus cannot outperform large firms. The first two of these three conditions permit the economies of scale that come from mass production and the possibility of lowering the quality of goods and services in order to increase returns. Mass production is not only the result of market control: mass production itself encourages a firm to seek market control because of the cost of capital tied up in mass production; market control makes it easier to keep investments working. Once a market breaks up into pieces that require different types of activities, such as frequent changes in production lines, for example producing nonformula motion picture films—see Storper (1989)—or generating new financial services, firms with integrated production will be threatened by new firms offering the new goods or services. To these we will finally turn.

## Nondependent Subcontracting

The next form in Figure 14.2—subcontracting—is a distinct new form that grew quickly in Japan from the 1960s on. It may also be well represented in Europe, but I am unsure about that. I will refer to it as the *nondependent subcontracting model*. Here the firm has a first line of subcontractors (perhaps 300 is the most that can be managed, even by a big auto firm), and these in turn have second and third lines of subcontractors, most of which are quite small. In some elaborate examples the second and third tiers have more than one customer, that is, the subcontractor will sell to two or more primary firms. Conceivably, the prime contractors can also have other customers. Note that the picture of the subcontracting model is a picture of an Integrated Firm (IF), except for the fact that all of these are independent firms. We lack the all-important line drawn around the firms, indicating ownership and retention of profits and responsibility for losses. Retaining their own profits instead of passing them on to headquarters may very well be the most important difference between the subcontracting and the IF models. But that again raises the question of why the parent firm does not just buy up the subcontractors and appropriate their profits. The most pleasant hypothesis is that the owners would not work as hard if they were employees, and the employees themselves would not work as hard for the big corporation as they did for the original owner of the small firm.

The Japanese favor the nondependent subcontracting model. In general, Japan has a higher proportion of small firms than does the United States, though the gross figure can be misleading. More to the point is the fact that, while General Motors (like most large European auto firms) makes 50 percent of the car, the average auto firm in Japan makes only 30 percent of the car. While GM deals directly with 3,500 parts suppliers, the Japanese firm deals directly with between 100 and 300 component suppliers. And these latter, in their turn, deal with about 5,000 subcontractors, arranged in tiers (Best 1991:163).

Subcontractors in Japan are no longer dependent upon the big organizations they sell to, according to Nishiguchi (1993) and Best (1991). They have a say in pricing and in design, they supply modules rather than single parts, their wage rates are nearly as high as their customers' rates, and they have several customers.

There is a quite depressing side to the Japanese miracle in terms of driving labor (Dohse, Jurgens, and Malsch 1985; Sakai 1990) and the exploitation of women, but they are not essential to the organizational form. They could be eliminated, and Best and others appear to believe that they have been mitigated to some extent.

## Small Firm Networks

Finally, there is the SFN. Imagine breaking up the Integrated Firm into units whose average number of employees is ten each. Instead of 2,000 employees in one firm, for example, there would be 200 firms of ten employees each. Figure 14.3 captures the essentials of this form. It is new to this half of the twentieth century, but existed already in the nine-

**Figure 14.3   Small Firm Networks**

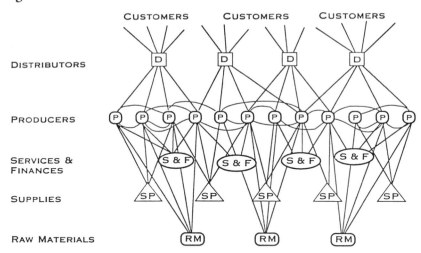

teenth century, as Sabel and Zeitlin (1985) and Best (1991) have argued.[3]

The firms are usually very small, say ten people. The firms interact with each other, sharing information, equipment, personnel, and orders, even as they compete with one another (see Figure 14.3). They are supplied by a small number of financial service firms and business service firms (which provide business surveys, technical training, personnel administration, transport, research and development, etc.). There are, of course, also suppliers of equipment, energy, consumables, raw-material suppliers, and so on. Finally, although some producers may do their own marketing and distribution, it seems to be more common for them to have a fair number of quite small distributors, which is especially striking since SFNs typically export most of their output.

The small firms are surrounded by an infrastructure that is essential for their survival and for their economies of network scale. This infrastructure consists of local and regional governments that provide roads, cheap land, educational services, and even financing; and of trade asso-

[3] The classic piece comparing "flexible production" through small firms (what I refer to as Small Firm Networks) in the nineteenth and the late twentieth century is that of Sabel and Zeitlin (1985). For a good account of the Springfield Armory as an SFN, or more accurately, as a network of small firms serving a final assembler as in the nondependent subcontractor model, see Best (1991:29–45). A striking comparison of the putting-out system in the eighteenth and nineteenth century with SFNs in the Modena knitwear industry today is found in Lazerson (1991).

ciations that provide economic information, training, financing, and marketing services. Both government agencies and trade associations, along with unions, monitor unfair business and labor practices.[4] Unfortunately, the notion of economies of scale that attach to a network of firms has not been much developed since it was first discussed in 1919 by Alfred Marshall (1919:283–288). One assumes that, although shared investments in equipment may be involved, most of the economies of scale come from shared information and efficient allocation of labor or human resources.

SFNs do not exist in heavy industry or extractive industry. In the final assembly for large goods, such as autos, we have the nondependent subcontracting form rather than a true SFN. SFNs, however, are said to exist in industries of clothing, food, light machinery, metalworking, electronics, and small- to medium-sized electronic goods, ceramics, furniture, auto components, motorcycles, small engines, machine tools, robots, textile and packaging machinery, mining equipment, industrial filters, and agricultural machinery. But it is not clear from the literature that in all these cases *networks* of small firms are involved, though in most of them such networks do exist.

There is a tendency to dismiss the importance of SFNs by tarring them with the brush of small firms in general, which are held to be exploitative, or by limiting them to consumer products from northern Italy, or even to simply textile firms in Prato, and to speak then of these as "sweat shops." But this is clearly wrong. Small firms are ubiquitous in all countries, and they are generally havens for low wages, dependency, and exploitation. But I am referring exclusively to *networks* of small firms with ties to each other and to multiple customers and suppliers. While there is some evidence of exploitation—often self-exploitation through ten- or eleven-hour work days—in textile firms in Prato and Modena in northern Italy, the literature almost always stresses the prosperity of the firms and the locality, as well as the skill of the workforce, when these economic issues are discussed.

---

[4]The literature on the infrastructure is now substantial, and this monitoring and facilitating it is one of two things that sharply distinguish *networks* of small firms from *clusters* of small firms about a dominant buyer. (The other is the minimal and very competitive contacts among small firms where they are dependent on a few big customers.) See one of the first articles on SFNs in Brusco (1982), as well as Brusco (1986), Brusco and Righi (1989) and also Herrigel (1988), Piore and Sabel (1984), Sabel (1989), and Trigilia (1986). Best (1991) provides some highly detailed discussion of infrastructure in northern Italy, with excellent accounts of business services and financing. Excellent details on computer clones and box-making and packaging-machinery industries can be found in Capecchi (1989). A detailed account of the role of unions in very small firms can be found in Herman (1990).

Ash Amin (1989), for example, finds that wages are high in "industrial districts" (which is another term for SFNs), and discredits the low-wage and exploitation thesis. Capecchi (1989) speaks at one point of "widespread" exploitation (without giving any details), but also notes some contrary facts about Emilia-Romagna. Child labor has declined; daycare centers have expanded (12 percent of children under three are in daycare in Bologna, while only 0.3 percent are in daycare in Naples); and there has been a sizeable decrease in the birthrate and in the proportion of "housewives." There has also been an increase in the educational level, with females surpassing males in high school and university studies; and a rising demand for instruction in physical exercise, nutrition, and so on. Emilia-Romagna has one of the lowest unemployment rates in Italy, and there is a growing demand for personal and household services. Taplin (1989) notes in his study of the textile industry in Prato, Italy that employment relations are largely nonadversarial, but that subcontractors who set up small workshops can impose long hours and poor benefits. Mark Lazerson, in an early draft of his 1991 manuscript, offered evidence of long hours and dangerous conditions for some young women in the knitting industry of Modena, but also noted the prosperity of the region. One should also note the failure of the exploited workers to seek work in nearby textile factories that offer better wages and benefits.

We have excellent empirical evidence, from Italian social scientists and others, about the reality and success of SFNs in northern Italy.[5] The next best documented case is a mountain town in Japan, which produces machine tools (Friedman, 1988). There is less detailed evidence, but at least some, from Germany, Denmark, perhaps Sweden, and France.[6] There is an emerging, struggling case outside of Madrid, in electronics (Benton 1986). There is a debate about the character of Silicon Valley in the United States (Florida and Kenney 1990; Saxenian 1991a),[7] and if we

[5] In addition to those already cited, see the just-completed dissertation by Kozul (1991), which contrasts the booming SFN furniture industry in northern Italy with the failing Integrated Production one in Yugoslavia.

[6] For several of these countries, see the general discussions in Sabel (1989), Piore and Sabel (1984), and Best (1991). For France, see Lorenz (1988). For mechanical engineering and machine tools in Germany, see all three Herrigel citations. The Swedish example, the area around Växsjö, is discussed in Johannisson (1990), but from the point of view of the entrepreneur rather than the relations among firms. It appears that there is no common product in this burst of small-firm industry in a thoroughly agricultural region of Sweden, but there is considerable sharing of entrepreneurial ideas and perhaps also of resources. This may be true of Jutland, in Denmark, as well, but the information is scanty.

[7] See Sabel's essay on studied trust in this anthology for an optimistic U.S. study in progress, and Saxenian (1991a) for a network description of Silicon Valley. But the account that Florida and Kenney give of the rapacious, short-sighted, individual self-interest

**Figure 14.4   Dependency and Independency in Networks**

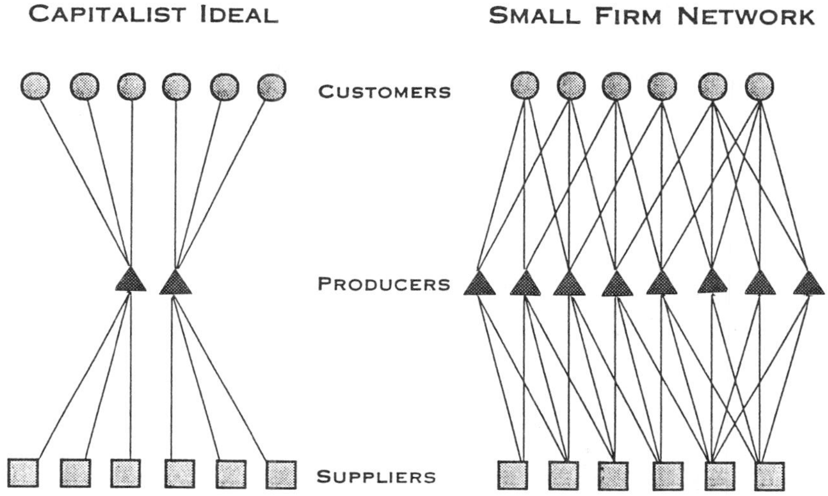

count it as an SFN, it is about the only case I know of in the United States. There is no evidence of SFNs in Ireland or Britain (as distinct from small firms; for the growth of these, see Keeble and Wever 1986; for the failure of flexible specialization, see Hirst and Zeitlin 1989). So the SFS phenomenon is not, as many still continue to think, limited to textiles or other soft consumer goods from northern Italy.

Though Figure 14.3, does not properly show this, an essential point is that any focal organization has multiple upstream and downstream ties with customers and suppliers. Figure 14.4 makes the basic point. Burt (1983) has done the most to explicate and demonstrate this empirically, but Pfeffer and Salancik (1978) have a cogent discussion of this phenomenon in connection with the resource dependency model, and the basic strategy is as old as capitalism. If you stand at the narrow waist, you can play several customers or suppliers off against each other. These are forced to trade with you—or with your nominal competitor. If you stand in the broad waist of the SFN, however, your customers have several choices, and so do your suppliers. A lot of potential power that is concentrated in the capitalist ideal is therefore dissipated in the SFN.

maximizing firms in Silicon Valley is very depressing, even if Saxenian is correct that the trusting network, while limited to the small firms, is still important. See Florida and Kenney (1990, chaps. 5–7). Christopherson and Storper (1989) and Storper (1989) find evidence of flexible specialization in the motion picture industry. An example from the New England fishing industry is discussed in the section "Welfare Functions" later in this chapter.

I should point out that this is a "structural" basis for cooperation. Firms have no option but to avoid deception and exploitation, because if they do not, someone else will get the business. The antitrust legislation in the United States was initially intended to create this structural condition, but failed to do so for a large number of reasons. But a multiple-tie network may exist not only because of the essentially negative reason that it forestalls maximizing self-interest with guile, but also for the positive reason that it makes the sector or industry more flexible, stimulates innovation, and maximizes sectorwide problem solving. The returns come first to the sector or the local industry, and the health of any single firm is known to be dependent upon the collectivity of competitive firms.

These positive reasons may account for the appearance of the highly successful subcontracting model in Japan. This type of organization seems to be able to gain the benefits of multiple ties without actually having multiple ties at all levels. In Figure 14.5 we can see an SFN existing up to the level of the producers, where it is replaced by a structure that permits the creation of highly dependent relations at the subassembly level and in its ties with final assembly in the parent firm. The fact that the parent does not appear to exploit the subassembly independent firms (nor do these exploit their strategic advantage over the producers) suggests that this aspect of trust can be produced without the structural condition of the previous figure—the broad waist. There is other evidence, for example, in German firms, of the dominant firm insisting that their subcontractors do no more than one-third of their business with the dominant firm, thus voluntarily giving up strategic power over suppliers in order to ensure the viability and health of those suppliers. This, of course, is just the opposite of the strategy used by the integrated firm, which controls its suppliers to the extent of absorbing them, and it contradicts the arguments of transaction costs analysis.

There exist other reasons why networks of small firms do not become "Chandlerized" and end up as one integrated firm. It is not that the members are less greedy or competitive than our industrial ancestors and their present offspring in the United States; it is rather that competition requires continual innovation in methods and products. This necessitates the full use and commitment of employees, and this is best achieved by reducing the gap between conception and execution, which is the gap introduced by Taylorism. Though the large firm is not incapable of reducing this gap (see Sabel 1991 on the Moebius-Strip firm), the small firm does so as a matter of course. The small firm thus can react more quickly and fruitfully to change in technology and markets. This has been

**Figure 14.5  Subcontracting Model**

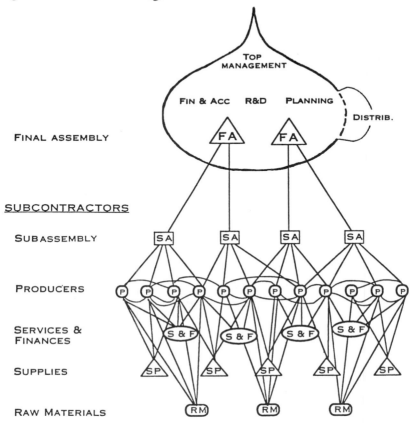

the consistent explanation for small firm networks since the initial work of Brusco, Sable, Piore, and Zeitlin.

## Explaining Small Firm Networks

Small as the phenomenon of SFNs is, it is theoretically implausible and violates established theories of industrialization of both the Right and the Left.

According to the Right, we should only have Integrated Production and multidivisional firms as described in the magnificent synthesis of Alfred DuPont Chandler (1977). He emphasizes that *technology* made it possible to greatly increase the size of vertically integrated firms and permit economies of *scale;* that vertical integration and technology permitted *efficient* throughput coordination from raw material to consumer outlet; and that *bureaucracy* made it possible to control exquisitely the mass of employees and the diversity of processes and products. We can include Oliver Williamson (1975; 1985) here, with his emphasis upon making sure that you will not be cheated in your transactions, which is solved by buying out your suppliers and distributors and settling disputes autocratically instead of by bargaining (see the critique of the markets and hierarchies approach in Lazerson 1988). But Chandler and Williamson have the problem of accounting for the apparent decline of the M-form (multidivisional form) and the large, Integrated Production form, and—unless it is exaggerated—the problem of also accounting for the appearance of so many SFNs around the world.

The problem with the account of the Right is the quite negligible role it assigns to trust and cooperation, or what is called "other regarding behavior," in economic affairs, and the dominant role it assigns to the maximization of individual self-interest. We cannot account for SFNs solely on the basis of varied and rapidly changing markets and the new technologies that allow for decentralized production. If this were the case, the big firms would find it profitable simply to decentralize and reward a multitude of small divisions for their flexibility, while retaining the "profit stream." They are trying this, of course. In fact, some on the Left feel the big firms will eventually displace SFNs as they spin off wholly owned subsidiaries. The Left argues this way because it has a power rather than efficiency explanation for the rise of Integrated Production and the M-form. Market power and political power supposedly account for their rise. While I share this emphasis on power, I also feel that the Left is burdened with an assumption that no longer applies.

The problem with the Left, then, is their view that, under capitalism and the capitalist state, change can only come from the *organization of the proletariat,* or the workers. The resulting change will be the reorganization of the *labor process* in order to eliminate exploitation and deskilling. The Left has little to say about firm size, interfirm networks, marketing techniques, product redesign, trade associations, competition, efficiencies, and the infrastructure that makes networks viable.

But those who created the SFNs were usually not alienated proletariats, but farmers, shopkeepers, and artisans; and instead of the organization of the proletariats, we find trade associations that facilitate commercial and industrial interactions. In some cases, especially in northern Italy, unions are important—but as regulators of labor conditions in small firms, as providers of business services, and as supporters of such things as autonomous work groups (Herman 1990). This effort by the unions has fallen on very rich soil, since the small firms already had strong inducements in that direction. No fight by workers against deskilling was needed; the production techniques and the changing market made skills necessary.

The Left, on the other hand, is correct that exploitation of labor always constitutes a problem, and especially so in small organizations. But *networks* of small organizations, which are supported and regulated by a revitalized local government, by trade associations of the small producers, and by unions in some cases, have managed greatly to limit exploitation in these regions. This job, no doubt, was made easier by the low unemployment levels and the remarkable prosperity of these areas.

Thus, powerful theories of both the Right and Left need to be questioned when we deal with SFNs. Both have neglected the economic power of three things that help to account for the success of SFNs: economies of scale through networks (still insufficiently theorized); trust and cooperation that both coexist with competition; and welfare effects that increase the efficiency of the region and industry. These may be as important as varied markets and new technologies.

## The Production of Trust

Let me elaborate on the production of trust in SFNs. The production of trust is difficult to demonstrate and even to illustrate. As Sabel notes in his remarkable essay in this anthology, trust seems only to be found retrospectively, and can never be created intentionally. I wish to argue that it is generated by structures, or contexts; and that these can be deliberately created, encouraging trust, even if trust itself cannot be deliberately created.

Here are some characteristics—all distinctive of SFNs—that are more likely to generate trusting than self-interest maximizing behavior in a group of firms:

- Information on markets, technologies, pay scales, and profits of firms is shared and discussed.
- Processes and techniques are sufficiently similar for firms to be able to understand and judge each other's behavior. (This is the difference between saying "I don't know how to make it, so I *have* to trust you," and saying "I know how to make it, so I *can* trust you.")
- Firms have experience of getting helped by another firm. (In fact, one should design incomplete organizations, so they have to ask each other for help.)

- The relationships between the firms are long term, though they may be intermittent.
- There is little difference among firms as to size, power, or strategic position.
- There is rotation of leadership when it comes to representing a number of firms.
- Similar financial rewards go to the firms and the employees within them.
- Firms collectively experience the economic advantages of increased sales and profit margins.
- There is an awareness of a bound community of fate, as generated by trade or professional associations, municipal service groups, unions, and the like.

Where these conditions exist, the possibility of trust is increased.

Elites have long known this, and ruling classes show many of these characteristics without the trust extending to those they rule. Employees of large firms generate some trust through unions, but it is small compared to elite cohesion and trust. One gets trust between owners and employees, and between owners in competing firms, when firms are small and networked. SFNs maximize the possibility for these conditions; the integrated production model does not, and the nondependent subcontracting model does so only partially.

## Welfare Functions

Big organizations did not invent *all* the curses of our times, but they certainly had a lot to do with the centralization of power and authority in modern societies. The larger the organization, the more power and authority at the top to hire, fire, develop, or enfeeble workers; to relocate; to influence politicians, influence elections, pollute, eliminate competitors, invest money, buy supplies from you or someone else, discriminate ethnically and sexually; and to corrupt. The bigger they are, the more power is generated, and the more concentrated it becomes.

If we take two furniture factories that each employ 5,000 people, and instead arrange them into 1,000 small firms with ten people in each, most producing furniture, but some marketing it, others delivering it, buying materials, doing the accounts, counseling employees, and so on, just think of the dispersion of power and authority. The example is not so far fetched as it might seem: the average firm size for the very prosperous furniture industry of the Lombardy province of Italy is under five (Kozul 1991; Best 1991).

Another thing that big organizations have not invented but have certainly perfected is hierarchy. Rights and privileges and authority and status are clearly defined and differentiated by rank or level in the organization, and movement from one rank to another is guarded by formal criteria. The big furniture firm will have a dozen major grades and many minor ones. These operate as a fine-tuning device as well as a rationalizer. But the small firm will have only two or three grades, and movement up and down them will be easy. A study of blue- to white-collar movement in Japanese firms found it very high in small firms, and low in very big ones (Friedman 1988). In Italy, people move back and forth from owner to worker to owner, as demand and styles change.

That takes care of two of the four horsemen of bureaucracy: centralization and hierarchy. The other two are formalization and standardization, which permit repetitive, high-volume production. Fortunately for small firms, formalization and standardization are minimized, simply because high-volume production is not a characteristic of the product markets that these firms service. Thus, the four dreadnoughts of bureaucracy will disintegrate when the large firm does, and they are neither reproduced in SFNs, nor do the networks find alternative ways to amass and concentrate power.

Another consequence of moving from integrated production to a network of small firms is that the distribution of wealth in society is affected, and thereby also the spending patterns. The heads of the small 1,000 firms in the furniture business will receive a great deal less in salary and benefits than the two heads of the two large firms. I support any development that will make the distribution of wealth more even without significantly changing the total amount, and if it can be done without taking taxes from the rich each year to provide inefficient programs for the poor—a politically expensive effort—all the better. Furthermore, one of the problems of uneven development and uneven economies associated with multidivisional and giant firms is that locally generated wealth is spent or invested nonlocally; it is taken from the city, province, region, or nation and sent elsewhere, enriching elsewhere and concentrating the wealth of the elsewhere. The wider distribution of wealth reduces this. None of the 1,000 owners is likely to make shopping trips from northern Italy to Paris and New York City, and they will use their village banks.

Finally, networks of small firms appear to be associated with strong local government institutions. SFNs seem to foster a more responsive educational system, more distributive policies regarding land use and city planning, a wider range of social services including child care, and perhaps also more political involvement of the citizens. These are particularly well discussed by Aydalot (1986) and Capecchi (1989). The network of firms and families also generate their own welfare functions in policing labor exploitation, lending money and equipment, and providing informal apprenticeships.

One of the most striking documentations of this comes from a comparison of two fishing towns, New Bedford and Gloucester in the United States (Doeringer, Moss, and Terkla 1986). In one of these, the fishing fleet was dominated by boats owned by capitalists who hired captains and crews. In the other, most of the fleet was owned by the individual captains, and family and friends and relatives made up the crew. The latter made longer-term investments in new equipment and methods, and shared work instead of using layoffs in slack time. When forced to lay people off, they chose the oldest who did not have growing families rather than the youngest or first hired; and when business picked up they responded more quickly, thereby benefiting the community.

## Size or Ties

In thinking about the positive consequences of SFNs that I have mentioned—the production of trust, the reduction of hierarchy, the wider distribution of wealth, and so on—I am at a loss to specify which of these stem from the "small" and which from the "networks" in the notion of SFNs. Clearly size is very important, and it is also the most convenient way of discussing bureaucracy. But small by itself is hardly beautiful. All of these propositions about consequences of size become unstable without ties, that is, networks. The small firms that are clustered about one or two mass marketers in the shoe industry in Alicante in Spain, as described by Benton (1986; 1989) do not cooperate through networks, and they compete fiercely and savagely for the few crumbs that the big corporations hand out. There is so little wealth generated among them that its distribution is insignificant; secrecy and distrust reign, as does the exploitation of workers and family members.

Perhaps it is not size, then, per se, that has welfare functions for society, but the network. Yet networks of large firms are familiar to us in the form of cartels, trusts, and interlocking directorates, and in the United States such networks are associated with concentrated power and predatory business practices toward small firms and consumers. Networks per se, then, have few welfare functions for society. An elite that generates trust among its members can be powerful and exploitive. The networks of large firms in Europe and Japan may not be as predatory as those in the United States, but I doubt that they generate many, if any, welfare functions on their own or that they welcome the state apparatus that requires it of them. Clearly, both characteristics are needed: small units that need to network to produce a good or service to which they all contribute.

The reader should also note that I avoid discussion of SFNs as a phenomenon of entrepreneurship. That is a formulation that suggests the primacy of motivation and the individual characteristics of leaders. While these are certainly important, I prefer a more structural approach. The key question is: what are the conditions under which an area is able to shape or give reign to motivations and leadership characteristics that are favorable to SFNs?

It should finally also be noted that in the way I have phrased the problem, the notion of successful small firm networks *directly* confronts the received theory of the multidivisional firm. It raises serious doubt that this type of firm, with its assumed economies of scale and of throughput, is economizing and efficient, and that autonomy is always required for the pursuit of self-interest.

## The Return of Civil Society?

My work on SFNs is a part of a larger project called "A Society of Organizations" (Perrow 1986a:49–52; 1991). In this project, I trace the development of the Integrated Production firm from the 1820s in the United States. This type of firm restructured our social landscape and generated externalities that spawned the public and nonprofit organizations that, by copying the bureaucratic form of the IP firm, generated further externalities. I argue that wittingly—but mostly unwittingly—the big organizations, public as well as private, increasingly perform more and more of societal functions such as socialization, providing occasions for social interactions, recreation, cultural productions, skill acquisition, and whatever else you wish to ascribe to "society." The units that once performed these functions were either weakened or made dependent upon the big employing organization. These weakened units are families, neighborhoods, schools, independent local governments, small and local guilds, and business and trade associations. Less and less social life existed outside the large employing organization or the flock of wholly dependent small firms clustering about them. In effect, society was being absorbed by the big organizations. Note that I am not referring to a welfare state government providing services, but to employers presenting society to their employees.

SFNs represent the possibility of a massive disengorgement from the big organizations, a spewing out of functions over delimited spaces where

## Figure 14.6  Activities that Could be Performed by Separate Organizations

| SOME PRODUCTION STAGES | BUSINESS FUNCTIONS |
|---|---|
| Retail distribution | Transportation |
| Wholesale distribution | Food Services |
| Final assembly | Legal Services |
| Final production | Accounting |
| Initial production | Advertising |
| Raw materials processing | Research & Development |
| Raw materials extraction | Purchasing |
| | Training |
| | Business Travel Services |

### CORPORATE SERVICES

| | |
|---|---|
| Medical & dental insurance | Retirement counseling |
| Fitness facilities | Career counseling |
| Sports programs | Legal services |
| Off-site recreational activities | Drug & alcohol abuse programs |
| Vacation planning, sites | Psychological counseling |
| Childcare | |

they can be picked up by small independent organizations. Small organizations are linked together by a sense of a community of fate, rather than a link based upon employees sharing the goals of the owners and top executives of a big organization. Figure 14.6 gives an idea of some of the opportunities for independent organizations that are today part of the big corporation. A similar figure can be put together for other huge employers, such as big government, big school districts, big unions, and big church bodies. If there exist different economies afforded by trust, networks, and the limitation of social externalities—if trust is an alternative way of reducing transaction costs, if networks are a way of achieving economics of scale, and if we can use community institutions as an alternative to externalizing social costs—then there is no need for one organization to do all the things as in Figure 14.6. Indeed, it would be a waste. Remember also that the fully integrated firm signifies the erosion of *civil society,* that precious area outside the big organizations, with a minimum of either market-driven behavior or of hierarchy. If SFNs represent a better alternative in this aspect, they warrant more attention than we have given them until now.

# References

AMIN, ASH. 1989. "A Model of the Small Firm in Italy." In Edward Goodman et al. eds., *Small Firms and Industrial Districts in Italy*. New York: Routledge, pp. 111–121.

AMIN, ASH, and KEVIN ROBINS. 1989. "Industrial Districts and Regional Development Limits and Possibilities." Working paper, University of Newcastle upon Tyne, England.

AYDALOT, PHILIPPE. 1986. "The Location of New Firm Creation: the French Case." In David Keeble and Egbert Wever eds., *New Firms and Regional Development in Europe*. London: Croom Helm, pp. 105–123.

BADARACCO, JOSEPH L., JR. 1988. "Changing Forms of the Corporation." In J. R. Meyer and J. M. Gustafson eds., *The U.S. Business Corporation*. Cambridge, MA: Ballinger, pp. 57–91.

BENTON, LAUREN A. 1986. *The Role of the Informal Sector in Economic Development: Industrial Restructuring in Spain*. Ph.D. dissertation, Department of Anthropology and History, Johns Hopkins University, Baltimore, MD.

———. 1989. "Homework and Industrial Development: Gender Roles and Restructuring in the Spanish Shoe Industry." *World Development* 17(2):255–266.

BEST, MICHAEL. 1991. *The New Competition*. Cambridge, MA: Harvard University Press.

BRUSCO, SEBASTIANO. 1982. "The Emilian Model: Productive Decentralization and Social Integration." *Cambridge Journal of Economics* 3:167–184.

———. 1986. "Small Firms and Industrial Districts: The Experience of Italy." In David Keeble and Egbert Wever eds., *New Firms and Regional Development in Europe*. London: Croom Helm, pp. 184–202.

BRUSCO, SEBASTIANO, and EZIO RIGHI. 1989. "Local Government, Industrial Policy and Social Consensus: the Case of Modena (Italy)." *Economy and Society* 18(4):405–424.

BURT, RONALD. 1983. *Corporate Profits and Corporation*. New York: Academic Press.

CAPECCHI, VITTORIO. 1989. "The Informal Economy and the Development of Flexible Specialization in Emilia-Romagna." In Alejandro Portes, Manuel Castells, and Lauren A. Benton eds., *The Informal Economy: Studies in Advanced and Less Developed Countries*. Baltimore: Johns Hopkins University Press, pp. 189–215.

CHANDLER, ALFRED D., JR. 1977. *The Visible Hand*. Cambridge, MA: Harvard University Press.

CHRISTOPHERSON, SUSAN, and MICHAEL STORPER. 1989. "The Effects of Flexible Specialization on Industrial Politics and the Labor Market: the Motion Picture Industry." *Industrial and Labor Relations Review* 42(3):331–347.

DOERINGER, PETER B., PHILIP I. MOSS, and DAVID G. TERKLA. 1986. "Capitalism and Kinship: Do Institutions Matter in the Labor Market?" *Industrial and Labor Relations Review* 40(1):48–60.

DOHSE, KNUTH, ULRICH JURGENS, and THOMAS MALSCH. 1985. "From 'Fordism' to 'Toyotism'? The Social Organization of the Labor Process in the Japanese Automobile Industry." *Politics and Society* 14(2):115–146.

FLORIDA, RICHARD, and MARTIN KENNEY. 1990. *The Breakthrough Illusion: Corporate America's Failure to Move from Innovation to Mass Production*. New York: Basic Books.

FRIEDMAN, DAVID. 1988. *The Misunderstood Miracle*. Ithaca, NY: Cornell University Press.

HARRISON, BENNETT. 1989. " 'The Big Firms are Coming Out of the Corner': the Resurgence of Economic Scale and Industrial Power in the Age of 'Flexibility.' " Paper delivered to the International Conference on Industrial Transformation and Regional Development in an Age of Global Interdependence, Nagoya, Japan, September 18–21.

HERMAN, BRUCE G. 1990. "Economic Development and Industrial Relations in a Small Firm Economy: the Experience of Metal Workers in Emilia-Romagna, Italy." Paper presented at the Conference on Economic Restructuring, Princeton, NJ, October 5–6.

HERRIGEL, GARY B. 1988. "The Political Embeddedness of Small and Medium-Sized Firm Networks in Baden Wuerttemberg: A Challenge From Above?" Paper delivered at the Workshop on Interfirm Innovation Dynamics, Stuttgart, West Germany, October 3–4.

———. 1989. "Industrial Order and the Politics of Industrial Change: Mechanical Engineering in the Federal Republic of Germany." In Peter Katzenstein ed., *Industry and Politics in West Germany: Toward the Third Republic*. Ithaca, NY: Cornell University Press.

———. n.d. "Industrial Order in the Machine Tool Industry: A Comparison of the United States and Germany." Conference paper at Social Science Research Council.

HEYDEBRAND, WOLF V. 1989. "New Organizational Forms." *Work and Occupations* 16(3):323–357.

HIRST, PAUL, and JONATHAN ZEITLIN. 1989. "Flexible Specialisation and the Competitive Failure of UK Manufacturing." *Political Quarterly* 60(2):164–178.

HYMAN, RICHARD. 1988. "Flexible Specialisation: Miracle of Myth?" In Richard Hyman and Wolfgang Streeck eds., *New Technology and Industrial Relations*. New York: Blackwell.

JOHANNISSON, BENGT. 1990. "Organizing for Local Economic Development." Working paper, Växsjö University, Sweden.

KANTER, ROSABETH MOSS. 1989. *Teaching Elephants to Dance: the Postentrepreneurial Revolution in Strategy Management and Careers*. New York: Simon & Schuster.

KEEBLE, DAVID, and EGBERT WEVER. 1986. "Introduction." In *New Firms and Regional Development in Europe*. London: Croom Helm, pp. 1–34.

KOHN, MELVIN, and CARMI SCHOOLER. 1983. *Work and Personality*. Norwood, NJ: Ablex Publishing Co.

KOZUL, ZELJKA. 1991. "Innovation and Industrial Organization: A Comparative Study of the Dynamics of the Italian and Yugoslav Furniture Industry." Working paper, Faculty of Economics and Politics, Jesus College, Cambridge, England.

LAZERSON, MARK. 1988. "Organizational Growth of Small Firms: an Outcome of Markets and Hierarchies?" *American Sociological Review* 53:330–342.

──────. 1991. "A New Phoenix: Putting-Out in the Modena Knitwear Industry." Working paper, Department of Sociology, SUNY-Stony Brook.

LORENZ, EDWARD H. 1988. "Neither Friends Nor Strangers: Informal Networks of Subcontracting in French Industry." In Diego Gambetta ed., *Trust: Making and Breaking Cooperative Relations*. Oxford: Blackwell, pp. 194–210.

MARSHALL, ALFRED. 1919. *Industry and Trade*. London: Macmillan.

MURRAY, FERGUS. 1983. "The Decentralization of Production: the Decline of the Mass-Collective Worker?" *Capital and Class* 19:74–99.

──────. 1987. "Flexible Specialization in the 'Third Italy'." *Capital and Class* 33:84–95.

NISHIGUCHI, TOSHIHIRO. 1993. *Strategic Industrial Sourcing: The Japanese Advantage*. New York: Oxford University Press.

O'FARRELL, PATRICK. 1986. "The Nature of the New Firms in Ireland: Empirical Evidence and Policy Implications." In David Keeble and Egbert Wever eds., *New Firms and Regional Development in Europe*. London: Croom Helm, pp. 151–183.

PERROW, CHARLES. 1986a. *Complex Organizations: A Critical Essay*, 3rd edition. New York: Random House.

──────. 1986b. "Economic Theories of Organizations." *Theory and Society* 15:11–45.

──────. 1991. "A Society of Organizations." *Theory and Society* 20:725–762.

PFEFFER, JEFFREY, and GERALD SALANCIK. 1978. *The External Control of Organizations*. New York: Harper & Row.

PIORE, MICHAEL, and CHARLES SABEL. 1984. *The Second Industrial Divide*. New York: Basic Books.

──────. 1988. "The 'Flexible Firm': Fixation or Fact?" *Work, Employment, and Society* 2(3):281–316.

POLLERT, ANNA. 1991. "The Orthodoxy of Flexibility." In Anna Pollert ed., *Farewell to Flexibility*. London: Blackwell, Chapter 1.

POWELL, WALTER W. 1990. "Neither Market Nor Hierarchy: Network Forms of Organization." *Research in Organizational Behavior* 12:295–336.

SABEL, CHARLES. 1989. "Flexible Specialisation and the Re-emergence of Regional Economies." In Paul Hirst and Jonathan Zeitlin eds., *Reversing Industrial Decline*. New York: St. Martin's Press, pp. 17–70.

———. 1991. "Moebius-Strip Organizations and Open Labor Markets: Some Consequences of the Reintegration of Conception and Execution in a Volatile Economy." In James Coleman and Pierre Bourdieu eds., *Social Theory for a Changing Society*. Boulder, CO: Westview Press.

———. 1992. "Studied Trust: Building New Forms of Cooperation in a Volatile Economy." Originally presented at MIT, August 7, 1990.

SABEL, CHARLES, and JONATHAN ZEITLIN. 1985. "Historical Alternatives to Mass Production: Politics, Markets and Technology in Nineteenth Century Industrialisation." *Past and Present* 108:133–175.

SAKAI, KUNIYASU. 1990. "The Feudal World of Japanese Manufacturing." *Harvard Business Review* 68 (November/December):38–49.

SAXENIAN, ANNALEE. 1991a. "The Origins and Dynamics of Production Networks in Silicon Valley." *Research Policy,* Special Issue on Networks of Innovators.

———. 1991b. "Response to Richard Florida and Martin Kenney 'Silicon Valley and Route 128 Won't Save Us.'" *California Management Review* 33:136–142.

SENGENBERGER, WERNER, GARY LOVEMAN, and MICHAEL PIORE, eds. 1990. *The Reemergence of Small Enterprise: Industrials Restructuring in Industrialized Economies*. Geneva, Switzerland: International Labor Organization.

SMITH, CHRIS. 1989. "Flexible Specialisation, Automation, and Mass Production." *Work, Employment and Society* 3(2):203–220.

STORPER, MICHAEL. 1989. "The Transition to Flexible Specialisation in the U.S. Film Industry: External Economies, the Division of Labour, and the Crossing of Industrial Divides." *Cambridge Journal of Economics* 13:273–305.

STYMNE, BENGT. 1989. *Information Technology and Competence Formation in the Swedish Service Sector: an Analysis of Retail Strategy and Development of the Finance Sector*. Stockholm: The Economic Research Institute, Stockholm School of Economics.

TAPLIN, IAN M. 1989. "Segmentation and the Organisation of Work in the Italian Apparel Industry." *Social Science Quarterly* 70(2):408–424.

THOMPSON, GRAHME. 1989. "Flexible Specialisation, Industrial Districts, Regional Economies: Strategies for Socialists?" *Economy and Society* 18(4):527–545.

TRIGILIA, CARLO. 1986. "Small-firm Development and Political Subcultures in Italy." *European Sociological Review* 2(3):161–175.

WILLIAMSON, OLIVER E. 1975. *Markets and Hierarchies*. New York: Free Press.

———. 1985. *The Economic Institution of Capitalism*. New York: Free Press.

WOOD, STEPHEN. 1988. "Between Fordism and Flexibility? The U.S. Car Industry." In Richard Hyman and Wolfgang Streeck eds., *New Technology and Industrial Relations*. Oxford and New York: Basil Blackwell.

# 15

# Future Alternatives of Work Reflected in the Past: Putting-Out Production in Modena

## MARK LAZERSON

Within both the Marxist and liberal paradigms of economic development, it has been widely accepted that, as industrialization preceded putting-out, small-scale production would eventually be superseded by larger and more complex organizational forms. Marx's description of this process, and his foreboding that the "country that is most developed industrially only shows, to the least developed, the image of its own future" (1977:19), were later to be mirrored by his severest critics who insisted the developmental patterns of all industrial societies were converging (Kerr, Dunlop, and Myers 1960). Indeed, the near disappearance of small-scale production in the United States, until recently the avatar of industrialization, was expected to be followed elsewhere.

But these expectations of unilinear industrial progress marked by ever larger industrial establishments have been undermined by the rather different experiences of several advanced countries, particularly Japan and Italy. There, small firms dominate important production activities from numerical control machine tools to textiles (Friedman 1988; Sabel 1982). Sometimes these small firms are the key actors, operating in sectors where, for a variety of reasons, large firms do not compete. In other cases, small firms perform essential production tasks as subcontractors for larger firms engaged essentially in research, development, and marketing. But even as regards subcontracting, the widespread view of small producers being at the mercy of large firms is often misleading, as is another that associates homework with sweatwork.

**403**

In this chapter, I examine Italian knitwear manufacturing in the province of Modena, an agro-industrial area of 600,000 people located in the Emilia-Romagna region of north-central Italy, where most production is based on putting-out. In putting-out production, outworkers use their own tools and work places to convert raw and semifinished materials owned by larger manufacturers into finished goods. Outworkers are self-employed and determine their own hours and work methods. Payment is by piece-rates. The persistence of this organizational form is surprising, for it was not thought that it would survive into late industrial capitalism.

Economic development theory has always viewed putting-out as seriously deficient because it allowed no role for management, which was supposedly necessary to improve efficiency (Williamson 1985). Indeed, economists widely accept the view that the very creation of the factory was necessitated in part because the absence of supervision in putting-out permitted impoverished workers to embezzle and loaf, reducing the manufacturers' profits (Landes 1969:56–60). This line of argument has been more recently refined by institutional economists such as Williamson (1980), who insists the factory was simply more efficient because it reduced transaction costs by eliminating dispersed putting-out stations. Ironically, Marxists have developed a parallel claim: that factory organization enhanced surplus extraction by improving discipline and surveillance of workers (Marglin 1976).

If economists criticize putting-out production for its economic inefficiencies, historians and sociologists condemn it for its harmful effects on workers. Essentially, putting-out production is seen by them as synonymous with sweatwork, labor-law violations, and the most negative aspects of capitalism (Bythell 1969; 1978; Schmiechen 1984). There are essentially two reasons given for this situation. One is closely related to the economists' claim that, because putting-out production is inefficient, wages must be lowered to enable it to compete with factory production. The second one is that, since putting-out production atomizes workers by eliminating collective structures, trade unions are unable to defend workers from the worst forms of exploitation. Indeed, the workers' movement has until now seen centralized production and ever-larger factories as necessary concomitants of its increased power in modern industrial society. Not surprisingly, the economic changes of the last decades of the twentieth century, which have witnessed a decrease in factory size and an increase in decentralized production, have been seen as an important explanatory factor in the erosion of trade union and left-wing political strength (Lash and Urry 1987).

But even if the epoch of centralized production is ending, there is no evidence that decentralized production represents a retrogression to past social conditions. Rather, new organizational models need to be conceptualized, models that link individual producers and smaller production links to collective services and associations. Piore and Sabel (1984) argue that in the emerging system of flexible production dependent upon rapidly changing designs and production methods, trade unions must abandon their emphasis on job security in any one particular firm and give greatest priority to assuring that their members obtain adequate job skills. In contrast to the view that decentralized production represents a return to unregulated capitalism, Piore and Sabel (1984:278) say that the foundations of flexible production are sociologically embedded in a communitarian and cooperative ethos. Highly specialized firms depend on collaborative relationships to manufacture completed products, and group solidarity prevents capitalist competition and instability from destroying the entrepreneurial environment (Lazerson 1988).

### Knitwear Putting-Out in Modena

Knitwear production in the province of Modena offers one example of how small-scale and home-centered production can provide a progressive alternative to a return to nineteenth-century sweatwork and Darwinian social policies. It also represents an excellent opportunity to reconsider the claims of Williamson and others who have insisted that putting-out production in the clothing and textile industries is highly inefficient.

Modena sharply refutes the orthodox connection between putting-out production and the initial phases of industrialization and primitive accumulation (Mendels 1972). In the same period that knitwear putting-out expanded, Modena was transformed from one of Italy's poorest provinces to one of its five richest (Forni 1987:37). Modena's social welfare indices are among the highest in Italy, allowing comparisons with Scandinavia (Brusco 1982). Actually, many of Italy's wealthiest regions are closely identified with extensive putting-out and artisanal production. On the other hand, in the relatively backward and economically deprived South, large firms are predominant and craft production is retarded (Weiss 1984).

Modena's knitwear industry employs approximately 16,000 people (it is the third-largest industry in the province after mechanical engineering and ceramics), and rests almost exclusively on putting-out. The industry's origins date from the mid-1950s with the growth of ready-to-wear clothing; the first manufacturers began with a network of putting-out workers employed in straw-hat production. Similar to the putting-out system in earlier times, when merchant-manufacturers provided household labor with wool and cotton to be transformed into finished or semifinished products

**Table 15.1 Typical Sequence in Knitwear Production**[1]

Manufacturers
Design and production of prototypes. Solicit orders from wholesalers and retailers. Buy raw materials to be transformed by subcontractors. Final shipment to buyer.

Subcontractors

| 1. Weaving | 2. Pre-pressing and pre-stitching | 3. Embroidery | 4. Assembly |
|---|---|---|---|
| Manufacturer's yarn woven into cloth, according to desired specifications. | If cloth is to be cut it must first be pressed and stitched together in order to lie flat. Homeworkers often used for stitching. | Computer-controlled machinery stitch designs on cloth pieces. Marginal phases sent out to illegal homeworkers. 3A. Illegal homeworkers Remove excess paper on reverse side of embroidery pattern. Hand embroidery. | Cloth pieces cut and sewn into garments. Sometimes cutting separate phase. Marginal phases sent out to legal and illegal homeworkers. 4A. Homeworkers Cuffs, collars, and borders are attached to garment. 4B. Illegal homeworkers Seams are hand-finished. |

[1] Unfinished goods are usually returned to the manufacturer following each production step and then immediately reshipped to the next subcontractor.

(Landes 1966:14), knitwear production commences with the manufacturer. The latter designs and produces the first prototypes and obtains initial orders from wholesalers or large retailers. With limited or no production facilities, the manufacturer depends on a vast array of highly specialized subcontractors to transform her materials into a finished product. These knitwear subcontractors contribute only their labor, skill, work place, and machinery. Weavers transform the manufacturer's yarn

## Manufacturers

Design and production of prototypes. Solicit orders from wholesalers and retailers. Buy raw materials to be transformed by subcontractors. Final shipment to buyer.

## Subcontractors

| 5. Fabric treatment | 6. Button-making | 7. Pressing and ironing | 8. Finishing, inspection, and packaging |
|---|---|---|---|
| Depending upon buyer's requirements and characteristics of cloth, cloth or garments sent for special softening, cleaning or dyeing treatments. | Buttons and buttonholes are added to garments. | Garments are pressed and ironed. Labels are usually added. Minor ironing of collars and waist borders sometimes farmed out to specialized artisans. | Garments are checked for defects, mended, folded, and placed in plastic bags. Some manufacturers inspect and package garments themselves to improve quality control. Often this phase is integrated with pressing and ironing. |

into cloth; assemblers cut and sew it into sweaters; and other subcontractors press, inspect, mend, and package them. Additional steps, depending upon the requirements of the buyer and the type of material, include the sewing and pre-ironing of the cloth prior to its cutting, the dying of the already assembled sweater or the washing of it to soften it and remove excess animal hairs, embroidery, and button-making. Subcontractors themselves sometimes rely on homeworkers. Especially low-paid marginal work is performed by illegal homeworkers who are not registered with the state employment office, but these represent a disappearing group, at least in Modena. Table 15.1 presents the actors and the production sequence.

FIRM TOPOGRAPHY.   Most of the province's 4,291 firms are extremely small, have only one plant, and are owned by artisanal subcontractors. The average size is 3.93 persons, including owners and family help. Excluding the latter, firm size falls to 2.39 (ISTAT 1985:15, 48). Though there was a slight increase in large firms' (firms employing more than 50 persons) contribution to employment until 1971, their share of the sector's work force plummeted from 38.9 percent to 19.4 percent in 1981 (see Table 15.2). This trend has continued through 1988.[1] In the same period, the proportion of microfirms with five or fewer persons has expanded from 21.7 percent in 1971 to 36.4 percent in 1981. Improved statistical collection and the legalization of many small artisans may account for some of these changes, but the absolute decline in large firms from 52 in 1971 and to 21 in 1988[2] clearly demonstrates a structural shift toward the putting-out mode of production as the knitwear industry matured and became a major exporter to other members of the European Economic Community and the United States.

Knitwear firms usually comprise only a single plant. Of the 33 firms including more than one plant in 1981, the single largest one had three units (ISTAT 1985:4, 16–17). The 89 percent of the sector's firms that are artisanal are legally limited to a single plant. In Italy, *artisan* is a legal classification granted to those entrepreneurs who own the means of production, are personally engaged in their firm's productive activities, and have no more than 22 in-house employees, including family members (Lazerson 1988). Artisans benefit from subsidized loans, special dispensations from labor and social security laws, and other economic incentives.

Artisanal knitwear firms are usually subcontractors engaged solely in production. Their small size is made technically possible by the extreme division of labor. This point is made clear in Table 15.3, based on membership data provided by the Modena National Confederation of Artisans (CNA), which represents between 50 and 60 percent of all knitwear firms in Modena. Except for firms specializing in "complete assembly,"

---

[1] Data supplied by Statistical Office of the Modena Camera di Commercio, November, 1988.

[2] Data from Statistical Office of the Modena Camera di Commercio, November, 1988.

**Table 15.2 Twenty-Year Change in Distribution of Modena Knitwear Firms by Workforce Size[1]**

| | | | Number of Employees | | | | | |
|---|---|---|---|---|---|---|---|---|
| **1981** | 1 | 2 | 3–5 | 6–9 | 10–19 | 20–49 | 50–250 | Total[2] |
| Firms | 2,145 | 858 | 634 | 308 | 232 | 78 | 36 | 4,291 |
| As percent | 49.9% | 19.9% | 14.7% | 7.1% | 5.4% | 1.8% | 0.8% | 100% |
| Staff | 2,145 | 1,716 | 2,339 | 2,234 | 2,892 | 2,337 | 3,305 | 16,968 |
| As percent | 12.6% | 10.1% | 13.7% | 13.1% | 17% | 13.7% | 19.4% | 100% |
| **1971** | | | | | | | | |
| Firms | 548 | 410 | 299 | 112 | 92 | 77 | 52 | 1,590 |
| As percent | 34.4% | 25.7% | 18.8% | 7% | 5.7% | 4.8% | 3.2% | 100% |
| Staff | 548 | 820 | 1,085 | 793 | 1,237 | 2,376 | 4,384 | 11,243 |
| As percent | 4.9% | 7.2% | 9.6% | 7.5% | 11% | 21% | 38.9% | 100% |

| | 1 | 2 | 3–5 | 6–10 | 11–20 | 21–50 | 51–264 | Totals |
|---|---|---|---|---|---|---|---|---|
| **1961[3]** | | | | | | | | |
| Firms | 678 | 259 | 196 | 88 | 53 | 27 | 25 | 1,326 |
| As percent | 51.1% | 19.5% | 14.7% | 6.6% | 3.9% | 2% | 1.8% | 100% |
| Staff | 678 | 518 | 737 | 678 | 749 | 862 | 2,369 | 6,591 |
| As percent | 10.2% | 7.8 | 11.1% | 10.2% | 11.3% | 13% | 35.9% | 100% |

[1]Workforce includes owners, family members, employees, and homeworkers. The knitwear category also includes production of socks and stockings. In 1981 only four firms and 59 persons were engaged in this activity.

[2]Percentages may add to less than 100.0 because of rounding errors.

[3]ISTAT 1964: 20–21. In this earlier census, the category "various other textiles not otherwise classified" was used instead of "knitwear." Since knitwear constitutes the only measurable textile production in the province, this category is essentially identical to the knitwear category contained in later census reports.

*Sources*: ISTAT 1985: 14–15; ISTAT 1975: 8–9.

**Table 15.3  Number of Knitwear Artisan Firms in the Province of Modena in 1988 by Number of Employees and Principal Phases of Production[1]**

| Production Phases | None | 1 | 2–3 | 4–6 | 7–10 | 11+ | Total[2] |
|---|---|---|---|---|---|---|---|
| Weaving | 229 | 29 | 32 | 13 | 3 | 4 | 310 |
| Percent | 73.9% | 9.3% | 10.3% | 4.2% | 1% | 1.3% | 100% |
| Complete Assembly | 88 | 17 | 26 | 30 | 31 | 32 | 224 |
| Percent | 39.3% | 7.6% | 11.6% | 13.4% | 13.8% | 14.3% | 100% |
| Partial Assembly | 267 | 30 | 33 | 24 | 16 | 4 | 374 |
| Percent | 71.3% | 8% | 8.8% | 6.4% | 4.3% | 1.1% | 100% |
| Fabric Cutting only | 33 | 10 | 2 | 1 | 1 | 0 | 47 |
| Percent | 70.2% | 21.3% | 4.3% | 2.1% | 2.1% | | 100% |
| Finishing, Inspection, Packaging | 73 | 7 | 21 | 4 | 5 | 3 | 113 |
| Percent | 64.6% | 6.2% | 18.6% | 3.5% | 4.4% | 2.7% | 100% |
| Laundry, Pressing, Fulling | 166 | 32 | 31 | 25 | 19 | 9 | 282 |
| Percent | 59% | 11.3% | 11% | 8.9% | 6.7% | 3.2% | 100% |
| Button Making | 37 | 4 | 6 | 5 | 1 | 2 | 55 |
| Percent | 67.3% | 7.3% | 10.9% | 9.1% | 1.8% | 3.6% | 100% |
| Embroidery | 70 | 10 | 18 | 11 | 2 | 5 | 116 |
| Percent | 60.3% | 8.6% | 15.5% | 9.4% | 1.7% | 4.3% | 100% |

Number of Employees

[1] Percentages may sum to less than 100.0 because of rounding errors.

[2] Data provided by the Modena CNA, which represents between 50 and 60 percent of all knitwear firms in Modena, as of October, 1988. The category "employees" includes homeworkers, but excludes family help.

production firms without employees ("None") compose a majority of the industry.

THE EXPLANATION FOR PUTTING-OUT.   Marketing, technological, and labor-market imperatives in large measure assure the survival and reproduction of small producers and subcontracting. Increasingly fickle consumer tastes, combined with unpredictable climatic changes, result in ever briefer product life cycles and numerous style changes. Accordingly, short production runs that preclude large economies of scale have become the norm in the knitwear sector. Abrupt cyclical changes are also more common in the knitwear industry than elsewhere, making factories with large amounts of fixed capital and many employees particularly vulnerable during economic downturns (Mariotti and Cainarca 1986:352).

Since the possibilities for automation of the most labor-intensive phases of knitwear production (garment assembly, pressing, inspection, and packaging) are limited, small firms and large firms share similar technologies. Indeed, in knitwear dye-works where capital investment requirements are far greater, firms with fewer than 20 employees are rare. Finally, sharply higher labor costs in the 1970s and increased industrial conflict over health conditions among laundry, pressing, and dye workers intensified the sector's already strong centrifugal tendencies. Manufacturers' reliance on small artisanal producers allowed the same technology to be employed without any diminution in the economies of scale, reduced costly investment in plant and equipment, and replaced much of the blue-collar workforce with self-employed entrepreneurs.

Although the putting-out system may be highly efficient, its existence and reproduction depend on three key, socially determined elements. First, state labor, social, fiscal, and business policies have established the structural conditions that allow large numbers of individuals, most of whom are ex-knitwear workers (ERVET 1983:32), to operate small firms with minimal organizational resources. Second, artisanal associations cooperate with the trade unions to discourage firms from violating contractual and legal norms that could lead to ruthless price-cutting and competition. They also provide their subcontractor members with administrative and technical services that a small firm normally would be unable to afford. Third, and perhaps most importantly, the industry depends to a great extent on the household as a unit and place of production. Because the rhythms of knitwear production often harmonize with those of household reproduction, the elderly and women are able to contribute their labor at minimal cost to the firm. The family firm also serves to transmit the necessary job skills, as well as insulate its members from the vagaries of the capitalist economic cycle.

# The Research

These noneconomic factors are important elements in my analysis of the putting-out mode, which is based primarily on field research conducted in the province of Modena in the spring and fall of 1988. I also returned to Modena in 1989 and 1990 to follow up my initial field data. In order to understand the organizational structure of the industry, I initially visited 44 firms (16 manufacturers and 28 subcontractor-artisans) covering every single phase of knitwear production, and used open-ended questionnaires to interview their principals. In two cases, I spent several days accompanying knitwear employers during their visits to contractors and subcontractors. I also interviewed eight homeworkers in their homes. Except for three firms located in adjoining provinces, the entire interview sample was based in Modena. Most of the interviews with the subcontractors were arranged by the National Confederation of Artisans (CNA). The Industrial Association of Modena (Confindustria) and the Association of Small Entrepreneurs (API) provided me with access to about half of the manufacturers I interviewed. Other interviews, including all those with homeworkers, were arranged through personal contacts. These interviews were supplemented by continuous discussions with industry and union representatives, principally those of the CNA and the Modena Labor Council (Camera del Lavoro), and statistical data obtained from government, union, and industry sources.

My discussion begins with a detailed analysis demonstrating that the alleged organizational weaknesses of the putting-out system have today either been overcome or else represent strengths. In this regard, the empirical evidence in Modena firmly rejects Williamson's claim that the putting-out system is burdened by excessive transaction costs. In the next section, I show how the flexibility of putting-out depends more on its social characteristics than its functional successes.

# The Putting-Out System Then and Now

## Theft and Embezzlement

If there is one link uniting nearly all accounts of the putting-out system, save that of Bendix (1974:203), it is that embezzlement and dishonesty by workers, especially in the cotton and wool industries, were widespread (Landes 1969:56–57). The dispersed form of production, which physically separated the owners of the material from the producers, meant that workers were able to substitute cheap wool for more expensive wool, wet the wool to distort its weight, work carelessly to increase their piece rates, or just simply steal. Legal measures to halt theft proved futile (Sayles 1983). Although Jones (1982:129–132) concludes that workers' embezzlement was a response to meager wages and employer abuses, Williamson (1983) points to it as an example of the need to subject human opportunism to strict hierarchical control in order to guarantee efficient economic arrangements. The relative importance of worker theft is also in dispute. Jones contends that losses due to embezzlement were an insignificant production cost, viewed customarily as part of the wage bargain. But Marglin (1976) and Williamson (1983) list worker embezzlement as one major reason for the collapse of the putting-out system.

But in Modena knitwear firms, theft and misappropriation of their property by artisans and homeworkers are so uncommon that manufacturers expressed surprise when I asked about it. Most manufacturers do take precautions against cheating. They normally weigh and count the woven pieces of cloth upon delivery by weavers, who are traditionally permitted a margin of between 1 and 2.5 percent for waste and lost material, depending upon the quality of the yarn. If there are any shortfalls they are immediately apparent, for each spool of yarn yields a precise number of cloths. As a further safeguard, some firms engage specialized laboratories to test the cloth's quality and thickness. But there are also manufacturers who own no scales and have neither the time nor personnel to weigh the material; they count only the pieces of cloth. Despite these measures, weavers could still manage to keep some yarn, but the amount would be inconsequential.

Opportunities for embezzlement also exist during the assembly phase, when the cloth is cut, leaving considerable waste. But when knitwear contains cashmere or other expensive materials, the yarn is often knitted to approximate the human form to avoid wasteful cutting of the finished cloth. Should high-grade wool be cut, the manufacturer would ordinarily request the subcontractor to sort the waste by color and return it. Since this increases labor expenses, the subcontractor will usually negotiate to keep some of the waste wool. More often, artisans are free to sell the waste, often composed of recycled wool and acrylics. The theft of finished garments by workers is equally rare, and if even one or two garments out of two or three thousand were to disappear, manufacturers would not always request reimbursement from the artisan. It should also be remembered that knitwear workers are allowed to buy most garments at cost from the manufacturers. In general, manufacturers eschew expensive and costly controls over their subcontractors because of established relations of trust and confidence developed over a long time, which few artisans would want to breach.

Where some manufacturers do take precautions against possible artisanal opportunism is in the protection of design secrets and of trade-marks. Indeed, preserving the secrets of production has been one expla-nation for the rise of factories (Chapman 1967:34). I did learn of one artisan subjected to civil prosecution after he misappropriated some ma-terial, reproduced it, and then used the manufacturer's patterns to make finished garments out of it. To avoid such problems, manufacturers who invest heavily in fashion design almost invariably produce the first pro-totypes internally, commissioning orders to subcontractors only after the buyers' initial orders have been received. Since many Modena manufac-turers invest little in fashion and rework the designs of others, plagiarism does not pose a substantial risk.

### Employee Idleness and Quality Control

If lack of supervision once encouraged embezzlement, it also impeded manufacturers from controlling how much outworkers worked. Landes says that the manufacturer "had no way of compelling his workers to do a given number of hours of labor; the domestic weaver or craftsman was master of his time, starting and stopping when he desired" (1969:58). This situation reflected the continued importance of subsistence agricul-ture to rural domestic workers (Sewell 1986:50), the widespread resis-tance in French and English society to market culture (Reddy 1984), and time-based factory discipline (Thompson 1967).

Today in Modena, material well-being and even social standing are difficult to separate from one's earnings. Nor is agriculture any longer a secondary source of income for most knitwear workers, although it once played an important part in the origins of the Modena putting-out sys-tem (Cappello and Prandi 1973). If anything, the putting-out system today appears to be the choice of those who value work far more than leisure, and it is the factory system with its five-day, forty-hour week that promises some reprieve from work without end. In one survey, knitwear artisans on average worked 2,428 hours annually, although weavers re-ported working 2,817 hours (ERVET 1983:34). Another study of Mo-dena's knitwear sector concluded that artisans "are prepared to be avail-able for long hours, almost without limits, at times even on holidays and Sundays" (Comune di Modena 1978:83). It should be understood, how-ever, that this predisposition to work long hours recalls the strong agri-cultural tradition in Modena, where intense periods of seasonal labor were the norm.

The absence of supervision has also been blamed for output of poor and uneven quality under the putting-out system. Quality control is a major concern of most Modena manufacturers, for the majority of garments are in the middle- to upper-price range. A few manufacturers reported that defects among put-out garments were slightly higher than those produced internally. Yet, the costs of defects under putting-out are still lower than under the factory system, for subcontractors, unlike employees, are liable for their own mistakes. Thus, despite the absence of bureaucratic supervision, subcontractors face greater pressures to satisfy the principals' standards than employees do.

OPPORTUNISM AND COOPERATION.    Nevertheless, the application of agency theory to knitwear putting-out (Alchian and Demsetz 1972) is subject to very precise limits because of the overarching need to preserve the long-term, stable relationships that are prevalent among 85 percent of subcontractors (ERVET 1983:57). If subcontractors were charged for every minor error or made to pay high prices for damaged garments, they would find other customers, thus impeding manufacturers' ability to achieve quality and efficient production through continuous interaction with their artisans. Similarly, the importance of cooperative behavior discourages attempts to exploit short-term changes in market conditions. Manufacturers who abandon subcontractors who refuse to lower labor prices during periods of excess demand risk being severely squeezed themselves during the seasonal rush, when deadlines are short and artisans can name their price.

### Transportation Costs

As in the traditional putting-out system, where the product had to be moved from cottage to cottage, transportation plays a crucial role in the organization of knitwear subcontracting. Knitwear lends itself to frequent movements, for it is light and relatively immune from damage during transport. Whereas in eighteenth-century England it was the manufacturers' responsibility to move the goods from one station to the next, in Modena subcontractors move the unfinished garments to and from the manufacturers' warehouses after each manufacturing step. Subcontractors' transportation costs are a function of their size, organizational structure, and proximity to customers. Transportation costs normally range from 2 to 10 percent of total expenses. But even if all transportation costs are eventually absorbed by the manufacturer, they amount to no more than 0.6 to 3 percent of total expenses, based on estimates that subcontractors' labor costs represent approximately 30 percent of a manufacturers' total expenses (Bursi 1987; 1989).[3]

---

[3] Data provided by the statistical office of the Camera del Lavoro of Modena, based on annual company statements filed at the Modena courthouse.

In contrast to the English putting-out system, which grew up in an area physically distinct from the factory (Jones 1983:65), 90 percent of all Modena knitwear firms are located in three townships, all situated within a radius of twenty-five miles from one another.[4] In Carpi, which is the second largest city in the province of Modena, and which accounts for about one-third of all knitwear production, where workshops protrude from the ground floor of hundreds of residential buildings, garments are frequently moved by handcarts from one subcontractor to the next. On the other hand, some firms use subcontractors located in the far south of the country.

### Other Transaction Costs

Williamson (1980) claims that theft, shirking by employees, and high transportation costs raised the transaction costs of the putting-out mode to unacceptable levels. He also says that putting-out needs larger buffer inventories to assure constant product-flow because of the long distances between work-stations. But, until recently, factories have maintained large inventories to guarantee full utilization of labor and adequate supplies (Jones 1982:127–129; Sayer 1986). In the knitwear sector, a just-in-time supply system is used: raw materials are purchased and then consigned to the producer only immediately after the order is received. If serious disruptions prevent a subcontractor from completing the work in time, the manufacturer can almost always find alternative subcontractors. Within a centralized production organization, the facility to jettison and substitute malfunctioning elements rapidly is limited. Thus, even if we accept Williamson's (1981:559) claim that internal hierarchies have greater access than market systems to information, the capacity of the latter to act on information is much greater.

One of Williamson's claims requires a longer view to adjudicate. He says that a weak decision-making hierarchy impedes the ability to "recognize and implement system innovations (of process, product or organizational kinds) . . ." (1980:23). Lazonick's (1983) study of the decline of the English cotton industry points to excessive decentralization for depriving it of the large integrated producers alone capable of providing the costly equipment needed to compete with new foreign producers. So far, the few significant technological leaps in the knitwear sector—such as the application of numerical-control computer technology to weaving, embroidery, and cutting—have been rapidly adopted by many

---

[4] Source: Provincia di Modena. June, 1987. *L'occupazione dipendente in provincia di Modena*, p. 49. Modena: Provincia di Modena.

small firms. Admittedly, the development and application by foreign competitors of automated equipment requiring massive capital investments could eventually undermine the putting-out model in Modena. But, as the following section demonstrates, the scope for automation and centralization in the knitwear sector is very narrow.

### The Manufacturers

Manufacturers, with their dual capacity to design and market a product, dominate the artisan-producers, who in turn now command most of the homeworkers. The sheer number of Modena knitwear manufacturers, however, dilutes the power of any single firm over subcontractors, and makes it impossible for any one to hold monopsonistic power. As of April, 1988, there were 597 industrial manufacturing firms,[5] in addition to probably 200 artisanal firms, many of which also have some production capacity and may serve as subcontractors for other manufacturers. Annual sales for manufacturers vary from under 1 million dollars for artisans to more than 200 million dollars for firms with international reputations.

Because of the heterogeneity of the Modena knitwear sector, most knitwear subcontractors normally work for several different manufacturers. This contrasts sharply with that of the knitwear industry in the Veneto region, where one producer—Benetton—dominates production and pressures subcontractors to work exclusively for it (Belussi 1987:28, 32). Though there are artisans in Modena obligated to work 100 percent of the time to repay manufacturers for loans or machinery given them to start their businesses, they are few in number. In my interviews, most manufacturers, whether large or small, believed artisanal dependence upon a single manufacturer undermined one of the aims of decentralization; that is, the separation of knitwear marketing from its production. Artisans also reported that manufacturers often referred them new customers. Within the city of Modena, which accounts for about 10 percent of all artisanal subcontractors in the province, the 1984 records of the Artisans' Register revealed that 15.3 percent of all knitwear artisans had only one customer (Commissione Provinciale per L'Artigianato 1987:47). A 1988 survey of 12 percent of Modena weavers revealed that 60 percent had from three to five customers and 21 percent had six or more.[6]

---

[5] Industrial manufacturing-firm data of April, 1988 provided by Camera del Lavoro of the Province of Modena.

[6] Source: CNA. September, 1988. *Indagine strutturale–congiunturale sul comparto della tessitura*. Modena: Confederazione Nazionale dell'Artigianato.

The vast majority of manufacturers now subcontract all phases of knitwear production. Manufacturers who were slow to subcontract were soon forced to follow their competitors because of lower profits (Bursi 1989). Normally manufacturers limit their direct involvement in production to the design and execution of the first prototypes and to the delivery of the finished garments to buyers. Some manufacturers at the upper-end of the market, but by no means all, package the finished garments internally in order to supervise quality control directly. Manufacturers who subcontract the design aspects of production are relatively few in number. Some of the larger manufacturers invest large sums in fashion design or else contract with prestigious Paris, Milan, and New York fashion houses. But for many others, one of the owners usually creates a prototype, invariably inspired by someone else's ideas. Theft of ideas is common in an industry that depends on appropriating the creations of others to make haute couture accessible to the masses.

## Artisans, the Embodiment of Flexible Production

Few knitwear subcontractors, no matter how skilled or advanced their machinery, can always satisfy the myriad tastes of the fashion industry. The knitwear industry's real flexibility is located in its totality rather than in its individual parts, and it rests upon a social and legal structure that insulates subcontractors from the worst ravages of the market's unpredictability. In the following subsections, I detail the elements that contribute to the sector's flexibility.

### Elements of Flexibility

TECHNOLOGICAL FLEXIBILITY.   During my research, many of the weavers I visited sat idle; their thick-gauge-needled looms were unsuitable for the finely woven cloth then in demand. The problem reflected the limited adaptability of knitting machines. Not even the most advanced numerical-control looms, manufactured in Japan and costing $150,000, weave yarn of more than one thickness. Any loom can be converted to a different yarn gauge for about one-sixth of its original cost, in addition to $400 in labor charges and two days' lost production for each resetting. Still, there is no guarantee that this new gauge will be useful when fashions change.

Numerical-control machinery can also be far less productive than older, traditional and less costly machinery. For example, during the fall of 1988, weavers with the most advanced numerical-control looms were able to produce the then-stylish classic-sweater model. But since these machines were not specifically designed for this sweater model, their productivity was far surpassed by the cheaper, traditional mechanical looms capable of producing only classic sweaters. In most other phases of production, where capital costs are significantly lower, there is more versatility but the number of applications is still limited. In knitwear assembly, where most machines cost an average of $6,000 new, specialized sewing machines that cut and sew fine knitwear are unable to cut and sew heavier knitwear. Nor can seamstresses in small shops, though far more versatile than the pin-makers studied by Adam Smith, easily switch from one material to another without sharp drops in productivity. Because of their small size and limited capital, most artisans offer only a modest range of services, even if collectively they are almost always able to meet the exigencies of the market. But, as a result, a large percentage of artisans remain idle for one to two months annually for lack of orders (ERVET 1983:75).

SOCIAL FLEXIBILITY. These brief periods of under- or unemployment in the knitwear sector are cushioned by heavy dependence on family labor, low overhead, extraordinarily long working hours, and less costly labor laws. Many of these advantages depend on the common juxtaposition of home and work place. More than 75 percent of knitwear artisans locate their work places either in the garage or on the ground floor of their homes (ERVET 1983:22). Most of the artisanal villages that dot the Modena landscape combine residential and industrial quarters. Thus few artisans pay rent; and special low-interest-rate loans for workshops also help subsidize their home building costs. The spatial integration of productive and reproductive spheres also permits artisans to rely on the casual labor of family members, particularly women and pensioners.

A remarkably high percentage of Italians in the region of Emilia-Romagna live in extended families. According to a random survey of 4,500 households, 26 to 32 percent of married sons (the frequency positively correlated to age) live in the same house or apartment building with at least one parent (Barbagli, Capecchi, and Cobalti 1986:18). The assistance of family members, combined with the proximity of home and work place, ease the burden of the long work days of artisans. Extended family arrangements also provide alternative sources of income when knitwear production enters the doldrums.

### Legal Inducements

Because of differences in pay, social insurance costs, dismissal protection, and sickness benefits, artisanal firms have lower labor costs than industrial firms.[7] Wages for artisanal and industrial employees in the province of Modena are about equal, though some large industrial companies pay as much as 10 percent more. But artisanal employees receive less for overtime, weekend, and night work, and if absent from work for illness are reimbursed only from the fourth day, unlike industrial employees who receive 100 percent of their wages from the first day. Artisanal employees also can be dismissed immediately, with only one month's severance pay, unlike industrial firms where dismissals are both more costly and time consuming. Industrial employees are also less likely to be dismissed outright, for a special insurance fund pays them approximately 80 percent of their take-home pay when temporarily laid off. These benefits are denied to artisanal employees. In addition, owners of small firms who work alongside their employees can closely supervise them, leading to 10 percent higher productivity than in large firms, according to studies by Benetton (Belussi 1987:31). In Modena, unionization rates of about 30 percent in knitwear artisanal firms are half those of industrial firms.[8]

A series of social-security laws encourage artisans to minimize their use of hired labor by relying on their own and family labor. Artisans are taxed at 26.39 percent of the employees' gross wage for pension benefits, above the employees' own contribution of 7.5 percent. But artisans themselves are only assessed 1.3 million lire annually plus 4.5 percent of declared income. Not surprisingly, their benefits are also lower; a flat 450,000 lire per month regardless of earned income, in contrast to employees, who receive 60 to 80 percent of their last monthly earnings. Artisans are charged payroll taxes of 14.1 percent for employees' health, sickness, and maternity insurance, but pay only 6.5 percent to insure themselves and their family members. Although artisans are uninsured for lost income due to illness, their maternity benefits are equivalent to those of employees. That part of artisanal payroll taxes based on earnings is reduced even further by widespread and substantial under-reporting of income by Italy's self-employed. This factor explains why factory workers appear as the third-highest paid occupational category according to Italian internal revenue data. In Modena, for example, a typical knitwear employee earned about $12,310 (gross) in 1987, whereas in the same period Modena artisans in the manufacturing sector reported average incomes of only $9,846.[9]

[7] *Contratto collettivo Nazionale di Lavoro per i lavoratori dipendenti delle imprese artigiane dei settori Tessile, Abbigliamento e Calzaturiero* (National Collective Agreement for Artisanal Employees in Textile, Clothing, and Shoe Manufacturing) June 6, 1984.

[8] Data from Camera del Lavoro, Province of Modena, November, 1988.

[9] *La Gazzetta di Modena.* October 5, 1988, p. 5.

Family members employed in artisanal firms are treated like artisans according to social security and health insurance regulations. The law presumes that any close family members (defined broadly to encompass first cousins, in-laws and their close relatives, and great-grandchildren) employed in the 76 percent of knitwear firms organized as individual companies (ISTAT 1985:6) are not employees but partners with a right to share in the firms' profits.[10] According to census data, family help constitutes 7 percent of all industry personnel (ISTAT 1985:48). In reality, the percentage is far higher, but government statistics fail to include the many family helpers who have second jobs, study, are retired, or have other reasons for hiding their gainful activity. Nevertheless, employers and family help still account for 39 percent of all those occupied in the knitwear sector according to the official statistics (ISTAT 1985:48).

## Market Demand

The character of market demand offers artisans an additional motive to prefer family labor to hired labor. The highly cyclical nature of the clothing industry, intensified further by the growth of the fashion-ready sector and its tight production schedules, results in extremely heavy and often unplanned workloads during periods of the year. As indicated above, long hours in the industry are common for artisans, yet financial and social reasons restrict overtime-work by employees. According to the national artisanal labor contract, a surcharge of 28 percent is applied to the first four hours of overtime, and 35 percent to any additional hours above those. In practice, however, overtime is traditionally paid off the books because employees want to avoid inclusion in a higher tax bracket and employers want to escape the 40 percent payroll taxes. But, even unburdened by payroll taxes, employers cannot afford unlimited overtime payments since undeclared wage costs are not deductible from gross income. A larger impediment to overtime work is the mostly female workforce whose members, in large part, are unable to accept extensive and unplanned overtime because of family obligations. For these reasons, an artisan and his family willing to work late into the night, and even on Saturdays and Sundays, often have a greater capacity quickly to fill sudden orders than an artisan completely dependent on hired labor.

## Cooperative and Public Associations

Cooperative associations also reduce many of the structural disadvantages of small firms by both reducing their organizational costs and increasing

[10] Italian Civil Code, number 230-bis.

their political cohesion. An elaborate network of store-front offices operated by the artisanal associations provide accounting and bookkeeping services at affordable rates for the many artisans that can not afford to pay bookkeepers or hire accountants. These offices also provide artisans with basic information about legal and administrative changes, as well as guide individuals who wish to become artisans. Most recently, the artisanal associations have actively attempted to connect manufacturers and subcontractors to wholesale and retail buyers. But even artisans who do not avail themselves of any of these services usually join the associations because of their links to political parties: the CNA, for example, has direct channels to the Communist (now called the Democratic-Left Party) and Socialist Parties that control the province of Modena and the region of Emilia-Romagna. Such contracts are important for resolving problems with the myriad of Italian regulatory agencies, all of which are highly inefficient and deeply politicized. Traditionally, the CNA also has had cooperative relations with the CGIL, the Communist-Socialist majority trade union. However, the former Communist Party's ability to harmonize relations among all the different social partners has noticeably atrophied, a result of its more pluralistic world view and deep internal conflicts.

Several different regional and provincial corporations have also been established to match subcontractors to manufacturers and to provide knitwear firms with highly specialized marketing, technical, and economic data. There are also regional associations that offer artisans information about new knitwear technology and organize technical courses.

## Conclusion

Putting-out in the Modena knitwear industry demonstrates that factory bureaucracy is not a requisite for economic success in the late twentieth century. Admittedly, the technical characteristics of knitwear production that favor small-scale production because of short product life cycles, unpredictable market demand, and minimum through-put efficiencies cannot be ignored. Nor can the particular characteristics of Italy's labor and social laws, which provide substantial incentives to self-employed individuals and their families. Nevertheless, the future scenarios of economic liberalism and neo-Marxism that depict ever-larger organizations preoccupied with various control strategies of employees seems to be overly influenced by the dynamics of the American economy rather than by any universal laws of capitalism (Edwards 1979; Williamson 1985). Nor does the extension of putting-out demonstrate any support for the claim that the capitalist labor process requires a relentless decrease in worker autonomy (Clawson 1980:116). On the contrary, capitalism can offer numerous opportunities to workers who wish to enhance their autonomy at work.

The arguments presented here—that putting-out is highly efficient, in the neoclassical sense of achieving maximum output with lowest possible input—may perhaps unintentionally make the reader believe that putting-out exists and is reproduced solely because it is more functional for capitalism. This highly asocial and ahistorical conclusion, however, is precisely the mistake that Williamson makes when he argues that firms with lower transaction costs will supplant those with higher transaction costs. Although economic efficiency is a crucial determinant of the survival of economic organizations, it is not the only one—nor can it be isolated from the surrounding social structure upon which it is dependent. If it were otherwise, one would expect to see the rise of putting-out production in the clothing industries of other countries, such as the United Kingdom where the large companies are in deep economic crisis (Stopford and Baden-Fuller 1989; Zeitlin and Totterdill 1989). But, because the success of economic organizations does not depend solely on their functionality, prescriptions for change are not easily implemented.

For example, in Modena the existence of cooperative and collective structures within a competitive system is an essential component of the knitwear industry. This is most probably determined as a consequence of the specific political institutions and historical formations within Modena, where left-wing parties have deep roots. Because of the hegemonic position of the left in Modena, artisans and other entrepreneurs accept the view that profit depends on improved design, organization, and production technology rather than on low wages. The relatively large numbers of manufacturers also makes it difficult for a few producers to impose prices on the many small artisans, thereby forcing the small artisans to undermine wages and working conditions.

The issue, then, is not the reproduction of the technical and organizational coordinates of knitwear production, but the social characteristics that underpin that model. Leaving aside the important legal entitlements granted to artisanal firms, entitlements that have their roots in the peculiarities of socialist cooperation and Catholic corporatism (Cavazzuti 1978; Weiss 1988), how can the communitarian and familial basis of Italian society be reconstructed elsewhere? Certainly, American families do not share the Italian conception of the extended family as an ideal (Pitkin 1985). Nor can trust and craft skills be so easily engendered and reproduced in the United States, where the average family moves every five years, instead of every thirty years as in Italy. Piore and Sabel (1984:275) rightly locate the success of craft production in the advanced society's preindustrial past. Unfortunately, as Polanyi (1957) has noted, the resuscitation of traditional social practices necessary for economic rejuvenation is an arduous task once those practices have been strangled by unregulated capitalist growth.

Support for this research came initially from a Jean Monnet Fellowship at the European University Institute and later from the Organization of Economic Cooperation and Development's Office on Local Employment Initiatives. Helpful comments on later drafts were received from members of the 1990–1991 Russell Sage Seminar on Economic Sociology, especially Mark Granovetter, Charles Perrow, and Charles Sabel. I am most indebted to Paolo Bignardi, who introduced me to the inner workings of the knitwear industry and gave generously of himself, and to the Modena National Confederation of Artisans (CNA), without whose assistance this research would have been impossible. The Modena Camera del Lavoro (FILTEA-CGIL), the Modena Association of Small Enterprises (API), and the Modena Industrialists Association (Confindustria) also provided crucial help.

# References

ALCHIAN, ARMEN, and HAROLD DEMSETZ. 1972. "Production, Information Cost, and Economic Organization." *American Economic Review* 62:777–795.

BARBAGLI, MARZIO, VITTORIO CAPECCHI, and ANTONIO COBALTI. 1986. *La mobilità sociale in Emilia-Romagna.* Bologna: Regione Emilia-Romagna, Assessorato Lavoro e Formazione Professionale.

BELUSSI, FIORENZA. 1987. *Benetton: Information Technology in Production and Distribution: A Case Study of the Innovative Potential of Traditional Sectors.* Sussex: University of Sussex Science Policy Research Unit.

BENDIX, REINHARD. [1956] 1974. *Work and Authority in Industry.* Berkeley: University of California Press.

BRUSCO, SEBASTIANO. 1982. "The Modena Model: Productive Decentralization and Social Integration." *Cambridge Journal of Economics* 6:167–184.

BURSI, TIZIANO. 1987. *Indagine sulle condizioni economico-finanziarie delle imprese emiliano-romagnole del tessile/abbigliamento (1982–1986).* Carpi: CITER.

———. 1989. *Piccola e media impresa e politiche di adattamento: il distretto della maglieria carpigiana.* Milan: Franco Angeli.

BYTHELL, DUNCAN. 1969. *The Handloom Weavers.* Cambridge, MA: Cambridge University Press.

———. 1978. *The Sweated Trades.* New York: St. Martin's Press.

CAPPELLO, STEFANIA, and ALFONSO PRANDI. 1973. *Carpi: tradizione e sviluppo.* Bologna: Il Mulino.

CAVAZZUTI, FRANCO. 1978. "Le piccole imprese." In Francesco Galgano ed., *Trattato di diritto commerciale e di diritto pubblico dell'economia,* vol. 2. Padova: Cedam, pp. 549–628.

CHAPMAN, STANLEY. 1967. *The Early Factory Masters.* Newton Abott (England): David & Charles.

CLAWSON, DAN. 1980. *Bureaucracy and the Labor Process.* New York: Monthly Review Press.

COMMISSIONE PROVINCIALE PER L'ARTIGIANATO. November 30, 1987. *Le imprese artigiane del comune di Modena.* Modena: Commissione Provinciale per L'Artigianato.

COMUNE DI MODENA. 1978. *Recenti evoluzioni del lavoro a domicilio nei comuni del comprensorio di Modena.* Modena: Dipartimento Interventi Economici, Comune di Modena.

CNA. 1988. *Indagine strutturale–congiunturale sul comparto della tessitura.* Modena: Confederazione Nazionale dell'Artigianato.

EDWARDS, RICHARD. 1979. *Contested Terrain: The Transformation of the Work Place in the Twentieth Century.* New York: Basic Books.

ERVET. 1983. *Le aziende artigiane del tessile-abbigliamento in Emilia-Romagna: i comparti della maglieria, delle confezioni e della pelletteria.* Bologna: ERVET Regione Emilia Romagna.

FORNI, MARIO. 1987. *Storie familiari e storie di proprietà: itinerari sociali nell'agricoltura italiana del dopoguerra.* Turin: Rosenberg & Sellier.

FRIEDMAN, DAVID. 1988. *The Misunderstood Miracle: Industrial Development and Political Change in Japan.* Ithaca, NY: Cornell University Press.

ISTAT. 1964. *Annuario statistico Italiano: 4th censimento generale dell'industria e del commercio 16 ottobre 1961. Dati sulle caratteristiche strutturali delle imprese e delle unità locali.* Vol. II No. 36 Provincial Data—Modena. Rome: ISTAT.

———. 1975. *Annuario statistico Italiano: 5th censimento generale dell'industria e del commercio 25 ottobre 1971. Dati sulle caratteristiche strutturali delle imprese e delle unità locali.* Vol. II No. 37 Provincial Data—Modena. Rome: ISTAT.

———. 1985. *Annuario statistico Italiano: 6th censimento generale dell'industria, del commercio, dei servizi e dell'artigiano 26 ottobre 1981.* Vol. II—Province of Modena. Rome: ISTAT.

JONES, S.R.H. 1982. "The Organization of Work: A Historical Dimension." *Journal of Economic Behavior and Organization* 3:117–137.

———. 1983. "Technology and the Organization of Work: A Reply." *Journal of Economic Behavior and Organization* 4:53–66.

KERR, CLARK, JOHN DUNLOP, FREDERICK HARBISON, and CHARLES MYERS. 1960. *Industrialism and Industrial Man.* Cambridge, MA: Harvard University Press.

LANDES, DAVID. 1969. *The Unbound Prometheus: Technological Change and Industrial Development in Western Europe From 1750 to the Present.* Cambridge, MA: Cambridge University Press.

———. (editor). 1966. *The Rise of Capitalism.* New York: Macmillan.

LASH, SCOTT, and JOHN URRY. 1987. *The End of Organized Capitalism.* Madison: University of Wisconsin Press.

LAZERSON, MARK. 1988. "Organizational Growth of Small Firms: An Outcome of Markets and Hierarchies?" *American Sociological Review* 53:330–342.

LAZONICK, WILLIAM. 1983. "Industrial Organization and Technological Change: The Decline of the British Cotton Industry." *Business History Review.* 57:195–236.

MARGLIN, STEPHEN. 1976. "What Do Bosses Do?: The Origins and Functions of Hierarchy in Capitalist Production." In Andre Gorz ed., *The Division of Labor: The Labor Process and Class Struggle in Modern Capitalism.* Sussex: Harvester Press, pp. 13–54.

MARIOTTI, SERGIO, and GIAN CARLO CAINARCA. 1986. "The Evolution of Transaction Governance in the Textile-Clothing Industry." *Journal of Economic Behavior and Organization* 7:351–374.

MARX, KARL. [1867] 1977. *Capital: A Critique of Political Economy,* Vol. 1. London: Lawrence and Wishart.

MENDELS, FRANKLIN. 1972. "Proto-industrialization: The First Phase of the Industrialization Process." *Journal of Economic History* 32:241–261.

PIORE, MICHAEL, and CHARLES SABEL. 1984. *The Second Industrial Divide: Possibilities for Prosperity.* New York: Basic Books.

PITKIN, DONALD. 1985. *The House that Giacomo Built: History of an Italian Family 1898–1978.* New York: Cambridge University Press.

POLANYI, KARL. 1957. *The Great Transformation: The Political and Economic Origins of Our Time.* Boston: Beacon Press.

REDDY, WILLIAM. 1984. *The Rise of Market Culture: The Textile Trade and French Society, 1750–1900.* Cambridge, England: Cambridge University Press.

SABEL, CHARLES. 1982. *Work and Politics: The Division of Labor in Industry.* New York: Cambridge University Press.

SAMUEL, RAPHAEL. 1977. "Workshop of the World: Steam Power and Hand Technology in Mid-Victorian Britain." *History Workshop* 3:6–72.

SAYER, ANDREW. 1986. "New Developments in Manufacturing: The Just-in-Time System." *Capital & Class* 30:43–72.

SAYLES, JOHN. 1983. "Embezzlement, Industry and the Law in England." In Maxine Berg et al. eds., *Manufacturing in Town and Country Before the Factory.* Cambridge, England: Cambridge University Press, pp. 173–208.

SCHLUMBOHM, JURGEN. 1981. "Relations of Production—Productive Productive Forces—Crises in Proto-Industrialization." In Peter Kriedte et al. eds., *Industrialization before Industrialization: Rural Industry in the Genesis of Capitalism.* Cambridge: Cambridge University Press, pp. 94–134.

SCHMIECHEN, JAMES. 1984. *Sweated Industries and Sweated Labor.* Urbana, IL: University of Illinois Press.

SEWELL, WILLIAM, JR. 1986. "Artisans, Factory Workers, and the Formation of the French Working Class, 1789–1848." In Ira Katznelson and Artistide R. Zolberg eds., *Working Class Formation: Nineteenth-Century Patterns in Western*

*Europe and the United States.* Princeton: Princeton University Press, pp. 45–70.

STOPFORD, JOHN, and CHARLES BADEN-FULLER. 1989. "Competitive Dynamics in Mature Industries." Working Paper Series No. 67. London: London Business School.

THOMPSON, EDWARD. 1967. "Time, Work-Discipline, and Industrial Capitalism." *Past and Present* 38:56–97.

WEISS, LINDA. 1984. "The Italian State and Small Business." *European Journal of Sociology* 25:214–241.

——. 1988. *Creating Capitalism: The State and Small Business Since 1945.* Oxford: Basil Blackwell.

WILLIAMSON, OLIVER. 1980. "The Organization of Work: A Comparative Institutional Assessment." *Journal of Economic Behavior and Organization* 1:5–38.

——. 1981. "The Economics of Organization: The Transaction Cost Approach." *American Journal of Sociology* 87:548–577.

——. 1983. "Technology and the Organization of Work: A Reply to Jones." *Journal of Economic Behavior and Organization* 4:57–62.

——. 1985. *The Economic Institutions of Capitalism.* New York: The Free Press.

ZEITLIN, JONATHAN, and PETER TOTTERDILL. 1989. "Markets, Technology and Local Intervention: The Case of Clothing." In Paul Hirst and Jonathan Zeitlin eds., *Reversing Industrial Decline.* New York: St. Martin's Press, pp. 155–190.

# Index

Boldface numbers refer to tables and figures.

**429**